The Heuristics Debate

The Heuristics Debate

Mark Kelman

OXFORD
UNIVERSITY PRESS

OXFORD
UNIVERSITY PRESS

Oxford University Press, Inc., publishes works that further
Oxford University's objective of excellence
in research, scholarship, and education.

Oxford   New York
Auckland   Cape Town   Dar es Salaam   Hong Kong   Karachi
Kuala Lumpur   Madrid   Melbourne   Mexico City   Nairobi
New Delhi   Shanghai   Taipei   Toronto

With offices in
Argentina   Austria   Brazil   Chile   Czech Republic   France   Greece
Guatemala   Hungary   Italy   Japan   Poland   Portugal   Singapore
South Korea   Switzerland   Thailand   Turkey   Ukraine   Vietnam

Copyright © 2011 by Oxford University Press

Published by Oxford University Press, Inc.
198 Madison Avenue, New York, New York 10016

www.oup.com

Oxford is a registered trademark of Oxford University Press

All rights reserved. No part of this publication may be reproduced,
stored in a retrieval system, or transmitted, in any form or by any means,
electronic, mechanical, photocopying, recording, or otherwise,
without the prior permission of Oxford University Press.

Library of Congress Cataloging-in-Publication Data
Kelman, Mark.
The heuristics debate /Mark Kelman.
p. cm.
ISBN 978-0-19-975560-8
1. Effectiveness and validity of law. 2. Heuristic. 3. Law—Methodology. I. Title.
K260.K45   2011
340′.11—dc22
2010030928
ISBN: 9780199746873

To Barbara Richman, always connected, always reflective, always a comfort, and to Ann, Nick, and Jake, just plain always.

CONTENTS

Acknowledgments ix

Part One: Introduction and Overview
1. The Framework 3

Part Two: The Controversy over the Nature of Heuristics
2. The Heuristics and Biases School 19
3. The Fast and Frugal Heuristics School 50
4. Fast and Frugal School Objections to the Heuristics and Biases Program 70
5. Objections to the Fast and Frugal School Program 90

Part Three: Implications for Law
6. Criminal Punishment and Cognition 119
7. Regulating Markets 152
8. Cognition and Value Incommensurability 178
9. Classical Orthodoxy and Legal Realist Responses Through the Lens of the Heuristics Debate 202

Part Four: Final Thoughts
10. Conclusion 229

Notes 243
Index 311

ACKNOWLEDGEMENTS

I have been working on this project for a very long time; in some ways, it seems fair to say that I started my professional career investigating the virtues and limits of rational choice theory back as a third year law student. And I still owe a great debt of gratitude to the people who worked with me on this broad project back when I was a student, and in my earliest days teaching here at Stanford, most especially Duncan Kennedy, Mort Horwitz, Paul Brest, and Tom Heller.

I started working, in a more focused way, on this book in particular a few years back and have received a great deal of help on this venture from a number of people, none of whom deserves any of the blame for all of the remaining misunderstandings and errors. Among the people who stand out in the psychology community who have been especially generous and helpful in stimulating thoughts about distinct aspects of this work over the years are Jared Curhan, Barbara Frederickson, Daniel Kahneman, Brian Knutson, Rob MacCoun, Lee Ross, and Norbert Schwarz (as well as several anonymous referees). Anthony Wagner stands out especially for giving both me and Nick Kelman (the co-author of the fifth chapter) a tremendous amount of guidance in working through the material on memory that is especially important to the discussion in chapter five. (Though, once again, I need to emphasize that problems and mistakes are ours, not his.) Many colleagues in the legal academy have given great feedback too, both in collective settings (at Berkeley, UCLA, Stanford, NYU, and Columbia) and one-on-one. I am particularly grateful to Paul Brest, Dick Craswell, Ronald Dworkin, Rich Ford, Barbara Fried, Mark Greenberg, Tom Grey, Deborah Hensler, Dan Ho, Russell Korobkin, Christopher Kutz, David Mills, Thomas Nagel, Jeff Strnad, Seana Shiffrin, Bill Simon, Susan Sturm, and Tim Wu. Many students and research staff here at Stanford have been helpful too, over the course of the project: most obviously, Nick Kelman (who co-authored one chapter and did research for others), Jason Hegland and Juan Carlos Sanchez (who each helped analyze experimental data), but also RAs Ashley Steinberg, Aaron Nissen, Kelly Lowenberg, and Elena Coyle. Jake Kelman, Abby Williams, and Katie Turner all helped in experiment administration. Stanford University in general and the Law School in particular has been a great place to work, especially on an interdisciplinary project like this one: Larry Kramer deserves a good deal of the credit for that (and many other things).

PART ONE

Introduction and Overview

1

THE FRAMEWORK

A. WHAT HEURISTICS RESEARCHERS HAVE IN COMMON AND HOW THEY DIFFER

At some high level of generality, there is considerable overlap in the way pretty much everyone interested in heuristics thinks about heuristics. At some level of generality, there is widespread agreement that people are employing heuristics whenever they make a judgment or reach a decision without making use of some information that could be relevant or some computational abilities that at least some people possess.

Again, there is agreement as well that using strategies that are plainly not formal optimization strategies is, sometimes, absolutely necessary. Many of us can "know" enough about the flight of a fly ball in baseball to catch a ball hit quite far from us even though there is lots of information about where a batted ball will land that we would never use at all (e.g., information about wind, spin, the force with which the ball was hit) and computations that many who catch fly balls either do not have the faintest idea how to perform or could not possibly perform nearly quickly enough to make use of them while pursuing a fly ball (e.g., about how far a ball will go if there is a particular angle of ascent). The one-input "gaze heuristic" we apparently use to "solve" the problem appears to work just fine. According to those who believe that we employ this heuristic, someone seeking to catch a fly ball first crudely estimates whether the ball will land in front of or behind him, then runs in that direction, fixing his eye on the ball. He adjusts his running speed so that the angle of gaze—the angle between the eye and the ball—remains constant or within a small range.[1]

At a high level of generality, too, everyone agrees that heuristics are often "functional." Using them produces answers that meet our ends well, however these ends are defined. Everyone agrees as well that they may also be used in situations in which their use is dysfunctional (again, given at least temporary consensus on the definition of dysfunctionality), though the two groups of researchers I focus on in this book do not agree on whether subjects are frequently or only rarely harmed by using heuristics. Moreover, there is widespread agreement that in a multiple-actor setting in which one agent may not treat another's interests as if they were her own, the fact that we employ heuristics can be exploited. Those who would exploit others have the capacity to manipulate an environment so it has, or appears to have, traits that trigger a particular judgment or decision, inducing behavior that the manipulator desires rather than the behavior that the agent would engage in if he either used a wider range of informational cues or encountered the single or simple cues that he would have encountered absent the manipulation. Thus, everyone who writes about heuristics worries, at least to some extent, about both advertisers and sneaky lawyers.[2]

At this same high level of generality, all agree that it is often easier or preferable to change the environment in which decision makers function or to delegate decisions from a badly positioned to a well-positioned decision maker than to try to change how each individual processes fixed cues: In that sense, there is consensus that the disposition to use even misguided heuristics may be recalcitrant, at least at times. If, for instance, patients are more likely to figure out how likely it is that they are actually HIV-positive given that they have tested positive when information is presented in one form rather than another,[3] it might be better to present it in the fashion that most people typically understand rather than to attempt to train them to "think better," remind them to focus more, or even give negative or positive incentives to do a better job.

Moreover, all of those who investigate the use of heuristics do so from a fundamentally similar *methodological* starting point, grounded in earlier work studying memory and perception done by psychologists trained in "mathematical psychology." Those studying memory assumed that accurate memory was a dependent variable and studied the conditions in which accuracy increased or decreased as a way to understand and model basic memory processes. Similarly, those who studied visual perception looked to see what parameters of an object produce a particular visual illusion or permit an object to be seen, and used these observations to create mathematical models of the visual perceptual system. All researchers who study the use of heuristics in making judgments and decisions use a fundamentally similar method, a method first employed by researchers in what is commonly labeled the "heuristics and biases" (H&B) school most associated with the Nobel Laureate Daniel Kahneman and with Amos Tversky.[4] They treat accuracy in judgment as the dependent variable and manipulate the choice-making environment to see what inputs produce both erroneous and true judgments. Doing this permits them to understand judgment and decision making more generally.[5]

The vast bulk of the literature in both law and the policy sciences relating to heuristics has drawn on the H&B school. My dominant aim in this book, though, is not by any means to add much to an already-voluminous literature that explores how that literature is relevant to policy formation, although I offer a brief conceptual overview of the contribution of the heuristics and biases literature to law and policy analysis at the end of Chapter Two and more detailed analyses of the contribution of the literature to policy formation, focusing predominantly on crime control in Chapter Six and regulating product safety and discrimination in Chapter Seven. Instead, I focus on an issue that has been almost entirely ignored in the legal academy and policy community: the *debate* between proponents of the heuristics and biases school and those associated with the "fast and frugal" (F&F) heuristics school, most closely linked with Professor Gerd Gigerenzer.[6]

Those in the H&B school emphasize the degree to which the use of heuristics often prevents us from choosing options that would maximize expected value in the way that conventional rational choice theorists believe we do, because we both miscompute probabilities that our choices will have certain consequences and misevaluate each of the end states that might arise. Those who think of heuristics as "fast and frugal" techniques to make decisions that achieve an organism's ends in a given environment, whether or not the problem-solving techniques are formally rational, are considerably less interested in "biases" or errors than in *achievements*. As I note later in this chapter, the most salient single contrast that the relatively small group of lawyers and policymakers who are aware at all of this debate have typically drawn between the schools is that those associated with the H&B school are more prone to believe that actors should be protected from making errors (as consumers, as voters) or cede decision-making authority to "experts" who might be less prone to make these same errors while those associated with the F&F school share rational choice theorists' optimism that subjects have adopted strategies that work well for them, even though they decidedly reject rational choice theorists' descriptive accounts of how it is that subjects are able to make good decisions.

In this view, the most significant contribution of the H&B school has been to detail a novel sort of market failure. While conventional rational choice theorists might see market failure in situations in which those making choices had inadequate information about the features of the options they were choosing among, H&B-influenced policymakers focused not on the external impediments to good choice (lack of information about the options) but the internal incapacity of subjects properly to use even the information that they have. F&F theorists, in this view, supported the rational choice scholars' intuition that people had good mechanisms to make good choices, even though the mechanisms they identified had little in common with those rat-choice theorists had identified. There is a great deal to be learned by drawing this contrast, but I believe I demonstrate over the course of the book that it is significantly incomplete and partly misleading as well.

As I explore in far greater detail later in the book, the distinctions between the schools do not merely go to the question of whether heuristics can better be seen as a frequent source of error or as the basic building block of intelligence and functional decision making. Scholars in the two schools think differently about why heuristics lead to mistakes when they do lead to mistakes, think differently about what it means to behave rationally, think differently about how the use of particular heuristics emerges, think differently about the processes by which we reach judgments when reasoning heuristically, and think differently about whether people are less prone to use heuristics when they have certain background traits (intelligence, disposition) or have more time or cognitive resources to reach a decision.

Take, just as an example, the issue of how to account for error. H&B theorists are likely to model the problematic use of heuristics in the following way: Using heuristics generates accurate judgments or good decisions in most circumstances, but not all. Actors might correctly believe a particular conclusion typically follows from some perceived reaction to stimuli, something that could loosely be described as serving the same role as an inferential "premise." The premises they rely upon are the most readily processed sub-set of a more complete set of input-premises, the cues that can be manipulated quickly and under high cognitive load that "substitute" for a fuller consideration of multiple factors. What gives rise to error is that the correct conclusion doesn't always follow from the most readily processed cues and reactions. The additional, harder-to-process factors and reactions—those that can *generally* be ignored with little cost to accurate decision making—may *sometimes* turn out to be crucial.

In that sense, H&B theorists are making arguments about error that are conceptually parallel to those typically made by lawyers critiquing the use of rules, proxies, or conclusive presumptions in decision making. Even those generalizations that are right on most occasions are not *invariably* right. Rules are inevitably over- and under-inclusive. Think of the canonical case of using a rule rather than a standard: ages of majority that determine when someone can vote, or buy liquor, or consent to sexual relations. In a sense, the use of a rule (those over 18 can vote) is very much like the use of an H&B heuristic: we substitute an easily made judgment—is the person trying to register to vote older of younger than 18?—for a richer, harder-to-determine true target attribute—is the would-be voter mature, reflective, politically sophisticated, and likely to care about the resolution of political issues? Naturally, some who are older than 18 are not very mature and some who are younger are quite mature.

The failure to make use of fuller, more sensitive judgment techniques may, but need not, generate significant net costs. Error costs might well at least sometimes outweigh the costs of using more tailored, effortful inference processes, but of course, this need not be true. Judgments made on the basis of just a few cues could be completely accurate or the gains that would accrue from making more accurate judgments might be outweighed by the costs of increasing accuracy.

I return to the discussion of how H&B theorists conceptualize error in discussing the "availability heuristic" in Chapter Two, but I preview the argument here because it provides such an easy and cogent illustration. It might well be true, most often, that if a certain sort of event X is "available"—that is, we can readily recall instances of X occurring rather than Y—then X is in fact the more common occurrence. Thus, we move, however unconsciously, from the readily processed judgment-making input—it is easier to recall instances of X than Y—to the conclusion that X is more common. Drawing this conclusion is generally sound because we typically recall things we have been exposed to frequently *and* we generally are exposed more often to things that actually occur more often. But it won't always be the case that the things we recall most readily are in fact more commonplace. We may recall things easily for other reasons (e.g., their emotional salience), and then misapprehend the relative frequency of X and Y, wrongly concluding that X happens more than Y because we easily recollect instances of X.

In a second view, more associated with evolutionary psychology generally, and the F&F school that is so heavily influenced by evolutionary psychology, we would model the problem of mistake quite differently. Traits—including the disposition to use particular cognitive methods, such as heuristics—that were adaptive in the particular *settings* in which they evolved (the "environment of evolutionary adaptation," or EEA) may sometimes have become dysfunctional in some modern settings. Evolution works slowly; there is adaptive lag. Think about the canonical illustration from evolutionary psychology: our taste for high-calorie sweets and fats—the taste is a decision-guiding "trait" that was perhaps functional in the calorie-poor environment in which our ancestors lived—may now serve even our gene-replicating ends poorly. This will be true if overeating and heart attacks have become a bigger threat to survival, or at least our capacity to insure we are around to protect our young until they reach maturity, than starvation. What is critical, though, is how we perceive and judge "error." In judging whether a heuristic has misfired, F&F theorists tell us to judge not why it may lead to *inaccurate* judgment as H&B theorists might—being accurate is not in the F&F view an organism's goal—but rather, whether or not the judgment occurs in the ecological setting in which it emerged. If it is, the judgment is presumptively fine, even if it appears "inaccurate," because evolved traits meet our "real" ends; if, and only if, it does not, it may be problematic. Naturally, for now, I set aside the question of whether it is apt to describe gene replication as an "end" at all, let alone whether we should be deemed to meet our ends if we replicate more successfully but fail to meet other conscious goals.

The H&B theorist, then, if conceptualizing the taste for sweets as a judgment heuristic, would believe that we had a target goal. Most plausibly, the theorist would posit that we were trying to determine, or make a judgment, about which foods we should eat that would improve our health. The theorist would further argue that the easily-processed cue we substituted for a fuller inquiry into that question—does the food "taste" good?—might well be misleading. Good-tasting is a generally accurate substitute for health-promoting (most toxins taste bad, for instance), but it can be inaccurate too on occasion. The F&F theorist would note, instead, that taste is a welfare-promoting guide only in certain environmental settings that might have changed since we developed the particular taste, not that taste was a misguided inferential cue.

There is another contrast between the approaches worth drawing upfront. While scholars in both schools believe many *decisions* are made more or less lexically,[7] scholars working in the F&F tradition are more strongly committed to the notion that decisions are frequently made without regard to all but a single dominant factor and seem uniquely committed to the idea that many *judgments* are made in a lexical, non-compensatory way. A *decision* is made lexically when a subject chooses A over B because it is judged to be better along a single, most crucial dimension, without regard to the other "compensating" virtues that B might have relative to A. Thus, for instance, one would have chosen some restaurant A over B in a lexical fashion if one chose it because it were cheaper and did not care about any other trait, like its quality, proximity, level of service, and so on. A *judgment* is made lexically when some proposition P is deemed to be true because P has some single feature that not-P lacks, even though not-P might have a set of features that outweigh, or "compensate," for the absence of the most salient differentiating feature. Thus, if we decide that city P must have a larger population than city R because we have heard of P and not of R, without regard to the fact that we have other reasons to believe or infer that P is a very small city and have learned that R has some trait or traits that we believe are typical of large cities, then we have used a lexical, non-compensatory method for judging city size, based solely on the familiarity of the city.

My hope in the second part of this book (Chapters Two through Five) is to explore the nature of the debate in a fair amount of detail, interpreting the proponents' positions dominantly in terms most relevant to policy analysts and lawyers rather than as expositors of particular views of cognition. At the same time, I hope to make some tentative evaluations of the positions each side has staked out.

In the third and final part of the book, I hope to explore some of the debate's implications for issues of both jurisprudence and policymaking. That this debate has implications for legal theory or policy is by no means obvious. I will certainly try to demonstrate that the disputes have this sort of bite, but I do not think that point is self-evident or, even upon reflection, clearly true. After all, as legal academics we are not *professionally* interested in describing human cognition accurately (either for its own sake, or, say, for purposes of figuring out more about what machines displaying "artificial intelligence" need to be able to do to solve the problems we hope they can be programmed to solve).[8] We are, though, interested in figuring out the implications of distinct views of judgment and decision making for a host of policy issues: Could we, for instance, devise more optimal modes of disclosure to consumers, surgical patients, and the like or better rules of evidence and jury instructions if we understand more accurately how people process information? Can we figure out how best to increase compliance with law if we understand how people make decisions whether or not to comply? Will democratically responsive bodies regulate risk better if we understand how public *attention* to particular risks is or is not related to actual risks?

B. THE STRUCTURE AND IMPLICATIONS OF THE DEBATE: LOOKING AHEAD TO PARTS TWO AND THREE

Naturally, I could not possibly review comprehensively each of the many heuristics that researchers in these schools have investigated, let alone comment on the degree to which each of the many studies in the field strikes me as convincing either in identifying how people make a judgment or reach a decision or in making the claim that the judgment is either acceptable or troubling. What is more, the studies that interest me raise innumerable issues about how to model cognition in detail that might be intrinsically interesting but bear relatively little on questions of interest to policymakers, who rightly invoke far broader brush accounts of how consumers or voters or jurors process information in making policy-relevant decisions.

I also recognize that when I describe the two "schools" of thought that I am contrasting, I am imposing more uniformity and somewhat false order on the work of scholars whose work is plainly more subtle, less mono-vocal, and far richer in its implications than I imply. I am constructing ideal types, and there is important detail that gets lost whenever one does that.

Furthermore, although I have referred earlier in this chapter, and will continue to refer, to commonalities of both substantive and methodological approach, I definitely highlight ways in which the schools have *competing* approaches. Because of this, I almost invariably understate the degree to which scholars in each camp qualify their views, for one sees far more commonalities when one looks at the concessions and qualifications than when one looks at the most interesting clashing claims. I also tend to set aside, largely or completely, certain themes that might bear significantly on legal and policy analysis either because I do not see any interesting contrast in views between the schools or because one or the other school largely ignores writing on the topic. Thus, for instance, there is a good deal of writing in the H&B tradition about how people establish particular norms about the fairness of transactions and how judgments of fairness may impact decision making—particularly leading people to behave in ways that are at first blush difficult to explain if people are narrowly selfish utility maximizers. The writing is important for lawyers and policymakers. It has, for instance, a close connection to work on procedural justice and alternative dispute resolution systems. But the work has not been subjected to extensive or systematic critique by F&F scholars, so it seems outside the purview of this book.

Moreover, I do not distinguish as carefully as one might between distinctions that are rigorously, analytically entailed by each approach and those distinctions that could better be described as growing out of weaker predispositions to emphasize one point over another. These sorts of predispositions or analytical "moods" might better be studied by those interested in the sociology of knowledge than those interested in discovering the analytical principles which define an approach. At the same time, this book arguably understates or ignores key aspects of "mood": I largely ignore the considerable rancor in these debates that I observe as an outsider to the field, albeit faintly. At times, where it appears analytically helpful, I make reference to the possibility that a certain argument is especially infuriating to the proponents of the competing school, and try to explain why it might be especially infuriating. Still, by and large, I studiously avoid noticing that there is a somewhat overheated feel to this controversy.

Finally, I need to emphasize what I am quite sure psychologists who might read this text will typically find all-too-noticeable, at best, and monumentally irresponsible or irritating, at worst. I am not a psychologist. I don't even purport to play one on TV. The hope, of course, is that having the perspective of a critical outsider permits me to see large patterns that insiders, rightly more concerned with detailed exposition, may largely ignore.[9] But the corresponding fear—that all of us outsiders will simply get things wrong that no insider would ever mess up—should be a hard one for the reader to discount or for me to shake.[10]

With these qualifications in mind, here is the basic plan. In Part Two of the text—Chapters Two through Five—I contrast the two traditions of thought I have adverted to: the "heuristics and biases" tradition and the "fast and frugal" heuristics tradition. I explain the F&F tradition partly by showing its similarities to, and distinctions from, theorists who believe that cognition is massively modularized (MM). (Very broadly speaking, MM is a general theory of mental functioning, designed, in essence, to revitalize the traditional idea that the mind possesses specific "faculties" each of which evolved to solve a fairly particular problem an organism faced rather than a more general capacity to learn and reason. These faculties—mental "modules"—have a number of critical features. Most important, modules are domain-specific, i.e., they are devoted to solving particular problems; mandatory, i.e., people do not have any more control over the cognitive outputs of the modules than they have control over whether their knee reflexively rises when it is hit; opaque, i.e., not amenable to self-conscious scrutiny; and, above all, *strongly* informationally encapsulated, i.e., drawing conclusions only from the delimited set of inputs the module is designed to process, even if other cues might seem rationally relevant to drawing a conclusion.)

More concretely still, I discuss the basic structural features of the H&B school in Chapter Two, and discuss the features of the F&F school, including its relationship to MM theory, in Chapter Three. One aim of Chapter Four is to further explicate the beliefs of the F&F school by attempting both to detail some particular critiques scholars in the school have directed at H&B work and to explain what I see as the broader common structural features of these more particular criticisms. At the same time, the chapter ideally serves to make readers more cognizant of some problems in the H&B literature. Similarly, Chapter Five—tracing through the structural features that a critique of the F&F literature would likely have, using a critique of Goldstein and Gigerenzer's work on the "recognition heuristic" as an illustration—should help readers understand some of the limitations in the F&F literature.

I am going to mention now, in the Introduction, the dimensions along which I think there are significant contrasts in each school's view of basic heuristic processes because I believe that it will help readers to be alert to what I see as the most significant areas of contention when they read Part Two. The most important distinctions among the schools can be understood if we see that they answer the following sorts of questions differently:

- What is each theoretical school fundamentally trying to explain? To what extent does the theorist start with an idealized picture of judgment and decision making and then look to see how frequently there are departures, why they occur, and how one would describe the non-ideal mechanisms? To what extent, instead, does the theorist start with the supposition that our judgment and decision-making processes evolved (or otherwise developed) to solve a concrete set of problems in the environments in which we must solve problems, so that our task is first to understand the *fit* between cognitive capacity and environmentally-established problems?
- What criteria does each school use in evaluating whether a judgment or decision-making process is "rational?"
- To what degree do theorists in a particular school believe that judgment and decision making are mildly, substantially, or absolutely "informationally encapsulated?" Are people capable of overriding heuristics or not when they make a judgment, using cues beyond the limited ones that would trigger a particular judgment outcome if they simply employ a particular heuristic? Do people use multiple cues when reaching *judgments* about the likelihood or value of

end-states? Do they make *decisions* by combining and weighing multiple narrower judgments or do they make decisions more lexically than they reach judgments?
- To what extent does the theorist believe that we can think about problems using "generalized," non-problem-specific cognitive mechanisms, and if the theorist believes that there are at least some general cognitive mechanisms, how should these mechanisms be described and what is their functional domain? Does the theorist believe, instead, that most cognition and decision making is better thought of as substantially domain-specific and modularized?[11]
- To what degree does the theorist see the use of heuristics as arising almost exclusively from limitations on internal mental processes—time, attention, computational power—and to what degree does the theorist emphasize not only the obvious limits of the human mind but the reasons that a significant number of important naturally occurring tasks could not be solved using ordinary optimization methods, even by an unlimited mind? Would we inevitably, sometimes, or never use heuristics less if we were somehow "smarter"?
- Does the theorist assume that all basically functional adults are equally likely to use both useful and dysfunctional heuristics? If some people with particular traits (e.g., higher intelligence, conventionally defined; certain personality traits that are generally associated with "open-mindedness") are less prone to use heuristics, or at least a sub-set of arguably dysfunctional ones, does this imply that we use heuristics because some, but not all, of us are computationally limited or unmotivated to solve problems "well"? Do individual differences, if real, suggest that heuristics are a response largely to internal limits, not features of the external environment? Does the purported existence of such limits imply, instead or additionally, that we have different capacities to override heuristics? If so, is it wrong to characterize heuristics as strongly informationally encapsulated cognitive responses to inputs? Finally, would the existence of individual differences in using heuristics imply distinct things about what rationality is and whether the use of heuristics is rational? Would it matter if "smarter" people used heuristics less when we tried to establish whether or not it is rational to use heuristics?
- Do people (often, rarely, or never) *consciously* employ the heuristics that we see them using? Are heuristics at least sometimes the deliberately chosen strategy of a cognitively generalist mind or do people use them without either being aware that they are using them or why it might be advantageous to be using them in a particular setting?
- To what extent should we expect significant problems to arise from the use of heuristics? To what extent should we encourage the use of new heuristics, assuming that heuristics can *ever* be adopted consciously?

In Part Three (Chapters Six through Nine), I illustrate, using what I take to be a small number of especially telling examples, some of the ways in which we can think about the implications of the debate. What I hope readers will see in working through the examples I have chosen to explore is how our views on a variety of policy and jurisprudential issues might be enriched by being aware that psychologists model heuristic reasoning in distinct fashions. Do certain policies appear more worthy if people reason as F&F theorists believe they do, rather than as either H&B theorists or conventional rational choice theorists believe? Can we understand certain ideas about legal reasoning and jurisprudence better if we see that advocates of particular jurisprudential positions may have implicit theories about how cognition works that correspond to the distinct theories that those in the heuristics debate adopt?

There is a reasonably commonplace, and not entirely inaccurate, view of what the implications of the heuristics debate might be to which I briefly alluded earlier in the chapter. In this view, what best distinguishes the schools is that the heuristics and biases people are conventional political "liberals" and that fast and frugal theorists are conventionally "conservative." This understanding grows from what is itself a view that is only partially true. In this view, what best differentiates the schools is that H&B people are fixated on error—and that they are then especially fixated on the possibility of both consumer error and manipulation/exploitation in unregulated markets—while F&F scholars see ordinary, heuristic-based judgments as excellent—and hence not in much need of correction by regulation.

But the disposition to identify each school with a political philosophy has other roots as well. *Everyone* notes, as I said, that the use of heuristics can misfire in particular situations. And nearly everyone, at least at times, provides a broadly similar evolutionary story for this, even though the evolutionary story is more *central* in F&F thought: Cognitive capacities that served us well, or well enough, in most of the circumstances we confronted in the hunter-gatherer environment in which they evolved may serve us more poorly in modern life where environmental conditions may differ.

It is no great surprise, though, that when optimistic functionalists like Cosmides and Tooby, whose work on modularity has been enormously influential among F&F theorists, search for an example of how functional hunter-gatherer capacities sabotage us in the modern world, they pick on support for a program, rent control, that conventional political conservatives attack for perfectly conventional politically conservative reasons: just another case of good-hearted, mushy liberals missing the unintended consequences of their misguided efforts to help the poor. But instead of *describing* this form of misdirected empathy as sentimental ideology gone bad or as a pernicious power-grab by self-interested state bureaucrats interested in expanding their own power or securing their jobs, they tell us it is the (rare?) case of misfit between our hunter-gatherer intuitions and modernity. So, our naturally selected intuition to help out those who are unlucky, rather than lazy or parasitic—developed so that others will help us out enough to pass our genes along when we are as unlucky as hunters and gatherers will inexorably be in a sub-set of food-gathering tasks—gets hijacked by proposals to control rents for those who might otherwise lose their housing because they cannot afford market rents, *even though that hurts those now homeless and those at risk of becoming so.*[12]

It is interesting for these purposes to note, first, that the example the authors pick to show that some traits that were adaptive for hunter-gatherers that are not adaptive now are *not* the sorts of reasoning traits that can be exploited by advertisers or those who would resist rational safety regulation that the "liberal" H&B people tend to highlight but misdirected mushy redistributive fervor. It is also interesting to note that the example they choose does not seem, in any obvious sense, to depend on the persistence of an outmoded adaptive trait. At the level of generality at which they describe the trait—a desire to help the unlucky—there is absolutely no reason to believe that those who possess the trait would be more prone to adopt the program they abhor (rent control) rather than the one they seem to favor more (housing vouchers). The fact that these generally self-disciplined authors seem drawn to using such a sloppy example can readily be interpreted in two distinct ways. For those who think ideology, conventionally understood, always overwhelms scientific detachment, this looks like an example of authors driven by entirely separate political predispositions to tinker with their method to get results they want. Alternatively, this is just another illustration of the degree to which the sort of modularized theories of cognition I discuss at some length in Chapter Three are vague and under-specified: It is simply not at all clear *what* a domain-specific algorithm to "help the unlucky" does and doesn't do in a world in which decisions don't come in neat domain-defined boxes. Does a proposal to back rent control rather than housing vouchers trigger this algorithm or not? If so, how?

At the same time, it is no great surprise that writers in the H&B tradition often throw the kitchen sink of familiar liberal complaints about Western market and political culture at you when they are ostensibly just trying to emphasize the point that even if our judgment heuristics were "good enough" to deal with most situations, they aren't good enough to deal with all of them. (Of course, the focus on error can emphasize either the general problem that proxies are inevitably inaccurate in some cases or, echoing the F&F theorists, the possibility that judgments that worked to solve so many of those tricky hunter-gatherer conundrums aren't quite up to the complex tasks of modernity.) Thus, the following is an entirely typical "defense" of the idea that non-adaptive uses are ubiquitous by a partisan of the H&B tradition, Keith Stanovich:

> Meliorists [the author's term for the people I am describing as proponents of the H&B program] see a world seemingly full of shockingly awful events—pyramid

sales schemes going "bust" and causing financial distress, Holocaust deniers generating media attention, $10 billion spent annually on medical quackery, respected physical scientists announcing that they believe in creationism, savings and loan institutions seemingly self-destructing and costing the taxpayers billions—and think that there must be something fundamentally wrong in human cognition to be accounting for all this mayhem.[13]

It is far easier to see that these "mistakes" are linked as "events that political liberals would believe can only be explained by error" than to see that they are cleanly linked together as outcomes of any well-theorized or experimentally demonstrated cognitive biases whose precise reach and domain are well understood. Sure, various forms of optimism bias can "explain," or at least name, what is going on when people spend a lot of money on a rather trivial chance of a good health or financial outcome, so we've got something on medical quackery and perhaps even the savings and loan crisis—though even here, we are a very long way from figuring out what limits on excessive optimism we will observe and when it will be counterbalanced by other rules of thumb. But Holocaust denial? Creationism?

I think, though, that it would be quite seriously misleading to view the distinct schools of thought about heuristics as dominantly *driven* by ideology or to think that the only significant *implication* of believing one or another story is to bolster an ideological program. For reasons we will see clearly, in Chapter Three, F&F theory tends to support—in the policy sphere—environmental regulations demanding the use of the "best feasible technology" rather than the sort of cost-benefit analysis typically advocated by politically conservative rat-choice economists. Is that a "conventionally conservative" implication? F&F theory also gives great comfort to those who believe that values are incommensurable (Chapter Eight), a view held fervently by many who think of themselves as on the political Left, conventionally understood, as a barrier against what they see as forms of cost-benefit analysis that sacrifice interests that ought to be sacrosanct and views that see it as acceptable to treat all end-states as properly bought and sold.

Ultimately, I think that in discussing the implications of the debate, it is at least as important to attend to distinct views about lexical, non-compensatory decision making as to the distinction in broad attitude about whether people are really good at making decisions. In a sense, one of the reasons I feel comfortable picking out a rather small number of policy implications to study is that I think I can illustrate the main issues with just a handful of examples. For instance, I think one can see adequately clearly (in Chapter Six) the enormous importance of attending to the ways in which F&F theorists believe in lexical decision making while H&B theorists believe that people engage in multifaceted decision making in which factual and evaluative judgments that need to be inputted into a many-faceted decision-making process are *distorted* simply by looking at the implications of each school's views for criminal punishment. So, in a sense, Chapter Six is meant to be in some part an inherently interesting contribution to the criminal law literature. After all, figuring out what sorts of steps state actors might take to increase compliance, or how we judge the degree to which one type of punishment should be considered more severe than another, are important issues and this literature bears on these questions, even if it does not come anywhere close to resolving them. But what it is mostly meant to be is an opportunity to see more clearly how the theorists in each school model human behavior and how certain models are inconsistent with certain views of efficacious intervention.

Similarly, I hope the discussion in Chapter Eight of the idea that values are incommensurable (incapable of being compared to one another) is valuable to those interested in that issue. But I also hope to show that those drawn to domain-specific models of cognition, models with an enormous resemblance to and influence on ideas that F&F people have about the use of heuristics, will find the idea that values may be incommensurable far more comprehensible than rat-choice skeptics of the idea, who have argued that the ability to form preferences and select among options belies claims that values cannot be compared, have implied. At the same time, I hope to demonstrate that it might well be comprehensible in a different way than philosophers who have defended the idea that values might be incommensurable have argued. Again, I am using this as a case study of the implications of believing in relatively domain-specific cognition as much as an occasion to study incommensurability, and hope that other scholars and readers would see how the arguments might be extended to other legal theoretical issues. The effort in Chapter Nine to draw homologies between classical legal formalism and the F&F school, as well as to demonstrate the ways in which Holmses's realism can be profitably reinterpreted by reflecting on H&B theory, gives us new insight into familiar debates about the use of both detailed narrow rules and broad principles designed to determine narrower practices.

I conclude, in Chapter Ten, with some summary remarks that will refer back both to my account of the significant distinctions in ideas about cognitive process and significant distinctions in policies that might be entailed by these distinct views.

PART TWO

The Controversy over the Nature of Heuristics

2

THE HEURISTICS AND BIASES SCHOOL

A. EXPECTED UTILITY THEORY AND THE HEURISTICS AND BIASES SCHOOL

What I think is most critical for lawyers and policymakers to understand about the heuristics and biases school (H&B) is that it can be framed, fundamentally, as a critique of the realism, but not the desirability, of evaluating options in accord with the dictates of classical rational-choice theory. I understand perfectly well that this is a significantly partial, and in some ways significantly misleading, portrait of what the researchers working in this tradition intended to do, and that it severely truncates our understanding of many of the school's achievements. H&B research was done by *psychologists*, not renegade economists, and their primary goal was to understand human cognition. In this regard, the study of both problematic judgment and decision making was designed to refine our understanding of how we think. Just as the study of perceptual illusions largely served to help us to understand perception more generally, so the study of biases was designed to illuminate judgment and decision making.[1] But, of course, there was no equivalent to rational-choice theory in perception, no one committed to the idea that people either *should* perceive "accurately" or tended to do so, either as individuals or because various collective processes—cognate to markets—tended to militate against the persistence of inaccurate perception in individuals.

At core, what rational-choice theorists both counsel and observe is that, as a prelude to a choice between two options, each of us should and often does assess the *probability* of each ultimate outcome that might arise if a particular action-option is taken and the *value* of each outcome. It is rational to choose that action-option that maximizes the expected value (probability multiplied by value) of the possible outcomes, weighting preferences about risk seeking or risk avoidance appropriately.

Parties plainly need not be indifferent between taking a course of action in which they will certainly receive an outcome valued at X and one in which there is a 50 percent chance of receiving an outcome valued at 2X and a 50 percent chance of receiving nothing at all, though whichever choice they make, the expected value of the action is X. It is an important point, in thinking about the contributions of the H&B school generally, but not so much in thinking about the debates between H&B and fast and frugal (F&F) theory at the core of this book, that H&B scholars believe that economists' traditional account of risk preferences is wildly inaccurate, so that modeling subjects as trying to maximize expected utility given certain attitudes toward risk is quite misleading. I do not doubt for a moment that work on how people evaluate uncertain outcomes is important for policymakers. I also acknowledge that there are genuine differences between the H&B material on the infirmities of the conventional rational-choice picture of risk proclivity and aversion—Kahneman and Tversky's "prospect theory"[2]—and the more recently articulated F&F response both to conventional expected utility theory and to prospect theory, work on the "priority heuristic."[3] But I remain skeptical that the distinction between the theories is enormously important for policymakers, whether one or the other is ultimately demonstrated to be descriptively more accurate.

Briefly, though, there are several crucial, defining aspects of prospect theory that plainly distinguish it from neo-classical economists' accounts of decision making given risk: First, people underweight outcomes that are merely probable compared to those that are obtained with certainty, contributing to risk aversion in choices involving sure gains and risk seeking in choices involving sure losses. Second, people ordinarily ignore features of an outcome that are shared by all prospects they are considering: This "isolation effect" makes it possible to elicit distinct preferences when the same choice is re-framed, in ways I return to exemplify later. Third, if people behave as prospect theory assumes rather than as expected utility theory assumes, subjects will not really assign "value" or "utility" to the "end-states" they ultimately experience or to the assets they will ultimately hold but, rather, to gains and losses. The value function is ordinarily concave for gains, convex for losses, and generally steeper for losses than gains. People are risk averse in the face of gains and risk seeking in the face of losses. Finally, while expected utility theorists assume that subjects assign probabilities to events, prospect theorists assume they assign "decision weights," which are generally lower than corresponding probabilities, except in the range of low probabilities in which they are higher. The overweighting of low probabilities helps explain the attractiveness of both gambling and purchasing insurance, though a party who simultaneously does both might be seen by expected utility theorists to exhibit inconsistent attitudes about risk.

I also set aside, until later in the chapter, the question of whether we should think of an option that a subject might choose to pursue as multifaceted or not. The prominent H&B theorist, Amos Tversky, argued early in his career that when an agent had to choose an option with many facets, he would not compute the value of the option by somehow summing the expected utility of each aspect but, rather, would do something more like deciding on the basis of distinctions in the "most important" distinguishing aspect.[4] In this sense, then, expected utility theory fails to describe behavior not merely because of mistaken *judgments*—fundamentally, most psychologically akin to mistaken *perceptions*—both about the likelihood that some aspect of a situation A will transpire rather than aspect B and about the value of A. It fails, in addition, because in making many concrete decisions, the decision to do X rather than Y, aspect A will inevitably be "bundled" with some aspects C, D, and E and computing the *total* utility of the choice X would be intractable even if we could correctly value A, C, D, and E separately and estimate how probable it really is that each of those states would eventuate if the subject chose X. These sorts of *decision-making* problems, though, occur *after* we have used—and sometimes misused—heuristic methods to evaluate aspects of decisions.

B. MISCOMPUTING EXPECTED VALUE: PROBABILITY MISESTIMATES

At any rate, if people are to perform the task of selecting an option that maximizes expected utility—setting aside both risk preferences and the multifaceted option problem—they must assess accurately the probability that each of a series of conceivable outcomes would arise if they choose a particular option.

Thus, the first aim of the H&B researchers was to show that people did *not* assess probabilities in a fashion that was likely to reflect the best available information about the probability of future events. People may have *thought* they were assessing how frequently some event X, not Y, would occur in the future on the basis of how often it had occurred in the past. However, their judgment of how often it had previously occurred inaccurately reflected the actual relative frequency of X and instead reflected things like its availability or its representativeness. It might also reflect the fact that people anchored to some prior estimate of frequency, even a rather transparently arbitrary and uninformed one, and adjusted inadequately.

At core, people *substitute* one feature of a cue (e.g., its availability or representativeness) for the more immediately, rationally relevant one (its probability). In earlier H&B experiments, such substitution was generally proven *indirectly*. Subjects demonstrably made irrational or false judgments, and the experimenters posited that the only plausible explanation for these mistakes was that the subjects had substituted a separate judgment. In some later work, H&B researchers attempt to get at the same point by noting, essentially, that there are high correlations between one subject group's ratings of the probability of a set of events and another subject group's ratings of, say, the representativeness of each event. This was a more direct way of testing the so-called substitution hypothesis. An illustration should help. In this sort of test of the substitution hypothesis, one group of subjects is given a vignette describing Tom W. and given nine graduate school fields: They are asked to rank order the degree to which Tom W. "resembles a typical graduate student" in each field, thus testing representativeness directly. The second experimental group is given the same vignettes and fields of study, and the subjects are then asked to rank how likely it is that Tom is a student in each field, thus testing probability estimates. The correlation between the two rank orderings is spectacularly high: 0.97[5]

When using the availability heuristic, individuals estimate the frequency of an event or the likelihood of its occurrence or recurrence "by the ease with which instances or associations come to mind."[6] So, for example, instead of using multiple cues to figure out how often people have contracted disease X rather than Y, and then using past frequencies to assess the probability of contracting each in the future, we estimate the relative probability of X and Y by comparing, implicitly, how available or readily recalled instances of each are. What makes using the "availability heuristic" accurate enough most of the time is that we typically recall things more readily when we have been exposed to them more frequently, and we typically are exposed to them more frequently because they are in fact more common. Using the heuristic can misfire, though, for example, in terms of measuring actual frequencies, when an event is readily recalled because it is emotionally salient, rather than common, or because it has been overexposed in the media. Because "available events" are deemed more probable than those less readily brought to mind, consumers, voters, and regulators may well fail to make optimal decisions affecting safety. They may, for instance, shy away from planes when cars are more dangerous because plane crashes come easily to mind, worry too little about the impact of diabetes relative to Amyotrophic Lateral Sclerosis (ALS), or demand or supply regulations to clean up well-publicized toxic spills while ignoring greater, less dramatized risks.

Within the H&B tradition, there is still disagreement about how the availability heuristic works. Broadly speaking, some think that the fact that one can recall X easily is itself the cue that X is common; on the other hand, subjects may instead recall all X- and Y-like outcomes that they can and use the recalled instances as a sample, assigning probabilities in accord with the recalled sample.[7]

It is not uninteresting to note that H&B researchers have been more interested in the *existence* of the heuristic than in understanding either its precise mechanisms or its origins, given their generally modest level of interest in figuring out ways in which particular capacities may have been adaptive, or otherwise evolved. This relatively low level of interest in the origins of the heuristics perpetually bothers F&F researchers: I return to this issue in Chapter Four, which focuses generally on the F&F critiques of H&B scholarship. Not surprisingly, too, the F&F people think that "availability" is so poorly defined that it is not clear whether there is a heuristic like it, or, if so, whether it is "fast and frugal" in some set of environments.[8] I return to the issue of imprecise definition as well in Chapter Four.[9]

Representativeness is a slightly more elusive concept than availability and has also been criticized for its elusiveness by F&F scholars.[10] Tversky and Kahneman note that "representativeness is an assessment of the degree of correspondence between a sample and a population, an instance and a category, an act and an actor, or, more generally between an outcome and a model." While representative events are often frequent events, they may better be thought of as ones that fit a stereotype or as diagnostic of group membership.[11] Experimental subjects are so prone to overestimate the probability of representative events that they may believe that a representative event is more likely to occur than a less representative one of which it is a sub-set. I flesh out this point soon, when discussing the possibility that subjects may make logical errors of judgment as well as factual mistakes.

People use an anchoring heuristic when they "make estimates by starting from an initial value that is adjusted to yield a final answer (when) adjustments are typically insufficient."[12] The existence of anchoring has been established by a procedure in which salient but uninformative numbers are first presented to subjects and the uninformative number influences a subsequent judgment. Thus, for instance, subjects' estimates of when Attila the Hun was first defeated in Europe were influenced by having been exposed to anchors constructed from their phone numbers; estimates of the number of countries in the United Nations are influenced by exposure to information about the number of doctors in the local phone book.[13]

Obviously, one can anchor in a fashion that leads to misestimates of more than probabilities and frequencies. Anchoring might, for instance, lead to misestimates of facts about how others would generally value an end-state. Hence, one commonly drawn legal implication—whether useful for trial practice or as a prod to law reform—is that jurors may award higher damages when the complainant simply asks for more, anchoring to a particular implicit estimate of how much someone in the plaintiff's position "lost" when the defendant harmed him.[14] More generally, in fact, while the early H&B studies focused largely on misjudgments of probability—biases that occurred in dealing with a world of uncertainty—most of the phenomena that were studied can be applied to misjudgments of both probabilistic and non-probabilistic facts, as well as value.[15]

It is important, then, to note that anchoring may also affect the second leg of the expected value calculus: one's own subjective valuations of end-states. Thus, for instance, when consumers value a bundle of X and Y, they may anchor to the more important item X and adjust valuation judgments inadequately, either up or down, for the presence of the second item, Y. Thus, when two items are "bundled together," the more important item may act as an anchor, and the overall evaluation of the bundle may not properly reflect the additional positive or negative value of the more trivial item bundled with the significant one.[16]

There is a straightforward legal application of this observation. One could readily argue that the hesitancy of traditional common law courts to let covenants run readily with the land is more defensible if one believes that the successors of initial covenantors don't adequately lower financial offers for the covenantor's land simply because ownership of the land—the important feature X—entails some burdensome obligation—the more trivial bundled feature Y. Thus, these successors to the initial covenantor are not adequately compensated through a price discount to perform the promise made by their predecessor in interest. They would have to be paid more to do Y, or forebear from doing Y, if asked simply to do Y or forebear from doing it, than they reduce their offer for the X-Y bundle because of the presence of Y. The value of the X-Y bundle is anchored to the value of X.[17]

Here is a typical example: J promises developer K that she and her successors will pay annual fees to be a member of the health club on the roof of J's condo or the golf course adjacent to J's home. J sells her condo or home to L; the legal question is whether L should be bound to keep J's promise as long as she has notice that it will bind her. The standard doctrinal alternative is to say that the promise does not run because it does not "touch or concern" the land or, in Third Restatement terms, because it is somehow "unreasonable." We will be more prone to think that L may be exploited if we allow this "covenant" to "run" to L if L will not re-evaluate the *big* item—the condo or the home—to account for the disutility of paying more for a service than it is worth to her when she computes how much she should offer J. There is, once more, not a tremendous amount of attention paid to the evolutionary origins of anchoring within the H&B tradition though there is some interesting work on its mechanisms.[18]

According to H&B theorists, people not only often fail to assess probabilities *accurately*, they often do so in a fashion that is *logically incoherent*. Naturally, it is easier to detect incoherence than inaccuracy, since assessing whether subjects have made *mistaken* estimates of the probability of an outcome requires that the experimenter herself knows the actual probabilistic distribution of the phenomena at issue. For example, people who judge probabilities on the basis of the representativeness of an outcome might believe that it is more likely that 1,000 people will perish in an earthquake in California in the next twenty years than that 1,000 people will perish in a natural disaster west of the Rockies, though an earthquake in California is included in the set of natural catastrophes west of the Rockies so it cannot be more probable than the set in which it is included. Natural disasters west of the Rockies is the conjunction of natural disasters in California and of natural disasters in states other than California west of the Rockies. Since the probability of the conjunction of two events with non-zero probabilities must be greater than the probability of either constituent, even the one more "representative" of disasters, people who make this judgment are exhibiting what is generally dubbed the "conjunction fallacy."[19]

Note, once more, the rather transparent implications of finding that people make this sort of error for insurance markets and the possible legal regulation of such markets: Insurance policies that actually cover more casualties may be incorrectly thought to cover fewer than those that actually cover a more limited range of casualties, as long as the explicitly covered casualties are more representative. The insured may thus mistakenly believe that it is less probable that the insured-against events will occur even though more events are in fact covered. Insurers might conceivably exploit that heuristic to write overpriced liability-limiting policies, and regulation of some sort might be needed to prevent this.

Note as well the less transparent implication for trial practice of the fact that subjects may be vulnerable to the conjunction fallacy. Jurors may find it more plausible that a certain event occurred for a particular reason than that the event simply occurred and thus underestimate the probability of events without clear motives and overestimate the likelihood of events where the defendant has a representative or prototypical reason to do something. Thus, for instance, even though it *must* be less probable that X killed one of his employees to stop him from talking to the authorities about X's illicit activities than that he killed one of his employees, in between-subject tests, people find the latter less likely. It is instructive in considering the debate between H&B and F&F theory to note that F&F theorists are skeptical that jurors who commit this "fallacy" are acting irrationally.[20]

C. MISCALCULATING EXPECTED VALUE: LABILE JUDGMENTS OF VALUE

i. Factual vs. normative "mistakes"

H&B researchers do more than detail ways in which people fail to assess accurately, or even coherently, the probability that certain outcomes will arise if they choose a particular option. They also attempt to demonstrate that people may make "mistakes" in *evaluating* the end-states whose probability of occurring, given any course of action, they have already assessed, however inaccurately. Given conventional commitments to maintaining a gap between "objective" fact and "subjective" value, it is naturally a bit trickier to demonstrate that an agent has *mistakenly* evaluated an end-state than that she has mistakenly assessed the probability of an event.

With certain qualifications I return to in a moment, it seems relatively easy to understand what we mean when we say that a subject may make *mistakes* in assessing probability. In the view of both the H&B researchers and conventional observers of probabilistic judgment, people plainly make mistakes when they make coherence errors. Thus, for instance, one *must* be wrong if one believes that there are more words ending in "ing" than words ending in "-n-." This is true even though many people indeed get the answer wrong, perhaps because more words ending in "ing" are available to memory. But what is critical to note is that one may be mistaken even when one makes perfectly coherent, contingent judgments. It *may* simply be wrong, for example, that there are fewer English words beginning with "r" than words whose third letter is "r," even though most of us think the opposite, because we can more readily recall words beginning with "r," but the belief is not *logically* wrong.

There is, of course, a substantial philosophical debate about whether probabilities of future events (rather than frequencies of already-observed events) are best thought of as objective or subjective (merely representing bets or beliefs). The debate is especially sharp when considering the probability of a single event rather than the frequency distribution of a future sample. In some views, it is sensible to think about objective probabilities when, but only when, there will be sampling. In this view, it is apt to speak of probabilities when one considers the number of green, not yellow, balls that will be drawn from an urn with eighty yellow and twenty green over 1,000 trials.[21] However, in this view, there is no such objective probability that it will rain tomorrow or that one will die in one sort of accident rather than another, merely subjective bets that people are willing to make about the likelihood of the outcome. The bets would take the form, for instance, of stating a willingness or refusal to bet $100 to receive $300 if it rained, expressing beliefs about both risk proclivity and subjective estimates of probability. The willingness to make or reject bets, like value judgments generally, cannot be "wrong" or "right." Both philosophers like Cohen who are strongly committed to the subjective view of probability[22] and the F&F scholars who are loathe to attribute irrationality to people and thus discount the possibility that any between-subjects test of probability judgments can reveal irrationality[23] because *no* probability estimate of a single event is irrational[24] have thus sharply questioned whether the H&B experiments demonstrate irrational probability judgments.

From the vantage point of subjectivists, it is thus not possible to discover "factual mistakes" in judgments of single-event probabilities, though they would agree that one could make a mistake in a frequency judgment of the sort that I mentioned, assessing the number of words with "r" as a first rather than third letter. I must confess that I have never been able to overcome my puzzlement at what "bite" the subjectivists think they are getting from this particular critique of the H&B school: It seems transparently the case that the *cognitive process error* that subjects who make the frequency *mistake* on the "words with r" problem are making is precisely the same mistake that they are making when they judge the probability of a unique event like dying from each of a series of distinct causes over the next year, and "overestimate" the probability of dying from a salient, available cause precisely because they misestimate the prior *death rate* from that salient cause. But of course, the belief about the prior death rate is a frequency judgment.

This point is put well by Sloman and Over:

> ... primitive people would have benefited from expressing and understanding degrees of belief or confidence about singular propositions, and one way to justify these single-case probabilities is through sample frequencies. Suppose that some primitive people have hunted 50 giraffes and failed in 40 of these attempts to kill one, and that they remember the sample frequency. Suppose also that they face the question one morning whether to hunt some specific giraffe in front of them. What is the good of recalling the sample frequency if they cannot use it that morning to justify the single case judgment that they will probably fail in hunting this giraffe?[25]

My skepticism about this attack is reflected as well in comments made Gilovich and Griffin: "An honest frequentist must concede that meaningful probabilistic statements can be made about unique events, such as the Yankees being more likely to win the World Series this year than, say, the Kansas City Royals..."[26] More generally, since many of the biases explicitly refer to finding other sorts of facts—rather than single-event probabilities—and most of the biases demonstrated in relationship to probabilistic reasoning seem to be sub-sets of more robust general heuristics that may mislead us in other settings, I think this particular critique of the H&B findings is largely a dead end.

Whatever one makes of statements about mistaken "factual" judgments, it is plainly often difficult to know just what to make of the proposition that principals misevaluate end-states, rather than misperceive facts, because they use heuristics: At some level, as preference-neutral liberals at least, we posit the existence of principals who articulate and evaluate ends that are by and large beyond rational reproach. These ends are fundamentally viewed as whimsical and arbitrary—that is, they need no justification. They are also subjective—they are not objects that exist in the external world that individuals apprehend as they perceive the natural world around them but rather come from the subject herself. Whether an end is "correct" or not can, in this view, be judged only by each individual subject himself, and the judgment of whether an end is "correct" is extremely limited. In essence, the subject can do no more than interrogate the authenticity and accuracy of the way in which he has articulated and come to understand his wishes. Ends cannot be judged from an external observer's objective viewpoint to be "wrong" in some transcendent and impersonal sense (e.g., because they interfere with a particular conception of human flourishing or fail to manifest what is most unique to human nature).

Though ends are mostly beyond rational reproach, there are certain rationality constraints on the formation of these ends that are ostensibly weak. Three are especially worth mentioning because it turns out to be the subject of controversy between the behavioral social scientists influenced by the H&B literature and rational-choice theorists whether real, rather than idealized, principles, form even these "minimally rational" ends. First, end-state preferences must be consistent and transitive; second, the presence or absence of irrelevant alternatives ought not to affect the choice between two end-states; third, and finally, if a good G is chosen over another good H, it should be done so regardless of how the goods are characterized or how the preference between the goods is elicited, as long as the "objective" features of each good remain unaltered. It is possible to argue that these three separate constraints can all be derived from a single model of the choice situation. In this model, principals have constructed, or can readily construct through introspection, a free-floating complete menu of rank-ordered end-states. The end-states on that menu are real, external objects whose true and discernible nature is insensitive to the way in which the objects are described. People choose higher ranked items over lower ranked items.

ii. Identifying Normative Errors: Incoherence, Frame-Sensitivity, and Regret

Overall, then, the criteria for questioning the validity of a value judgment are at once both narrower and almost invariably more controversial than the criteria for critiquing a factual judgment. Value judgments are most obviously troublesome when they violate coherence rationality—they are, for instance, intransitive or they violate dominance rules. Not surprisingly, then, H&B researchers frequently attempt to demonstrate that the use of heuristics generates intransitive preference orderings or violations of dominance rules. Thus, for example, when presented the rather transparent choice between (1) a 25 percent chance to win $240 and a 75 percent chance to lose $760 and (2) a 25 percent chance to win $250 and a 75 percent chance to lose $750, subjects know to choose (2). Choice (2) dominates (1), promising *both* higher gains and lower losses at equal levels of probability. However, if asked to make the following pair of concurrent decisions between (3) a sure gain of $240 and (4) a 25 percent chance to gain $1,000 and (5) a sure loss of $750 and (6) a 75 percent chance to lose $1,000 and a 25 percent chance to lose nothing, the vast majority of respondents choose the combination of (3) and (6) over (4) and (5), though combining choices

(3) and (6) yields dominated option (1) while combining choices (4) and (5) yields the dominant option (2).[27]

Further, and more significantly, the H&B theorists typically argue that they need not have substantive views on what tastes are "objectively preferable" to argue that people are not evaluating end-states properly if the evaluation of such end-states is frame-sensitive. H&B theorists have been especially adept at exploring situations in which some end-state X is evaluated as better than Y if the outcome X is described in one fashion but not another or if X is evaluated as better than Y only if there is some irrelevant third alternative Z present as part of the option set.

Assume that agents will use one of the most familiar H&B heuristics, grounded in "endowment effects" and "loss aversion." We should expect that they will judge the same mortality outcome either preferable to or inferior to some other outcome depending on whether the outcome is *described* as saving a certain number of lives or resulting in a certain number of deaths. Thus in one scenario, subjects choose between two programs designed to respond to a disease expected to kill 600 people described as follows: "If Program A is adopted, 200 people will be saved. If Program B is adopted, there is a one-third probability that 600 people will be saved and a two-thirds probability that no one will be saved." In the other scenario, the same subjects choose between Program C ("If Program C is adopted, 400 people will die") and D ("If Program D is adopted, there is a one-third probability that nobody will die and a two-thirds probability that 600 people will die."). It is quite common to choose A over B and D over C, displaying the sorts of risk-seeking preferences in the context of "avoiding a loss" and risk aversion when dealing with "gains" that those drawn to "prospect theory" predict. This is true even though A and C are identical and B and D are at least intended to be identical by the experimenters in the sense that in the first program, the certain mortality rate is two-thirds in each case, and in the second, there is a two-thirds chance of 100 percent mortality and a one-third chance of zero mortality.[28]

Similarly, H&B researchers assert that as a result of what they dub "contrast effects" that influence decision making, a particular legal outcome X might be preferred to another outcome Y depending on whether the choice between them is coupled with the option of selecting a clearly inferior outcome Z that is somewhat similar to X. We know in these experiments that Z is clearly inferior to X because no, or nearly no, subjects select Z. Such a decision violates one core principle of rational choice: Options are selected based on the presence or absence of irrelevant alternatives. Thus, experimental subjects are more likely to choose that a convicted white-collar defendant be punished by being placed on probation rather than ordered to serve time in jail when a third option, an especially silly and pointless *form* of probation, is offered as an additional option, because sensible probation most clearly contrasts with "silly" probation. Their judgment appears precisely the same as the judgment of experimental subjects who are more likely to choose a Mark Cross pen over $6 when they are also given the option of choosing a markedly inferior pen.[29]

At the same time, the proportion of subjects who select X as the proper outcome may depend on whether X, rather than Y, is the "compromise" outcome compared to some other potential outcome Z that is more severe than X rather than some Z that is less severe than Y. Thus, experimental subjects are more prone to convict a defendant of murder, not manslaughter, when murder is the choice intermediate between manslaughter and capital murder options than when the choices are involuntary manslaughter, manslaughter, and murder, though the factors that a rational actor is directed to account for in distinguishing murder from manslaughter are unaffected by the presence of either third option. This judgment in the legal context echoes decisions made by consumers, who are more prone to pick a good when it is intermediate between a higher price and lower price item.[30]

We see similar sorts of frame sensitivity in other settings as well. Experimental subjects acting as legal decision makers are likely to choose to "grant" custody to Spouse 1 rather than Spouse 2 if Spouse 1 has a lot of markedly positive as well as markedly negative traits while Spouse 2 is described in uniformly flatter, more humdrum terms. At the same time they are prone to "deny" Spouse 1 custody if asked to which spouse they would *deny* custody, rather than being asked to which spouse they would *grant* it. This is true even though denying custody to Spouse 1 is merely another way of framing what it is to grant it to Spouse 2. This sensitivity to frame appears to occur because when asked whether to deny custody to one spouse, people using a "reason based" decision heuristic focus on negative traits, those that give them a "reason" to deny custody. When asked to "grant" custody, they similarly seek reasons to do so.[31] Subjects do not appear to be capable of simply evaluating end-states—who gets the kid?—in the fashion that rational-choice theory suggests they must. Instead, elicitation procedures, framing identical outcomes in distinct ways, matter. Once more, elicitation sensitivity of precisely this form is by no means restricted to situations in which people are making legal judgments rather than, say, ordinary consumer choices.[32]

H&B proponents have shown a proclivity to critique evaluative mechanisms even when they do not either generate incoherent preference orderings or demonstrate irrational frame sensitivity. While unwilling to adopt full-blown perfectionist critiques of "substantively bad choices," they often argue that the choices made by subjects who are "misusing" heuristics are apt to regret their choices, and that the regret bespeaks a substantive problem. Obviously, whether regret truly bespeaks "error" (or even something that could be called troublesome) is hardly obvious. It is not demonstrably true that the reflective self who regrets a choice is better equipped to judge the propriety of the choice than was the person who was ostensibly confused when he made heuristic-influenced evaluations. People may regret choices because they undervalue the experiences of now-bygone selves or because they overvalue certain forms of self-presentation compared to experience, just as they may make mistakes when they make decisions with future consequences, unduly discounting the utility of "future selves" or underestimating the hedonic consequences of harshly evaluating one's overall life course.

It is pragmatically, or at least rhetorically, significant, though, to find that the choices agents subject to "biases" make often do not survive reflection. Not surprisingly, then, H&B researchers frequently note that heuristic-influenced end-state evaluations are subsequently renounced, that those making heuristic-based choices often incorrectly predict how they will ultimately come to evaluate the outcome they claim to desire, or that their heuristic-based evaluative schema could not possibly survive reflection.[33] In this regard, it is interesting to note that Kahneman's first important theoretical work in hedonics—the psychological study of the meaning and causes of "happiness"—sharply distinguished between subject's choices and their experienced utility on the explicit assumption that evaluations made at the time of choice might well prove to be poor predictors of the actual evaluated quality of lived-out experience. Economists and modern-day preference utilitarians typically were concerned with what Kahneman calls "decision utility," in part because all that could be reliably observed is whether an agent *chooses* X rather than Y, not whether he "truly" enjoys consuming X. Kahneman argued it was important to attend to and try to measure "experienced utility" as well, in part because he assumed heuristic-using imperfect decision makers would often make choices that worked out poorly.[34]

Here is a version of the problem of "renounced choices" with transparent legal policy implications. Assume that we want to do a cost-benefit analysis of a program that will save some migratory birds, in part by eliciting contingent valuations from members of the public about what they would pay to avoid the loss of life of some of the birds. Absent income effects, the upper bound of what subjects should ordinarily be willing to pay to save X birds should be the sum of what they are willing to pay to save X-k birds plus what they would pay to save k birds.[35] But, in fact, researchers find substantial scope neglect that is not likely explained by declines in the marginal value of additional saved lives: Subjects' willingness to pay to save migratory birds scarcely varied if one was going to save 2,000, 20,000 or 200,000 jeopardized birds through some costly action.[36] This is plainly not a strictly *incoherent* preference order, but H&B researchers note that it is quite unlikely to survive reflection. Instead, it almost surely arises from the sort of attribute substitution that H&B researchers so often emphasize. Rather than thinking directly about the value of the bird-saving action, people access their affective reaction to the pictured event—birds dying—and the harm associated with this "event" is sensitive not to scope but to the salient representative instance, the picture of a single bird stuck in an oil spill.[37]

Similarly, H&B researchers note that heuristic-based judgments of overall life satisfaction or happiness are woefully inaccurate; in this same sense, they are quite unlikely to withstand even cursory reflection. Thus, Kahneman, relying in significant part on ongoing work by Schwarz, notes, for instance, that people may report, and even believe, that they are happy because the affect-relevant events that are readily retrieved from memory or *available* are favorable ones, or that they anchor their judgment of how happy or unhappy they are to their appraisal of the first affect-relevant event or domain that comes to mind. Thus, people may report higher *overall life satisfaction* merely because they have recently picked up a lost dime planted by the experimenters or learned that the team they root for just won a game. It is almost impossible to believe that anyone would, on reflection, believe that his life, overall, was truly better because he had just found a dime. Similarly, the correlation between "overall life satisfaction" and dating "success" radically increases if subjects are asked how often they have dated in the last month before, rather than after, they are asked how satisfied they are, presumably because the happiness-relevant data they recall is about dating only when they are first asked about that life domain.[38] These sorts of unstable, readily disclaimed misjudgments may well lead people to believe that they have made good general life choices when they have not, or bad ones when they ought not to change course. It makes it tricky to evaluate the hedonic impact of a host of policy interventions, too, if our outcome measure, reported happiness, is so unstable and unreliable.

Generally, then, the H&B researchers are more or less committed to the idea that people behave more rationally when they follow the dictates of conventional rational-choice theory. This is not to say that they believe departures from rationality are invariably "costly" at all, that any real embodied people even have the capacity to behave rationally on all occasions, or that the gains from behaving more rationally—assuming we would be capable of doing so—are generally worth the cost and bother. But they believe that it is better, all else equal, to make veridical judgments than false ones. This includes judgments about probabilities of future outcomes arising from particular actions, but it is not restricted to probability assessment. They believe that logically incoherent judgments can never be veridical, and that it is better to evaluate end-states in a fashion that is both coherent and insensitive to the ways in which the end-state is named or the decision context in which it is evaluated. At the same time, though, they believe that we will frequently fail to achieve the reasonable goal of behaving more rationally (in these senses). Why?

D. WHY DO PEOPLE BEHAVE IRRATIONALLY?

There is no simple or uniform answer that H&B researchers give to the question of why people behave irrationally. Many would almost surely think it inappropriate to give *any* general answer, believing it more plausible that distinct heuristics are best understood as reflecting quite distinct cognitive processes. Still, I think there is a dominant general story about the place of heuristic thinking in overall cognition that goes something like this: Our brains have two "systems." Cognition that occurs in System One, including most of the rationality-distorting heuristics, is associative, effortless, unreflective, rapid, intuitive, and fairly automatic or tacit rather than conscious. System Two, on the other hand, is at core rule-based, analytical, and explicit.[39]

It is a very difficult issue for me to assess, in even the most preliminary fashion, whether H&B theorists generally think of Systems One and Two in wholly metaphoric terms, or believe that each system corresponds to something in the physical brain. Is System One thinking associated with particular specified neurological processes or with the workings of distinct brain regions? Would we expect some or all System Two processes to break down if there were lesions in particular brain regions in the same way that we think that certain forms of memory or visual perception are compromised when there are lesions? Some H&B scholars might believe that describing something as System One cognition represents nothing more than a summary conclusion about the nature of the thought process we observe, while believing that thought processes with certain qualities can emerge from a quite disparate array of underlying neurological mechanisms. For instance, we could say that any time we observe thinking that is rapid or non-abstract or more likely to be the output of a person acting under high cognitive load, we are observing System One thinking. This is quite different from making the claim that there are any particular known neural correlates to each of the rapid, context-based, non-abstract thought processes that we dub System One processes.

This "physicalist," less metaphoric claim would surely be harder to defend. It seems that it would have to rely on any number of propositions that might be tricky to define, let alone defend. First, it would either have to rely on the idea that the brain is fundamentally divided into only two functionally differentiated regions, a proposition that is manifestly untrue, or on the proposition that the multiple regions we have identified can each be classified as "belonging" to one of two larger systems. Second, it would seem to rely on the idea that there is a fairly sharp discontinuity between conscious and reflective practices and unconscious intuitions. Third, it might rely on the proposition that each judgment or decision is made by a single brain region, rather than picturing decisions as the output of multiple interconnected processes. It is not merely the case that I am dubious that any of these propositions is defensible, since I obviously put little or no weight on my views about neuroscience. What is far more important is that I am dubious that H&B theorists who have used the System One/System Two metaphor have really committed to any of them.

At any rate, whether those who refer to Systems One and Two mean to refer to two physically distinguishable pathways to certain judgments or decisions or as metaphoric descriptions of either the process of reaching judgment or the sorts of judgments and decisions that emerge, H&B theorists who use the concept have differentiated the systems along many dimensions. For instance, they believe that virtually all functioning adults engage in System One cognition pretty much equally well. Many H&B theorists—though this is not anything like a consensus or even majority position—seem to believe that System One thinking is sufficient to meet most "primitive survival tasks." Thus, to the extent that our thinking is evolutionarily adaptive, it is System One thinking that is most plainly adaptive in this view,[40] though it is hardly uncommon for H&B psychologists to emphasize that System Two rationality permits the sort of flexibility to deal with novel situations that may radically increase inclusive fitness.[41]

Many, but again, by no means all, H&B theorists believe that System One thinking is highly contextual rather than abstract. People engaging in System One thinking are unable to draw inferences about situations they have not directly experienced simply on the basis of the formal features of the situation. The canonical example comes from anthropology. An illiterate Uzbek—ostensibly showing high reliance on System One thought—is presented with a syllogism: "In the Far North, where there is snow, all bears are white. Novaya Zemlya is in the Far North and there is always snow there. What color are the bears there?" The respondent could not answer but merely stated that he had only encountered black bears in his own experience and could not speculate on what bears would look like in places he had never been.[42]

System Two thinking is, in this view, pretty much the opposite. It requires hard work and tends, therefore, unlike System One thinking, to be disrupted by distractions, stress, and time pressure. It is conscious. It is less sensitive to the factual content and context of propositions than to the formal analytic properties of these propositions and what the propositions logically entail. Generally, H&B theorists imagine that System Two works to insure more rational judgment by sometimes overriding and sometimes accepting System One intuitions,[43] though like many of the F&F theorists, many H&B people seem to assume that the choice to use a heuristic is sometimes conscious and deliberately processed rather than automatic.[44]

At any rate, some H&B researchers have also argued that the capacity to engage in System Two thinking is influenced not merely by situational mediators, like time pressure or distraction, but by innate or learned individual distinctions in the *capacity* to engage in System Two thinking in more situations. As a result people who are trained in statistics are more likely to override the use of many heuristics.[45] Similarly, people who are more "intelligent" (in the sense measured by traditional "g-loaded" tests that purportedly measure "general intelligence," like IQ tests or the SATs) use many of the heuristics less frequently.[46] The point, for the group of H&B theorists most interested in individual differences, is not that the "sort" of intelligence that g-loaded tests measure is the only sort of relevant intelligence, or even the most important sort, but that it is a genuine measure of *something*. That something appears to be the capacity to manipulate non-contextualized formal symbols in accord with the dictates of conventional rational-choice theory.

For instance, subjects with higher SAT scores less frequently err in making veridical probability judgments, especially when subjects' judgments are non-veridical because logically impossible. Thus, for instance, subjects with higher SAT scores are less prone to commit the conjunction fallacy that results from the use of the representativeness heuristic. I discussed this fallacy earlier, noting that people think it more likely that 1,000 people will die in a San Francisco earthquake than in a natural disaster west of the Rockies. There is another "conjunction fallacy" test that is widely discussed in the literature. Subjects responding to what is widely known as the "Linda problem" are given a description of Linda as a left-wing hippie intellectual ("Linda is 31 years old, single, outspoken, and very bright. She majored in philosophy in college. As a student, she was deeply concerned with issues of discrimination and social justice, and also participated in anti-nuclear demonstrations"). They are then asked what it is likely she is doing now. Many more people in between-subject tests, and somewhat more in within-subjects tests[47] say that is more likely that she is a "feminist bank teller" than say that she is a "bank teller." This is true even though feminist bank tellers are a sub-set of bank tellers and that it is a necessary truth that it is no more probable that someone is a member of a sub-class than the class in which it is contained. In the probabilistic (but not the frequentist) version of the problem, the mean SAT score of the subjects who committed the conjunction fallacy in within-subjects tests was 82 points lower than those who avoided it.[48] Those with higher SAT scores are less vulnerable to many other manifestations of what H&B researchers see as irrationally biased judgments as well.[49]

There is some evidence as well that people with certain forms of innate or learned personality dispositions (that might be characterized as "thinking styles") are also more prone to override their heuristic "intuitions." Most interestingly, people who might be described as "open-minded" rather than dogmatic, especially in the sense that they accept the possibility that their own thinking is fallible and that they feel obliged to evaluate the quality of arguments without much regard to their predispositions about how an issue ought to be resolved, are less prone to make many of the errors that the H&B researchers have identified as "biases." If one wants to get a quick, intuitive feel for the sorts of dispositions one might be trying to measure here, think about how two subjects might evaluate the statements; "people should always take into consideration evidence that goes against their own beliefs" and "No one can talk me out of something that I know is right."[50]

Most H&B "two system"—or dual-process—models assume that System One thinking inevitably or automatically occurs and is simply sometimes overridden by

System Two. It appears that most H&B researchers assume that when we "cognize" a problem, the "systems" engage in something like temporal order. Accounts of when, why, and how "correction" occurs are not terribly lucid or developed in the H&B literature, in precisely the same way that we will come to see in Chapter Three that accounts of the "domain" of domain-specific responses is poorly specified in F&F theory.

It would, of course, be possible to imagine, instead, that the tasks that "fully rational" people must perform are often quite difficult, and that some—but not all—use "easy techniques" rather than harder ones to solve problems. But they do not "begin" with the easy ones, and then override them if they have the System Two-based ability to do so; they merely solve the problem in a fashion that approximates the rational-choice solution *as best they can given their capacities*. In this view, what the dual-process theorists call System Two capacities is simply a summary of capacities that are less uniformly distributed across individuals that permit a sub-set of people, say, to think about probability through statistical inference, processing available evidence rather than some substituted judgment.[51]

Those H&B researchers who advocate the idea that there are individual differences—particularly "intelligence" differences—in the use of a fairly substantial sub-set of heuristics employ that observation to make a number of points. First, and most important, they argue that the fact that "more intelligent" people avoid the biases to refute a claim frequently made by F&F proponents that I discuss in detail in Chapter Four. The F&F claim is that experimental subjects who have "erred" in the eyes of H&B researchers have construed the task in a fashion that is somehow *more rational* than the way the researchers have. (For instance, they think that those committing the conjunction fallacy in the Linda problem are picking up on more subtle conversational cues and answering the "real question" better.) Stanovich and West respond in a quite typical fashion:

> [We] should resist the conclusion that individuals with more computational power are systematically computing the *non*normative response. Such an outcome would be an absolute first in a psychometric field that is 100 years and thousands of studies old.... [G]iven that positive manifold is the norm among cognitive tasks, a negative correlation (or, to a lesser extent, the lack of a correlation) between a probabilistic reasoning task and some standard cognitive ability measures might be taken as a signal that the wrong normative model is being applied to the former task or that there are alternative models that are equally appropriate.[52]

At the same time, when these researchers find that conventionally defined "intelligence" does *not* correlate with performance on a task that H&B researchers have identified as a bias, they are considerably more likely to look to for what the F&F people far more frequently look for, and expect to, discover: a good reason for a rational person to make use of the heuristic strategy at issue. Thus, for instance, it seems that high SAT subjects exhibit what social psychologists like Ross have identified as the "false consensus" effect as often as lower SAT subjects—assuming their own beliefs are more representative of general public opinion than they really are.[53] That may well be the case because in a world of limited information, it really is a good guess that one will believe what most people believe, barring some additional information about why one is atypical. Thus, if I knew nothing about X—and for these purposes, I might well imagine that *I* am X—it would be prudent to think that whatever X believed is what most people believe since X is simply sampled randomly from the whole population in an implicit public opinion poll and is therefore more likely to belong to the larger sub-group.[54]

Finding that "smarter" people use many heuristics less often plays somewhat the same role as finding that subjects typically *endorse* the "formally rational" response rather than the one that manifests some form of F&F "ecological rationality" once each response is explained to them. The argument that H&B researchers have made goes as follows. If subjects really thought that what conventional rational-choice theorists would call the non-normative responses were better, they would stick to them once the best arguments for the non-normative and for the normative responses were presented to them. Because far more people switch from conventionally non-normative to conventionally normative responses than do the opposite once one assists them in reasoning reflectively by providing arguments for each response, H&B theorists argue that the subjects they viewed as prone to "biased" judgment did not have a different end or task construal in mind but merely did the assigned task in a less satisfactory fashion.[55]

For reasons that I expect will be substantially clearer when I work through F&F critiques of H&B research in Chapter Four, this is not a particularly powerful argument. F&F theorists might justifiably resist this interpretation, even without positing, as many have on occasion, that subjects would *not* perform more conventionally "normatively" if given more information. (Occasional F&F claims that "intelligent" people respond just like others or that subjects do not shift to conventionally normative responses after being given explanations of the problems in their thinking are really quite weak.[56]) If, though, the F&F theorists are correct that the "right" response to the abstract paper-and-pencil logic tests that the H&B people give in experimental settings is the conventionally rational answer simply *by definition*, then it is not surprising that *highlighting* the purely formal and logical properties of the problem will get people to criticize their heuristic responses. It is also not surprising that those with higher levels of conventional "intelligence," measured as the capacity to manipulate context-free abstract logic puzzles, are more prone to answer questions without regard to context. But it is only if one reduces the problem to its symbolic logical components—that is, if one strips it of semantic and pragmatic context—that the "right" answer is inevitably the normatively preferred response.[57] I attend to this debate most explicitly in Chapter Four, but it is important for now to point out that the debate is not resolved simply by noting which answers people stick to when given certain information about the problems they have answered.

E. A VERY BRIEF NOTE ON "BUNDLED" DECISIONS AND "ELIMINATION BY ASPECTS"

Frequently, we cannot make decisions that permit us to combine more-desired end-states with one another. If I choose to go to a tapas bar tonight, I may have to drive further than if I choose to go to an Indian restaurant, or spend more on parking, or deal with the familiar rude waiter at the available tapas bar. It may be quite difficult to decide which restaurant I "prefer" even if I am quite sure I prefer tapas to Indian food, a shorter to a longer drive, cheaper to more costly parking, and kinder or more obsequious waiters to rude ones. It is easy to see that many decisions are "bundled" even if it is hard to know precisely what it might mean to break decisions down into their fully discrete aspects. Is the "discrete" desire to eat Indian food tonight better thought of as a decision that itself combines judgments about "taste," with judgments about the health risks of butter-heavy food, with judgments about the symbolic social meaning of eating one food rather than another, and so on?

The H&B literature I have discussed thus far largely helps us understand how we would evaluate the expected utility of the discrete aspects of decisions, but it does not directly address how we make choices when these aspects cannot be "unbundled." So the H&B literature I have discussed might help us understand why we do or don't estimate the health risks of butter-rich food properly, or recognize *whether* Indian food is butter-rich or not, and help us understand how we evaluate health risks, given the context in which this evaluative judgment is made and our preferences elicited. It will help us, for instance, attend to questions of the following form: With what do we contrast the particular health risk we face if we eat certain foods? The health risk of other foods? The morbidity or mortality risks of other leisure activities that also could be said to generate "utility"?

Academics associated with the H&B school, though, have been interested not just in these sorts of perceptual judgment issues but in comprehending how people make decisions when discrete choices involve selecting bundles of attributes. One would expect that the decision-making process posited by full-blown rational-choice theorists—that the person could assess the expected utility of all the bundled attributes and simply add them up as a prelude to selecting the utility-maximizing option—would be one that a cognitively limited decision maker might not engage in. There might well be "heuristic-like" methods to select the best choice without assessing and combining the value of all features inevitably associated with a particular choice, and one would not be surprised to find that H&B theorists have modeled such heuristics. As Frederick notes, though, these sorts of decision heuristics are likely consciously chosen System Two heuristics, deliberately designed to cope with the problem of undue informational and computational demands, rather than System One, unconscious heuristics that are closer to intuitive and perceptual.[58]

The most prominent such attempt to model the way in which we reach decisions when alternatives have multiple attributes is Amos Tversky's early theory of elimination by aspects (EBA).[59] A subject making decisions using the EBA method sees each alternative that she might select as a set or bundle of aspects. At each stage in the decision-making process, a single aspect is selected. An alternative is thought to have a "positive" aspect value if it possesses some virtue above some threshold level of acceptability. All the alternatives that do not "include" the aspect (i.e., in which the value is below the threshold) are eliminated, and the process is continued, one aspect at a time, until only one alternative remains.

The intuition behind the theory—if not its mathematical structure—and the ways in which it contrasts with conventional rational-choice theories that subjects choose the alternative that maximizes expected value, can be explained without difficulty. Assume that you are picking between three restaurants: an Italian restaurant one block south of your apartment and two equally appealing Chinese restaurants, one of which is a block south of your apartment and the other a block north. Assume, too, that you are indifferent between having Chinese food and Italian food this evening, and indifferent between traveling one block north and one block south to dinner. Expected utility theory predicts that the chances that you will choose to go to each restaurant is one in three, because the expected utility of each choice is the same. But elimination by aspects theory suggests, quite persuasively, that the chances of going to the Italian restaurant is 50 percent and the chance of going to each Chinese restaurant is 25 percent, because the choice among alternatives is made on the basis of the most significant aspect first (what kind of food do I want tonight?), eliminating one or the other sort of food, without regard to the second, markedly more trivial aspect (do I want to go one block north or south?)

Moreover, the theory implies a point that I return to discuss in thinking through the problem of incommensurability in Chapter Eight: the fact that we might make the choice between the two equally tasty and inexpensive Chinese restaurants a touch easier (imagine one is *three* blocks north, the other just a single block south) so that one Chinese restaurant clearly dominated the other would not make the chance of picking the one-block-south Chinese restaurant 100 percent if it were in a pair-wise comparison with the Italian one. For example, if the decision maker learned at the last moment that the more proximate Chinese restaurant were closed for the evening, she would not inevitably go to the Italian restaurant though she had thought of herself as essentially indifferent between the proximate Chinese restaurant and the Italian one.

Think, too, of an example that Tversky uses. Imagine one cannot decide whether to go to Paris or Rome on a vacation. The fact that one could easily decide to go to Paris *plus* be given $5 rather than merely go to Paris does not mean that it is easy to decide whether to go to Rome or go to Paris plus get $5. Choice probabilities approach 0 or 1 only when there is a clear divergence between the utility of the choices or an easy basis for comparison of utilities when they are proximate.

A decision maker who chooses from a multifaceted, bundled set of alternatives using elimination by aspects simply ignores all features shared by all alternatives or absent in all and then eliminates any alternative lacking a virtue (or, more precisely, possessing "it" below a threshold level of acceptability) associated with the aspect that has the highest probable decision weight. The process is sequential and lexical. The bases for aspect ordering are not obvious or specified. They may be influenced by others (e.g., advertisers who attempt to direct consumers to focus on the traits that all of the advertiser's competitors lack). They may be established in the first instance in accord with some expected utility calculation that is itself more global and compensatory, For instance, I think I will *first* discriminate among cars on the basis of price, eliminating all those above a threshold, but I got to that point by making a judgment involving compensatory thinking about the probable impact of higher price on my judgment of expected utility.

I am highly skeptical that decision makers use EBA, rather than compensatory decision-making processes, *invariably*. I do not doubt that we can find situations in which people appear to be using EBA, especially in situations in which "secondary" aspects are unlikely to have a major impact on aggregate utility, either because they are trivial or because they vary little across alternatives. But what is more critical to note is that Tversky conceives of the use of EBA in decision making in much the same way that he conceives of most other heuristics in judgment: Its use is a function of limited information-processing capacity; it may well work pretty well lots of the time, and it may misfire badly.

Let me illustrate the latter, and more important, point: EBA, like any short-cut method, may harm its users. In explicating this point, Tversky discusses an advertisement for a company that provides computer programming training that is plainly intended to prod consumers to use EBA. In the ad, there are several dozen eggs, each representing a competitor, and one walnut, representing the advertised company. The voice-over tells people that not all companies have on-line training facilities while some eggs are removed, job placement services while some more eggs are removed, or allow people to use veterans' benefits to pay for the training. At this point, only the walnut is left.[60] As he notes, "there may be contexts in which [EBA] provides a good approximation to much more complicated compensatory [mechanisms] and could thus serve as a useful simplifying process." But at the same time, he recognizes that the decision maker might be making a bad mistake if he eliminated some programs because they lacked a feature of no moment to him (e.g., he is ineligible for veterans' benefits anyway) or lacked a feature that mattered but which was outweighed. For instance, placement services might matter, but if one of the schools that the choice maker eliminated because it lacked placement services had radically superior training, it might well be better to choose that and find jobs on one's own.[61]

My descriptive skepticism about whether decision makers in fact invariably use EBA comes in two flavors, the first of which I quite tentatively believe Tversky shared. First, *if* the decision about the proper sequence of aspects is dictated in some significant part by decisions about the likelihood that an aspect will change the relative expected utility of choice alternatives, it is hard to figure out in what way the decision-making process is not one that in significant part *estimates* expected utility by *first* establishing a *general* compensatory scale that is then applied lexicographically. Thus, for instance, if I am looking to go out to a "normal" modestly inexpensive dinner at an ethnic restaurant, being located in Palo Alto, Mountain View, or Menlo Park may be a first-order lexical aspect. I simply do not consider going to restaurants in Napa or Sonoma (two hours away). I *do* consider restaurants in Sonoma or Napa when I am thinking about expensive "special" dinners, so location is not the lexical discriminator in relationship to restaurants but only a sub-set of restaurants. If that is the case, though, wouldn't it be more accurate to say that I am trading off quality and convenience non-lexically in deciding how and when to apply a lexical EBA rule to a sub-set of seemingly "similar" cases? My knowledge that no distinctions in the quality of Thai food would overcome the inconvenience of the long drive *is* a decision made non-lexically, an expected utility-based decision that comes out differently when it comes to very fancy restaurants.

I think, though, that I have further disagreements with what I take to be Tversky's position, to the degree that he implies that EBA is, descriptively, a near-universal strategy. It is simply not the case that once I decide I am willing to drive to Napa or Sonoma for a fancy meal—that is, that all fancy restaurants in the broadly defined Bay Area "share" the trait of being "close enough" that none will be ruled out through an EBA strategy—*either* restaurant quality *or* travel distance is a lexical cue. I may still make expected utility trade-offs in which distance is a negative factor. Even though all fancy restaurants in the "Bay Area" are not "eliminated"—in the way that a Los Angeles restaurant would be—the fact that going to some restaurant R necessitates a four-hour round-trip drive remains a strike against it, a strike that must be outweighed by greater virtues along some other dimensions of quality, novelty, and so on. Thus, EBA, in my view, has no clear domain, not only in terms of whether it generates satisfactory results but whether it represents the best descriptive picture of decision making. But it is instructive in helping us think about the limits of making simple expected utility calculations.

F. THE INFLUENCE OF H&B RESEARCH ON LEGAL THEORY, POLICY, AND PRACTICE: A BRIEF CONCEPTUAL OVERVIEW

However we come to see that H&B theorists understand what an irrational "bias" might be and how such biases arise, we must recall that the picture of decision makers as imperfectly self-serving transformed many of the policy debates that went on in the law schools over the last thirty years. In this section, I do not give anything resembling detailed accounts of the particular disputes that were filtered through the more general debate between rational-choice and H&B theory. To some extent, I have already given some exemplars of the influence of H&B theory on law, and I give many more in Chapters Six and Seven. I obviously will, however, make brief reference to specific controversies in this section: For instance, can consumers or regulators properly appraise risk? Can jurors adequately assess the *ex ante* negligence of a party who was revealed, *ex post*, to have caused harm? Will seamless Coasean bargaining occur after injunctions are given or will people "overvalue" the end-state they are granted by injunction as a result of endowment effects? My main aim, instead, is to describe in broad-brush terms the *pattern* of work influenced by H&B research.

At core, the H&B-influenced literature focused on people in two distinct roles. People could be characterized as principals, as subjects making decisions designed to meet their own ends, or as agents, subjects who at least ostensibly seek to meet the ends of some principal or principals whose ends they feel, or should feel, duty bound to meet. Principals in this view are the primary decision makers who are essentially unfettered by explicit rules in making their decisions. They are the source of commands rather than those asked to follow commands. Agents are persons asked to implement some principal or principals' plans. Thus, in the standard picture, the principals are, in the conventional commercial economic realm, consumers picking among commodities or workers deciding what job, if any, to take; in the political realm, voters selecting desired public policies and desired collective goods; in the social realm generally, individuals deciding how many, if any, children to have, drivers deciding whether to drive more or less cautiously. Agents might be jurors, asked to follow a judge's explicit instructions or judges asked to be faithful to legislative commands; legislators attempting to follow the appropriately weighted preferences of their constituents (if following a fundamentally pluralist rather than republican model of a legislator's duties); managers trying to maximize the value of shareholders' interests.[62] The legal literature that has drawn on H&B scholarship has focused on the degree to which both principals and agents may frequently fail to meet their ends.

It is, then, a literature focused at core on *failure*. It is focused on why market failure is more common than one would suspect if one examined only situations in which information is absent, rather than processed poorly. It is a literature that focuses on the possibility that regulators respond to salient problems and risks that are less significant than less salient, but more serious, ones. It is a literature that tends, to various degrees, to suggest that technocrats might often profitably displace decentralized decision makers—whether consumers in markets or democratically responsive administrators or legislators.

Broadly speaking, agents and principals will fail in two distinct ways. First, they will misperceive "facts." Early research focused to a considerable extent on the misperception of facts about the probability of distinct events, but many heuristics that lead people to misjudge probabilities lead them to misjudge both other sorts of facts and to make unstable judgments of the value of end-states. As I noted earlier, errors in judging probability have the same basic structure—instead of perceiving as best as the rational mind could the actual past frequency of an event type and projecting that frequency into the future, unless there is reason to expect change, the decision maker *substitutes* some more readily processed surrogate for probability.

Several examples might be useful: So, for instance, instead of figuring out how often people have gotten disease X rather than Y and then using past frequencies to assess the probability of contracting each, we estimate the relative probability of X and Y by implicitly comparing how available or readily recalled instances of each are. This may affect the steps people take in role as "consumers" or "social actors" to prevent each disease, and affect as voters how they believe research funds ought to be allocated. We may, in the same way, choose either to clean up toxic waste dumps, mandate costlier cars that emit less carbon monoxide, or build roads with more expensive median dividers to avoid head-on collisions. Our judgments about which project is most urgent or most cost-justified may depend on mistaken judgments about relative risks, and judgments about whether risk-reducing expenditures generally are worthwhile may be impacted by forms of "optimism bias" that lead people to downplay their vulnerability.

At the same time, a juror—acting as an agent, applying collectively determined rules to facts that she should find as accurately as possible—judging whether a tort defendant acted negligently in failing to take a certain precaution might also have to make a risk estimate. How likely was the defendant's conduct, given the precautions she took, to result in a particular level of harm?

Or recall the "anchoring and adjustment" heuristic, in which people's perception of real quantities—including probabilistic frequencies—may be established by an initial cue, whether the cue is relevant or not. We know, experimentally, that it influences subjects' estimates of the number of physicians and surgeons listed in the local yellow pages to write the last four digits of their social security number: Their estimates were strongly correlated with their social security numbers. It might well then be that judgments about, say, the amount of compensation top executives at Fortune 500 companies receive, which may well be germane to voter judgments about appropriate income taxes or proposals to limit compensation for corporate managers generally or those managing companies receiving government aid, are affected by anchoring rather than more thorough investigation.

Similarly, anchoring might impact judgments about the *value* of certain end-states. I mentioned that experimental and actual jurors often set the damages that they award for a particular injury—judging in essence the disutility of the outcome that the plaintiff suffered—in part by anchoring the judgment to the amount that the plaintiff *requested*. Similarly, in responding to contingent valuation questions of the form, "How much is it worth to you to protect a particular wetland?" the use of bounded scales with distinct end-points may have a large influence on the answers people give because people anchor to one of the end-points.

What was most important in "reforming" the legal literature was the novel emphasis placed on the observation that principals fail not solely for the reason posited by conventional rational-choice theorists. Rational-choice theorists had long noted that there are external impediments to perceiving reality, that information is scarce and that it is costly to obtain more of it. Instead, what H&B-influenced writers emphasized was that they will, *internally*, process a good deal of readily available information in a fashion that leads to erroneous conclusions because their cognitive processing methods, though likely functional in a range of typical circumstances, are grossly imperfect in many important situations they actually confront. This is especially true given the presence of other agents prone to exploit others by presenting the factual world or option set in a way that nudges others to choose what the manipulators wish they would choose.

Having honed and developed a disposition to be suspicious of the most optimistic accounts that consumers and voters could make decisions that truly served their own interests, H&B-influenced policymakers were hardly uniform in recommending responses to the perceived problems. Still, there was certainly a standard menu of interventions that policymakers influenced by the H&B literature have suggested at various points The errors made by the worker or consumer at least suggest the possibility of certain *forms* of mandatory disclosure—giving information that is more likely to be processed correctly. And, if processing errors are ubiquitous even when we take maximally effective steps to reduce them, we may need uniform term quality regulation: The standard argument is that heuristic biases in estimates often cannot be overcome and that the products consumers choose given prevailing incorrect estimates do not meet the stable ends of the consumer as well as the mandated product would. Naturally, in ways we return to consider in Chapter Seven, the attractiveness of this option depends in part on the degree of heterogeneity in underlying consumer preferences.

Voters (principals, again) subject to manipulation by "availability entrepreneurs" may overestimate the risk of bad events that are persistently brought to their attention and underestimate risks that get less coverage. Law reformers may believe that "expert" risk regulation by administrative agencies is less likely to be grounded in such misperception and urge greater deference to experts in many settings in which the most serious sorts of long-term risks are likely to be less salient.

We are obviously not, though, worried that the juror (an agent) will not meet his own long-term ends. Instead, reformers influenced by the H&B literature worry that whatever policy ends would be met if the juror found facts correctly—optimal deterrence, corrective justice whatever—will not be met because the agent cannot do the job she is asked to do. We might choose to displace the jury's decision-making role: once again, the possibility of looking to "technocratic expertise" as a rescue. We might merely alter evidence rules or jury instructions; in this regard, for instance, we may observe or want to tinker with rules that minimize the manifestation of one aspect of hindsight bias, the tendency to believe that others should have foreseen what eventuated. A "reformer" might recommend bifurcating trials so that juries considering damage measurement, who know precisely what ended up happening, do not make judgments about whether defendants negligently ignored undue risks in the first instance.

Second, as I noted in some detail earlier, principals will misevaluate end-states, either in the relatively strong sense that their evaluations fail to meet minimal rationality requirements, like transitivity, or the somewhat weaker sense that the heuristic-based evaluations that they make at a particular point of time are especially prone to be not only unstable but the object of something we conceive of as well-considered regret. As I noted, it is often difficult to know just what to make of the proposition that principals misevaluate end-states, rather than misperceive facts, because they use heuristics. At some level, as preference-neutral liberals at least, we posit the existence of principals who articulate and evaluate ends that are by and large beyond rational reproach.

Academic lawyers and policymakers were often influenced by claims that people frequently violated simple rationality norms, making judgments as principals or agents that were internally incoherent, most typically by choosing A over B and B over A simultaneously, depending on how each option was described or by adding some irrelevant alternative C to the mix. Generally, rational-choice theorists resisting this claim that we observed such irrationality typically argued, though, that the goods *are* different in the two distinct settings in ways the critics are simply missing, or that the agent has met *some* intelligible goal, even if he has failed to meet the goal that the behavioral researcher attributed to him. I discuss at length in Chapter Four variants of this criticism offered by scholars associated not with rational-choice theory but with the F&F school. In each case, those skeptical of the H&B school allege that the scholars in that school misapprehend the functional skills of actual decision makers.

For now, I simply want to mention that this particular reply by rational-choice theorists has indeed seemed to me especially plausible in response to certain findings criticizing the rationality of experimental jurors, the agents most typically studied in the legal literature. Take, for example, the finding that jurors suffer from one particular sort of context effect—extremeness aversion—that causes them to reach irrational "compromise" verdicts. To put this point in the terms I have been using to describe the structure of claims that people make biased judgments, subjects who are averse to picking extreme options substitute a readily-perceived cue—is option O the intermediate option—for a more complex judgment—is it really the best option, all things considered? Thus, in a study I co-authored with Rottensteich and Tversky, experimental jurors were asked to judge whether a defendant was guilty of manslaughter rather than murder when he shot an off-duty policeman moonlighting as a shopping center guard who used racist epithets in confronting and detaining the defendant though he had committed no crime. The group of jurors who were told that *murdering* an off-duty policeman is *capital murder*, rather than ordinary murder if it is murder at all, because of the victim's identity as a police officer, was far more prone to convict of murder than manslaughter, even though the victim's identity did not bear on the only relevant question the juror/agents were *directed* to answer in distinguishing murder and manslaughter. The answer to that question turns *solely* on whether the defendant acted under the influence of extreme emotional disturbance for which there was a reasonable explanation or excuse when he killed. But a rational-choice theorist would correctly note that it is not clear that the *overt* instructions given to these "agents"—attend only to whether the defendant was acting under the influence of reasonably explicable emotional disturbance in grading whether the homicide is murder or merely manslaughter—are truly *complete*. The ends that these agents might reasonably think should be met in setting penalty levels for homicide may include other supplementary or even contradictory ends. The *fuller* homicide-grading ends may be described as an effort to *balance* two distinct forms of culpability. In one form, we focus on the defendant's level of self-control and premeditation. In the other, we focus on the heinousness of the crime. If we believe that killing an "ordinary" victim is not as bad as killing someone we decide to label a police officer, it is *appropriate*, not irrational, to compromise between capital murder and manslaughter by punishing a party more severely if he has killed a policeman impulsively or reactively than if he killed an "ordinary" victim in that way.

I am quite skeptical, though, that rational-choice theorists will invariably be able to make these sorts of plausible claims that H&B scholars have simply failed to see that the subjects' ends are more complex than they might at first blush appear. Changing elicitation procedures and contexts may simply really matter. Take a case I raised, in text and in a note, earlier in this chapter. The principal may be asked a single functional question—whether he prefers Vacation A or Vacation B—in three distinct ways. He may be asked whether he will cancel plans he has made to take Vacation A (without financial penalty), and substitute Vacation B, cancel B (without penalty) and substitute A, or book one or the other assuming he has made no plans. Or an agent—an experimental juror—may be asked a parallel set of questions in two distinct ways: will he give custody of a child to parent A' or B'? He may be asked whether he will deny custody to A', which is tantamount to granting it to B', or whether he'd be prone to grant custody to A' or B'? If vacation A (or parent A') has many markedly bad and many markedly good traits while B (and B') is blander, he is prone both to cancel A (deny custody to A), showing a preference for B (B')—and to book it (grant custody to A')—showing a near-simultaneous preference for A (A'). He will not typically cancel B, or deny custody to B'.

As I noted, the standard explanation for this behavior among behavioral social scientists is that principals engage in what is dubbed "reason-based" decision making, which is quite distinct from *rational* decision making. If asked to take what looks like an affirmative step, like booking a vacation, they seek affirmative reasons to take the step; if asked to take a negative step, like canceling a vacation, they look for reasons (A's salient negative features) to take that negative step. The "normative" decision maker in classical rational-choice theory of course simply adds up the value of the positive and negative traits in Vacation A and determines whether or not he prefers the sum of those traits to the sum of the rather neutral traits of Vacation B. The decision maker using heuristic short-cuts rather than engaging in compensatory, multicue decision making to evaluate which outcome is preferred and less preferred ends up behaving inconsistently.

Now, it is always possible for rational-choice theorists to describe the chosen end-states in these cases so that rationality norms simply *cannot* be violated. For instance, one can say that one end-state is "having cancelled vacation A" and another is "booking vacation B" rather than that the end-states are the vacations themselves. But this sort of response seems unhelpful if applied this facilely. Because it is difficult to specify any genuine external features of the option that have been altered simply by re-naming the option, the notion that the decision maker has behaved rationally is hardly plausible.

As law reformers, then, those suspicious of the rational-choice theorists' account may worry that choices can be too readily manipulated by putting distinct options in particular contexts. We should worry about, and possibly regulate, retailers who push people to buy the highest profit margin item by presenting it alongside a more expensive and a cheaper item, or by presenting it next to an ostensibly similar item that it clearly dominates. Outside our "reformer" mode, when we are, say, merely guiding students in a trial practice setting, we may simply note without approval or condemnation that fact finders *can* be manipulated by the way in which an outcome is characterized (e.g., deny bail or grant it) or by the context in which an option is placed (e.g., as the intermediate or extreme penalty)

Think, too, about another example from the context-dependence literature. A context-dependent principal, selecting among settlement offers in a lawsuit, will be more prone to select a particular offer P rather than another offer Q when a similar but markedly inferior offer P' is added to the menu. In our experiments, we offered one group of experimental subjects the choice between two settlements for a nuisance suit in which the defendant "club" had created a nuisance by msking too much noise. Fundamentally, the choice was between a promise to abate the noise and an offer to pay the plaintiff to stay in a hotel over the weekends when the club was at its noisiest and give the plaintiff $120/week in cash as long as it operated as a nuisance. The second group was given these two options plus a third that was a "bad" version of the second: instead of getting $120 in cash in addition to the hotel stay, he would get $40 in cash plus $85 in credit to be used only at this or three other dance clubs. The subjects are told that the plaintiff attends such clubs only three or so times a year. While 53 percent of the subjects choose the promise to abate the noise in the group given just two options, only 26 percent choose it if given the three-option set. No one takes the third (clearly dominated) option.[63]

The preference-elicitation procedure thus affects the rank ordering of P and Q, though it cannot affect their real traits. Should we ask, in our law reform mode, whether judges should supervise settlement conferences to preclude these sorts of preference-manipulating offers? Or, in our "teach tactics" mode, should we simply inform our students that this technique might work to help them meet their clients' desire to have the person on the other side of the table choose what the client prefers her to choose?

G. CONCLUSION

It is most profitable for policymakers and lawyers to think of H&B theorists as treating conventional rational-choice models as normatively appealing but descriptively inaccurate. For a variety of reasons, people often misperceive the world around them. At a very general level, they have some perception P that they believe is a proxy for some fact-of-interest F, and judgments about P *substitute* for more considered judgments about F. Quick, relatively effortless heuristic judgments based on the substitute variable rather than the full range of information that is available may be accurate enough, most of the time, but people using them may act just like uninformed consumers and voters would act. At the same time, heuristics may lead people to evaluate end-states in ways that are either plainly problematic (incoherent or frame sensitive) or at least arguably troublesome (prone to be regretted).

It might well be the case that there is a hidden rationality to some of the judgments that H&B theorists deride—experimental subjects may sometimes have different ends than those the researchers ascribe to them, seeming inconsistencies in judgment may at times be a result of reinterpreting experimental prompts—but if the H&B theorists are persuasive, then biases and errors are often real and costly. Since much of conventional policy science is grounded in the supposition that people will generally be able to choose from among available options those that maximize value, the discovery that people will often misestimate probabilities and misevaluate the end-states of the options that could result if they chose a particular option was naturally quite a challenge to the common wisdom.

3

THE FAST AND FRUGAL HEURISTICS SCHOOL

I hope and assume that readers have already picked up a good deal about my conception of the structure of the fast and frugal (F&F) research program by reading the first two chapters. I tried to set out some contrasting F&F positions as a way of highlighting precisely what the heuristics and biases (H&B) theorists believe. I hope, then, to be able to give a somewhat more whirlwind account of the critical features of F&F thought in this chapter without any loss of depth.

A. ECOLOGICAL, NOT LOGICAL RATIONALITY

H&B theorists typically start with the assumption that people do and should seek to make conventionally rational decisions, and they fail to do so because they lack what are usually thought of as sufficient *internal* resources—time, attention, and computational power. F&F theorists emphasize instead that making formally rational decisions does not inevitably serve the organism's goals. Thus, we should not optimize in the fashion suggested by H&B theorists, even if we had limitless computational powers.

Gigerenzer puts the criticism of the H&B position lucidly:

> *People use heuristics only because they have limited cognitive capacities.* This much-repeated phrase incorrectly locates the reason for heuristics exclusively inside the human mind.... However... external reasons (e.g., that a problem is computationally intractable, the future is uncertain, and the goals are ambiguous) are sufficient for minds and computers to rely on heuristics... Limits of attention, memory, and reasoning can, of course, contribute to the use of simple heuristics, but external reasons are sufficient.... [l]imited capacities can in fact

enable cognitive functions, not only constrain them ... [E]very optimization model is optimal only relative to a set of mathematically convenient assumptions. To the degree that these assumptions do not hold in the real world, the outcome of optimization can be disappointing. In these cases, optimizing theories are second best.[1]

Naturally, F&F people frequently and forcefully emphasize that optimizing is typically not feasible because of limitations that would plainly be described as internal—that full-blown optimization would require that people had the minds of super-computers.[2] Interestingly, but not surprisingly—in terms of *rhetorical strategy*—Gigerenzer typically chooses to call such imagined minds "demonic," though one could imagine a rational choice theorist interested in the impact of internal limitations referring to such capacious minds as "God-like" or superhuman. Gigerenzer himself sometimes does.[3] In fact, F&F researchers are even more prone than H&B theorists to disparage the way in which economists and other rational choice theorists understand bounded rationality. Economists typically understand heuristics as consciously chosen rules of thumb to be employed when the "costs" of gathering and processing more informational cues would outweigh the expected benefits of achieving increased precision in decision making.[4] If that view were correct, say the F&F theorists, then people would require even more superhuman powers, because determining the expected net value of investing in acquiring additional information requires truly enormous amounts of information and processing capacity.[5]

At the same time as they share the H&B theorists' concern that rational choice theorists are wrong to assume that people generally have the internal cognitive capacity to make optimal "rational" decisions, F&F researchers emphasize two further points to a far greater extent. First, they contend that many of the tasks that people actually confront in the world are not really amenable to optimization solutions. Second, they argue that many tasks that are formally amenable to optimization can be solved nearly as well through the use of heuristics, so that using the heuristic would, all things considered, be preferable given that the trivial accuracy gains would be outweighed by the massive losses in speed and processing ease.[6]

They make a third, more critical point, too, at the intersection of these two points: Sometimes heuristic decision makers will be *more* accurate than those using conventional rational strategies. This presumably occurs when the use of optimizing methods is ill-suited to a task and when a heuristic decision maker can act on a cue that gives adequate information to permit a successful decision (e.g., the easily processed cue directs the decision maker whether or not to eat a certain food, and the cue correlates well with whether the food is indeed toxic or edible while those trying to reason using a range of cues will incorrectly assess the safety of the foodstuff). In these situations, the F&F researchers frequently invoke one of their principal mantras: Sometimes, "less is more."[7]

Broadly speaking, the F&F researchers believe that one *cannot* employ optimizing methods when a decision task has some or all of the following traits: The problem may be computationally intractable, payoffs from the projected outcome are ambiguous, and the future is uncertain.[8] It is not clear to me that computational intractability is ever, as the F&F theorists suggest, properly characterized as a feature of the decision-making environment. One can plainly argue that things are computationally intractable only relative to the computational powers of particular computing agents. If that is true, then computational intractability is always at core an internal feature of the subject trying to compute, not simply of the environment. Nearly *everything* standard optimization theorists require we do is "computationally intractable" from the vantage point of, say, a worm. It would be odd to say that worms cannot figure out how far the sun is from the earth because that fact is *intrinsically* computationally intractable.

And it is not obvious that payoffs really are ever properly characterized as "ambiguous" in the way that the F&F theorists seem to take for granted. I am dubious that one can so easily resolve the contentious debate I discuss at some length in Chapter Eight between critics and supporters of the idea that values may be incommensurable. Certainly, one can argue that people are always capable of providing ordinal rankings for all outcomes, should they need to choose one or the other, and it is possible to devise a decision-relevant payoff system from any complete set of ordinal rankings.[9] Moreover, it is hard to figure out what it even means to describe the experience that options are incommensurable as a trait of the options themselves or of the decision environment, rather than a disposition or thinking style of the decision maker.[10]

Furthermore, the fact that the future is uncertain—at core, an argument that change is ubiquitous—seems to be less of an argument against the use of optimization techniques than it is an argument against the desirability and perhaps the evolutionary plausibility of modularization. If your mind is modularized, you will respond to certain cues a certain way even if they are no longer probative or if other agents manipulate signals to control your actions in ways that serve their ends rather than your own.[11] But, of course, modularized cognition is just the extreme form of heuristic-based thinking.

Often, though, it seems that the F&F argument about the uncertain future is not really so much an argument against general efforts at optimization but an argument against particular forms of statistical reasoning. It is, Gigerenzer repeatedly and rightly notes, troublesome to rely on regression equations that fit, or, as he rightly puts it, overfit, a particular data set. His definition of overfitting is lucid and instructive:

> Overfitting occurs when a model with more parameters fits a sample of data better than a model with fewer parameters but makes less accurate predictions

for a new data sample than the simpler model. Complex models with many free parameters, such as multiple regression or Bayesian methods, tend to overfit in environments where information is noisy or fluctuating, particularly when forced to make predictions from small samples.[12]

It can indeed be misleading to establish relationships between some dependent outcome variable V and a host of factors that have been present or absent in the past when V occurred if our goal is to predict whether V will occur in the future. This is true because many of the factors that seemed to influence the occurrence of V were accidentally related on a single, non-recurring occasion, or the relationship between some of these factors and the occurrence of V will alter. There may, instead, be a small number of cues that persistently co-occur with V, even in a changing world, but many others that do not: Heuristic decision makers may focus on the few best cues that turn out to be persistent.[13]

Sometimes, too, the solution that the fast and frugal decision maker arrives at, though identical or near identical substantively to the solution a "rational" decision maker might also reach, is preferable because it is the only one that can be reached in the limited time the organism has available to make a decision. Even if we could do a somewhat more *accurate* job distinguishing approaching predators from harmless interlopers using a non-heuristic method, any mechanism that doesn't tell us quite quickly whether or not to skedaddle is pretty useless in terms of meeting the organism's survival ends. And once more, what is critical to emphasize is that we act rationally from the F&F vantage point if we meet our goals, not if we are more accurate. F&F theorists typically assume—arguably, without adequate supporting data—that a decision would be made more quickly if made on the basis of fewer discriminating cues. Some have questioned, on both empirical and theoretical grounds, whether there is a necessary connection between the "number" of items of information the organism must process and the speed with which the organism would reach a decision. It might sometimes be slower, not faster, to decide on the basis of a single cue.[14] Sometimes, too, the heuristics-based solution is better not because of the urgent need to act but simply because the gains to the organism in accuracy would be outweighed by the costs in time, attention, and cognitive burdens that using a less informationally impoverished mechanism would entail.

What one can see, more generally, is that F&F people do not start with the assumption that our goal is or should be to be logical—to follow abstract, context-free reasoning norms. We do not and should not seek *logical* rationality; we do and should seek *ecological* rationality. We do and should seek to use our inevitably limited capacities in such a way that we meet our ends, and we do so by having developed cognitive capacities that fit our environment (i.e., that permit us to process cues discernible in this external environment in an apt time frame to reach decisions that meet our goals). When an environment provides certain readily processed cues that can lead to judgments that induce action-path choices that meet our ends, it is of little moment whether or not these underlying judgments are as logically consistent as they might be or as veridical as they could be if we accounted for more cues.[15]

It might help further clarify the distinction I am drawing between H&B and F&F conceptions of rationality to consider an argument that F&F researcher Bruce Burns made. Burns was responding to the finding that people typically fallaciously believe that a player who has made many recent shots in a basketball game would continue to make them (the so-called hot-hand fallacy).[16] Burns acknowledges, at least for argument's sake, that conventional H&B researchers were correct to assert that people are mistaken to believe in the "hot hand" in basketball. That is, people are wrong to believe that the probability that a player will make his next shot is dependent on whether that particular player has made or missed his previous shots.[17] But Burns argues that it is nonetheless *ecologically rational* to take the action that belief in the hot-hand "fallacy" suggests one should take: to pass the ball to the "hot shooter" and try to insure that the shooter with the hot hand gets as many shots as possible. It is a rational belief because it entails adaptive action. Even if the reason that one does the right thing is that one mistakenly believes that his shooting percentage will be higher if he is "hot" rather than "cold," as long as following the hot-hand heuristic meets the overarching rational ends of the team—to score more points—the "fallacy" is rational.

Burns claims that acting on the basis of the fallacious belief is efficacious without regard to the obvious reason it might be: that passing to a person who has made his or her recent shots makes it more likely that one is passing to someone who is, over time, a better shooter, given that a better shooter is more likely to be on a hot streak than a poorer shooter. He claims that the success of the heuristic is not based on acting on this separately available information about global shooting ability, information that one might, as a non-heuristic-using rational chooser, seemingly be able to process without recourse to the belief in the hot hand. (Even if this information is available in theory, it could still be true that people do not learn, or act on, general shooting percentage data but do readily perceive, and act on, hot and cold streaks.)

I think he is just flat wrong in making this claim about why the heuristic arguably "works" to increase team scoring: I think he simply does not see how assumptions that the team ordinarily ignores aggregate shooting prowess, unless guided by the hot-hand fallacy, are embedded in his equations about each team's *ordinary* shot selection process. But that is really not my point for now. One can certainly *imagine* a situation in which a plainly non-veridical belief—for example, a belief that a certain toxic food should not be eaten not because of its known toxicity but because it is irrationally associated with wholly imaginary demons—can lead to action that meets the agent's ends. My only point for now is that F&F theorists call such beliefs rational.

B. THE STRUCTURE OF HEURISTIC REASONING

F&F researchers not only posit that boundedly rational thought arises in a particular fashion—the organism "fits" its adaptively evolved capacities to environments in which the use of a particular capacity will meet its proximal needs—but that boundedly rational thought has typical structural features. At core, one can readily summarize the structural features that characterize what F&F researchers typically dub a "fast and frugal tree"[18] in modeling the most basic F&F take-the-best strategies. The subject first follows a simple search rule. This rule tells her what cues she should initially look for. She then employs a simple stopping rule that tells the subject that she need not search for more cues, either because she has learned enough to make a decision that reaches an aspiration level or because she has found an informational cue that provides her with adequately accurate information to make a satisfactory factual judgment. Finally, she uses a simple decision rule that directs her to take the action that the positive cue value specifies.[19]

Think in this regard about one of the simplest and most basic of the heuristics— the recognition heuristic that I explore in detail in Chapter Five in the context of making judgments about the relative population of two cities. Structurally, what I want to emphasize here is that the subject using the recognition heuristic implicitly employs just such a simple search rule (search first to see if one recognizes each city), a simple stopping rule (stop looking for other cues to city size if one recognizes one city in a pair but not the other, i.e., stop looking as long as the decision objects are distinguished in terms of this first potentially discriminating cue), and a simple decision rule (decide that the recognized city is more populous). In that sense, the recognition heuristic is an ideal exemplar of the structure of F&F heuristics, even though Gigerenzer classically describes the use of the recognition heuristic as *preceding* the search for cues that differentiate two items that are each recognized, presumably because one does not precisely "search" one's own memory to discover whether one recognizes a city or not.[20]

It also has a second key structural feature, typical of F&F heuristics. Users of the heuristic co-opt a basic psychological capacity to solve a problem that was not necessarily confronted when the capacity developed, given the features of the novel environment. In this case, the capacity they draw upon is the capacity to recognize, to know whether or not they have confronted in the past an object they are now confronting. They then implicitly "search" within memory to see if a city is recognized because the recognition cue permits them to resolve the novel judgment task, determining the relative population of the cities, since it turns out that a factual feature of the environment they are acting in is that recognition correlates with larger population.[21]

At any event, the search/stop/decide cognitive process envisioned by F&F researchers is not strongly informationally encapsulated in the sense used by massive modularity (MM) theorists that I describe briefly later in this chapter.[22] A decision about relative city size, for instance, is not committed to a module that processes only recognition information, a module that cannot be penetrated by any other information. Were there a full-blown city population-determining module that was triggered once a subject discriminated between two cities (one recognized, one not), he simply could not alter his judgment of the relative size of a recognized and unrecognized city even if he learned, from a book or Wikipedia, that the unrecognized city was much more populous. But heuristic-based cognition is "softly" informationally encapsulated in the sense that people *typically* will not incorporate any additional information once they have passed their "stopping point." I explore in Chapter Five the rather unambiguous finding—both in my own experiments and the experiments of other researchers—that subjects do not use this single-cue, lexical procedure. Instead, they actually frequently use non-recognition information in a compensatory fashion when making many assessments (e.g., assessments of species populations or relative airline safety), including assessments of relative city size. That is, they *sometimes* do believe that a non-recognized city is bigger than a recognized one, implying that they are accounting for non-recognition cues rather than "stopping" once they have found the discriminating single cue.

The interesting, structural point for now is how F&F researchers have reacted to this finding—on the occasions when they do not simply reject it thoroughly—in terms of how they model heuristic reasoning. Some argue that the relative city size judgment is only *sometimes* made heuristically, and that when it is, it is made without the use of non-recognition information. Thus, from this vantage point, the interesting question is how we define the *domain* in which we will use heuristics or a particular heuristic, not what it means to use a heuristic *if* we are using one.[23] Whether this threatens to turn the debate over whether users of heuristics inevitably follow the search/stop/decide method into an argument resolved by tautology—they are simply not using heuristics *unless* they do so—is open to question. Presumably, one could argue, as Pachur and Hertwig do,[24] that we can determine whether or not a subject is using heuristics not only by definitional fiat—she only is doing so if she follows the canonical lexical decision-making process—but by reference to other aspects of the decision *situation* (is she rushed or not? is she under cognitive load?) and other aspects of her decision *process* (does she make the decision more quickly? in the context of the recognition heuristic, does she use, exclusively or dominantly, parts of the brain associated with recognition memory so that we could describe the recognition heuristic as a heuristic used only when inferences are solely memory based?).

Their approach is certainly sensible, but it has both empirical and conceptual problems. Empirically, for instance, it is dubious that subjects actually make recognition-based decisions more quickly (Volz et al., though generally sympathetic with the F&F position, do not find that they do).[25] Worse still, any particular finding that subjects make recognition decisions atypically quickly compared to decisions made through some other mechanism might not be robust. Even if we found, for instance, that subjects made recognition-based decisions more quickly than they made decisions about the relative size of two cities they recognized whose size was in fact fairly close, on the basis of a multiplicity of cues, none of which was enormously probative, this would hardly tell us much. We would need to compare how quickly subjects make recognition-based decisions with the whole range of other "easy" city size decisions. For instance, we could investigate whether they are made more quickly than judgments based on readily retrieved semantic information (e.g., that recognized New York City is bigger than recognized Boston). We could compare whether they are made more quickly than judgments based on other good cues that one of two recognized cities is larger (e.g., its relative "prominence," the presence of professional sports franchises in one of two recognized cities).

Conceptually, the problem is one that I explore in the section of this chapter on the relationship between MM theory and the F&F school: If people need non-modular (or "slow and informationally rich" rather than "fast and frugal") cognitive processes to determine *whether* to assign a cognitive task to a module or heuristic decision-making process and, if so, to what module or heuristic to assign it, then it is not at all clear that we should describe *cognition* on the whole as either modularized or heuristic. Conventional rational choice theory also contemplates that subjects will use single-cue rules of thumb *when* the decision maker thinks them apt or sufficient. If F&F and MM theorists differ from rational choice proponents—with or without the sorts of heuristic-based biases H&B scholars highlight—it is because subjects need not generally *choose* what sort of decision-making process or how many cues they will use.[26]

It is important to note, as well, that from the vantage point of most F&F researchers, heuristics have this basic structural form even when they are consciously chosen decision rules rather than automatic responses that those who use them are utterly unaware of. In F&F-school thought, heuristics are not by any means the exclusive province of less deliberative parts of the mind. Because one can *choose* to use cognitive processes with this structural format (simple search, stopping, and decision rules), it is worth considering whether we do so as often as we should. Thus, for instance, medical professionals making decisions in an emergency room about which patients must be sent to the coronary care unit and which could be treated in a regular ward could select a protocol with a lengthy laundry list of cues. Each "factor" could be difficult to measure individually, and it could be even more difficult to combine and weigh the factors in a fashion that really predicted medical need. Instead, they might make use of a very small number of discriminating cues. Not surprisingly, F&F researchers have extolled the conscious adoption of medical care screening systems with very few, simple on/off discriminators.[27]

In the H&B tradition, of course, the basic *structural* feature of heuristic thought is that the heuristic thinker engages in some sort of unconscious, automatic (System One) "attribute substitution" that is sometimes "corrected" by more labored System Two overriding. System One thinking is not conscious, but, given the possibility of System Two override, the *problem* that the agent is trying to solve is not ultimately committed to either a strictly informationally encapsulated module or a softly informationally encapsulated decision process. When the decision maker portrayed in the H&B tradition is judging the relative past frequency or future probability of distinct types of accidents and makes use of the "availability heuristic," he may not be searching for a cue in the environment, whether we characterize it as an external environment or characterize his memory, more metaphorically, as a kind of environment that he must search. He is not necessarily searching to discover how easily recalled one accident type is, and he is certainly not searching for an external environmental cue. Nor is he necessarily treating the answer to the question "is accident A more easily recalled than B?" as a cue that permits him to infer at least as a good enough approximation that what is more easily recalled is more likely.[28]

When one engages in "attribute substitution," one may not be picking the single best cue from a list of potential cues that the fully rational subject would also use. Instead, one may be simply substituting a cue that the automatic, less labored system can readily process. The distinction between the schools on this issue may be slim, though, in practice. The F&F people may often believe that the best cue available is *not* the single most statistically predictive cue but the most predictive cue that permits fast and frugal processing. In this sense, the F&F heuristic user may be engaged in something very much like attribute substitution. He is approximating rationality as best he can under serious time constraints. Once more, though, the rhetorical emphasis may be considerably different. The H&B researchers are sure the substituted attribute is *easy* for System One to process—and they are certain that it would not have stably evolved unless helpful and correct enough in most situations—but that its ease of use is sufficient to explain its use. They do not believe there is any reason to believe that the mechanism will typically be used only when its use in a particular environmental context meets the organism's needs, however the needs are defined.

Finally, just as F&F researchers have had an extraordinarily difficult time answering the question of how we should describe the mental processes that permit us to decide whether to use a heuristic and how to decide which heuristic to use, H&B researchers have a remarkably undeveloped picture of why System Two sometimes does and sometimes doesn't override System One. Only MM theorists avoid this problem: For reasons that I am about to explore, they believe they can dispense with the idea that organisms need to *pick* a decision-making mechanism and reject the proposition that informationally impoverished decision-making mechanisms are consciously chosen. Because they are not consciously chosen, according to MM theorists, there is no need to posit a generalized cognitive capacity to assess the utility of using an informationally impoverished mechanism on one occasion and not others. Instead, selection pressure favors more adaptive over less adaptive modularized responses to cues, and it is these, and only these, responses that we will observe.

C. ILLUMINATING THE F&F SCHOOL BY BRIEFLY EXPLORING THE MASSIVE MODULARITY HYPOTHESIS

I should begin this section with an important qualification: It is not clear that anyone at all believes the unqualified MM thesis that I am about to present and discuss rather critically. The notion that there are cognitive scientists who believe that the brain is massively modularized, rather than that there are many modules, or that what it means to believe the brain is "modularized" is to suppose more than there is substantial functional specialization in cognitive functions,[29] is to a significant degree an ideal-type construct offered up by those who are most suspicious of highly modularized theories of cognition. Cosmides and Tooby—who did much of the most interesting early work on the centrality of modular thought—arguably now endorse something closer to the "dual process" theory I associated with H&B research in Chapter Two, though their System Two provides considerably less constant oversight of modularized System One reactions.[30] Moreover, I present the "classical" form of the MM hypothesis not because it is intrinsically important to a policymaker's understanding of heuristic reasoning but because understanding it is, I think, tremendously helpful in understanding the scholarly program of F&F researchers.

MM theorists occasionally addressed the heuristics debate directly, and their express forays into the debate doubtless influenced the ways in which F&F theorists came to be dubious of the H&B focus on bias and error. They argued that it is unlikely that people would use heuristics that would have failed to meet their ends in the so-called environment of evolutionary adaptation (EEA).[31] Thus, to the degree that H&B experimenters found that experimental subjects frequently gave non-normative responses to problems, MM theorists often argued that the subjects did so because H&B researchers either picked problems that were of little significance to our ancestors, or posed them in a fashion that our minds had not evolved to solve. In this sense, the *direct* contribution of MM theory to the heuristics debate that I address in this book has merely been to support certain aspects of the F&F critique of the H&B school that I discuss at length in Chapter Four, expressing considerable skepticism about studies that show sub-optimal levels of functionality in cognitive processes.

But MM theory was not just another optimistically functionalist theory about the wonders of our cognitive system, so what is most important to understand for my purposes in this chapter is how it differs from F&F, not from H&B. This section, then, is largely meant to help augment our understanding of F&F scholarship.

i. What are modules? Why must we use them?

MM is, in essence, a general theory of mental functioning designed to revitalize the traditional idea that the mind possesses specific "faculties" rather than a more general capacity to learn and reason. These faculties—mental "modules"—have a number of critical features. Most important, modules are domain-specific, mandatory, opaque, and, above all, *strongly* informationally encapsulated, and while F&F heuristic users most typically reveal a "weakly" modular mind, F&F heuristics are not in the final analysis identical to modules along any of these dimensions.

What does MM theory mean by domain specificity? The basic idea behind the claim that our cognition is domain specific is that we do not cognize a range of problems using general skills but employ algorithms processing a limited number of cues devoted to solving very specific problem types. The key to understanding domain-specific theories of the mind is to understand that if they are true, certain classes of informational cues are processed by dedicated mechanisms.

In some ways, one alternative intuitively credible view of domain specificity—that cognition is domain specific in relationship only to bodies of knowledge—is either trivially true or too vague to fathom. If one said that we had a specific *topical* domain of knowledge (say, knowledge about cats), it would be tautologically or trivially true to the degree that each of us could say something about cats that he or she would not say about some broader categories (animals, objects that are spatially extended). But domain-specific theories of cognition almost surely imply not just that we have access to information about narrower, rather than conceivably broader, subject categories, but that there are distinct algorithms to process cues about the category.[32]

MM theorists believed, though, that all or virtually all problems in which making use of different "solutions" would have distinct implications for inclusive fitness are solved by unique, problem-sensitive, domain-specific algorithms. In their classic account of massive modularity, Cosmides and Tooby put it as follows:

[T]he more important the adaptive problem, the more intensely natural selection specializes and improves the performance of the mechanism for solving it.... [N]atural selection tends to produce functionally distinctive adaptive specializations.... Simply to survive and reproduce, our Pleistocene ancestors had to be good at solving an enormously broad array of adaptive problems—problems that would defeat any modern artificial intelligence system. A small sampling includes foraging for food, navigating, selecting a mate, parenting, engaging in social exchange, dealing with aggressive threat, avoiding pathogenic contamination, avoiding predators, avoiding naturally occurring plant toxins, avoiding incest, and so on. A woman who used the same taste preference mechanisms in choosing a mate that she used to choose nutritious foods would choose a very strange mate indeed.... These different adaptive problems are frequently incommensurate: They cannot, in principle, be solved by the same mechanism.... Even a restricted consideration of hunter-gatherer tasks suggests that it is unlikely that any single general computational system could solve them all.... (Indeed, it is difficult to imagine a domain-general computational system that could solve *any* of them.)[33]

There are two obvious and related questions that the standard MM account of domain specificity raises, and these prove relevant in thinking more carefully about F&F heuristics as well. First, at how fine a level of granularity should we portray the domains that algorithms are purportedly specifically designed to handle?[34] (Think, too, about this in relationship to F&F heuristics we have examined. To what degree do we think people make judgments only about the size of cities based on recognition? If we only made judgments about size, would size mean population only, or include judgments about area? Do they instead make judgments about the relative virtues—performance level? height? price?—of all sorts of objects based on recognition?)

Second, how do we assign cues to the appropriate module or cognitive domain that we simply, in the first instance, merely *perceive*? When the mate-selector needs to figure out whether her would-be seducer is going to bolt without caring for the kids (the paradigmatic evolutionary psychology doomsday scenario), does she simply employ a narrowly grained fixed algorithm that permits her to determine whether any would-be lover will stick around? Or do women have finer-grained modules still that help them answer that question in distinct ways for older men, for those their own age, for the forceful and the polite, for those who already have mated, for widowers? Is her evaluation task done instead by a far *broader* social exchange module that helps us detect cheaters, those who will try to get a benefit without reciprocating? Couldn't we describe men seeking sex and bolting without taking care of the kids as just a sub-set of the larger set of defectors or cheaters? And if there are *different* modules in the brain for cheater detection in the EEA equivalent of the exchange economy and for sexual selection in the EEA equivalent of the bar scene, how do we know where to process the cue we directly *perceive*? Which module gets triggered by a voice with a certain tone that asks, "What's your sign?" or says, "I've never met anyone quite like you?"[35] In talking about how people make decisions to comply with legal commands in Chapter Six, we note that F&F theorists believe that people frequently choose either simply to follow their habits or to mimic others. But do they believe one is more appropriate to making decisions about complying with laws regulating speeding than complying with tax laws or with rules on insider trading? And if we decide to mimic, how do we know which of the many people in the world acting differently from one another we should mimic? Perhaps, too, we mimic *more* than legal compliance decisions because compliance decisions are in some sense *like* some other set of decisions, but how many more?

For now, it is not especially important whether MM theorists have *good* answers to these two questions. But it is certainly important to note, first, that in order to think they can answer these questions satisfactorily, they must believe that the world external to our minds has detectable structural features (i.e., features available to purely perceptual systems) that enable us to assign events in the world to the appropriate processing system.[36] And, while it is ultimately not crucial to the task of better understanding F&F theory to *resolve* these issues, it is also certainly worth noting that I share Fodor's sense that they have nothing close to good answers to these questions.[37]

What is most important for now is to highlight that domain-specific MM cognition is related to, but not precisely the same as, the sort of "adaptive toolbox" cognition described in F&F scholarship. In Gigerenzer's seminal F&F view, people do not merely use one particular sort of recognition memory as a solution dedicated to a particular domain-specific adaptive problem. That is, they do not merely employ an algorithm grounded in recognition that permits them to distinguish food less likely to be toxic from food more likely to be so. Instead, once they have developed the *capacity* to recognize, it functions as a more generalized capacity that can be brought to bear on problems that are not readily characterized as being in the same topical domain. Thus, as I have noted, and as I discuss at length in Chapter Five, people can co-opt the generalized capacity to recognize to pick a more populous city from a list of two, even though they might not have developed the capacity unless they had needed to solve the problem of recognizing toxins, and certainly did not develop it because there was inclusive pressure to recognize larger cities. They will use a capacity as long as it is ecologically rational to use the capacity in that fashion.

But it is implausible to imagine that there is a domain-specific module or single simple evolved capacity that would make us realize that at least some instances of the problem of figuring out which of two cities is larger is adequately solved by using the recognition heuristic. MM theorists need not face that problem, because the toxic food recognition adaptive challenge *alone* is simply remitted to a dedicated cognitive mechanism that happens to work through something that could be described as recognition. F&F theorists have therefore had to spend a good deal more energy figuring out how people decide whether to use a heuristic and which heuristic to use.[38]

The argument that the brain is massively modularized is generally thought to imply further that thought processes are essentially *mandatory* rather than deliberately chosen. Think in this regard about fearing snakes that one knows are not poisonous or loving sweets though one knows one doesn't need the caloric hit to survive the long spells of hunger our ancestors faced. The MM hypothesis further implies the claim that cognitive processes are *opaque*, which further implies that they are not consciously chosen. That is, for instance, that we have no idea why we fear snakes, even without prior exposure to them or any obvious "learning." (In general too, we would associate the case for modular capacities with "poverty of the stimulus" arguments that are familiar from Chomsky's account of language acquisition. In all such arguments, the subject seems to demonstrate competence beyond that which he could have learned given the slim inputs he has been exposed to. Thus, we learn grammatical rules without having been exposed to enough instances that instantiate them to have learned them by "generalization"; we fear snakes before we have enough experiential data to do so.)

In that sense, of course, MM theorists also seem to differ from F&F theorists who believe that we somehow have the capacity to *choose* on at least some occasions to use heuristic reasoning. F&F theorists doubtless share with MM theorists the idea that the particular heuristic "selected" from the adaptive toolbox to be used when it is ecologically rational to do so may not be selected by a conscious reasoning process, though, as I note in a bit, they have other theories of less-than-conscious "learning" to use the apt heuristic. At the same time, however, they posit the possibility of conscious selection, and many of their bureaucratic and legal reform proposals are grounded in the idea that people can consciously elect to use heuristics.

What all this means is that F&F theorists face a problem that the MM theorists can readily duck: how to account for the capacity to select the right heuristic or any heuristic at all. For MM scholars, what I might dub a quasi-heuristic or the modular algorithm has been assigned to each particular problem, and it need never have been selected by any individual who had to assess the goodness of fit of the heuristic to an environment. Instead, those who used the quasi-heuristic in a particular domain-specific setting survived at higher rates than those who did not; the *mandatory* heuristic is selected by evolutionary pressure, not some inevitably underspecified meta-cognitive process.

While a good deal of F&F work has gone into specifying the appropriate meta-cognitive processes, even Gigerenzer acknowledges that there is only scant progress in solving the problem. ("Had Dougherty et al. ... argued that the present knowledge of heuristic selection, as opposed to models of heuristics, is rather vague, then they would have made a fair point. However, there is progress on the issue of selection as well.")[39]

Not only does the fact that MM theorists posit that the heuristics are mandatory and opaque permit them to avoid having to postulate the sorts of capacious mental capacities that F&F theorists usually derisively describe as "demonic" just to recognize when it is ecologically rational to use a heuristic; it also permits MM theorists to put plausible limits on the types of heuristics that people might use. Take a typical F&F heuristic: Take the Best. This is precisely the kind of heuristic that an MM theorist would find overbroad and hard to interpret. There is presumably some set of domains in which inferring the existence or desirability of Y from some single cue A is markedly superior to trying to combine information about A, B, C, and D to decide whether to infer or prefer Y. (There must be some class of cues A–D in which B–D are largely redundant, or unstably related to Y in a changing environment.) But while MM theorists could postulate that evolutionary pressure led people to "Take (some domain-specific piece of information) A" to infer some domain-specific conclusion Y, it is far less clear how it could have resulted in a general mental capacity to determine whether the *procedure* of taking the best cue would do well enough in dealing with each sort of novel problem.

At the same time, if the F&F brain can generalize tools *sometimes*—it might have taken the best cue about a potential mate's fertility, or the presence of a predator, and somehow developed a more general capacity to Take the Best when deciding, say, whether or not an incoming heart patient needed to be sent to the coronary care unit—it is far from clear why it doesn't do it other times, or what it even *means* to generalize a cognitive "procedure."

In a similar vein, MM theory explains why quasi-heuristics are "rational"—in a gene replication-maximization sense at any rate, if not precisely in either of the senses that F&F or H&B theorists employ—at least as long as the relationship between input cue and mental output has not altered since the EEA. But there is no good reason to assume that F&F heuristics will be employed rationally any more often than they will be applied irrationally, unless we posit that the brain has a really good heuristic selector capable of assessing whether there is a good fit between "tool" and "external environment." But at that point, the *source* of rationality, if there is one, is the good selector, not the heuristics. As I noted, Gigerenzer seemingly now believes that heuristics are best "selected" either through direct evolutionary pressure (just as MM theorists might), through imitation of other subjects (so that the "imitation heuristic" becomes in a sense the meta-heuristic that explains the use of other heuristics), or through individual learning,[40] but the viability of the last two strategies seems dubious in the absence of a non-heuristic brain to evaluate their efficacy.

ii. A brief note on modularity's key: strong informational encapsulation

In many ways, then, the MM hypothesis purges F&F theory of many of its most galling problems. But it does so, alas, by positing what many find implausible mental processes that are strongly informationally encapsulated: They are not just softly informationally encapsulated in the way that F&F theorists posit cognition is (i.e., people typically employ "stopping rules" so they don't search for or attend to further information once they have processed an adequately discriminatory cue), but, rather, information that is not processed by the localized algorithm simply cannot be processed at all.

But modules *must* be informationally encapsulated, essentially as a matter of definition. What a module *is* is an informationally encapsulated cognitive process, so whether the mind is wholly composed of modules or modules are a small part of cognition, wherever they exist, they are, tautologically, informationally encapsulated. Fodor explains the point lucidly:

> Imagine a computational system with a proprietary ... database. Imagine that this device operates to map its characteristic inputs onto its characteristic outputs (in effect, to compute a function from the one to the other) and that, in the course of doing so, its informational resources are restricted to what its proprietary database contains. That is, the system is "encapsulated" with respect to information that is not in its database....[41]

One might best understand this input-to-output transformation by considering the limits on the information that modularized theorists of language acquisition posit, recognizing that modularized theories of language acquisition are somewhat less controversial than MM theories of cognition more generally. In order to parse the *structure* of certain linguistic inferences, one need not know many further, contextual facts about the world. Thus, we may know that the sentence "John swims and Mary drinks" is true if an only if both statements are true. We need not know what either verb means (what is swimming? what is drinking?). We need not know who John is or who Mary is. And even if we know who they are and what the verbs mean, we need not know whether the statements are actually veridical to know that the sentence is not true unless both statements are true.[42] What it means to have a modularized computational theory of mind is that the brain works in precisely this way in making all judgments: It processes certain semantic representations according to rules without regard to potentially relevant further facts about the representations.[43]

Thus, Fodor continues:

> Its operations are defined with less than full generality or its informational exchanges with other processing mechanisms are constrained.... In a nutshell: Modules are informationally encapsulated by definition. And, likewise by definition, the more encapsulated the informational resources to which a computational mechanisms has access, the less the character of its operations is sensitive to global properties of belief systems. Thus, to the extent that the information accessible to a device is architecturally constrained to a proprietary database, it won't have a frame problem[44] and it won't have a relevance problem... Frame problems and relevance problems are about how deeply, in the course of processing, a mind should examine its background of epistemic commitments. A modular problem-solving mechanism doesn't have to worry about that sort of thing because, in point of architecture, only what's in its database can be in the frame.... To a first approximation, nothing affects the course of computations of an encapsulated processor except what gets inside the capsule, and the more the processor is encapsulated, the less information that is. The extreme case is, I suppose, the reflex; it's encapsulated with respect to all information except what's in the current input.[45]

Naturally, anyone influenced in any serious way by rational choice theory, including H&B scholars, is already dubious that people ever use even soft forms of informational encapsulation like voluntarily chosen lexical decision-making processes that simply ignore potentially relevant cues, employed by those completely lacking the capacity to override the assumption that the single cue is adequate even when that supposition doesn't seem to fit. Such thinkers will be at least equally suspicious of MM theory that posits that virtually *all* cognition radically restricts the range of processed cues. It is not clear that the encapsulation story works all that well even if one looks at phobias and reflexes, the standard illustrations of encapsulation outside the production of perceptual input (e.g., through the visual system). It is hard to figure out why I'm not scared of the pythons and boa constrictors behind the glass at the zoo, unless we think I am able to combine information (the snake is behind the glass though it is proximate) with the fear-producing, apt-action-inducing module (see a snake, panic and scoot). The attack on the prototypical F&F claim that people often use cues in a non-compensatory manner is obviously an attack as well on the cognate idea of strong informational encapsulation.[46]

Solving some of the vexing problems of F&F through MM theory has its costs: We may solve the heuristic selection problem only by positing an implausible picture of cognition.

D. A BRIEF NOTE ON ESTABLISHED LAW AND POLICY IMPLICATIONS

H&B literature has percolated for decades through the legal academy, as well as policy schools and economics departments influenced to some degree by the behavioral economics work that derives almost wholly from H&B scholarship. That does not mean that it is easy to summarize the impact of either the general structure of H&B thought or the reform implications of particular insights. To some extent, I hope, the last part of this book (Chapters Six to Nine) explores more fully just what sorts of claims an H&B orientation entails or facilitates. Still, one can say, with fair confidence, that H&B theorists have alerted policymakers to new forms of market failure—situations in which people with reasonably full information about the external world cannot process that information in a fashion that permits them to draw accurate conclusions either about the external world or their desires. At the same time, it has highlighted novel forms of regulatory failure—situations in which political actors respond to an irrationally selected sub-set of social problems and measure how citizens value public goods in ways that are unduly sensitive to the manner of elicitation. One can say, too, with rather less confidence, that H&B scholarship has been associated with the "technocratic" turn in policy formation. It has tended, to some extent, to favor, or at least be more tolerant of, expert displacement of both market choices and democratic preference expression.

F&F theory has made scant inroads on existing policy analysis, and to the limited extent that it has been influential, its findings—somewhat wrongly—have been subsumed in arguments that fuller disclosure to consumers, patients, and so on, will result in information overload rather than better decision making. Because it has percolated less, it is probably harder to give a quick and dirty summary of its basic impact on legal theory and policy. Once more, I hope the discussions in the last part of this book will illuminate the implications of F&F scholarship for jurisprudence and policy in ways that we have not yet seen, but I still thought it worthwhile to sketch a plausible cursory summary of how users of this research would be likely to intervene in both law and public policy schools.

Here would be the most general picture: First, F&F theorists would be far less wary of the decisions made by both consumers and voters, radically less prone to believe that they have adopted decision-making mechanisms that serve their ends poorly, even when they seem to be making judgments that can, described in certain ways, appear irrational. To the degree that H&B extends the policy domains of consumer protection and the philosophical domain of justified (and non-illiberal) paternalism, F&F attempts to retract it. Even where the F&F scholars observe error, they are more disposed to believe that errors are not intractable, but could be corrected by supplying information in the forms that people most readily process it, permitting them to retain higher levels of negative autonomy.

Second, F&F theorists would be very suspicious of experts who purported to rely on case-by-case detailed cost-benefit calculations to select ideal action courses. F&F-influenced theorists are predisposed to believe that easily applied rules that rely on discerning just a few decision criteria are to be preferred to standards or multifactor balancing tests. (I return at greater length to a variant of this point in the discussion of the move from Langdellian Formalism to Legal Realism in Chapter Nine). They are thus suspicious of the cost-benefit analysis favored by most rat-choice scholars in part because its adoption falsely implies that some group of experts has the capacity to understand complex causal relationships that ordinary people lack. Instead of worrying about the intuitive judgments of laymen, they worry that those who reason statistically most typically merely overfit regressions to the random data from a particular period that they have collected. At the same time, they are suspicious of technocratic cost-benefit analysis because those who practice it falsely believe that different sorts of gains and losses can be readily made commensurable. (For a fuller discussion of how F&F scholars might conceive of, and endorse, the idea that values are incommensurable, see Chapter Eight.)

Thus, not surprisingly, in the legal *reform* role we have already observed, the F&F theorists are at least as likely to stress situations in which we should urge the use of new heuristics that have not typically been employed as they are to look to protect people from being led astray by heuristics.[47] For instance, if we want to increase organ donation by those who may be in fatal accidents, we should merely make donating the default since "don't change the status quo" is an operative F&F heuristic.[48] More elaborate alterations in the payoffs for donation are unlikely to be processed and acted upon. (For a far fuller discussion of how both H&B and F&F theorist thinks about guiding behavior, e.g., compliance with criminal law, see Chapter Six.) Similarly, those committed to environmental clean-up programs that nonetheless account for the fact that resources devoted to such cleanup might have alternative, and better, uses might still wisely adopt a simple heuristic ("do the best that you can" or "do the best that is currently technically feasible"). They might do so not only because the process of trying to figure out which possible clean-up steps are actually cost-justified in full-blown rational choice terms is so intractably hard that it leads to agency paralysis, but because, in application, the "simple rule" may do a more-than-adequate job distinguishing worthwhile from manifestly overcostly clean-up programs.[49]

E. CONCLUSION

Those researchers who believe that people make use of fast and frugal heuristics recognize that those using these heuristics may, on occasion, serve their own interests poorly. But what they have been committed to emphasizing is the substantial degree to which using a heuristic is a good way of solving practical problems. People have certain underlying mental capacities; the world has certain discernible features that we can process in making judgments and decisions. By and large, evolutionary pressures guarantee that we will process environmental cues given the capacities that we have available in such a way as to maximize inclusive fitness. We will generally do a good job making good choices and solving problems, and we will do so even when we make judgments that could be described as illogical or when we fail to account for some available information.

Thus, in the view of F&F scholars, heuristic users are typically ecologically rational—the tools they employ are well-suited to good decision making in the actual environments in which they operate even if they seem suspect in some abstract or logical way. The tools they use can be employed quickly and economically, and that is inherently advantageous. More strikingly, they often produce answers that are plainly superior to those that would be generated by more effortful or informed agents because readily processed single cues, or small numbers of cues, more consistently predict a feature of the world the subject must ascertain than do multiple cues. People often spontaneously and un-self-consciously develop these single or minimal cue judgment or decision-making processes—using simple search rules that tell them what cue to look for that will help them discriminate between one judgment or decision and another, stopping rules that tell them to look for no further discriminating cues once they have found sufficient discriminating ones, and decision rules that tell them which judgment to make or what course of action to take once the judgments or actions have been differentiated. They may also, more self-consciously, *choose* to use simplifying heuristics to make judgments or decisions rather than multifactor balanced judgments.

It is doubtful that F&F theorists have adequately accounted for either the persistence of maladaptive heuristics—except by recourse to rather flimsy stories of adaptive lag—or, more urgently, subjects' ability to recognize when the use of any heuristic, let alone a particular heuristic, will serve their interests. But the basic message remains clear. People have always treated certain delimited cues as judgment and outcome determinative (and they should); they have co-opted basic psychological abilities developed to make judgments about some particular set of evolutionarily significant features of the world, and they have used them to process some novel set of cues in situations in which the use of these co-opted basic abilities proves valuable.

4

FAST AND FRUGAL SCHOOL OBJECTIONS TO THE HEURISTICS AND BIASES PROGRAM

What I hope to do in the next two chapters is to explain why psychologists associated with the fast and frugal (F&F) school are ultimately so dismissive of the work done by the heuristics and biases (H&B) researchers, and why the heuristics and biases scholars ultimately return the (dis)favor. The task is a bit daunting. Without being unduly reductionist, I want to distill a wide array of focused and detailed attacks on particular findings and studies to a small set of structurally similar claims about the perceived weaknesses of a general approach.

Moreover, the approach I take in these two chapters is not especially symmetric. In this chapter, I largely try to identify recurring problems that F&F researchers have explicitly noted in the studies done by H&B scholars. While I follow the same approach at times in Chapter Five, I do so only to a very limited extent because I am not sure it would be either feasible or fruitful. First, H&B scholars have penned far fewer explicit attacks on F&F work; there is simply little critical work to summarize. Second, even when I try to *construct* what I take to be the implicit criticisms of the F&F approach by H&B researchers, I find they typically simply mirror the critiques that have been leveled at their own work. Thus, instead of emphasizing what I believe H&B academics would likely see as recurring structural flaws in F&F scholarship, I present a "case study," using work on the recognition heuristic—both original research and work done by others—to illustrate the sorts of objections that I believe those working in the H&B tradition have to aspects of F&F scholarship.

In this chapter, though, I simply attempt to identify and categorize the main hesitations about H&B work that have been explicated in the F&F literature.

A. IRRATIONALITY STAYS INSIDE THE LAB

At core, the most basic critique that F&F theorists level at H&B research is that subjects *seem* to perform sub-optimally in H&B experiments only because they are given problems in these experimental settings that do not accurately mimic problems that they would confront in natural environments. Much of what draws many rational choice theorists to the work of F&F scholars, whether or not the F&F psychologists embrace the endorsements, is that Gigerenzer's work can be invoked to support the idea that anti-paternalist pro-market stances make more sense than H&B interventionists imply, given their fixation on error in judgment and decision making.

What ultimately *causes* the gap between performance on "real-world problems" and laboratory problems is that the mental capacities that evolved are the capacities to solve recurring problems that increase inclusive fitness, not the more diffuse capacity to be an abstractly better calculator (e.g., of expected values). In this view, what is wrong with H&B research is that the H&B investigators have fashioned lab problems that merely test formal problem-solving capacity and then interpret formal failures on these problems as functional failures of cognition. Gigerenzer puts the general point quite clearly: "... the means and ends of social intelligence are broader than consistency (coherence) and accuracy—the accepted norms of logic and statistics."[1] More generally still, Gigerenzer notes that "rationality" is not an end but a means to other ends: "From a functional view ... consistency in choice and judgment is not a general norm to follow blindly, but rather a tool for achieving certain proximal goals."[2]

Implicit, too, in the supposition that there is likely a disjunction between "poor" laboratory performance and "impressive" human capacity is the commitment to the idea that capacities are generally, if not always, domain specific. F&F theorists, who believe that cognition is significantly domain specific, would not expect people to have gotten better at solving problems that impact inclusive fitness simply by developing more generalized cognitive capacities that they could utilize to solve *any* set of novel problems. Rather, F&F theorists expect that they would have developed the capacity to succeed by utilizing narrower algorithms that solve a narrower set of problems that they really face. Implicit, as well, in this critique of the H&B school is the claim that H&B psychologists do not pay nearly enough attention to the adaptive advantages of using particular problem-solving techniques, given particular environments. They focus far too much on abstract, general reasoning capacity and not enough on the *fit* between narrower capacities and the way in which real-world problems actually present themselves. They misperceive critical features of real-world problems, overestimating both the quantity and quality of available data and underestimating how quickly data must be processed to do the subject any good.

Whatever its ultimate *origins*, the gap between good real-world performance and bad lab performance may be *manifest* in four distinct ways. First, F&F theorists claim that H&B researchers often present problems in a cognitively intractable *form*. Second, they claim that H&B theorists often present problems that are mathematically equivalent to problems people have learned to solve contextually, not mathematically or formally, when there are important reasons to solve the problem and then express unwarranted surprise that people cannot solve the formal equivalents of these genuinely significant problems. Third, they present problems with formal payoffs that differ from the payoffs in real-world "games" that closely resemble the games that they have subjects play. They then express unmerited surprise when their subjects play them by the rules of the real-world game that the lab games most closely mimic rather than playing them by the formal, novel lab rules. Fourth and finally, subjects appear to H&B researchers to make mistakes because they reinterpret the experimenter's instructions in a fashion that makes their responses reasonable. Their reinterpretations actually demonstrate the subjects' conversational competence and the experimenter's tin ear.

Before proceeding, though, to detail the ways in which the scholars associated with the F&F school believe that H&B theorists underestimate the actual problem-solving capacities that people exercise in the natural environments in which they must solve real problems, I want to mention a fairly parallel critique that most of the F&F researchers are *not* making. Some scholars—influenced more by sociology and the study of organizations than by the alternative view of individual capacity proffered by the F&F theorists—would make an argument of the following general form: People often face and solve problems collectively, rather than individually. Collective decision making is not best seen as a simple summation of individual decision making; organizations establish procedures, customs, and techniques to approach and solve problems that may not simply combine the insights that isolated individuals would produce. It is particularly likely that if individuals bear the negative consequences of biased decisions, they will try to work collectively to establish decision-making mechanisms that do better than they would each do as isolated decision makers.[3]

Here is a simple, perhaps crude, conceptual example: H&B researchers might study the degree to which experimental jurors, acting individually, exhibit hindsight bias (e.g., in judging whether those who have injured others should have foreseen that the precautions they took were inadequate to avoid injury; to determine whether police who actually found contraband had probable cause to search). But it is possible that even if individuals *typically* are prone to exhibit such bias, *juries*, rather than artificially isolated experimental mock-*jurors*, avoid hindsight bias through processes of deliberation, reason giving, and attending to diversity of viewpoint. Moreover, the level of hindsight bias exhibited by the collectivity might be sensitive to both voting rules and decision-making procedures.[4] (It is, of course, possible that juries will exhibit more bias than their constituent members as well.)[5] In a less straightforward fashion, sociologically inclined critics of H&B might either model or describe institutions that do better making decisions that serve stable interests than the individuals who comprise them would do acting alone. In Chapter Seven, I briefly describe an instance of this approach in considering the heuristics-influenced literature on unconscious bias.

For now, though, I want to identify and explicate what F&F theorists see as four distinct distortions in the way H&B scholars describe infirmities of human judgment and decision making.

- *H&B theorists may present material in a fashion that is formally mathematically equivalent to an alternative presentation that subjects would find more tractable.*

In experiments that the F&F theorists believe are vulnerable to this particular critique, subjects indeed make what even F&F theorists concede are "mistakes." That is, in this class of cases, the F&F scholars are not arguing that the subjects' answers are "better than rational." However, the mistakes, they say, come from the artificiality of the way in which the problem is presented. The fact that the subjects make mistakes in the lab setting does not imply that they will typically make mistakes coping with problems of a similar sort in ordinary life. (At core, this could be seen as a form of external validity critique.) Moreover, the material the H&B experimenters present might be more tractable if presented in the manner that it is, at least ostensibly, confronted in natural settings generally, or at least in the natural settings that were prevalent when humans developed their cognitive capacities.

This criticism was perhaps most prominent in disputes over whether people would exhibit the base rate neglect that H&B theorists had demonstrated if the information they needed to process had been presented in frequentist rather than probabilistic fashion. Base rate neglect is an error that occurs when the probability that some hypothesis H is true, given some evidence E, is assessed without taking sufficient account of the prior probability that we will confront E. (For instance, we learn that we have tested positive for a disease and assess whether we have the disease without thinking about how many people who are not sick would test positive for the disease, even if the test has few false positives, as long as the base rate of the disease is quite low.)[6]

Here is one account of the basic debate: According to F&F theorists, as well as some massive modularists (MM), people indeed have a great deal of trouble processing information presented in the following probabilistic form that H&B researchers had conventionally used in testing for the prevalence of base rate neglect: "99.8% of those who are HIV-positive test positive. Only 0.01% of those who are not HIV-positive test positive. The base rate for the disease among heterosexual men with few risk factors is 0.01%. How likely is it that a particular low-risk factor heterosexual man is HIV-positive if he tests positive?" On the other hand, most people find it relatively easy to handle properly the same information presented in the following frequentist way (i.e., stated in terms of how often some X occurs compared to the sum of X and not-X): "Think about 10,000 heterosexual men with few risk factors for acquiring HIV. One is infected, and he will almost certainly test positive. Of the remaining 9999 uninfected men, one will also test positive. So what are the chances that the person who tests positive is infected?"[7] (It is well worth noting that the debate has some direct, fairly obvious implications for evidence law. If jurors process information better when it is presented in frequentist form rather than probabilistic form, judges ought to cabin the presentation of statistical evidence accordingly. Thus, for instance, jurors might process how probative DNA evidence is far better if it is given in the second form.[8])

As I said, those presented with the first form of information typically exhibit what H&B proponents have called irrational "base rate neglect," failing to account adequately for the fact that because extraordinarily few people have the underlying disease, even a low false-positive *rate* among the extraordinarily high number who are disease-free will still impact a non-trivial number of people,[9] and focusing entirely, instead, on the facts that the very few people who do have the disease will rarely be misdiagnosed and that false-negative rates are also low.[10] One might believe—with both Gigerenzer and Cosmides and Tooby—that our evolved ability is to deal with data presented in terms of "natural frequencies" because we had to make judgments in our adaptive environment about false negatives and positives based on "natural sampling" of a discrete set of events rather than probabilities (though there appears to be nothing resembling evidence in any of their work that EEA (environment of evolutionary adaptation) hunter-gatherers confronted or processed data in terms of such natural frequencies.) They note too in this regard that the concept of probability developed quite late in human history. Thus, concededly irrational base-rate neglect can be made to disappear if data is presented in the form it would purportedly have been confronted through the vast bulk of human history.[11]

It is not surprising that H&B researchers have been largely unimpressed by this line of argument. They are extremely skeptical of the empirical claim that frequentist presentation in and of itself radically improves performance and the associated claim that it does so because our ancestors confronted data in frequentist form and learned to work with it in that form. But, for our purposes here, what is most critical is the structure of the F&F critique, not the question of whether it is perfectly accurate or framed in the most felicitous way.[12]

Gigerenzer further believes that the gap between our natural facility with frequentist data and our clumsiness with manipulating probabilities helps explain why subjects exhibit the conjunction fallacy in the "Linda problem" that I discussed in Chapter Two. (Recall that most experimental subjects, given a description of "Linda" as a hippie politico in college find it more likely—i.e., more *probable*—that she is now a feminist bank teller—a category of which she is a prototypical or representative instance in Kahneman and Tversky's view—than that she is a bank teller. This is the case even though feminist bank tellers are sub-sets of what logically must be the larger set of bank tellers.) For reasons I first mentioned in Chapter Two and return to discuss in some detail later in this chapter, F&F theorists believe that subjects who believe this are arguably properly interpreting conversational cues (e.g., cues that imply that a "mere" bank teller is *not* a feminist bank teller), but, oddly perhaps, Gigerenzer *also* believes that if one asks subjects in within-subject tests questions about Linda's profession in frequentist form, they will not commit the conjunction fallacy. That is, if the same subject is first asked, "If there are a hundred people with descriptions like Linda's, how many are bank tellers?" and then asked "How many are feminist bank tellers?" very few will state that a larger number will be feminist bank tellers.[13] (Oddly, too, while Gigerenzer criticized H&B theorists for failing to recognize this, Tversky and Kahneman performed the same basic manipulation, with the same results, in their initial paper on the conjunction fallacy.[14])

- *Two problems may be formally, mathematically identical, but we are able to solve only the problem with "practical" significance in increasing inclusive fitness. We have learned to do so "informally" though, rather than by developing generalizable mathematical skills; we should not be surprised to find, then, that we cannot solve the formally identical problem for which we never developed an informal solution mechanism.*

Once more, the basic idea motivating this argument is that we solve the problems that we solve using dedicated problem-solving algorithms, not by reducing all problems to a form in which they are tractable for a general computing machine. We can thus demonstrate that people are poor problem solvers if we give them problems they have little reason to solve in real life (or at least real life in the environment of evolutionary adaptation, or EEA). This is true even though accurately responding to the questions posed in the laboratory seems to involve no more formal math skill than solving problems that they figure out readily when the problems must be solved to meet a practical end. We do not really solve those practical problems by first reducing them to abstract, generalized mathematical form; instead, we have domain-specific solution techniques to handle them.

Not surprisingly, given the prominence of the task in debates over the general persuasiveness of evolutionary psychology, one of the key disputes raising this issue centers on poor performance on the "four-card" Wason selection task. Though the task does not directly involve either judgment or decision making, the structure of the dispute over the "reality" of poor performance is unaltered. In the formal task, subjects are told that the rule whose veracity they must test is, "If a card has an even number on one side, it has a vowel on the other" and they are given four cards: One has an even number face up, one has an odd number, one a consonant, and one a vowel. They are asked which cards they must turn over to verify or falsify the proposition.[15]

At the high level of abstraction that H&B theorists associate with System Two thinking, *all* selection task problems might be seen as the same. (I return to discuss, in a very cursory fashion, why some H&B theorists are skeptical of the claim that all "selection task" problems are indeed formally identical, but my main point for now is to clarify the F&F critique, so one should assume that it is at least plausible to describe them as invoking the same formal solution procedures.) If given a proposition of the form, "If P, then Q," a person who wants to take the steps necessary to discover whether the proposition is true must investigate both whether the Ps he encounters always entail Qs *and* whether some of the not-Qs he encounters are accompanied by Ps. He need not, though, investigate whether some not-Ps are accompanied by Qs *or* whether some Qs are accompanied by not-Ps because the rule is not violated in either of those cases. This is true if the proposition is of the form, "If a card has an even number on one side, it has a vowel on the other" (the four-card Wason selection task form): one must turn over cards with an even number facing up to see if they have vowels on the other side (P accompanied by Q) and check whether the card with a consonant has an even number (not-Q accompanied by P). One need not check whether the card with an odd number has a vowel on its back or the card with a face-up vowel has an odd number since it would not violate the rule if they did.

The same formal procedure is useful in verifying whether a liquor license holder is following the rule: "If you are drinking beer, you must be over 18" (the "cheater detection" form). One must check both known beer drinkers to see if they are over 18 and underage patrons to see they are not drinking beer; however, it does not violate the rule for a soft drink imbiber to be an adult or for an adult to have a soft drink, so we needn't check the soft drink user or the adult.

People do quite badly figuring out what steps they need to take to find out if the first, more abstract four-card selection task proposition is true. Most subjects know that they have to turn over the card showing an even number to discover if there is a vowel on the other side, but very few recognize they have to turn over the card with a face-up consonant to make sure it doesn't have an even number on its flip side. On the other hand, far more people solve the problem in the second "cheater detection" form. They know that they must check both known beer drinkers (beer drinking is the "face-up" information) to make sure they are over 18 *and* known 17-year-olds to make sure that what's in their glass is root beer, not beer.

This finding has given rise to the conclusion among MM theorists, echoed in the F&F literature, that there is an evolutionarily adaptive "cheater detection module" whose function, in terms of inclusive fitness, is to permit people to reap the gains from social exchange by recognizing the distinction between defectors from cooperative games and those who will continue to play nicely. Thus, in a social exchange relationship, the "If P, then Q" relationship may be illustrated by a proposition such as, "If you now have the goat I delivered to you, then I should have some of your berries." I know to check whether I have your berries when you have my goat (P entails Q)—the situation in which you have cooperated in the social exchange—but I also readily know I need to check whether you sometimes have my goat even though I don't have your berries (in that case, not-Q is accompanied by P and the "rule" is violated) because you breached your obligation.

There is an enormous debate, filling many journals and books, about how one should best *define* the sorts of tasks that people do well and those they do poorly that arguably resemble the "abstract rule" four-card task and those that either arguably resemble the "cheater detection" task or arguably invoke other domain-specific problem-solving skills. I do not think it crucial for my purposes here to rehearse more than the smallest fraction of that debate. My deliberately narrower point is rather to indicate, structurally, what *types* of arguments F&F researchers make when expressing skepticism about claims that people are cognitively less competent than one might expect and what forms the H&B counterarguments take. For that purpose, the key message is that one critical argument takes this particular form. Let me emphasize again what this form is: *We readily know how to look for cheaters because it is significant to be able to do so even if we don't have general cognitive skills that enable us to use a formally parallel technique to test the veracity of conditional statements.* The critical argument, at this level, is indeterminate about how to describe the domain-specific competence. One could be committed to the idea that one uses a general technique of proposition verification only when one is adequately motivated to do so and that adequate motivation is triggered only by certain domain-specific problems. One could instead argue that subjects never cognize the abstract rule verification task but merely know the more precise steps to take to detect a particular form of rule violation; in this view the algorithm is quite domain specific. For purposes of understanding this criticism of the H&B literature, it is of no moment which, if either, of these interpretations more accurately reflects the beliefs of most F&F researchers or which, if either, is true.[16]

Still, it is worth noting that it is not easy to define what the salient traits of either the abstract rule four-card Wason task *or* the cheater detection version of the task really are. Assume first that we are evaluating statements that are best defined as indicative conditionals (i.e., those in which we are evaluating the truth or falsity of an "If P, then Q" statement) rather than deontic conditionals (e.g., "If you are drinking beer, you must be over 18") in which finding a 17-year-old with a beer does not *falsify* the statement but represents a breach of a socially defined obligation.

We must still figure out if it is realistically *feasible* to test whether any particular indicative conditional we confront is true by checking not-Qs. For instance, it is ordinarily, in the real world, a truly stupid waste of time to investigate all the not-Qs in trying to assess the truth of most propositions that have the abstract indicative conditional "form" that the four-card selection task has. Assume, for instance, that the proposition to be tested is "All ravens are black" (formally, "if a raven, then black"). It may well be worthwhile to check whether the ravens you confront are black and necessary to check at least some of them, but inane to investigate all things that are not black to see if any is a raven. There are simply far too many non-black things to check.[17] If this is true, the relatively "bad" performance on the Wason four-card selection task might arise not because we are formally illogical but have the specific capacity to detect cheaters especially well but because the cheater detection task cues a rather restricted range of not-Qs to test while the typical indicative conditional verification task cues us to expect a near-endless set of not-Qs to explore.[18]

Obviously, too, it is not clear what to make of the fact that people deal differently with at least some indicative conditionals and deontic conditionals. Arguably, the distinction reflects some special capacity to ensure that one is gaining from social exchange. But indicative and deontic conditionals *are* different. The statement, "It is obligatory that P" does *not* logically imply that P is true though the statement that "it is logically necessary that P" does imply P is true. As Over notes, one cannot get very far in the world without realizing that obligations are not necessarily fulfilled.[19] (A statement that P is obligatory may only imply that P is permissible or, more ambiguously, feasible.) But what is critical from Over's (H&B) vantage point is that reasoning about deontic conditionals is, or at least could be, at a high order of context-independent generality. This is true even if the reasoning rules people use in dealing with these deontic conditionals are distinct from those used in relationship to indicative conditionals.

In Over's view, this explains why subjects do just as well figuring out whether conditional precaution rules are being followed ("If a man cleans up spilt blood, he must wear gloves") as they do handling "cheater detection" tasks ("If a man cleans up spilt blood, he must have a license."). A man not wearing gloves while cleaning up blood is not a cheater, though he may be endangering himself. MM and F&F theorists, confronted with such evidence, have responded that there may yet be another module to deal with precautions and hazard identification.[20] One of the strongest pieces of evidence that those committed to MM and/or F&F views that we have separate faculties to reason about precautions and to detect cheaters—though each seems to involve pragmatic reasoning about deontic conditionals—is that there appears to be at least one patient with lesions whose performance on cheater detection tasks is significantly compromised despite looking like an ordinary subject when reasoning about precautions.[21]

Perhaps just as significantly—especially if our goal here is to understand, rather than evaluate, the debate between F&F and H&B theorists—Over notes that the modularized view of either cheater detection or hazard identification copes poorly with our plain capacity to *reason* about cheating. (To put it in the terms I have been using, it ignores our ability to make use of information in a compensatory fashion, rather than having a mildly or strongly encapsulated response to delimited inputs.) We not only must identify rule-violating cheaters but must cope with and evaluate an extraordinarily wide array of more-or-less acceptable excuses for non-performance of obligations in order to understand the real mechanisms of social exchange and cheating.[22] Some such excuses may even come from informational cues we purportedly process as a hazard ("If it is foggy, slow down" may also be seen as a reason to *violate* the most straightforward version of a social exchange rule: "If you made an appointment to see me at three, you must be there by three.").

- *Subjects may make what appear to be "mistakes" playing games in laboratories with formal payoff rules because the "games" resemble real-world problems in which the payoffs are subtly distinct from the payoffs that are defined in the formal game. People solve the real-world variant of the problem that they have been presented, rather than the precise problem they have actually been presented*

Once more, in this class of cases, the F&F researchers concede that the experimental subjects perform poorly on the task they have been given. That is, once more, the behavior is not "better than rational" given the precise payoff structure of the laboratory game. Fundamentally, they do so, however, because they ignore the instructions they have been given—they have confronted them for the first time in the experimental setting. Instead, they assume that they are playing a game that they either play often in real life—or that their ancestors played often in the EEA, when people developed relevant cognitive capacities—that *resemble* the laboratory game but have a different set of payoffs.

The debate over "probability matching" is instructive in understanding this aspect of the dispute between F&F and H&B researchers. Assume that experimental subjects are shown an urn with seventy green and thirty yellow balls. They are told that ten balls will be drawn from the urn, and the ball that is drawn will be put back in the urn after it is drawn. Subjects are asked to guess which color ball will be drawn on each of the ten occasions. They win a prize for each correct answer. Rational subjects should pick green all ten times unless the subject has nonmonetary goals (e.g., a desire to keep himself more interested in the contest). The expected value of choosing green for all ten selections is seven correct selections (you've got a 0.7 chance each and every time.) Most people, though, choose green seven times and yellow three; that is, they engage in what is usually dubbed "probability matching" for the set, making their choices match the most probable outcome of ten draws. They do so even though the expected value of that choice is 0.7 × 7 + 0.3 × 3 or 5.8 correct guesses rather than 7.

People *could* figure out what choices to make using some general cognitive mechanisms that permit the calculation of expected values in all sorts of situations. Alternatively, people might have developed at least relatively domain-specific cognitive mechanisms to solve the problem of picking an optimal mix of distinctly risky gain-seeking activities from a small option set that dictates that one will engage in probability matching. F&F theorists, echoing evolutionary psychologists who believe that people have developed narrow domain-specific "answers" to problems that presented themselves to our ancestors facing evolutionary pressures, argue, for instance, that the "cognate" problem to the urn problem in a natural environment is to pick between foraging sites with distinct probabilities of finding food. The optimal strategy in that setting may not be to maximize expected value, though, but to balance both the need to get more food now and to learn more about unexplored environments for the future, at least when one is satisfied that one has gone to enough sites with higher odds of finding food to guarantee that one will be a bit flush with food.[23]

Assume, at least for argument's sake, that the F&F theorists are correct to note that our ancestors may have been rational to forage (at least when they were not extremely hungry) both in places with a high chance of success and those with a lower chance of success because doing so permitted them to both get enough food and to gather useful information about which of the relatively improbable places to find food actually turns out to be a good place to find it. It is still plain that this strategy makes no sense when trying to maximize the return one gets in the betting game that the experimenters have presented. When there are thirty yellow and seventy green balls in the urn, and the selection procedure appears fair, picking the yellow 30 percent of the time will teach you nothing about the probability of getting a good result on some future occasion, even if foraging in three 30 percent-chance-of-success sites may teach you where to go and where not to go in the future.

I must confess that I am simply befuddled by the claim that the foraging "game" so closely and transparently resembles the probability matching draw-a-ball-from-an-urn game that one should *expect* experimental subjects to substitute the foraging payoff rules for the rules the experimenter has established. Even if one is not generally skeptical of claims that we can readily assess which "modules" people will assign tasks to, I think one would be hard-pressed to defend even the intuitive plausibility of the claim that payoff expectations from foraging would seem close to applicable to a game in which no further agency by the subject would ever be required, nor would he learn anything at all about his future prospects (or anything worth knowing at all) through "trial."

In my view, then, it is not surprising to find, as Stanovich and West found, that people who do better on g-loaded tests like the SAT are less likely to engage in "probability matching" than those who do more poorly on the SAT.[24] Should we describe the situationally rational and conventionally "smarter" people as more capable of overriding "intuitions" when they are inapt? (Recall the standard H&B image of System Two overriding System One "intuitions.") Should we think of them as people better able to "assign" a decision-making task to the apt decision-making algorithm? However else we should describe them, we would, I think, be loathe to describe them as making decisions that lack ecological rationality since they alone are accurately discerning the fit between algorithm and the *actual* environment the subjects are confronting, yet that is precisely what the F&F critique implies.

- *Subjects may appear to make computational "mistakes" because they reinterpret the experimenters' instructions or assume that the experimenter has implied more than he has explicitly stated. Making these sorts of conversational implications is a necessary part of being able to communicate, and, of course, being able to communicate is adaptive.*

F&F psychologists often argue that H&B researchers have assumed, incorrectly, that subjects are giving non-normative responses to the set of questions that they intended to ask, when they are really giving normatively appropriate responses to the questions that socially adept communicators, interpreting linguistic cues as they would ordinarily be interpreted in real conversation, believe have been posed. It is important to note that two separable points are embedded in this argument. First, subjects may be giving perfectly good answers to the questions they infer have been asked, even if there is no compelling explanation for them to interpret the questions as they do. (If I hear you ask me what two plus two equals and I say, "Four," I have not made an *arithmetic* error even if you clearly said "What is two minus two?" and the breakdown in communication is entirely attributable to my inattention or bad hearing, not your failures as a communicator.) Second, F&F scholars argue that, as a matter of fact, the subjects' interpretations of the questions the experimenters pose are typically more sensible, given general norms concerning how we should draw implications from literal language that are necessary for communication to proceed.

One can probably best understand this general controversy by reflecting on two particular disputes. First, one might look at certain F&F critiques of the conjunction fallacy experiments that I have discussed. Second, one might look at F&F critiques of experiments purporting to show that preferences about end-states were irrationally sensitive to framing (most particularly, experiments in which outcomes were framed, alternatively, as either gains or losses).

Recall, first, the point I initially mentioned very briefly in Chapter Two: F&F critics argued that those who ostensibly committed the conjunction fallacy in the "Linda problem" did not do anything problematic, even though they believed it more probable that Linda was a feminist bank teller than a bank teller, though the former is a sub-set of the latter and cannot, therefore, be more probable. (Recall that they did so, from the vantage point of H&B theorists, because Linda was first described as having had traits in college far more prototypical of a feminist than an ordinary bank teller. They then made judgments of the probability of the "outcome" based on its "representativeness.")

Instead, F&F scholars claimed, the subjects were actually behaving more intelligently by observing the standard Gricean norms about conversation and reinterpreting the "intended" question. Grice posits that those committed to a cooperative principle of conversation that permits listeners to draw proper inferences from words spoken in a conversational context assume that what we offer our conversational partners must be relevant.[25] According to the F&F critics, rational social creatures recognizing the cooperative nature of Gricean conversation would think that the experimenter would not have offered information about Linda's left-wing politics or countercultural style *unless* the experimenter intended to signal that she was indeed a feminist bank teller now. (Maxims of both relevance and quantity are implicated.) Thus, the "conjunction fallacy" response is normative, not irrational, in accounting for implicit information that those who avoid the fallacy simply neglect.[26]

Another way of putting the point—more useful, in my view, for purposes of the present exposition—is that the subjects "hear" a different question than the experimenters claim to have asked, given their Gricean interpretation of the prior "conversational" inputs. At core, the claim is that those who make appropriate inferences from the prior "conversation" in which they have already been told about Linda's past political/cultural identity, information presumed to be both relevant to the conversation and not part of a needlessly long-winded monologue, is to hear or read the explicitly uttered phrase "Linda is a bank teller" as "Linda is a bank teller but not a feminist." It is equally plausible, in this view, that subjects hear the statement "Linda is a bank teller" as an implicit conditional (i.e., "*If* Linda is a bank teller, she is a feminist.").

It may well be the case, as H&B researchers note, that experimental subjects express regret or embarrassment about their initial response once alerted to the fact that it cannot be more likely that Linda is a feminist bank teller than a bank teller. That is, they renounce the response that rationalists would consider non-normative. Still, for F&F theorists, that renunciation is essentially beside the point. *Of course* people can be made to feel that their response to the Linda problem was mistaken if the "explanation" of the alternative answers the experimenters present is completely context-free and *defines* one response as a sub-set of the other so that judging that response more probable is simply wrong.[27]

Consider the following, though. A friend shares all sorts of information that makes it sound like he went on a thoroughly terrible date. We would likely hear his statement in the course of the negative description of the evening that, "Dinner at the expensive restaurant my date took me to was edible" to imply that it was *no better than edible*, that the fact that he said it was "edible" *rules out* the possibility that it was fabulous. We would do so, even though we could construct a formally logical view of the statement in which edible and fabulous *could* be seen, formally, as a sub-set of edible and thus would not be *excluded* or ruled out by the statement that dinner was edible. Obviously, "edible and fabulous" is *not* a sub-set of "edible" if edible *means* "edible but not fabulous" just as a feminist bank teller—or, to put it a tad more formally, feminist *and* bank teller—is not a sub-set of bank tellers if bank teller means, "non-feminist bank tellers." Whether this commonplace F&F response is adequate to deal with the Stanovich/West finding that more conventionally "intelligent" people do not construe the task in the fashion Gigerenzer thinks is ecologically rational is, as usual, another tricky question.[28]

Similarly, F&F critics contend that experimental subjects I first mentioned in Chapter Two who choose a program that is said to *save* 200 of 600 people while rejecting a program in which 400 of the 600 people will *die* are not irrational in evaluating end-states. Recall that once more, H&B scholars contend that they are irrational, picking or rejecting the precise same outcome depending merely on whether it is described or framed as a gain or a loss. Instead, F&F-influenced psychologists believe the subjects are more conversationally astute than the experimenters who saw the responses as irrational. The subjects are, in this view, reading inferential subtext as well as literal text, rather than displaying their vulnerability to the sorts of framing effects that H&B theorists highlight in demonstrating how labile end-state value judgments can be. It is the experimenters who believed they were asking the subjects to evaluate the same program, merely described in two distinct frames, who misunderstood the task. In this view, when one *says* that a program will save 200 people, it leaves open the possibility that more still will survive (e.g., as a result of other programs); on the other hand, when one says that 400 people will die, they are goners.[29] Given that interpretation, a program that saves 200 of 600 *is* superior to one in which 400 of the 600 die.

B. INADEQUATELY THEORIZED AND SPECIFIED HEURISTICS

While the most powerful and significant criticism lodged by the F&F school at H&B researchers is that they see irrationality where it does not ultimately exist, or find it in settings of little or no practical consequence, it is important to note that they also repeatedly complain that the H&B theorists neither explain why people use the precise heuristic problem-solving mechanisms that they allegedly use nor typically define the mechanisms in adequate detail. Their *explanation* for this second deficiency in the H&B program is pretty similar to the explanation of the perceived failure of H&B theorists to test performance on real-world problems. Like all academics influenced by variants of evolutionary psychology, F&F theorists start with the idea that mental capacities are adaptive and think we are most likely to be able to identify mental capacities/mechanisms not simply by observation but by reasoning backward from the inclusive fitness "need" that the organism had to meet to the capacity it must have developed.

Because, for example, H&B theorists do not typically even attempt to specify precisely what adaptive *role* it might have played to make certain forms of purportedly bad judgments (e.g., to neglect base rates, to encode gains and losses asymmetrically, to assess probabilities on the basis of availability), they purportedly have more difficulty describing the *form* these phenomena would take. On the other hand, the F&F "adaptive toolbox" approach *starts* with the supposition that we can identify a series of tools, with some precision, that would have been useful in increasing reproductive success. These *are* the basic heuristic mechanisms, and these cognitive capacities are either used in settings in which they were originally adaptive or co-opted—most often with good results, sometimes not—when it is possible to use the capacity to cope with an environment that is novel from the vantage point of those who utilized only the basic capacities in the EEA.

Whatever the *cause* of these problems that purportedly beset H&B research, it is plain that F&F theorists frequently note critically that the H&B heuristics are poorly defined, very hard to operationalize, and—as a result—give us little to work with if we want to make predictions that can be falsified or verified. I noted in Chapter Two, for instance, one exemplar of this kind of critique: F&F writers are skeptical that the concept of "availability" is defined clearly enough for us either to accept or to reject the idea that people misestimate probabilities or frequencies based on the "availability" of an event whose probability or frequency they are asked to assess.

First, they note that the H&B theorists fail to provide an "evolutionary psychological" explanation for a cognitive capacity to retrieve particular events from memory more readily. When some H&B researchers implied, in ways I return to discuss in Chapter Five, that the "recognition" heuristic essentially relied on the fact that objects that F&F researchers believed were "recognized" were merely more "available," one of the reasons that the F&F researchers so strongly resisted this interpretation was that they believed that there *was* an adaptive reason to believe that people had developed the capacity to "merely" recognize. They strongly believed that what differentiated them from the H&B researchers is that only H&B scholars feel no obligation to provide some such similar reason to believe that we have an evolved capacity to retrieve some sub-class of events more readily than others.

More important, for these purposes, they believe that availability has no precise definition: The most obvious candidates—data in a category is more "available" if subjects could retrieve the first instance of a category more quickly, or could retrieve more such instances in a fixed time frame—had not been rigorously tested by H&B theorists. When F&F researchers tested whether categories that H&B researchers had assumed were more available (e.g., words beginning with the letter "r" rather than those whose third letter was "r"), they found that they were not more available in these senses.[30]

Once more, the substance of this debate is of relatively little significance for my purposes at the moment, but I must say that this F&F finding does little to undermine my belief in the notion that "availability" is a genuine cognitive phenomenon. If asked to estimate as many specific cases as possible of words whose third letter is "r" in a *short*, finite time rather than words whose first letter is "r," it is not all that surprising that three-letter words seem more, not less, "available" (thus defined.) As soon as one thinks of one such three-letter word, one can quickly list words that rhyme with it: One thinks of "bar" and readily gets to "car," "far," "jar," "mar," and "tar" in a big hurry. Still, one immediately knows that the whole "r" section of the dictionary is made up of many, many words beginning with "r" (so not only *instances* are readily available but the existence of a large category is available) while it is more difficult to picture the existence of words with "r" as a third letter outside the discrete words and word types one explicitly remembers. Moreover, there are many word types whose third letter is "r" that are both truly difficult to recall quickly and don't generate, once recalled, further instances by obvious rule. Think in this regard about words that are far longer than three or four letters, that do not fall into easy categories or categories that generate other instances (e.g., words like sartorial, harass, marvelous, and string). If, instead, one thinks of equally "random" words *beginning* with r—like random—the recollection will generate, explicitly or implicitly (a form of meta-availability), a set of words that are roughly in alphabetical order with the first word recalled (e.g., ranch, rancid, rancor, and randy).

I am not claiming that I have specified or could specify a *definition* of availability in making this point, only that it is not surprising that Kahneman and Tversky were able to predict, accurately, based on arguably underspecified intuitions about ease of retrieval, ways in which subjects would misestimate probabilities. They did not merely look to see which items were overestimated and declare them, *ex post*, to be the more available ones.

The claim that H&B theorists are hampered by their failure to investigate the adaptive role that particular cognitive techniques might serve can be seen even more clearly if we look at how F&F theorists have responded to another set of H&B findings. Many of those in the H&B school imply both that people sometimes mistakenly believe that recent events will recur with abnormal frequency when they won't (the so-called hot-hand fallacy) and sometimes wrongly believe that random events will self-correct—that a head will be tossed because a string of tails needs to be "counterbalanced" (the so-called gambler's fallacy). The alleged problem that F&F scholars think the H&B theorists face here is that they are simply cataloguing what they see as errors, but they cannot *specify* when people have "positive recency" (i.e., believe things that have happened recently will likely persist) and when they have "negative recency" (i.e., believe things that happened in the recent past will likely stop). They are unable to reconcile these findings or predict the domains in which we should observe positive rather than negative recency because they neither have an adaptationist theory of why people should make certain sorts of assumptions about distinct sorts of events, nor—partly as a result—have they specified the precise domain or nature of heuristics like the "hot-hand fallacy."

F&F theorists argue, at core, that there are adaptive reasons to distinguish intentional events—events created by the actions of other actors, especially persons, capable of acting deliberately—and non-intentional events, generally involving no animate objects. In this view, we *should* attribute positive recency to intentional events because it would be useful to believe that people reveal disposition, like skill or clumsiness, through conduct. At the same time, it would meet our ends to assume that non-intentional events, over time, are random over enough trials, if not one.[31] They thus predict that subjects will infer negative recency in situations in which the pattern appears to be of inanimate origin and positive recency if these situations appear to involve human skill, while H&B theorists are left to claim, in some underspecified fashion, that both the hot-hand and gambler's fallacy are caused by "representativeness."

Note, too, that resolving the controversy has some implications for legal regulation. Do consumers underestimate the probability of product danger or of product underperformance because most of their encounters with products have been unproblematic, making a mistake akin to the hot-hand fallacy?[32] Or do they overestimate that such problems will arise in the future to "correct" for their undue good fortune, making an error akin to the gambler's fallacy?[33] Do we need stricter product performance regulation because of systematic underestimates of product failure or should we expect consumers will overestimate the true risk of product failure? H&B research may tell us little. The F&F scholars seem to imply that if and only if consumers perceive product failure as arising from the manufacturer/person rather than the inanimate product will they underestimate risk having had generally good experiences with products. What we need to investigate is how consumers perceive the products with which they have experience.[34]

C. COMPUTATIONAL LIMITS OR THE LIMITS OF COMPUTATION?

There is one last structural critique that F&F theorists regularly make that I will note briefly. F&F psychologists allege that H&B theorists (and perhaps to an even greater extent, economists who speak of "bounded rationality") overestimate the problems caused by the mind's computational limits and fail to account adequately for the fact that the *best* way of solving many problems even for a computationally unlimited mind is to use a scaled-back computational *method*. Thus, they argue that those in the H&B school ignore the degree to which fast and frugal heuristics can outperform decision-making rules that utilize more information as long as the information that is available is of a certain form.

I have already discussed several variants of this argument. One that I think Gigerenzer finds especially powerful is that in a world in which the relationship between observables and outcomes is shifting or unstable, a mind that was capable of limitless computation might well be able to fit a regression equation that purportedly accounted for all factors that influenced outcomes. This would be a mistake. A mind that instead made use of the "Take the Best" heuristic, either consciously or unconsciously, might well do better, because the "best" cue to predict an outcome might well be more *stably* causally connected to the outcome, rather than coincidentally related in the few observed trials.

Thus, for instance, to take a case I noted briefly in Chapter Three, doctors must triage patients who might or might not be eligible for the coronary care unit. The University of Michigan used an elaborate Heart Disease Predictive Instrument, which required probability calculations for fifty variables and a logistic formula to weight and add the predictors. The fast and frugal alternative was to use a single question to make an initial admission decision: If the patient has a certain anomaly in the ST segment of his electrocardiogram, he is immediately admitted to the coronary care unit. If not, he is admitted to the regular nursing bed unless, first, his primary symptom is severe chest pain *and* one of four other factors exists. Even though the fifty-variable Predictive Instrument contains all the information elicited in the fast and frugal method, it is *less* accurate in classifying whether a patient is about to have an actual heart attack, because regression weights are heavily skewed and the outcome highly unpredictable.[35]

It is worth noting, though, that using the heuristic system generated many more false alarms than using most versions of the complex formula did—the multifactor system was tweaked to generate different numbers of false positives and negatives in a fashion that the heuristic system could not readily be. It is not clear, as a result, that the heuristic system is actually a "better" or more rational system, given resource constraints, nor that its improved capacity to recognize those actually having heart attacks is not largely a simple product of its overinclusiveness. It is also not obvious that it is the cheapest or most accurate "overinclusive" system that one could create or implement if one chose to move in the direction of reducing aggregate mistakes but to skew mistakes toward false positives. The hospital seemingly never tried to develop a multifactor test that would identify a still-higher proportion of those who would actually subsequently have myocardial infarctions at the expense of admitting still more parties to the coronary care unit who would not. We know instead that they initially developed the complex inventory as a response to overcrowding in the coronary care unit.

F&F theorists also often note that if people attempt to use lots of information, they will merely use information that is undependable or inaccurate, thus revising judgments that they would have made with more accurate single pieces of information in an unfortunate direction. In some ways, the Goldstein and Gigerenzer view of the recognition heuristic, which I discuss at great length in Chapter Five, is that parties who think they know a lot about city size (either from direct, but poorly recalled or vague semantic knowledge or by making inferences based on undependable cues) may implicitly revise estimates of relative city size that would be better made if they could only rely on a single cue (whether they recognize the city), a cue that is ecologically valid because differential recognition correlates more highly with relative size than do any of the other cues that people might try to use. Of course, one *cannot* use recognition if one recognizes both cities, but one could use parallel, "Take the Best" cues (e.g., the "prominence" of the two cities) rather than try to recall or infer more information about population size. The structure of the F&F claim is quite clear in this regard as well; its accuracy, as I explore, is more dubious.

E. CONCLUSION

F&F theorists have criticized the work associated with the H&B school largely because they think the H&B theorists have exposed frailties in judgment and decision making that are at core artifacts of poorly designed experiments. Poor performance in these experimental settings does not imply poor performance in natural environments. The experiments are poorly designed in the sense that they often present problems in a cognitively intractable form rather than the more tractable form that the problems would take in natural environments. They are poorly designed in the sense that they ask people to solve, through abstract methods, problems of no practical significance that formally resemble important problems that they solve without using formal logic. The experimental prompts are also subject to two sorts of revision by the subjects. At times, subjects will substitute a payoff structure from the real-world variant of the "game" that resembles the "game" the experimenters have established with its own unfamiliar payoff structure and, at other times, people will reinterpret the language of instructions they are given because they draw implications from the quasi-conversation with the experimenter that are not literally present.

At the same time, F&F scholars believe that the heuristics that the H&B scholars have identified are both undertheorized—there is no adaptationist account of why any of the cognitive mechanisms they identify would have developed—and underdefined. As a result, they claim, it is hard to predict how people will behave, in any given problem domain, if they behave as users of H&B heuristics. Instead, H&B researchers tend to note departures from idealized rational choice theory and then merely give an unfocused, *post hoc* explanation to account for the gap. Moreover, H&B theorists are inadequately sensitive to the possibility that computationally limited actors who make use of good, albeit limited, information may outperform actors able to combine considerably more, if poorer, informational cues.

At core, all of these more detailed critiques derive from a single conceptual critique. F&F scholars believe that H&B researchers have not paid adequate heed to the ways in which people developed domain-specific problem-solving techniques to cope with a discrete set of survival challenges. At the same time, they fail to focus on the fact that we also have the capacity to make use of the evolved capacities to make good judgments in novel settings when we perceive that we are in environmental settings in which exercising the capacity facilitates fast and frugal judgments.

5

OBJECTIONS TO THE FAST AND FRUGAL SCHOOL PROGRAM*

Most of the attacks that fast and frugal (F&F) researchers have made on the research in the heuristics and biases (H&B) tradition have been explicit. In that sense, the task in Chapter Four was considerably easier than our task will be in this chapter, for, with relatively limited exceptions,[1] the H&B objections to F&F work must largely be inferred, not merely reported and systematized. At their core, though, the most fundamental H&B critiques of the work associated with the F&F school simply mirror or flip the F&F critiques presented in Chapter Four.

Thus, while F&F theorists deride H&B theorists because they purportedly fail to account adequately for the ways in which cognition is adaptive to the problems people actually face, our tentative view is that the H&B theorists believe in turn that the F&F scholars' fixation on the ways in which capacities *must* be adaptive may lead the F&F theorists on occasion to misconstrue observed behavior and to overestimate the practical optimality of observed performance. It may also lead them to expect universal use of similar problem-solving methods, to expect convergence on the imagined adaptive strategy when there is no such convergence. We try to articulate these general claims extremely briefly, and then illustrate them at considerably more length in our discussion of one of the most basic, exemplary and clear of the F&F heuristics, the so-called recognition heuristic.

* with Nicholas Richman Kelman

A. DO F&F THEORISTS OBSERVE TRAITS OR DEDUCE TRAITS THAT "MUST" HAVE EVOLVED?

The most contentious claim that H&B scholars arguably make is that F&F theorists are simply wrong when they declare that they offer descriptions of the heuristics people use that are both more detailed and more accurate than those that H&B theorists provide. Instead, the critics suspect, the heuristics the F&F people identify are frequently inaccurate idealizations of actual capacities or cognitive strategies—ungrounded both in behavioral observations and in neurobiology—that merely posit a solution to some imputed adaptive *goals* as if these solutions were observed capacities. To put that point another way, H&B scholars arguably believe that the F&F theorist too typically describes a cognitive process without regard to its real nature, but only as the projected solution to the adaptive problem the F&F theorist *imagines* the organism both needed to solve and must have solved in the fashion the theorist posits.

It is vital to recognize that this sort of derogatory observation would merely echo a perfectly common refrain in critiques of evolutionary psychology (EP) more generally. Instead, of observing a trait, say critics of EP, EP researchers selectively observe behavior and "see" the attributes that they believe they ought to find, given the adaptive needs they believe they have identified. This is troublesome in part because it is very difficult to figure out precisely what our adaptive needs were and how they might or might not have been met. It is troublesome too because the solutions to adaptive problems that are in fact in place need not—in fact, typically *cannot*—be the hypothetically optimal solutions that EP theorists generate because developmental biological limits constrain the realistic traits an organism can develop through mutation.[2] It is also bothersome, of course, because if researchers are indeed describing "observed" traits as they hope or suspect they will be, rather than as they have been observed to be, that would simply be bad science.

We, and many far more expert others, have offered examples of this critique of EP outside the heuristics domain.[3] Take for example the standard criticisms of the veracity of EP descriptions of how and why both rape and rape avoidance purportedly developed to meet adaptive needs. EP theorists assert that men with few opportunities to have fully consensual sex are the most likely to rape because these theorists see rape as an adaptive reproductive option that becomes more attractive when other options are foreclosed.[4] However, the data they use to *demonstrate* this as a valid description of actual rapists are inadequate to demonstrate it to be the case. Instead, they demonstrate that it *should* be the case if rape plays the role they believe it plays in increasing male inclusive fitness.[5] The *direct* evidence that rapists have atypically few opportunities for consensual sexual contacts is extraordinarily weak: It turns out that rapists seem to have had an average or slightly above-average amount of voluntary sexual contact proximate to their attacks.[6] And the *indirect* evidence the EP scholars employ—that rapists are those who are not likely to be voluntarily chosen by women because they are atypically likely to be the sort of poor resource providers that women purportedly abjure—unduly downplays the commonplace association between poverty and all forms of antisocial violence, sexual and nonsexual alike.[7]

We return in some detail, later in the chapter, to explore this point in the context of the recognition heuristic, but here is the key observation we try to elaborate there that hopefully elucidates this particular critique: In discovering the recognition heuristic, Goldstein and Gigerenzer arguably *start* with the proposition that it would serve adaptive ends to have the "capacity" to merely recognize or fail to recognize things, very hastily, in a simple on-off binary way. This form of "recognition" is the adaptive tool in the Gigerenzian toolbox that people will purportedly be able to make use of. They then assume the capacity is used to make judgments about city size based on the recognition heuristic: Subjects will identify immediately which of two cities one "recognizes" (if one recognizes but one) and then decide, without further reflection, that the recognized city is larger, simply building on "this capacity." One of the questions we explore is whether subjects actually use the capacity they have identified—the ability to make item recognition or familiarity judgments—when they confront the task of comparing city sizes by "recognizing" a city, and whether they have accurately described how item recognition works, even in cases in which it is the capacity in play.[8]

B. PERFORMANCE VARIABILITY

Chapter Two summarizes claims that different people, with different cognitive abilities and "thinking styles," may systematically use heuristics differently, noting the typical claim that "smarter" and "more open-minded" people simply use them *less* in situations in which their use results in errors.[9] Such claims are at least mildly incompatible with a number of aspects of the F&F view. Systematically differential use of heuristics is hard to square with the claim that we should almost invariably understand heuristics far less in terms of computational deficits and far more in terms of locating apt fits between computational capacities and the external environment. If less is (indeed) more, one might expect smarter people to make use of less information, more frequently. But they do not: People with more computational capacities use the heuristics that depend on processing fewer cues less often. The data does not suggest that they are "smart enough" to figure out that their use is optimal given the external environment more frequently than less "intelligent" people are able to realize.

But what we wanted to highlight here is that heterogeneity in the use of heuristics—without regard to the question of whether the nonusers are likely doing "better"—is not readily reconciled with the claim that adaptive pressures dictate the use of mandatory heuristics. Of course, this need not be true: One *could* develop a distinct, if not obviously more plausible, adaptationist picture than the F&F theorists offer that there is a game-theoretically stable equilibrium with a particular population mix of heuristic users and non-users, parallel to the stable mix of Hawks and Doves that can emerge in standard evolutionary game theory accounts. It also would not be true if we ultimately find interpersonal differentiation occurs only in responding to poorly designed laboratory tasks, but not in responding to actual tasks with adaptive significance. In this regard, F&F theorists are likely simply to reiterate the claim that H&B "biases" and "mistakes" are artifacts of unrealistic experimental prompts.

One would expect, as noted in Chapter Two, that this last counterargument would be the one that F&F theorists offer to the claim that the pattern of differentiated heuristic use makes it difficult to argue that the use of heuristics is *hyper-rational*. Here is how the argument would likely be developed: It could be the case that g-loaded tests measure the capacity to reduce contextual information to symbolic representations best handled by abstract formulas—and that the H&B researchers are treating such reductions as normative—but that those who succeed on g-loaded tests are actually *failing* to meet their considered ends when answering as they do. It is also more plausibly the case that one could believe (as above) that g-loaded tests measure the capacity to translate tasks into rational choice abstractions *and that this is the proper strategy to employ when, and only when, solving H&B experimental tasks* but that the use of heuristics in real-world settings is more universal and more adaptive.

C. THE CRITIQUE ILLUSTRATED AND EXTENDED: THE RECOGNITION HEURISTIC

Goldstein and Gigerenzer's seminal work on the so-called recognition heuristic[10] is not just significant as an attempt to model a particular decision-making task—assessing which of two cities has a larger population when one lacks precise semantic knowledge of each city's population. More important, it is emblematic of the general F&F approach to heuristics. As I have noted repeatedly, the key point is that it is critical for Gigerenzer and his associates, in describing a heuristic—a fast and frugal decision-making mechanism that may outperform more cumbersome, multi-cue compensatory decision-making strategies—first to find a mental capacity that humans have developed, because developing that capacity ostensibly increased inclusive fitness. The next step is to discover situations in which using the developed capacity exploits structures of information available in the environment to reach sound judgments. Those who are naïve or ignorant enough to be able to make use of the recognition heuristic, because they confront city pairs in which they recognize one but not both members of the pair, ostensibly do precisely that. According to

Goldstein and Gigerenzer, people who are frequently able to rely on a single cue—whether they recognize the name of one city in the pair but not the other—will do a *better* job answering questions about which city is more populous than those who know a good deal more about the cities. Thus, for instance, Germans more frequently correctly stated that San Diego is more populous than San Antonio than do Americans,[11] who know far more about each city, because they can and do rely on only one cue, whether they have heard of one city only.

It is critical to note three points if we are to understand the more general structure of H&B critiques of F&F theory that are embedded in the controversy over the recognition heuristic. First, the critics argue that the account of the evolved capacity that subjects allegedly use to begin to solve the city size assessment task is not, as F&F scholars like to claim in describing their methodology, at all precise, or based on careful observation. In fact, once one unpacks what it is that the subjects in Gigerenzer and Goldstein's experiments actually do when they claim to recognize one city rather than another, one would see that there is little space between what F&F theorists believe to be the psychologically well-specified capacity to recognize and what they claim to be the poorly specified H&B tendency to find one memory more "available" than another. Second, the critics believe that the interesting F&F claim that people solve the size comparison problem using a single cue, disregarding additional information that might cue city size, is simply false, and that attempts to rescue the claim by arguing that they do so only when they are exclusively making use of memory-inference-based heuristics reduce the claim to an uninteresting tautology. While it is often difficult to distinguish the predictions of those who believe people are using conventional rational choice methods making use of limited information and those who believe subjects are employing heuristics, it appears in this case that those who believe the city size assessment task is solved by rational choice methods are far closer to being correct. The idea that we have a "dedicated informationally encapsulated module" that co-opts the "recognition capacity" and uses it exclusively in ways that are cognitively a-rational though they meet our ends to make useful judgments is belied by the data. Third, critics note that there are systematic differences in the ways in which more academically successful subjects approach many aspects of the city size assessment task; these suggest, though do not prove, that the use of any aspects of the "heuristic method" (binary judgments of "familiarity," one-cue decision making) is not "compulsory" in the way one would assume it would be if it served adaptive functions.

Finally, Goldstein and Gigerenzer seem to us ambiguous on another critical point. When subjects have no other information but recognition, or recognition-like, information, they use it exclusively regardless of whether there is reason either to intuit or to have learned that it is ecologically rational to do so. That point is uncontroversial; after all, what else could they do? However, the F&F notion that we co-opt developed capacities to solve problems quickly and frugally when the opportunity presents itself rather than to rely on multicue strategies depends on the existence of some unspecified mechanism that permits us to tell *whether* we are in a situation in which the use of the heuristic is ecologically valid. Gigerenzer and Goldstein are ambiguous, especially in their early writing regarding the heuristic, about whether and how people have the meta-cognitive capacity to select heuristics when and only when they are adaptive to the precise task they are charged with performing. They are unclear as well in specifying what environmental cues would be available to tell them whether or not they are in a domain in which the heuristic is properly employed. Naturally, it is possible that they simply do not have such a capacity. Like most theorists who imply or state that cognition is at least modestly domain-specific, Gigerenzer and Goldstein are very vague about how to describe the relevant domain to which the cognitive ability is specific: Do people use recognition to make judgments about city size? Or, is city size either too broad a category—they make judgments about the size of certain sub-sets of cities but not others or about city *population* size but not city *area*? Might it instead be too narrow a category because they use something like recognition to make judgments about all size judgments (e.g., the population of species) or every comparison judgment that has any "evaluative dimension" (e.g., better/worse; bigger/smaller; more fertile/less fertile)? Obviously, one can construct experimental environments in which recognition indeed correlates with criterion value—the German and American city size experiments present one such experimental environment—but one can also construct environments where it does not. Recognition in fact negatively correlates with most lists of species population. Lions are famous, hardly any of the near-endless but awesomely populous species of insects are. There is almost no correlation between recognition by American subjects and the relative size of "second-tier" large Asian cities—those with populations between two and six million—most of which are cities in China and India that very few Americans recognize.

Given this ambiguity, it seems reasonable to assume that Goldstein and Gigerenzer must believe *either* that subjects will not use the recognition heuristic when it is ecologically invalid, because they have the adaptive meta-capacity to co-opt the evolved mechanism only when it successfully exploits information structures in the environment, *or* that they will always use recognition to assess relative city sizes (species population? who will win a soccer match?), whether it is ecologically valid to do so or not. While it is clear in their more recent writings that they believe that subjects can make use of a variety of meta-cognitive methods that guide them as to whether to use a heuristic, and which heuristic to use,[12] it remains ambiguous whether the theory predicts that subjects would or would not use the heuristic in the wide range of situations in which it generates bad results, ranging from large but not enormous Asian city size to species population. However, it is quite explicit in making what amounts to the tautologically true observation that if the correlation between recognition and targeted attribute is low (lower than 0.5), then the use the heuristic is not *effective*.

We do not address this important concern in this chapter, however, since this issue was at the core of the discussion of the relationship between F&F theory and the massive modularity hypothesis that was already explored in somewhat more detail in Chapter Three. It is worth noting, though, that it is addressed, in more direct relationship to the recognition heuristic, by scholars like Richter and Spath, finding that subjects do *not* assess the relative population size of different animals or the relative safety of two airlines based on recognition, where correlations between recognition and criterion value are in fact weak.[13] It is addressed as well in works by F&F theorists like Pachur and Hertwig, who offer certain "boundary conditions" in which the heuristic would be used,[14] and by Volz et al., using fMRI (functional magnetic resonance imaging) data to argue that different portions of the brain are used to determine *whether* to use the recognition heuristic than are used in either simply recognizing items or in employing the heuristic.[15]

We discuss, then, only the first three of these problems in F&F work: accuracy in identifying cognitive capacities, the hypothesis that subjects do not use more than a single piece of information, and the possibility of systematic variability of performance across experimental subjects.

- *Are Goldstein and Gigerenzer correct that their subjects "merely recognize" cities as previously confronted and that their judgments about whether they do so are on/off binary judgments?*

Goldstein and Gigerenzer's first basic task, both in the article setting out the case for the use of a recognition heuristic and as a matter of general method, is to identify an evolved human capacity. In this particular case, they start by noting that the capacity merely to recognize is such a capacity. In fairness, it is difficult to determine whether they are primarily drawn to the idea that such a well-evolved, readily understood capacity exists because it purportedly serves obvious reproductive success functions. (Most important, they note, if we recognize food as familiar, we can eat it because we know it did not poison us when we ate it before. Secondarily, they note that the capacity to recognize people will alert us to those who might have social power.) They do not, though, unambiguously "derive" the existence of the attribute from its evolutionary desirability. They also rely on *observation*. There is substantial experimental data that demonstrates our rather extraordinary ability to recognize items that we know very little about (e.g., people exposed to 10,000 photos for five seconds can, two days later, pick out of a pair of pictures the one that they were so briefly exposed to

8,300 times) and from studies of head-injured patients who recognize pictures of celebrities even when their memory is otherwise severely impaired.[16]

How, though, do they operationalize the idea that subjects asked to compare city size draw on the capacity to label one city "recognized" and the other "unrecognized"? Here is there basic claim: *When a subject is confronted with two city names, he makes a simple binary judgment, grounded in this well-evolved human capacity to "merely" recognize objects, including proper names, as familiar or not, that he has either seen the city name before or not. His or her initial "search" (to use the familiar search/stop/decide process) is simply to "search" memory to determine whether or not the city name is familiar.* Though many psychologists have criticized the proposition that subjects use this sort of recognition as the *exclusive* mechanism to judge the relative size of two objects, including cities,[17] there was little or no research questioning this basic picture of recognition, so we present here original experimental research designed to question this conception.[18]

It is important to note that it is much more clearly the case in the original Goldstein and Gigerenzer article on recognition that the authors believed that they were identifying and describing a form of memory as *the* evolved adaptive capacity that subjects could "use" in making city size judgments.[19] Over time, it has become less clear that that they are committed to *any* particular picture of how people "remember" whether they have confronted a particular city name, arguing—more or less—that the recognition heuristic describes a way in which people *use* information retrieved from memory, however the "memory" is encoded in the first instance.[20] To the degree that they are no longer committed to any particular picture of memory, the relationship of the recognition heuristic to the "adaptive toolbox" approach becomes considerably less lucid. It is also not clear that subjects who "retrieve" information from memory that permits them to judge whether an item is "more than familiar enough" (i.e., familiar above some threshold level) to trigger the use of that judgment in drawing a conclusion about city size are making a fast or frugal judgment, or that the judgment they are making is especially distinct from the allegedly poorly defined, difficult-to-operationalize judgment that the name of one city is more available than the name of the other.

- *Familiarity versus recall: Do subjects merely recognize city names in the same way they recognize non-words, as previously confronted symbols, or do they "recall" the city (knowing further contextual facts about it)?*

What we found is, first, that to the degree that subjects are simply judging whether a city is "familiar" or not, most do not judge whether the city is merely a previously confronted proper name. Making a judgment that a proper name has been confronted before is what would be conventionally be dubbed a familiarity or item recognition judgment. Such judgments are rightly associated in their articles with the recognition of non-words, the capacity to distinguish in forced-choice situations previously encountered non-words from non-words that had not been confronted. Instead, they make a more cognitively complex, neurologically distinct judgment *recollection* or *recall* judgment and attempt to recall the context in which the proper name was confronted, to cognize the cue *as a city*. We return to discuss the fact that more academically successful subjects are even more prone than less academically successful subjects to distinguish between recognizing that they have confronted the cue as a proper name (a familiarity judgment) and recognizing the cue as a city (recalling context): The fact that there are systematic differences across groups in performing these differentiated tasks suggests further that the tasks are indeed distinct and that Goldstein and Gigerenzer were wrong to assume that the universal adaptive capacity to merely recognize is the capacity that all will use to begin to solve the city size assessment problem.

We first address the experimental evidence for this proposition: Responding to a prompt in one of the experiments that we ran, forty-one Stanford University subjects were asked to pick seven proper names (both places and persons) that would appear in an American history text from a list of fourteen proper names. All forty-one circled the proper name "Roosevelt." On the other hand, across the many experimental surveys in which subjects were asked to circle cities that they recognized, only 10.7 percent of the 215 Stanford subjects recognized the *town* Roosevelt, New York. (Interestingly, a substantially higher proportion of our other experimental group, less academically successful students at Foothill College, the community college most near to Stanford, conflated proper name recognition with town recognition: We return to this issue in assessing systematic differences across subjects.)

One can thus reject Goldstein and Gigerenzer's implicit proposition that people merely assess whether a proper name is recognized as having been confronted in the past, in the fashion that most closely parallels the story they tell about familiarity with food, briefly encountered photos, or recognition of non-words. In ways we discuss after presenting evidence that subjects in these situations do not make binary judgments, subjects appear to reveal not merely whether city names are "familiar" but rather whether they "recollect" the city name *as a city*. It is, to put it mildly, no great surprise that people would "recognize" Roosevelt as a president but not a small town on Long Island. We merely follow convention in demonstrating experimentally, rather than merely noting, this self-evident point.

We must make this obvious point, though, in order to respond to Goldstein and Gigerenzer's seminal article. Goldstein and Gigerenzer believed that one of the critical features that distinguished the work of the F&F school from the H&B school was that those in the F&F school alone specified the underlying cognitive or psychological mechanisms that people drew upon in making heuristic-based judgments or decisions. And the mechanism they identify for the recognition heuristic is, quite unambiguously, what conventional memory researchers call "familiarity" (or sometimes "item recognition") memory (though for reasons we have never discovered, they called it "recognition memory"). The problem that we are addressing is that people making use only of familiarity memory *don't* know that Roosevelt is a president; they merely know that they have confronted an a-contextualized stimulus (like a word, a picture, a face).[21]

We view this point as a perfectly friendly, relatively minor amendment to Goldstein and Gigerenzer's work. In our view, there is no reason for them to rely on the proposition that the recognition heuristic was founded in one particular form of human memory. It would perhaps be an unfriendly amendment, though, only if one makes at least one of two suppositions. First, it might be that Goldstein and Gigerenzer believe that only familiarity judgments are adequately fast and frugal to form the basis for a fast and frugal heuristic; recollection memory, requiring retrieval of context, might conceivably be thought of as too cumbersome or slow. Second, it might be that Goldstein and Gigerenzer worry that the memory processes that recognition heuristic users drew upon cannot be adequately specified unless they are using familiarity memory, and F&F theorists remain wedded to the notion that they alone specify these underlying processes carefully.

- *Do subjects who do not circle a city when asked whether they recognize it actually have some familiarity with cities that are more widely explicitly recognized and known by other subjects (so that we should presume they have actually come into contact with the information that it is a city)?*

What is more significant to explore is that, even if one assumed for argument's sake that subjects were making familiarity judgments of the proper name rather than recalling the city and contextual information about it, familiarity judgments are not binary, though Goldstein and Gigerenzer explicitly assert that they are in their initial formulation of the heuristic. People in fact recognize cities as more and less familiar. A city may be familiar enough that a subject will pick it out as a real city from a list that also includes both made-up and truly unfamiliar cities in a forced-choice test but not familiar enough that the same subject would consciously assert that she recognized the city if merely asked, as Goldstein and Gigerenzer do, whether or not they recognize the city. Thus, if the initial "search" rule were as simple as Goldstein and Gigerenzer posit—a search drawing on the evolved capacity to "recognize" cities that are minimally familiar—their purportedly "ignorant" subjects would frequently be unable to make use of their ignorance because they are not in fact fully ignorant in the way the authors assert.

There is no ambiguity in Goldstein and Gigerenzer's initial claim that their subjects either do or do not "recognize" a city they confront. Goldstein and Gigerenzer are quite explicit on this point. They state, "[T]he recognition heuristic does not address comparisons between items in memory, *but rather the difference between items in and out of memory*.... The recognition heuristic treats recognition as a binary, all-or-nothing distinction . . ."[22] If, however, people "recognize" something as soon as it is familiar *at all*, then people actually recognize in this binary sense many cities that they claim not to recognize. (Moreover, it is the capacity to know "merely" that something has been confronted or not that plays the purported simple evolutionary role that the expositors of the recognition heuristic emphasize.) We return to discuss problems with a more plausible, revisionist version of the claim that recognition is "binary."

The following experimental findings demonstrate the basic point that people are familiar with names that they say they do not recognize. Subjects are first asked in Part One of a questionnaire to circle each German city they recognize. In Part Two of the same questionnaire, they are given a list of thirty-two cities, and told that sixteen are real: They are *forced* to circle the sixteen cities that they believe are real, to distinguish sixteen real from sixteen imaginary cities.[23] The first, rough way of seeing that people actually "recognized" cities that were not so familiar that they *realized* that they recognized the city name is to compare the proportion of those who said they did not recognize a city that is famous enough to be recognized by the bulk of other survey subjects who nonetheless circled it in Part Two with the proportion of those who pick less famous or made-up cities in the forced-choice condition. (The idea, of course, is that cities that many respondents have heard of are likely to be publicized enough that even those who do not think they recognize the city have indeed been exposed to the city, so that the city name is actually stored in memory. Cities that few or nearly no subjects have heard of may be cities to which other subjects have actually never been exposed, or exposed so infrequently that they are indeed scarcely familiar with them.)

To illustrate, fifteen of thirty-nine Stanford student subjects do not overtly and explicitly *recognize* Leipzig when asked to circle cities that they recognize in Part One of a survey (i.e., they do not recognize it in the sense that Goldstein and Gigerenzer measure). But 80 percent of those fifteen circle it when forced to pick out the sixteen real German cities in Part Two. On the other hand, none of these same thirty-nine subjects recognize the far less famous city of Reutlingen in Part One; just 18 percent of those thirty-nine pick it out in the forced-recognition condition.

While there are somewhat more precise ways of presenting the data,[24] the bottom-line message is precisely the same when one presents it in the simplest fashion. For the four real cities most commonly consciously and explicitly recognized, there are thirty-two opportunities for subjects to circle the cities in the forced-recognition condition when these subjects had not consciously recognized the city: twenty-three of thirty-two (71.8 percent) recognize the city in the forced-recognition condition. For the three rarely recognized real cities, they are recognized in the forced-recognition condition in only 29 of 108 opportunities (27 percent). The forced-recognition rates in the second part of the survey of "made up" cities are lower still. The ability of subjects to recognize a city that they ostensibly do not recognize in the forced-recognition condition essentially varies in a linear fashion with their probable actual exposure to the city, measured by the proportion of respondents who consciously recognize the city. If subjects were simply unfamiliar in a dichotomous way with all the cities they purportedly do not recognize,[25] they would be no more likely to pick out the cities others consciously recognized at greater than chance or "guessing" rates.[26]

What is vital to note is that if Goldstein and Gigerenzer were actually trying to ascertain whether their subjects were familiar with particular cities in the way that memory researchers try to ascertain whether a subject is familiar with a non-word or once-confronted photo, they would have relied *solely* on these sorts of forced-choice tests. (We recognize that doing so would have been impossible, though, were one to test how people used "recognition" in making size judgments because their subjects would then all have recently been exposed to all the city names.) Forced-choice recognition is not only a form of item recognition, it is the form conventionally used in establishing whether people are familiar with pictures they have seen and non-words they have confronted.[27]

It is possible to reformulate Goldstein and Gigerenzer's argument in a way that does less violence to the well-established finding in the memory literature that recognition memory is not really binary. It is tautologically the case that we could describe recognition versus non-recognition judgments (or any judgments for that matter) as binary if we say that a person describes an object as recognized only if the level of recognition is above some threshold. Obviously, all continuous judgments are binary if one establishes a break or cut-off point. This is more-or-less the reformulation offered by Schooler and Hertwig, F&F theorists trying to defend the psychological plausibility of a binary recognition heuristic, grounded in the claim that we cannot access all memories but experience "sensations" that a memory is somehow intense enough to activate a "recognition judgment."[28]

The first, and quite overwhelming, problem with this reformulation is that the threshold level would surely vary depending on the payoff structure the subject faces when asked to state whether or not he recognizes a city. As false positives become relatively more costly compared to false negatives, the subject should set his threshold level higher. But Goldstein and Gigerenzer give no indication what they believe the costs of false negatives or positives are in the context of either their own city recognition experiments or city recognition more generally, or any other tasks for which the recognition heuristic might be used in more naturalistic settings. Nor do they offer any explanation of why the judgment about the apt threshold level would itself be a fast and frugal one. The second problem is that the notion that the cut-off threshold can be intuited by the sort of sensation Schooler and Hertwig posit is that our experimental subjects are able to shift thresholds almost instantly, when moving from responding to the question "do you recognize city C?" to having to select city C in a forced-recognition setting.[29] Which of these two quite-distinct "threshold" judgment subjects employ when making cue value differentiations in assessing city size is utterly unclear. Why don't German subjects who might well "recognize" San Antonio in a forced-recognition test have just as much trouble as Americans distinguishing the recognition cue-value of San Antonio and San Diego?

Once again, it is not immediately obvious whether this is a friendly or unfriendly amendment to the Goldstein-Gigerenzer view. Traditional data and theory suggesting that recognition judgments are not best seen as binary or dichotomous could be interpreted in at least two ways. First, the observation could be used to note that people know how familiar an item is because there is differential neural activity when items are more familiar than when they are less so. Second, it is possible that we keep some sort of not-entirely-conscious "count" of how often we have confronted a cue in the past, based on the strength of the electrical activity that occurred when it was most recently confronted, permitting us to make reasonably accurate judgments about the *degree* to which an item is familiar. In this sense, Goldstein and Gigerenzer might have argued that the "familiarity" judgment need not be binary to be fast and frugal. If the first step in a revised account of the recognition heuristic were to identify a city as quite familiar or only vaguely so, it would seem that subjects have the capacity to do that readily and quickly. In this sense, employing a more conventional picture of memory would not have radically interfered with their underlying aims; it would merely have made their picture of the relevant cognitive processes more plausible.

I suspect that they might find the amendment unfriendly precisely because it would make their account of recognition and the account of availability in H&B work converge a great deal. Each would be on a more-or-less continuum, and in each case, a judgment would follow from a comparative judgment. (San Diego is more available to memory than San Antonio; it is *so* available that it is above some threshold that subjects might describe as "recognized" in responding to questionnaire requests to distinguish recognized from unrecognized items.) If this account is right, though, it may lead us to reflect on the possibility that, once again, H&B theorists are especially irked by what they see as false claims of novelty in F&F work. The recognition heuristic might just be another variant or instantiation of the already-discovered availability heuristic. It has the same problems of specification. It might then, too, like that heuristic, be good enough to reach accurate judgments on many occasions but lead to biased judgments on other occasions. We would need to investigate whether people overestimated the probative value of finding one name more available than another, and in what settings they might do so.

There is also a more general point to be made here, though, that is hard to treat as a possible friendly amendment. Put narrowly, it seems to be the case that the work on the recognition heuristic at least arguably misrepresents the sorts of memory that subjects confronting two cities whose size is to be compared would make use of. Put broadly, though, the critique belies one of the most basic claims about the superiority of F&F work over H&B work on heuristics. The basic psychological *processes*—in this case memory—are *not* described in a more careful, detailed, or experimentally tractable way. If it is indeed difficult to say when an H&B subject finds data "available" or "easily recalled," it is equally difficult to say when a recognition-heuristic user actually *recognizes* a city, in the way that Goldstein and Gigerenzer think should facilitate the use of the heuristic. If the H&B theorists do not describe the processes that underlie heuristic use in a fashion that draws on standard psychological accounts of cognitive capacities, Goldstein and Gigerenzer's description of the cognitive task their subjects perform similarly fails to account for much of the mainstream work on memory, though it purports to be a description of how memory can be used to make fast and frugal judgments.

Goldstein and Gigerenzer's accounts of the city recognition task do not track conventional memory research in several key respects. Conventional memory research distinguishes more precisely than Goldstein and Gigerenzer do between recollection—the capacity to recall information associated with a target cue, often including information about the context in which the cue was confronted—and familiarity—which merely triggers a feeling that the cue was confronted, though no additional information or context need be available.[30] The most common finding in the literature is that patients are able to make familiarity judgments, particularly in relationship to items confronted on only one or a few occasions, but not recall information well, when they have damage to the hippocampus, but not damage to the perirhinal cortex[31] Similarly, fMRI studies often find that one can predict success in making these sorts of episodic item recognition judgments if the perirhinal cortex, but not the hippocampus or parahippocampus, is activated while activation of the hippocampus and parahippocampus predicts later success in recollection.[32] It is these sorts of studies that Goldstein and Gigerenzer are relying in distinguishing, rather imprecisely, between recall and "mere recognition."

But Goldstein and Gigerenzer assume, far more than the conventional memory literature warrants, that recall and familiarity judgments are wholly separate, unduly relying on the idea that they play distinct functional, adaptive roles.[33] More important, it is consistent with conventional research that our subjects who claim they recognize a city do not merely recognize it as a proper name at all: They are making use of recollection capacities generally associated with the hippocampus rather than MTL (medial temporal lobe) in cases of single or small exposure episodic memory. At any rate, they recall something about the context in which they confronted the name, and/or they have learned relevant facts associated with the name. The fact that they are capable of doing that suggests that they are capable of identifying the "recognized" cues not only as cities but as large cities.[34]

More generally speaking, still, the claim that the "recognition capacity" is well-defined in the piece is a difficult one to accept. Not only is there little attention paid to the question of whether the experimental subjects are actually using recollection rather than item recognition memory (or how, exactly, those might differ), there is little attention paid to the live question of whether all forms of item recognition memory either serve the same function or are performed in the same fashion neurologically.[35]

- Are Goldstein and Gigerenzer correct that subjects use "recognition" cues lexically, or do subjects integrate additional information as well in making a judgment?

Both rational choice theorists and H&B scholars—to the extent that they saw no or limited proof that subjects "substituted" a judgment of "recognition" for a fuller judgment about relative size—would doubtless agree that there is a normatively sensible, *non-heuristic* use of information that closely resembles what Goldstein and Gigerenzer believe is "recognition information." If the subject "recognizes" one of two proper names not only as a place name but as the name of a "large" or "populous" place, and does not recognize the other place name, the rational subject *ought* to infer that the proper name *recognized in that way* is larger than the other place name. Most unrecognized places are not populous, so a rational subject would readily infer that the newly confronted place name is smaller than any city recognized as "large."

But the rational chooser would not use "mere recognition" *exclusively* or lexically to make city size judgments even in situations in which she "recognizes" only one of two cities in the set whose size she is asked to compare. If she either firmly knows or is able to infer that the recognized proper name is a small place, and if she simultaneously infers that the unrecognized (or, more accurately, less familiar) place is not especially small (e.g., because it is named "X *City*" or because she has been told it is home to a minor league team or is the capital of a state), she ought not, if "rational," to infer the recognized city is larger.

At the same time, a rational choice theorist would argue that a subject working with very limited information should rely on whatever information he had about city size, even if the information did not in any way depend on making use of the supposed evolved capacity to recognize or involve the use of simple binary cues. Thus, subjects who make cognitively complex judgments that one of two cities—each of which she recognizes—is *more* "prominent" (not either "prominent" or "not prominent") than the other should, according to rational choice theorists, be prone to believe the more prominent city is larger in the absence of further information to the contrary. Subjects should do this in precisely the same way that those who "recognize" one city rather than another do, even if not necessarily with the same level of confidence, In fact, it may well be that judgments about one's own familiarity with a city are best seen merely as an input into making more complex judgments about a city's prominence rather than as simple "recognition" judgments.[36]

We present a brief summary of the experiments that we performed that both confirmed and extended a host of prior experimental findings that subjects will use non-recognition information to make judgments that are more accurate than they would make if using the recognition heuristic alone. What we find, that others have not previously investigated, is not particularly surprising: People use such information more frequently when it is more easily tractable and clearly probative, *and* more academically successful subjects use such information more often, and do so markedly more often when the additional cues are difficult to process and more ambiguously probative.

At the same time, we performed novel experiments to indicate that people use single-cue judgments almost as often as they use recognition judgments that are not themselves grounded in simple evolved capacities. In many, but not all, cases, informed people make very similar judgments to one another about which of two cities is more *prominent*, even when they recognize both cities. These widely shared prominence judgments do not implicate anything like the ostensibly basic, domain-specific evolved psychological "capacity" to recognize but instead involve far more complex judgments grounded in a mix of semantic knowledge and inference. We predicted that subjects would use these decidedly non-fast and frugal initial judgments about relative prominence in much the same way that they use recognition/familiarity judgments. When they have no other information about city size, they do what a rational choice theorist would posit that they should do—assume prominence correlates with size and select the more prominent city as larger.

- *Do subjects generally use non-recognition cues in making city size judgments at markedly higher rates than Goldstein and Gigerenzer posit?*

Goldstein and Gigerenzer report that more than 90 percent of inferences are consistent with the use of the recognition heuristic even when non-recognition information is available that would suggest that the inferences subjects might make solely on the basis of recognition memory might be unreliable. (The additional information they offered was that the recognized city was not the site of a soccer team. In our view, this information permits only a weak inference that the city without a soccer team is small, and an even weaker inference that it is smaller than an unrecognized city. It is not terribly surprising that given the weakness of each of the inferences, few depart from inferring that more prominent cities are larger based on that additional information.)

Like many researchers before us, who tested whether subjects used non-recognition information they learned in the lab setting or used such information that had been learned in naturalistic settings,[37] we find substantially higher uses of compensatory processes requiring additional information than do Goldstein and Gigerenzer in all the conditions we tested (each of which permits a stronger inference that the recognized city is smaller than the unrecognized one). Non-recognition information is used by nearly all subjects in some conditions. In Part One of all three relevant questionnaires, subjects were asked to do just what they are asked to do in Goldstein and Gigerenzer's surveys: to identify those towns or cities on a list of towns or cities that they "recognize." Some of the cities were made up (e.g., Harglade); some were real towns so small that recognition rates were below 5 percent (e.g., Chilmark); some were moderately large cities that we nonetheless assumed (from pre-tests) and found in the actual experiments that few respondents would have heard of (e.g., Elizabeth City); some were very small towns that were recognized, and recognized as small, by a nontrivial number of respondents because they were famous either for their association with an historical event (e.g., Kitty Hawk) or as small tourist destinations (e.g., Taos), or because they were small towns proximate to the sites of the experiment, Stanford University and Foothill College (e.g., Los Altos Hills). The rest were among the fifty largest American cities.

In Part Two of the first two surveys, subjects were again asked to circle which cities they recognized. In one survey, these sixteen cities were correctly labeled as state capitals. We assumed and found that some would nonetheless be unrecognized by large numbers of respondents (e.g., Frankfort, Kentucky; Dover, Delaware). In the other survey, subjects were told that all the fifteen cities were the homes of minor league baseball teams. To ensure that people were answering seriously, one was made up, the rest real. Again, we assumed from pre-tests and found in the actual experiments that many of these cities would not be recognized by most subjects (e.g., Kinston, North Carolina; Dunedin, Florida.)

In Part Three of these two surveys, subjects were asked—just as they were in Goldstein and Gigerenzer's work—to circle which city in a pair had a larger population. The key questions in the first survey were those in which subjects would compare recognized small cities (e.g., Los Altos Hills, Wounded Knee) with unrecognized state capitals. The rational choice inference that the unrecognized town is large is direct and relatively easy in the sense that all state capitals must be modestly large merely to house those who work in state bureaucracies and service them. In the next survey, the key comparison questions were those in which subjects compared recognized small cities with unrecognized hosts to minor league teams. The inference that the unrecognized town is large is very indirect, difficult, and not enormously dependable. Essentially, the inference process is both indirect and difficult in the following senses: It is indirect in the sense that subjects must figure out that it would not be economically viable to put a stadium someplace in which there were not lots of available fans. It is not enormously dependable in the sense that it is possible that a minor league stadium would be located in a very small town that is adequately *proximate* to populous areas.

Part One of the third survey was essentially the same as Part One of these first two; subjects were asked to circle recognized cities. In the second, and last, part of the survey, respondents were asked to pick which of two cities in a comparison set had a larger population. The significant pairs for purposes of this issue involved comparisons designed to test judgments comparing towns recognized to be small with unrecognized towns whose *names* cue the likelihood that they are at least moderately large (e.g., Johnson *City*).

What stands out in analyzing the aggregate data is that, just as rational choice theorists would predict, subjects use non-recognition information more often when the additional information relevant to the judgment task at hand is both easier to use and more strongly probative. If people either did or did not use the recognition heuristic rigidly when confronting a particular sort of task, as Gigerenzer posits, we would not expect such variation. Our results mimic findings in the prior research in this regard.[38] Thus, subjects make simple inferences grounded in highly probative cues about the large size of unrecognized cities more often than they make complex inferences based on less probative information.[39] More specifically, in the sub-class of cases in which the subjects received easily processed plainly probative additional information and the inference to be drawn from the information was direct (the unrecognized city was a state capital), subjects scarcely ever believed that the recognized city was larger.

Our findings essentially flip Goldstein and Gigerenzer's results: We find non-recognition cues dominate the use of recognition cues nearly as often as they find that recognition cues are used exclusively. Nearly 88 percent of *responses* (309 of 352) were that the unrecognized state capital was bigger than the recognized small town. Moreover, 84.7 percent of *respondents* thought the unrecognized capital was larger in 75 percent or more of the cases in which they compared the size of a small recognized town and an unrecognized capital. In the sub-set of cases in which the compensatory process was relatively easy to use, modestly probative but essentially indirect (the unrecognized town was named "X" *City*), 55.5 percent of responses were inconsistent with the use of the recognition heuristic. The unrecognized towns (Elizabeth City, Rapid City, and Johnson City) were thus circled in more than half the circumstances in which a subject was comparing them with recognized smaller cities. However, only 30 percent of respondents made this judgment more than 75 percent of the time. Finally, in the sub-sets of cases in which cues were most difficult to process—the situations in which the cue was that the unrecognized city was the home of a minor league baseball team—subjects less frequently thought the unrecognized city was larger. Subjects correctly identified the unrecognized city as larger in only 40.4 percent of responses and only 16 percent of respondents answered that the larger unrecognized city was larger more than 75 percent of the times they had to make that choice.

It is possible to reformulate Goldstein and Gigerenzer's hypothesis to say that our subjects were no longer making inferences solely from memory, while the subjects in their experiments who were indifferent to learning that a recognized city had no soccer team were indifferent because they were making memory-based inferences. Our subjects are making inferences about cities (unrecognized cities that they learn are state capitals for instance) that were not previously stored in memory. This reformulation reduces claims about the recognition heuristic as a lexical decision-making device to an uninteresting tautology: People use only memory-based cues when and only when they exclusively make memory-based inferences and do nothing else to solve the size comparison problem. But unless subjects have reason to infer that an unrecognized city is *larger* than a recognized one—not merely that the recognized one is smaller than they might first have intuited—of course they will simply use recognition as a cue.

- As rational choice theorists would predict, subjects use judgments of prominence in the same way they use "recognition" cues because judgments of prominence, though not grounded in a simple "evolved capacity," are rationally relevant cues and may, like recognition, be the sole such cue available.

We needed to determine experimentally if people used transparently non-binary, cognitively complex, non-recognition-related "prominence" judgments to assess city size when they had no other information about city size upon which to rely. We hypothesized that they would do so in the same way that a rational choice theorist would predict that they would use what Goldstein and Gigerenzer identified as "recognition" in their experiments (i.e., when they also had no other information to use). To do so, we first had to ascertain whether "prominence" judgments can be robust and widely shared. Subjects were instructed to label a city as more prominent if they believed a higher proportion of randomly surveyed Americans would recognize it and if a random sample of people would be more likely to mention it in a conversation or discuss it.

We did not ask the same subject if she thought City X were *both* bigger and more prominent than another, because the judgments might then be simultaneously determined. Instead, we asked one group of subjects to name the more prominent city, to determine whether these judgments of prominence were so widely shared that we could presume subjects not asked about prominence were very likely to share them, and then see if a second group of subjects made relative size judgments that conformed to the first group's relative prominence judgments.

We found that prominence judgments made by the twenty Stanford subjects for certain city pairs are remarkably widely shared though they are plainly grounded in complex cognitive judgments, requiring subjects to combine and weigh a great deal of semantic information, rather than in a "fast" simple input grounded in a single, straightforward adaptive "tool," as "recognition" is argued to be. We do not believe that prominence judgments would necessarily be widely shared for the majority of large city pairs. Our point instead is that there are predictably shared prominence judgments that would help us predict city size assessment in the absence of non-prominence cues nearly as well as cognitively faster and more frugal recognition judgments would.

We tested prominence judgments for eleven pairs of cities whose relative size would be assessed in a separate questionnaire. Even among subjects who recognized both cities, there was widespread agreement about which was more prominent, and each time subjects accurately picked the city more of their fellow respondents actually recognized as more prominent. The meaningful results are fairly straightforward: Overall, of respondents who had heard of both cities in the pairs, 92.5 percent agreed on which city was the more prominent one.

Even though the more prominent city was actually smaller in the first eight but not the last three cases, and even though some sub-set of subjects who recognize both cities in a comparison pair must have enough semantic information available to enable them to choose the larger city even though they believe it to be less prominent, the fact is that prominence judgments dominate city size judgments in a substantial majority of cases, as rational choice theorists would expect, given the paucity of available semantic information about actual city size. Stanford subjects pick the more prominent city as larger, even when they recognize both cities, in 78.3 percent of cases. If one excludes the two cases in which subjects made judgments involving Honolulu, a city that Stanford students seem to know is prominent but small, Stanford subjects pick the more prominent city 84.5 percent of the time and picked it more than 90 percent of the time in five of eight cases.[40] In the Goldstein and Gigerenzer study, the mean proportion of inferences in accord with the recognition heuristic was barely higher (90 percent).

- *Are there systematic distinctions in the ways in which distinct subjects both employ memory (in terms of the distinction between item recognition and recall) and use compensatory processes?*

We did not measure the individual traits of survey participants. We initially thought that we would simply look at each respondent's SAT scores, as researchers conventionally do in looking to measure individual differences in "intelligence," conventionally defined, but this proved impracticable because a large proportion (57 percent) of Foothill students responding to the relevant surveys had not taken the SAT, compared to less than 12 percent of the Stanford sample. There are many reasons to think the Stanford students and nearby community college students we sampled are quite distinct from one another in terms of general academic achievement, though, as well as access to semantic knowledge. If one looks at the SAT scores of respondents who *did* take the SAT, one sees dramatic differences in these scores across groups: 71 percent of Stanford respondents received a score on the Verbal and Math portions of the test between 1400 and 1600, 13 percent received between 1300 and 1400, and only 3 percent received a combined score of less than 1100. On the other hand, only 28 percent of Foothill respondents who had taken the SATs received a combined score above 1300, 53 percent received a score less than 1200, 38 percent received less than 1100, and 25 percent received a score of 850 or less. Stanford students also seem to have a good deal more geographical knowledge: For instance, the mean number of capital cities that Stanford subjects recognized was 11.9 of the 16 tested state capitals; the mean for Foothill subjects was only 6.32.

The Foothill students performed significantly differently from the Stanford students in two ways. First, quite interestingly, a substantially higher proportion of Foothill students conflated proper name recognition with town recognition: While only 10.7 percent of the 215 Stanford subjects who answered all questionnaires that permitted them the opportunity to identify Roosevelt as recognized or not recognized the *town* Roosevelt, New York, 22.9 percent (40 of 175) of the Foothill students believed they recognized the town of Roosevelt. The distinction must dominantly be a function of increasing levels of false city recognition. It is implausible *a priori* that the Foothill students, nearly none of whom come from the East, actually recognized a small town near New York City more often than Stanford students, faculty, and staff, many of whom *do* come from the New York area. Moreover, *a priori* logic is supported, albeit tentatively, by other data: Foothill students generally recognize small towns outside the San Francisco Bay Area at far lower rates than the Stanford subjects. For instance, 42.3 percent of Stanford subjects recognized Cooperstown, New York, compared to 13.6 percent of Foothill subjects. (The comparable numbers for Kitty Hawk, Taos, and Wounded Knee were: Stanford 50.9, 33.1, and 36 percent versus Foothill 15.3,

14.5, and 10 percent.) The distinction in what we posit to be false recognition rates between Stanford and Foothill subjects is statistically significant: (p < 0.001 in a two-tailed chi-square test).

What stands out as even more interesting in analyzing the data, in terms of studying systematic differences across the two distinct subject populations, is that the academically more successful Stanford subjects use a compensatory, non-lexical process far more frequently when the subjects must make an indirect, complex inference to infer that the unrecognized city is a relatively large one (the unrecognized city is home to a minor league baseball team). In terms of responses, 51.1 percent of Stanford responses assess the unrecognized home of the minor league team as larger than a recognized small city while only 22.6 percent of Foothill responses assess the unrecognized minor league host as larger (p < 0.001). In some ways, the disparity seems even more striking when one looks at the response patterns of individual respondents in each group: Only 5.4 percent of Foothill respondents assess the unrecognized minor league town as larger in more than 75 percent of the chances that they have to do so while 64.7 percent do so less than 25 percent of the time. On the other hand, 25.7 percent of Stanford subjects do so more than 75 percent of the time and only 22.9 percent do less than 25 percent of the time. The distinctions are still modestly pronounced (and at the borderline of statistically significant; p < 0.098) when the inference is mildly complex (i.e., the unrecognized city is named "City"), 109 of 183 (58.4 percent) of Stanford responses and 46 of 84 (48.4 percent) of Foothill responses state that the unrecognized town is larger. What is most critical to note is that the distinctions in use of compensatory information nearly disappear, though they remain statistically significant, due to the large sample size (p < 0.006) when the inferences are simplest (i.e., when the unrecognized town is a state capital). In those cases, 85.9 percent of the 78 Foothill responses versus 90.5 percent of the 274 Stanford responses correctly compensate for the recognition cue.

Some theorists associated with the H&B school would likely posit that the more academically successful subjects would use compensatory processes more often because those with higher scores on g-loaded test like the SAT are systematically more likely to use so-called System Two "deliberative" processes to override the use of more automatic System One-based heuristics.[41] In doing so, such theorists essentially attribute the use of heuristics more generally to the internal processing limits of people rather than their "good fit" with the external environment. They also typically argue that System One capacity is more equally distributed across the population than System Two capacity and argue that those with more internal processing resources are more likely to "override" System One.

However, more academically successful subjects may perform better for a variety of other reasons. While we entered the study suspecting we would find systematic differences across our two groups of subjects, we were agnostic about the roots of the distinctions we would observe: Our ultimate finding, that how differentiated the capacity to make inferences about the size of unrecognized cities would be across groups would depend almost exclusively on the complexity of the inferences that must be drawn, was no more plausible to us, *a priori*, than any of three alternative hypotheses. It seemed possible that Foothill subjects would be less motivated to solve the size assessment problem in an effortful fashion; less capable of using System Two "overrides" to intuitions; or lacking in semantic knowledge that certain recognized cities had small populations.

Because the Foothill students use a compensatory process in the same way Stanford students do when the additional information is clearest and most readily processed, it appears that Foothill subjects are only trivially distinguishable from Stanford subjects along any of the following dimensions: motivation to answer the questions correctly; semantic knowledge that the recognized small city is indeed a small city; and general proclivity to use non-recognition information or non-lexical *methods*. Instead, it appears that what differentiates them from the Stanford subjects is dominantly, though not exclusively, slight distinctions in semantic knowledge: the fact that the Foothill students recognize so many fewer cities strongly suggests but does not prove that they know less about the cities that they do recognize.[42] Also, and more important, they seem to differ in the capacity to make certain convoluted rational inferences.

- *Assessing the recognition heuristic.*

Overall, the evidence we examined suggests that subjects make judgments about relative city size in more or less the fashion that a rational choice theorist thinking about subjects acting with limited information would predict.[43] Sometimes, but rarely, they may have detailed semantic information that permits confident assertions about the relative size of two cities, each of which they recognize. Thus, of the sixty-seven Stanford subjects who recognize both Boston and New York City, sixty-six correctly state that New York City is larger. Of the sixty-eight who recognized both Oakland and Chicago, sixty-five correctly identified Chicago as larger. Subjects rarely have such detailed knowledge, though. In fact, populations of large American cities are fairly clustered, so it would be quite surprising if they did: Twelve of the fifty largest American cities have populations between 500,000 and 600,000; thirty-two of fifty have populations between 400,000 and 800,000.

If a subject does not *know* the size of each of two cities, she can nonetheless attempt to infer their relative size. If she is certain that she knows that each city is, broadly speaking, a "large" city, she may make use of prominence judgments and infer that the more prominent city is larger. If she is certain that she knows that one city is large, and infers that the other city/town is small because it is not familiar enough that she is even immediately confident that she recognizes it as a city/town at all, and most unknown places are small, given the large number of cities/towns there are in the world, she should plainly choose the *known* "large city" as larger. If a subject is certain she recognizes a city/town as small but knows nothing about the other city/town, it is a hard call as to how to guess: It is no longer obvious that randomly sampled places are smaller than the known small place, but the opposite is not obvious either. If one place name is known to be a small city/town, and the subject can infer that the other place name is the name of a large place, even though it is unrecognized, whether she infers that because of its name or because she has been given some information about it that signals it is likely to be large, she ought to infer that the "recognized" small placer is smaller.

What is most interesting, though, descriptively, is that F&F scholars seem to employ a far more impoverished account of rational choice theory than do the H&B theorists. The concern is that their account misrepresents how subjects with limited information may make rational choices using rules of thumb; the use of rules of thumb is distinct from the use of Gigerenzian heuristics because those who employ rules of thumb do not *ignore* relevant information. What H&B theorists would add to the rational choice account that we just traced is that it is worth investigating whether subjects typically "overvalue" recognition. They would want to know whether people make rationally indefensibly inadequate use of non-recognition information, because they substitute a generally probative cue (i.e., cities I am confident I recognize are bigger than ones I don't confidently recognize) for case-by-case judgment. Our experiments do not permit us to say how frequently recognition is overused, though it seems to be a result of what H&B researchers would probably label a "bias" that *anyone* thinks a speck of a nearby town like La Honda is bigger than any state capital. (In fact, if one were to argue that a, if not the, chief distinction between the F&F and H&B school is that the former concentrates on human prowess and the latter on human frailty, looking at the distinct ways in which the experimenters in each school treat recognition/availability might be a prime bit of evidence. H&B researchers *could* have run experiments noting that subjects correctly assessed mortality rates from diseases using the availability heuristic; cancer *is* both more easily brought to mind and more frequently fatal than lupus. Instead, they chose to run experiments comparing the incorrect mortality estimates of airline and car crashes. F&F researchers *could* have run experiments where people will asked to declare which of two large, but not extremely large, Asian cities is more populous or asked subjects to compare the size of nearby tiny towns and unknown state capitals; had they done so, they would have demonstrated recognition/availability *bias*.)

What is peculiar in the F&F argument generally, outside the recognition heuristic context as well, is that it relies heavily on the idea that if decision makers were *not* to follow the softly informationally encapsulated strategy but instead to follow the non-lexical strategy they rightly insist rational choice theorists believe that people actually follow, they would be forced in one of two untenable directions. First, they claim, decision makers might have to process a near-infinite amount of potentially relevant data about facts or values. Alternatively, they would need a brain with near-limitless computational power to ascertain whether the value of additional information they might acquire to help them make a decision would outweigh the cost of acquiring it.

This is misleading. The rational choice theorist would assert only that the decision maker will account for probative facts that she is aware of or cognizes could readily be acquired that change her rule-of-thumb decision weights. The rational choice theorist does not claim that someone trying to assess relative city size makes use of all available information that might alter the probability that one listed city is bigger than another. The subject may well ignore information about the typical size of cities in a particular state, at least some information about which infrastructure features, such as airports, convention centers, and "major league" ball teams, are present in each city. The rational choice theorist merely asserts that the subject may depart from *any* particular rule of thumb (the recognized city is larger, the more prominent city is larger, unknown cities in China and India are likely bigger than unknown cities in Malaysia or Belgium, etc.) when confronted with reasons to believe he is not in the typical situation covered by the rule of thumb.

It is also not the case that rational choice theorists adopt an *a priori* commitment that people can always, in all situations, recognize the distinction between the general run of cases and the particular case, and this problem is acknowledged with even greater force in H&B theory. One would expect, for instance, that if they are under time pressure to make decisions, they particularize less. But the rational choice theorist, and H&B theorists, merely adopt an *a priori* theory that people frequently maintain the cognitive *capacity* to particularize.

Finally, a brief comment on the claim that the relative success of parties who are more ignorant than other parties shows that, at least under certain conditions, "less is more": that it is not better to be either smarter, more computationally sophisticated, or more informed on all occasions. That claim might well be correct, but it needs to be sharpened. It is not at all clear that it is apt to say that the Germans who recognize one of two American cities and correctly assess its size actually are less informed than Americans who get the city size comparison wrong although they know much more about each city. Imagine that Americans know just as well as Germans do that more famous cities are likely to be larger than less famous ones and that everything else they know about the sizes of the cities they are asked to compare is nearly worthless twaddle. Still, they are missing a critical piece of information that is readily available to the Germans by a simple inference process: The Germans can infer, "X is more famous than Y because I have heard of X and not Y." If the Americans had more information—for instance in addition to knowing what they already know, they were told that twice as many Germans recognized one city rather than the other—then they might well do as well or better than the Germans in assessing city size. It is simply not at all obvious that we should describe those people who lack the most probative piece of semantic information as more knowledgeable. Obviously, we understand that F&F theorists would resist this rational choice translation. They would not agree that Germans know or infer that the unrecognized city is less famous but rather that they employ a heuristic that is less knowledge and inference dependent. But unless we found that the uninformed did better on these size comparison tests even when more informed people learned about recognition rates by the naïve, we think it remains difficult to reject this possibility.

D. CONCLUSION

While F&F scholars have explicitly criticized H&B research on many occasions, it is less certain how H&B scholars respond to the F&F program because there is far less research by the H&B theorists that specifically responds to that program.

Still, it seems fair to believe that H&B scholars reject or reverse the accusation that they give vague or misleading descriptions of the basic cognitive processes that people using heuristics are employing. Instead, they suspect that F&F researchers do not so much *describe* cognitive processes in careful detail as imagine processes that would serve imputed adaptive ends. In discussing the recognition heuristic, for instance, we noted the possibility that the F&F description of the basic cognitive capacity that recognition heuristic users purportedly employed—the capacity to make dichotomous item familiarity judgments—was substantially misleading. Subjects actually were using "recall," not "familiarity" or "item recognition" memory, and find cities more or less recognizable, not recognizable or not.

At the same time, H&B theorists are suspicious that heuristics users will almost invariably outperform those using conventional rational choice strategies. F&F theorists overestimate the degree to which evolved performance mechanisms are optimal. It may be helpful to note that, on occasion, "less is more," especially if it were clearer what it meant to have less relevant information or computational wherewithal. But quite often, however less is defined, "less is less." People who use one-cue decision-making methods will get the wrong answer in a large class of fairly simple city size assessment tests: They will think that tiny towns right near where they live are bigger than state capitals they have not heard of. F&F theorists know they should not do this—when recognition does not correlate with an attribute, it should not be used—but if one has to know that recognition correlates with size before one decides to use recognition information exclusively, one needs a less-than-fast-and-frugal method to determine whether to use a fast and frugal judgment tool.

But, of course, the H&B theorists believe that far fewer people use these single-cue strategies than F&F theorists posit. Nearly no experimental subjects actually use recognition information lexically when asked to compare the size of known small towns with unknown state capitals. There are patterns, too, to *whether* one uses lexical decision-making methods, though identifying those patterns with precision is no easy task. H&B theorists conventionally argued that, across the board, people deemed "smarter" (in the sense that they did better on g-loaded tests) were typically less prone to use heuristics. It might be, though, at least in the case of the "recognition heuristic," there is no systematic tendency for more academically successful subjects to use compensatory *processes* but that all people use additional information less often when it is more difficult to assess and evaluate and that more academically successful subjects use only the more difficult-to-process information significantly more often.

PART THREE

Implications for Law

6

CRIMINAL PUNISHMENT AND COGNITION

In this and the next chapter, I show that those drawn to one or another view of how people are likely to use heuristics in decision making approach certain classical legal policy issues in distinct ways. In this chapter, I address the issue of designing an optimal system of criminal punishment, and in the next I deal with a handful of issues about the regulation of markets, focusing especially, though not exclusively, on information disclosure.

It is important to recognize, right from the start, the considerable limits on our capacity to use insights from cognitive psychology to frame policy. When I discuss deterrence in this chapter, for instance, I do not mean to imply that we could ever hope simply to *deduce* the empirical relationship between particular policy interventions and the level of offenses by better integrating psychologically based theories of how people process cues and/or make decisions. What we can hope instead to get from psychological theory—from all theories of human behavior—are two things. First, the relationship between empirical social science data and theory is invariably dialectic. Empirical studies are never fully persuasive on their own: Every econometric study has some degree of insoluble problems of omitted variable bias and co-linearity, every "natural experiment" is imperfectly controlled. To some degree, then, we "test" the plausibility of data by whether it makes sense given a convincing underlying theory of behavior. At the same time, the plausibility of any general theory is "tested" by its fit with available data. Second, I believe that developing new theory helps us to generate testable empirical hypotheses that we might not otherwise generate. For instance, without thinking about the "theoretical" possibility of hedonic adaptation and peak-end hedonic reporting that I discuss in some detail later in this chapter, my claim is that one would not likely think to investigate the empirical possibility that longer sentences might *diminish* specific deterrence.

The problems of using the insights gleaned from the heuristics debate to help frame criminal law policy—even in the very limited ways I have just described "using theory"—are even more severe. The applied psychological literature is still quite undeveloped, and, at this point, rarely tethered to empirical studies, either at the macro data level or the micro experimental level. So, in a sense, all I can hope to do in this chapter is describe the broad sorts of policy-relevant suggestions that would grow out of the "heuristics and biases" (H&B) and "fast and frugal" (F&F) literature respectively.

The most significant point I want to explore in this chapter relates to what is traditionally referred to as the "deterrence" function of criminal law—the role that punishment plays in diminishing the frequency of proscribed, undesirable acts. The claim I make is that those associated with the H&B school will, like rational choice theorists generally, believe that the behavior of those deciding whether to violate criminal statutes is at least to some significant extent grounded in calculations about the expected value of offending.[1] At the same time, H&B scholars will believe that these calculations of expected value—based on judgments about how probable the would-be offender believes it is that he will be punished if he disobeys the law, the value of what he expects to gain from the commission of the crime, and the "disvalue" of whatever punishment he might receive—are all likely to be systematically distorted. The level of effective deterrence is plainly a function of the *perceived* expected value of offending, and we should not assume that the perceived value is congruent with the "objective" expected value. The "objective" expected value, as understood by rational choice theorists, is derived by multiplying the objective probability of each outcome by the invariant, frame-independent subjective evaluation of the gains and losses from successful or unsuccessful criminal efforts.

Scholars associated with the F&F school, on the other hand, are likely to be highly skeptical of the idea that would-be offenders calculate the expected value of offending at all. Thus, decisions about how to behave, about whether or not to comply with legal rules, are likely to be based on responses to an extremely delimited set of cues. Given this view, manipulating either objective expected punishment or perceived expected punishment is skew to the goal of increasing compliance with law. Instead, we need to manipulate the signals that people actually use in making fast and frugal judgments about how to behave.

At the same time, I also discuss briefly how distinct ideas about how people use heuristics play out in thinking about retribution—the notion that punishment is justified as an apt response to prior wrongdoing, regardless of the forward-looking consequences of exacting punishment. I do so only in discussing one aspect of retributive thought: assessing whether a particular punishment is proportionate to the criminal's wrongdoing, rather than excessive or unduly lenient. I further explore, also briefly, some problems that those with particular views about the use of heuristics in decision making are likely to see in implementing criminal punishment systems designed to "incapacitate" offenders—to prevent those deemed prospectively dangerous from harming the non-incarcerated population by isolating them.

A. DIMINISHING THE CRIME LEVEL: THE F&F APPROACH

• *Contrasting F&F pictures with those in which putative criminals are perfect or imperfect value-maximizing actors*

F&F theorists are extremely skeptical that people would make a decision about how to behave by performing the type of conventional cost-benefit analysis that rational choice theorists assert that those contemplating committing offenses do. Their skepticism about the capacity of actors to engage in such analysis is not grounded in the familiar idea that the sub-set of the population seriously considering criminal activity is especially unlikely to calculate. The failure to calculate is not in their view dominantly a function of internal limits at all, let alone internal limits that vary significantly across persons.

So the F&F critique of the descriptive realism of deterrence theory is not grounded in the commonplace ideas that those who commit at least some subset of "conventional," if not white-collar, crimes might be atypically unintelligent and bad at calculation, atypically likely to be using intoxicants that compromise both the capacity to calculate and the motivation to attend to anything but the satisfaction of impulsive desires, or atypically flooded with the sorts of emotion like rage that interfere with the capacity to calculate.[2] Similarly, it is not grounded in the possibility that rational choice theorists would acknowledge: Actors may often lack the information necessary to make decent calculations about expected punishment levels, both because they do not even know what nominal punishments are imposed for convicted violators and because there is little information available about objective risks of apprehension, prosecution, and conviction.[3] In this regard, I also set aside the concern that will clearly preoccupy those influenced by the H&B school—that is, that people will systematically misuse available information so that perceived probabilities will diverge from the best estimates of objective probability that could be made using the information to which they do have access.

Instead, F&F skepticism about conventional deterrence theory is grounded in the more general claim that all people typically use lexical, not compensatory, decision-making processes. People will act as if there is a single best cue to search for in deciding how to behave—and the decision whether to commit a particular offense (speeding, failing to recycle, whatever) is such a behavioral decision. If and only if there is no information about the value of the dominant cue that permits them to stop searching for more information and to make a decision, they will go through a second search/stop/decide process, looking for the presence or absence of a second cue (and so on.) But the cues they use need not act, as H&B theorists would imagine, as "substitutes" for expected value calculations; that is, they need not be the best method of approximating what they would learn using a fuller cost-benefit measurement procedure were one feasible. Instead, following these heuristics in making decisions might simply meet some other ecologically rational goal, for example, permit the maintenance of reciprocal relationships that best protect one's offspring from harm.

In the final analysis, the hypotheses that particular F&F theorists make about the compliance decision are less significant to me than the *form* of the hypotheses, in part because the "applied" policy literature in this area is still so new and underdeveloped. Here is an argument of the proper form, though. One can imagine that an F&F theorist will believe that the typical search order for determinative, lexical rules that an actor uses—at least in some domains—is that the actor will first figure out what she has done before and do that again (habit). If the actor has never confronted the choice before, she might then check whether the behavior violates known, strong internal norms. Failing to find an answer to that second question, she might look to see what others around her are doing and imitate social practice.

Note that there are a variety of forms of "imitation" heuristics. This is true whether actors *first* look to imitate or, as in this schema, do so only if they cannot follow habit or strong internal norms. One can imitate the first person or most proximate person one sees, imitate the majority, imitate those one thinks are "successful," or do the opposite of those one has observed when there is feedback that they are "unsuccessful." What should be obvious is that as these imitation "heuristics" require more and more complex evaluation of the results of the conduct one is supposedly merely mimicking in a fast and frugal way, the distinction between these purportedly heuristic strategies and rational choice strategies grounded in analyzing the inevitably limited information available gets very slim. If I only imitate those I deem successful, I need to figure out what I mean by success. Presumably, I will imitate something like those persons who behaved similarly who got "good outcomes" (outcomes where gains exceed losses?) most often. How this differs from doing my best to make an expected utility calculation is, to put it mildly, murky.[4]

These sequential search/stop/decide schemas can readily incorporate formal law, but they typically incorporate it as something like a last resort. Only if habit, internal norms, and social imitation fail will the agent look to see what the formal legal norm demands.[5]

It need not be the case that F&F theorists believe that the sequential search for non-lexical cues is the same in every setting. In some settings, one might first look to imitate others. For instance, in making decisions about how fast to drive, people might match the speed of prevailing traffic. Then, only if that extremely fast and frugal strategy is unavailable, the decision maker might look to follow some other fairly simple habit-based norm (e.g., go 15 kph faster than the posted speed limit).[6]

The most prevalent F&F argument that people *must* make these sorts of decisions heuristically is grounded in what strikes me, and others coming more from the rational choice tradition, as a *non sequitur*. The F&F theorists rightly note that *full-blown* rational choice calculation would require the decision maker both to have too much unavailable information and to make overly difficult computations. Imagine a driver trying to figure out how fast he should drive using such methods. To calculate the optimal speed as rational choice theorists allegedly hypothesize, the decision maker would need to know an enormous amount. He would have to know how much faster he can get where he is going if he drives faster and the value of the "saved" time. He would have to know the number of speeding tickets he would expect to receive if driving (each incremental amount) faster and the cost of the speeding tickets. He would have to know the number of extra accidents he would cause if he went faster and the costs of those accidents. Even to the degree that accidents generate only purely financial costs, he would still need both to know the pecuniary damages he would suffer uninsured and the injuries to others he would generate, the likelihood of being caught and sued, and the range of jury verdicts as well as know about his liability insurance coverage. He would need to be able to place a determinate and commensurable subjective value on the "thrill" of fast driving.

But this account of rational choice theory is misleading. Rational choice theorists do *not* require that actors fully calculate the expected value of each action in that way. Rational choice theorists acknowledge that actors may well use any of a variety of starting places or rules of thumb—and they would hardly be surprised if past action or the actions of those around them are perfectly good candidates to serve as rules of thumb.

All that rational choice theorists assert that is inconsistent with the F&F picture is that the actor will be sensitive to *shifts* in expected value and make decisions in a compensatory, non-lexical way. Thus, the driver will slow down, all else equal, if he sees a police car up ahead, changing the probability of detection, even if no one else around him sees the police car so that all the drivers he purportedly imitates without further reflection keep driving fast. He will speed up, all else equal, if he is rushing to an important meeting rather than driving to the airport to catch a plane that will not take off for hours. He will slow down, all else equal, if his windshield wipers are working poorly during a storm, and he is more than typically scared that he will get into an accident if he is driving more quickly. Those who make use of softly encapsulated heuristics lack the capacity to integrate any such facts into judgment because they are not themselves judgments generated by any domain-specific algorithms.

When one thinks about "decisions" to commit serious crimes—robbery, murder, and the like—the F&F idea that they occur as responses to single lexical cues seems especially implausible. People seem to assault or kill when they are especially enraged or stand to gain a great deal from the victim's death. That is, they do so when the subjective gains of the behavior are atypically high, not because they do so habitually. Not even serial killers murder *that* often or mimetically. People commit property crimes when the chances of detection are atypically low or when they face immediate "need" for resources, as drug addicts might. Of course, they might use rules of thumb in which a single-cue value *substitutes* for elaborated judgments about the expected value of committing a particular offense on a particular occasion; for example, a burglar might typically break into houses with the lights off. But if he hears people inside the dark house with the lights off, rational choice theorists, but not those committed to the idea that criminals make lexical judgments, predict he might forebear.

It seems quite plausible, though, that the changes in expected punishment that the legal system can realistically generate either by shifting nominal penalties or by altering global, but not locally and immediately perceived, rates of apprehension are especially unlikely to influence behavior. The proposition that policy meant to shift expected punishment will be inefficacious seems reasonably persuasive even if it were utterly daffy to think that actors are unable to use multiple bits of information in making compliance decisions. It is not obvious that the fact that Town T catches 15 percent of speeders and City C only 12 percent will influence speeding decisions in the same way that seeing a police car around the bend will, or that levying $250 fines rather than $100 fines for speeding will have the impact on expected costs that realizing one cannot see very far through the storm has. The barriers to processing all these incremental shifts in expected punishment may or may not be the sorts of limits to perception specified by H&B theorists that I discuss shortly. It may be true, however, that within a wide margin, shifts in expected punishment are simply of very limited moment. If that is the case, though, then we should use alternative strategies to increase compliance, if increasing compliance is our goal, rather than to fuss with rules that might abstractly appear to shift expected punishment.

- *Fast and frugal legal compliance mechanisms*

It is less important at this point to study and evaluate the precise mechanisms that scholars influenced by F&F theory have suggested might help increase compliance than to think about the types of strategies they are considering. As I have noted, the literature applying F&F theory to legal compliance is essentially too new and too thin to have generated many well-developed or empirically tested suggestions. Still, there are a few points worth noting.

First, F&F theorists are likely to share with a variety of legal scholars the view that positive law works best when it mimics pre-existing social norms. For these limited purposes, what drives this belief is not the idea that social practice tends to evolve in functional ways but simply the idea that if law is to be effective, it must be obeyed. For law to be obeyed, it must either be known (and people can readily learn law only if they have already learned most of its content in the course of ordinary moral education)[7] or obeyed without reference to law, but by reference to the observed behavior of others. The behavior of others, of course, likely tracks—or perhaps defines—social norms.[8]

There is a narrow legal doctrinal implication to this observation, as well as the broader policy recommendation to tailor law to norms. Traditionally, a defendant's mistakes about the content of the criminal law's basic governing laws—his erroneous belief that his behavior is permitted rather than criminally punishable—are of no moment. This "doctrine" has two formal parts. First, neither knowledge of the governing law nor recklessness or negligence in being unaware of the content of that law is ordinarily an element of an offense, needed for conviction.[9] And, in much the same way, ignorance of the law does not constitute an exculpatory *excuse*.[10]

Some commentators have argued that legal ignorance ought to be irrelevant because citizens can and should learn their duties by explicit study of rules that regulate the behavior they are likely to consider performing. For these commentators, it is rightly considered a bad argument that no one could possibly know *all* the legal regulations in the world. Most of us need not consider, say, how the interstate shipment of toxics is regulated because we are not considering doing anything that might possibly run afoul of that law. Those of us who operate in heavily regulated areas *can* find out about our legal obligations.

But if the F&F theorists are right, *no one* is really learning their legal obligations through such explicit study anyway. It is *only* reasonable to expect a defendant's compliance with norms that could be followed by observing and mimicking social practice or, if the F&F-influenced "moral realists" such as Mikhail are correct,[11] because some sub-set of legal rules track moral rules that are known without being taught. This observation not only has implications for expanding "mistake of law" defenses in the relatively rare sub-class of cases in which defendants raise "cultural defenses"—claims that behavior made illegal in the jurisdiction in which they have committed an offense is tolerated or encouraged in their own culture. In such cases F&F academics would be amenable to the claim that they should be exculpated because they took the same steps as members of the dominant culture take to learn *their* obligations (i.e., they, too, simply have learned to mimic observed behavior).[12] It also has implications for treating mistakes of law as exculpatory even in more routine "mistake of law" cases in which defendants may argue that the ordinary modes of communicating obligations are not operative, or at least not yet operative.

Second, F&F theorists are likely to believe that one can generate compliance with new laws only by investing heavily in making compliance habitual. In this regard, the success of the German government in generating high levels of waste separation by households for purposes of facilitating recycling was *not* grounded in setting meaningful penalties for noncompliance or rewarding those who did what was desired. Even if these "expected cost" altering mechanisms were generally effectual, they would have been impractical strategies to adopt in this context, given the high transaction costs of imposing fines or rewards and the incongruence with norms of household privacy that would have been entailed in observing each household's behavior in order to reward or punish it.

Instead, household behavior was initially changed from the ground up. There was enormous effort spent indoctrinating school kids from kindergarten on about the necessity to separate waste with the hope that parents would not disappoint their children's moralistic expectations. There was also a fairly high level of advertising aimed directly at adults. The need for making these start-up efforts has gradually eroded, though, because waste separation has become so habitual that Germans merely follow the first lexical rule ("what have I done before?") in making decisions about how to handle household waste.[13]

Third, compliance may often best be induced by altering the potential violator's immediate *capacity* to violate norms. While it is possible to think of "barriers" to noncompliance as merely raising its costs, F&F theorists seem to think that those who comply because it is immediately difficult not to do so are making decisions based on a single cue—is action A readily achieved?—rather than "costing out" the difficulty of taking the non-preferred action as a prelude to making an overall calculation of the relative costs and benefits of noncompliance. In this regard, one should think of using speed bumps, rather than higher fines, to restrain speeding or seat belt interlock systems rather than laws that impose penalties for driving without belts. More subtly, perhaps, one might imagine that the use of certain road markings and curves in the road make people perceive themselves as going faster than they actually are and thus induce people to slow down.[14]

Fourth, and finally, F&F theorists typically do not disdain the use of either formal state punishment mechanisms such as fines or imprisonment or informal social control mechanisms, such as gossip, negative reputation, guilt-provoking educational messages. But they typically argue that these are effective in the long run only if they help implant habits that individuals follow, using the "what have I done before?" search rule, or "social norms," that work if people follow some sort of imitation heuristic.[15]

I am unsure how, within this picture, punishment establishes habits or norms in the first instance, unless it operates through rational choice mechanisms. More important, I am unsure why punishment would cease to generate rational choice-based compliance over time if it once altered behavior in such a way that we developed a new set of habits. The theoretical answer is clear. Lexical thinkers do not use secondary cues if first cues are adequate for decision making. If there is a habit to follow, the decision maker need not attend to a further cue. But even if one accepts the dubious notion that people do not use additional information and process only the *simplest* cues first, it is not clear why it would invariably be simpler to recall all of one's past actions than to make a transparent cost-benefit calculation when the balance was hardly close.[16]

I think what is clearest, though, overall, is that tinkering with prices (marginally higher punishments, marginally higher probabilities of imposing punishment) is of little moment to the F&F theorist. Habit, mimicry, and difficulty of noncompliance rule the day.

B. THE H&B APPROACH TO DETERRING CRIME

- *Perceived versus actual expected value of committing offenses*

Rational choice theorists and H&B theorists agree that what is relevant to a decision maker is the *perceived* expected value of a decision, even if the perception is inaccurate for some reason. Thus, for conventional rat-choice theorists, for instance, a would-be violator will not be deterred by the prospect of punishment unless she knows that she might be punished. H&B theorists, of course, focus less on the external impediments to accurate perception—the lack of available information—and more on internal barriers to processing available information.

The expected value of offending depends in part on the perceived probability of various outcomes: how likely one is to succeed in committing the crime; how likely one is to be apprehended; how probable it is that one will be subjected to each level of punishment if apprehended. It also depends on the perceived value of each possible outcome: how good will it be to "succeed," how bad will the experience of each sort of possible punishment be. To the degree that there are internal barriers to processing information about probabilities accurately or problems evaluating outcomes in a fashion that is logically consistent or stable, the perceived net gains of crime may be higher or lower than they would be if information were processed better and outcomes evaluated in a different frame.

Although not central to the specific contributions of H&B theorists, it is helpful in thinking about the gap between perceived expected punishment and "objective" expected punishment to consider first the problem of limited information. It is important in thinking about whether would-be offenders *know* the law to distinguish between the proposition that people know in some general sense that many things they consider doing are punished and the proposition that they will be aware of *changes* in the details of law of the sort that those policymakers attempting to manipulate behavior might consider. Thus, a legislature might increase the objective expected punishment for burglary by increasing mandatory minimum sentences and permissible upper ranges, but if all people ever cognize is that burglary is punished "pretty harshly," then the details of the scheme are irrelevant.[17] Similarly, if legislators intend to deter particular conduct that is not universally known to be punishable by declaring it illegal in the particular jurisdiction for which they enact the criminal code, it may have little effect. There are empirical findings, for instance, that citizens of states in which it is illegal to use deadly force to thwart unarmed burglars are no more likely to think it is illegal to use such force than citizens of other states in which it would in fact be legal.[18]

There is widespread agreement that the existence of punishment deters. (Even F&F theorists may believe it ultimately deters by triggering avoidant behavior that in turn becomes habitual, normative, and/or imitated.) But the consensus over this broad proposition breaks down if one reads it to imply the further claim that government officials can deter crime more effectively by increasing nominal punishment *levels*. Still, even those skeptical of the notion that legislatures can typically do much to manipulate perceived punishment by incremental shifts in rules believe that certain *stark* rules with transparent binary consequences (e.g., that one first becomes punishable *at all* for a whole range of crimes when one attains adult status) will result in many would-be offenders desisting from committing crimes as adults that they had committed as juveniles.[19]

What H&B theorists in particular emphasize is that manipulating perceived expected severity may depend more on knowing how people actually make judgments given available information than on manipulating objective factors in the environment. While the H&B literature on how would-be violators may actually both assess probabilities and evaluate outcomes is slightly more developed than the F&F literature on the roots of legal compliance, it is once again more important for my purposes to look at the *forms* of argument that H&B theorists have suggested than to assess the persuasiveness of any particular proposition. My sense is that the possible distortions in probabilistic thinking are more obvious to those who have thought about the standard H&B heuristics than the problems of end-state evaluation, and hence, less thought-provoking, if no less important for policy formation purposes. At the same time, there are a standard set of arguments grounded in the H&B literature to suggest that those implementing the law will be misled by the usual biases into giving unintended signals about what behavior is appropriate and inappropriate.

- *Expected punishment miscalculation: misestimating the probability of punishment*

I offer some exemplary accounts of the ways in which H&B theorists suggest that would-be violators may misestimate the actual probability of each particular level of punishment. The point, once more, is not so much to evaluate particular arguments as to illustrate the *types* of arguments that these theorists are likely to find worth investigating:

First, there are findings in the H&B literature that suggest that people will systematically *overestimate* the risk of punishment because people often exaggerate the possibility of low-probability events.[20] At the same time, if people suffer from an "optimism bias"—as most H&B researchers suggest they do—they might underestimate the probability of *bad* events.[21] Since punishment for offending is both rare *and* bad, it is indeterminate, *a priori*, whether people typically under or overestimate true punishment probabilities. It might seem that making instances of punishment more salient and hence more available—assuming that could be done without violating separate moral and legal norms—would increase popular estimates of the likelihood of punishment. But it is certainly open to question whether other forms of conscious, and otherwise-acceptable, state action can mute the optimism bias. We know that optimism bias will diminish to some uncertain extent if actors believe that bad events are thoroughly out of their control. This is the case because the bias seems to turn in part on mistakenly believing that one is better than average at manipulating those aspects of the environment that are controllable in a fashion that favors one's interests. Thus, the well-publicized use of enforcement techniques like random audits or searches that diminish the capacity of the genuinely skilled to evade punishment may be effective in muting the bias because those wrongly believing they *are* the genuinely skilled will no longer assess their chances too optimistically.[22]

Second, unless the probability of punishment is "fairly high," some argue that there will be little deterrent effect because low-probability events have little impact on behavior, even if people accurately cognize the probability of such events. We need not, in taking this view, imagine that there is some threshold of probability below which people will be thoroughly undeterred. We need only imagine that the marginal efficaciousness of punishment falls rapidly as the probability of punishment drops.[23]

Third, H&B theory suggests the possibility that people who have been recently punished may falsely believe that the probability of getting punished is lower for them than it would be for a random violator.[24] Their biased perception—an instantiation of the gambler's fallacy[25]—is that is it highly improbable one will be "caught again" if one has just been punished. To the degree that this H&B-influenced view is true, rather than merely theoretically plausible enough to be worthy of empirical investigation, it seems decision makers are being especially irrational since it is plainly considerably more plausible that ex-offenders will be apprehended by the police *more* frequently than random violators, given that they are on suspect lists and have had criminal confederates who might gain by informing on them.[26]

It may be the case that a number of other biases I will soon discuss suggest that convicted criminals—especially, perhaps, those recently released—will *over*estimate the probability of detection and punishment. However, the presence of something like the gambler's fallacy might help explain why, acting purely from a deterrence vantage point, we aggravate punishment for recidivists. If those who have been punished systematically underestimate the probability of detection if they offend again, their perceived expected punishment will be atypically low unless we aggravate punishment levels.

Fourth, at the same time, one might expect those who have been punished, especially if they have been punished recently, to overestimate rates of punishment because the possibility of punishment is atypically salient and available, while those who have not been punished might underestimate the probability of punishment because they cannot so readily bring to mind instances in which committing crimes has negative consequences.[27] One might think the tendency to discount true punishment probabilities would be especially pronounced among those who have committed crimes but not been punished since non-punishment in the face of violation is then the most available outcome. (Once more, we see the problem of "theory" generating competing predictions without any metric to predict the relative strength of the competing effects, or rubric to ascertain the domain of one or the other phenomenon: The fact that there are theoretical reasons why the recently released should overestimate the probability of detection—availability—and reasons they should underestimate it— the gambler's fallacy—does not permit us to infer behavior from theory.)

Whether the tendency of the never-punished to underestimate the odds of punishment can be overcome by making the punishment of *others* more salient (without the use of morally dubious and constitutionally impermissible punishment spectacles like the stockades and public hangings) is obviously open to question. Not surprisingly, those influenced by H&B try to find ways to increase the salience of law enforcement without crossing these sorts of moral lines. They might, for instance, argue that it is sensible to make sure that parking tickets be large, bright, and visible so that by-passers see that others have been ticketed or like the idea of having visibly marked police cars regularly appear in neighborhoods, even if officers riding in marked cars actually apprehend fewer criminals and thus lower the objective expected punishment level at any given level of spending on police.[28] Here, of course, the underspecification of the traditional H&B heuristics once more makes it difficult to generate policy applications. We know at some level that people overestimate the probability of salient or available events but have a weak idea about what the roots of salience or availability might be. For instance, one could imagine that if the prospect of jail were incredibly aversive, the experience of seeing any criminal imprisoned would be incredibly salient in memory for that reason alone. Were this true, though, threats of very bad events would always seem realistic.

- *"Frame sensitive" end-state evaluation*

At the same time that H&B theorists develop descriptive accounts of both the divergence between the objective probability of punishment and its perceived likelihood, and suggest some policy tools that might help overcome the tendency of would-be criminals to underestimate the odds of punishment, they argue that we should be more attuned to the ways in which potential violators are likely to evaluate both the rewards of successful criminal activity and the pain of potential punishment. We should be alert in thinking about the evaluation of punishment to distinguish general deterrence effects—in which would-be violators evaluate projected punishments that they have learned about but have not directly experienced—from specific deterrence effects for those who have experienced punishment in the past and are now considering whether or not to violate the law again.

Once more, I am more interested in the *structure* of the arguments that H&B theorists have made that emphasize that there may be no context-independent, frame-independent method of ascertaining how people will react to a particular fine or term of imprisonment than I am interested in the *persuasiveness* of particular accounts. There is even less developed H&B-influenced literature focusing on how labile evaluative reactions to punishment may be than there is literature on biased probability estimation, but it is nonetheless worth sorting through some of the arguments that have been made, directly, as well as those that might follow from the literature on biases.

- *The timing of rewards and punishments*

First, there is no doubt that the decision about whether or not to commit a crime, if made in significant part in response to calculations about the costs and benefits of disobedience, might be different if the expected punishment were more immediate, or the benefits of offending more delayed. The "negative" value of punishment is obviously blunted because it occurs in the relatively distant future—after apprehension and a fairly drawn out criminal process that is not likely to resolve itself, whether through plea bargain or trial, for quite a while after the initial offense occurred. There is some substantial reason to believe that people process distant and immediate rewards in different parts of the brain.[29] At the same time, many criminologists have long believed that those prone to commit crime are especially impulsive, exclusively or nearly exclusively processing proximate consequences, and prone to discount the future atypically steeply. Their behavior is best described by a hyperbolic discounting function in which events that are "immediate" are fully weighted while those at any point in the future are immediately discounted with less regard to how far in the future the events may be.[30]

Still, it is by no means clear that we should describe such discounting as "frame sensitive" decision making. Actors would plainly be frame sensitive if they reevaluated expected punishment that would occur at the same time differently depending on how the punishment was *named* or reevaluated it because of the presence or absence of an irrelevant alternative. It is not obvious, though, that the timing of a good or bad event *should* be described as an irrelevant fact about the event. It is hardly apparent that it is merely a way of "framing" the *same* event. So, if we are to describe would-be violators as irrational or biased in some fashion when they think about the timing of either the rewards of criminality or the punishment, we must mean that they are using discount rates that are dynamically inconsistent or irrational, not merely that they are using discount rates that could be described as overly high from some perspectives.

The standard argument that the hyperbolic discounter is "irrational" or frame sensitive is that she does not consistently discount an event that comes one year later than some other event but rather treats events a year apart in the distinct future as far less distinguishable in affective terms than events a year from the present. For instance, when offered the choice between $1,000 now and $1,500 a year from now, many people will choose the immediate $1,000. However, given the choice between $1,000 in five years or $1,500 in six years almost everyone will choose $1,500 in six years, even though that is the same choice seen at five years' greater distance, seen in a different frame.

Obviously, *any* discounting is in part a function of risk aversion; I may not be around to enjoy the greater sum of resources I am promised in a year. (I might also be *certain* that I will enjoy any given level of resources less as I get older.) But people have distinct information about immediate and distant risks, so treating the year five/year six gap differently than the present/one-year gap, would not necessarily be irrational. It is sometimes logically reasonable to assume that there is an implicit risk that the reward will not be available at all at the future date, and furthermore believe that this risk decreases with time. Consider a party to a contract who will accept $100 from you now or $120 in a year when he is pretty certain, but not absolutely certain, both that you will still pay and he will still care. He may demand a higher annualized interest rate to receive the money in twenty years—a higher discount rate—as uncertainty grows, but in making the choice between receiving the money twenty-one rather than twenty years from now, the discount and interest rate for that additional year will fall because he may believe that nearly anyone who could pay in twenty years will be able to pay in twenty-one years. Still, in cases where both alternatives are fairly certain to occur, this pattern of discounting is dynamically inconsistent, and therefore inconsistent with standard models of rational choice, since the rate of discount between time t and $t+1$ will be high at time $t-1$, when t is the near future, but low at time t when t is the present and time $t+1$ the near future.

- *Contrast effects and intermediate punishments*

Second, there is some suggestive evidence—looking at the punishment-imposition patterns of experimental jurors—that judgments about how serious a penalty is *are* indisputably frame sensitive. Experimental jurors are more likely to convict a hypothetical defendant of the less severely punished crime of voluntary manslaughter rather than murder if the choice set from which they choose contains the even less severely punished option of punishing for involuntary manslaughter, even if the involuntary manslaughter option is "irrelevant" in the sense that it does not fit the facts and scarcely any subjects choose to impose it, than if the option set instead contains not involuntary manslaughter but capital murder, even if *that* option is also rarely chosen, because it also poorly fits the facts.[31] The fact that experimental jurors believe the *intermediate* punishment is more *apt* (i.e., appropriately strict or lenient) suggests, though it does not prove, that would-be violators might also think the punishment for manslaughter is more *severe* if they believe it is the intermediate punishment available than they would believe it to be if it were the lowest one conceivable.

Similarly, experimental jurors attend to irrelevant alternatives not only when they choose a punishment option more frequently because it is intermediate between other options but when, as a result of "contrast effects," they choose an option more frequently when a third option that few choose is offered which is similar to, but clearly dominated by, one of the "realistic" options. Thus, experimental jurors were far more likely to believe a violator deserved only traditional probation, rather than jail time, if offered a third option (a silly, "New-Age" form of probation that virtually all reject) as well as the two conventional options.[32] Once more, this suggests, but does not prove, that a punishment like probation may seem more severe to would-be violators—just as it seems severe *enough* to experimental jurors—if it is merely an option that is available alongside a similar but manifestly insufficiently punitive or senseless punishment.

In policy terms, this suggests perhaps that a short prison term might seem to be more severe if presented alongside the very remote possibility of receiving the same short term with all sorts of possible release conditions, none of which the would-be violator believes he would be able to avail himself of. The short prison term—without "fake" release possibilities—would both become the "extreme" punishment and would "dominate" the punishment to which it is similar. It might thus appear both more sensible to those who impose it, and more punitive to those who experience it.

- *Hedonic adaptation and desensitization*

Third, the simplest assumption that legislators, members of sentencing commissions, or judges imposing imprisonment terms might make is that the value of each month or year spent in prison would be relatively invariant. Were that the case, doubling sentence length would impose twice as much pain or displeasure. If it is not the case—if the marginal level of either experienced or remembered disutility changes in more unpredictable ways—then sentencing policy must be more nuanced. Obviously, too, the degree to which we can measure the *experienced* disutility associated with punishment may be relevant in making judgments about whether punishments for distinct crimes are proportioned correctly, in retributive terms. It might also, if actual disutility levels are perceived by would-be violators *ex ante*, affect the level of deterrence associated with each punishment. Questions, though, about how prisoners themselves will experience long terms of incarceration, and whether their perceptions are in some sense "biased," how would-be violators will estimate how they would come to perceive such terms if punished, and whether perceptions of either group are policy tractable are among the most complex questions in this area. They are not, however, especially well addressed in the existing literature.

As a preliminary matter in addressing these questions, it is useful to note that it is probably more plausible to argue that *specific deterrence*—the impact of experiencing punishment on the calculations of potential recidivists—is affected by either experienced or recalled punishment disutility than to argue that general deterrence signals depend on the experience or memories of others who have been punished. Actual or perceived disutility of punishment would affect generally perceived "price signals" only if those who have been imprisoned effectively communicated their views of how they experienced the punishment each had received to never-punished would-be violators who would otherwise rely on naïve projections about how they would react to distinct punishments.

It is important to note, as well, that F&F-influenced theorists might be especially skeptical of the claim that actual disutility levels impact the perceived severity of punishment. Although I have found no writing to this effect, I am nearly certain that F&F theorists would believe that to the degree that would-be violators are sensitive to punishment levels at all, the would-be offenders would perceive punishment levels in terms of a single, readily processed cue, and imprisonment length is the most plausible such single cue. Would-be violators would not try to figure out, more precisely, using additional information of various sorts, how they would likely *feel* about punishment of different lengths. In a "Take the Best" cognitive universe, the single cue that would best signal psychologically experienced severity is length of sentence, and additional cues (e.g., that studies tell us that people typically discount the increased severity of longer sentences because of hedonic adaptation) will simply never be processed.

There is nothing in rational choice theory to tell us whether or not the marginal *disutility* of a year in prison declines as prison term grows as, say, the marginal utility of income ostensibly declines with growing income. What H&B-influenced literature might do is to identify several reasons why we should expect both sharply declining marginal disutility, as a result of hedonic adaptation, and perhaps even more sharply declining marginal disutility for those who have had prior experience in prison, as a result of a form of desensitization. It might be the case that even short terms of imprisonment "immunize" those who have experienced them to longer terms, perhaps in part by desensitizing them to *variations* in punishment. It is not obviously the case that either hedonic adaptation or desensitization should be considered "biases" of the precise sort that H&B theorists have discussed. Still, I think there is a reason that H&B scholars have been interested both in studying how poorly people predict their hedonic responses to the paths they choose—their decision making is in many traditional ways "biased"—and in studying hedonic adaptation and desensitization—their evaluations of end-states depend not on the abstract qualities of the end-states but the frames in which the end-states are evaluated.

At the same time, H&B researchers argue that we should expect people who have been punished to misperceive and misremember, and most plausibly to *under*estimate, the displeasure they "actually" experienced when punished. If that is true, longer terms of imprisonment may "really" hurt offenders—and perhaps be therefore justified as appropriate in retributive terms for more serious crimes—but they are unlikely to pack additional deterrence punch. Oddly, I think the H&B literature simultaneously suggests that those who have not experienced prison at all will *over*estimate, rather than underestimate, how aversive they will find it because they will not properly anticipate hedonic adaptation or desensitization.

If all of these undertested empirical propositions are true, the ordinary American pattern of punishment for "professional criminals"—widespread use of low sentences for juveniles and young adults who commit rather minor offenses in the early portions of their criminal "career" followed by harsher penalties for later, more serious offenses—could hardly be worse from a deterrence vantage point. Few people considering committing serious offenses do so from a naïve position in which they overestimate, rather than underestimate, the pain from punishment and many have been "immunized" so that they scarcely register punishments that once would have seemed highly aversive. Similarly, the fact that prisoners often are punished less harshly as their terms come to an end—they gain privileges if they have behaved reasonably while incarcerated—may make sense from the vantage point of prison administrators interested in giving incentives for prisoners to be cooperative, but it may blunt specific deterrence, because people will, in complex ways I return to, overweight their last days in prison in recalling how the experience on the whole felt.

Conceptually, it is clearer that misperception and distorted memory are *biases* or errors than that those who hedonically adapt are either irrational or "misperceiving" an external state.[33] Instead, observing hedonic adaptation simply reminds us that reactions to abstract "goods" or "bads" are context dependent. While I come back to discuss controversies over what hedonic adaptation might really be, broadly speaking, one is said to hedonically adapt to a situation when something that once gave pleasure stops giving as much when it has become routine or familiar and one stops experiencing as much disutility from a bad event that one has acclimated to.

Just as we cannot assess the abstract value of a decontextualized good, like the Mark Cross pens that experimental subjects I discussed in Chapter Two evaluated more favorably in the presence of a cruddy comparison pen, so we cannot assess the value of a year of imprisonment five years from now without knowing whether that year of prison will be the fifth successive year of imprisonment or will interrupt a life of "freedom." But the context dependence we see in the imprisonment case does not violate rationality canons as it does in the pen selection case. Subjects who treat a year of prison more favorably if it is familiar do not reevaluate the end-state simply because it is renamed or coupled in an option set with irrelevant alternative options. Instead, the end-state simply *changes*—or, to put it more accurately, it was inadequately specifically described in the first instance. There is no *a priori* reason a rational choice theorist would think that the "good" that we call "one year of prison five years from now" is fully specified. Correlatively, there is no reason to expect it would be evaluated identically if it were aptly characterized as "a fifth year of prison" rather than "a first year of prison five years in the future."

"True" hedonic adaptation occurs when people's "actual experience" of the events in their lives are highly path dependent in a particular way: Events that are at first bad seem less bothersome if they become routine and expected, and events that were once good seem less pleasurable once taken for granted. The most famous, albeit highly problematic, empirical findings on hedonic adaptation were that those who win lotteries are far less happy than one would think after the small initial bump of excitement and that those who sustain serious injuries that leave them paralyzed are not nearly so unhappy as one might expect once they get over the initial shock.[34]

It would seem to make a great deal of sense, *a priori*, that one's affective reactions would diminish once any state—bad or good—were stable. To the degree that the primary role of emotions is to induce action, to impel efforts to change the situation one is in when there is pain, and to maintain or seek states that produce pleasure, it makes sense that one would have strong emotional reactions only to *shifting* circumstances, because once a state is persistent, it appears likely that there is little we can do to change it.[35] Hedonic adaptation to the immutable leaves us room to be sensitive to small, incremental local changes that are now most likely to be action relevant. Looking forward, I may dread, roughly equally, confinement in a nine-foot or a seven-foot cell. If I hedonically adapt to my actual ongoing state—say, confinement in a seven foot cell—I may work to achieve a realistic goal, moving to the nine-foot cell by behaving well in prison.

"True" desensitization occurs if, over time, one becomes less sensitive to distinctions in end-states than one once was. That one might adapt without becoming desensitized can be seen if one considers that a prisoner might hedonically adapt to life in a seven-foot cell, while becoming *more sensitive* to the distinction between being confined in a nine- and seven-foot cell. The opposite is possible too. One *could* find it harder to distinguish between ten- and fifteen-year jail terms once one has been in prison while finding the average day in prison *increasingly* painful, meaning instead of adapting to the familiar, bad things *could* become worse if they persist.

Policymakers influenced by the hedonic adaptation literature have tended to argue that increasing prison terms is likely to be surprisingly ineffectual if the policymaker's goal is to increase the disutility of punishment.[36] Longer terms may even, when coupled with duration neglect, peak/end reporting effects that I discuss below, perversely *decrease* specific deterrence and punishment by making long prison terms seem *less* painful than shorter ones.

At the same time, there is a particular form of effect that arguably mixes desensitization with adaptation that could have profound impact on optimal punishment practices. Assume that a person would, at first exposure, find a "short" (e.g., three-month) prison term fairly bearable and ineffectual as a deterrent but would find a moderate term (e.g., two years) to be significantly painful enough to deter crime. If she *first* experiences the non-deterring three-month sentence, though, she may no longer be deterred by a two-year sentence; the response to that marginal cue is simply dampened. These sorts of "adaptation to intensity" desensitization effects have been shown in animals—for example, pigeons may be deterred from seeking a reward by a shock of 80 volts if that is the first shock that is ever administered but if they are first administered a sub-deterring jolt of 60 volts, they may seek the reward even when shocks go as high as 300 volts. As I noted earlier, our most conventional punishment practices— very low punishment for very high numbers of first-time offenders, particularly youthful offenders—may only serve to make actors indifferent to a broader range of punishments, even when they would otherwise find longer punishment noticeably different and worse.[37]

It is important to recognize, however, that researchers such as Kahneman, associated with the H&B school, have expressed skepticism about whether hedonic adaptation is "real" or merely a reporting artifact. The view that it is a reporting artifact is a complex one that I explore at some length, but at core, what lies behind this understanding of the phenomenon is the idea that people who seem to be adapting hedonically are merely using typically biased cognitive heuristics to *report* a cognitively inaccessible state of affairs, their level of happiness. Thus, when thinking about the classical heuristics studied by H&B researchers, we recognize that there is some true feature we seek to identify (e.g., the probability of events in the prototypical H&B scenario, one's "true" hedonic state in this case) and that one instead *substitutes* more readily cognitively accessible attributes for the hard-to-discern real attribute. So the (proto)typical H&B subject *tries* to identify whether more words end with "-n-" or "ing," but answers illogically that the second ending is more common because words with that ending are more available and she substitutes easily made judgments of availability for a difficult, reasoned approach to assessing probability.

Similarly, the person seeking to know how she reacted hedonically to her time in prison cannot readily summarize or access her experiences; she thus substitutes various conventional "happiness reporting" proxies. For instance, the person who might appear to adapt hedonically may merely figure out if her most recent or salient experience is better or worse than she *expected*—and expectations are readily established by experience—and *declare* herself happy if the experience meets or exceeds her diminished expectations.

This is ultimately not an easy argument to sustain, though it may well be at least modestly persuasive. It is easy to know what Kahneman means when he says that people misestimate the number of words ending in distinct letter combinations or misestimate the probabilities of available and unavailable forms of accidental death. Moreover, it is important to note that there *are* situations in which *reported happiness* is plainly influenced by factors that could not possibly impact experienced happiness. In those cases, the traditional heuristics and biases account seems most persuasive. People *mean* to report how happy they have been over some extended period but are heavily influenced by extremely temporary states that are much more readily recalled (e.g., whether they have recently found a dime, whether the weather is good). Or, their responses are highly sensitive to the way in which questions are framed. If asked first to say how many "dates" they have had in the last month, and then to state how happy they are, the number of dates correlates highly with reported happiness. If one reverses the question order, the correlation nearly disappears. The explanation for this question order effect is that subjects who have been asked about dates first fix on information about dates in evaluating their overall state because such information has been made highly available to memory.[38] Their responses to questions about happiness levels also change if they are asked to construct negative or positive counterfactuals before answering questions about their hedonic state.[39]

But it is not nearly so clear what Kahneman means when he says that those who appear to hedonically adapt have merely changed their aspiration levels, that they have not changed their hedonic experiences. How do we know that "true" happiness is not happiness relative to some set of expectations? What does it mean to have a true hedonic experience that we not only do not, but seemingly cannot, know?

It does mean something to Kahneman. To him, hedonic reactions to life events are essentially involuntary binary responses, with a natural zero point. People like the situation they are in and wish it would persist; dislike it and wish it would end; or are indifferent.[40] Even if they cannot readily make cardinal judgments about precisely how good or bad an end-state is, they *cannot help but make* this sort of good/bad/indifferent judgment. What Kahneman is claiming, then, is that long-term prisoners continue to find their daily situation just as full of aversive situations as the newcomers do but simply misreport that hard-to-discern fact because they are able only to *report* more cognitively tractable information about satisfaction relative to ever-shifting expectations. Whether this is consistent with robust findings that almost all prison suicides occur in the first few days of imprisonment[41] is hardly clear, but for now, I am assessing the theoretical point more than the empirical one.

Kahneman argues that there is a strong theoretical reason to believe that the judgment of good and bad has a single zero *point*. He argues that judgments of "happiness" are like judgments that a hue is neither dominantly green nor dominantly red, but "white." Such judgments have a single zero point, even though our ability to discern where that point is located alters with context. (Those exposed to strong red light just before they are asked to label a stimulus will call light with a higher proportion of red "white.")

They are unlike judgments that a line is "neither short nor long" (though, once more, judgments about whether a particular line is short or long depends on the length of lines one has been exposed to prior to the stimulus). His claim is that the length judgments are driven by the need to communicate in relativistic language, while the color and pain/pleasure judgments are driven by shifts in sensory mechanisms. Another way of expressing this insight is to note that respondents to the color experiments think that all the "white" lights they see look the same, while those who describe two lines they describe as "neither short nor long" can still differentiate the lines' length. Moreover, he argues that pain/pleasure/indifference judgments, like color judgments, are bipolar rather than unipolar. (Length is continuous from shorter to longer, not on one side or the other of a zero point.) He also argues that distinct physiological mechanisms triggering approach and avoidance are present when we perceive good and bad states, and that we can observe approach or avoidance without requiring the subjects to communicate their feelings at all.[42]

Kahneman thus puts great stock in the idea that those who historically reported surprisingly high happiness levels in the "old hedonics literature" (like paralyzed accident victims, or the elderly, or long-term prisoners) did not actually "adapt" to their poor circumstances but simply *reported* higher levels of happiness relative to diminished expectations. Kahneman refers to this as a "satisfaction" treadmill rather than a hedonic treadmill; people who have more bad experiences may declare themselves satisfied with a poorer distribution of good/bad/neutral experiences but the number and nature of good/bad/neutral experiences does not alter as a result of past experience. He argues further in this regard that if hedonic adaptation were thoroughgoing—rather than hedonic reporting being labile—we would not observe, as we do, that certain experiences—such as cutting oneself shaving—are always unpleasant, no matter how often they are repeated.

Still, if the most significant impact of adaptation is to broaden the indifference band, and to broaden it systematically to include more events that were historically hedonically charged, then the purported distinction between "reporting errors" and "unmediated" responses largely disappears. Kahneman's theoretical argument would then be, in my view, quite unpersuasive. Even if good/bad judgments are bipolar and nonrelativistic, there is no reason to believe that the "neutral" (zero point) area does not increase in size. Thus, it may be the case that those who have experienced lots of misery find a wide range of once-miserable experiences too ordinary to condemn or avoid, or that those who have done lots of wonderful things become jaded in the sense that a far larger range of experiences are not attractive but neutral. If this is true, the "hedonic treadmill" is real, rather than a satisfaction-reporting treadmill. It will simply be manifest as a wider zero point for once-pleasurable experiences.

My tentative sense is that this problem is related to the distinction I tried to draw between "true adaptation" and "true desensitization." Frederick and Loewenstein note, "it is important to distinguish between adaptive processes that diminish subjective intensity by altering the stimulus level that is experienced as neutral (shifting adaptation levels) and adaptive processes that diminish the subjective intensity of the stimulus generally (desensitization)."[43] If people just adjust adaptation levels, they should still be able to sense distinctions between stimuli. My cautious intuition is that desensitization among some range of the options that one actually most typically experiences might be one way of describing a radical increase in the no-response area.

I understand that Kahneman's view is not only that desensitization is not a very important part of the hedonic treadmill process but that people do not really adjust adaptation levels either. Rather, the subject simply changes how he reports the "summary" of any given level of actual satisfaction. Note, though, that there are some indicators that what psychologists have perceived as adaptation is not simply a reporting or memory problem, but is manifest in non-communicative behavior: For instance, Krupat finds that prior exposures to threats not only lowers subjects' reports of how dangerous the situation they now face is but reduces galvanic skin conductance, a physiological measure of fear.[44]

Whether hedonic adaptation is best described as diminishing something we would consider "real" negative hedonic reactions to long-term imprisonment or merely "reported" negative reactions, it is important to recognize, when thinking about the *ex ante* impact of future punishment, that would-be violators will almost surely discount the actual level of hedonic adaptation. When making affective *forecasts*, subjects typically underestimate the degree to which they will get used to bad situations and stop appreciating good ones, whatever it means to "get used to" such situations. People naively suppose they will believe or report themselves to be persistently happier if they get tenure or win a prize and persistently unhappier if they endure a tragedy—even losing a child or being sent to a concentration camp—than they have been in the past when they have had positive or negative experiences. Broadly speaking, H&B researchers who have been especially interested in the failure to predict adaptation think that most people remain "relatively happy" most of the time and external events do little to change that for long.

These researchers think that subjects overestimate the durability of the affective shifts that accompany negative events for six broad reasons: First, they often misconstrue the events, unable to imagine them with an adequate degree of specificity (they may, for instance, think broadly about "going blind" but cannot imagine that they will have gone blind in a particular context, e.g., slowly as a result of a congenital disease or as part of a heroic effort to save a child). Second, they embrace inaccurate general theories about the sources of happiness and attach them to their hedonic forecasts (for instance, they wrongly think that "money is the key to happiness" and prospectively overestimate the impact of financial success or failure). Third, they are "defensively pessimistic" about bad events so that real life will be better than they expected. Fourth, because they can most readily imagine the strong immediate reaction they will indeed have to a negative event, and then anchor their estimates of the hedonic impact of the event to the anchoring point, they overestimate long-term consequences. Fifth, undue "focalism"—the tendency to forget that many other things, good and bad, will happen after the salient event on which they are focused—tends to distort one's impression of the impact the salient event will have on overall happiness. (Even if one wins the lottery, your kids might get sick; even if one gets in an accident, your kids may marry really great people.) Finally, and perhaps most significantly, there is a residual sort of "immune neglect," a tendency to underestimate the degree to which organisms do not maintain a perpetually gloomy state once they recognize that the gloom cannot produce action that will alter the environment.[45]

Hedonic adaptation may be relevant to punishment practices in a further way. There is substantial reason to believe that people may adapt better, and hence "feel" better, when they are *sure* something bad has happened than when they are 95 percent sure but still can imagine that there might be a way out. In this regard, those who receive bad HIV reports or a firm diagnosis that they have Huntington's disease seem better off than those not yet informed, but highly wary, of their status.[46]

This may seem counterintuitive at first glance. Under one view, of course, the person with a 100 percent chance of something bad happening is just like the person with a 95 percent chance except that as to the last 5 percent, he is in worse shape. One way of putting that is that state X is being 95 percent certain that one is HIV positive, and that state X is present both in those who are certain that they are HIV positive and those who are not yet informed but are fairly sure that they are HIV positive. If state Q is "a lottery ticket with a 5% chance that I learn that I am HIV positive" and state R is "a lottery ticket with a 5% chance that I learn that I am HIV negative," one plainly prefers R to Q, but one may not in fact prefer the sum of X and R to the sum of X and Q. Alternatively, one could frame this point by noting that it is clear that the subject prefers state E, HIV- status, to D, HIV+ status: but that ordinarily implies that the expected value of a 95 percent chance of D plus a 5 percent chance of E is valued more than a 100 percent chance of D.

The fact that this set of preferences seemingly violates ordinary rationality conventions can be seen if we imagine the state E being "winning" $1 million (parallel to HIV status) and state D being winning only $100 (the lower valued HIV+ status). It would plainly be better to have a 95 percent chance of D and a 5 percent chance of E than a 100 percent chance of D, and we would think we would be able to infer that from the fact that E is preferred to D. The conventional rationality principle that those who prefer "certain" bad news violate is Savage's "sure thing" principle—the principle that if one is offered a lottery X and a lottery Y which differ only with respect to the fact that X contains prize A as one prize and Y contains B, that one rationally "must" prefer X to Y if one prefers A to B.

My main point for now is that Savage's sure-thing principle apparently does not precisely apply when subjects are adapting to very bad news. Once more, the reason the "mathematical" rationality model seems to fail is that it does not seem to deal with the "integrating" experience agent—the "ego" that adapts to bad news and somehow goes on, or suffers from prospective anxiety as long as he possesses lottery tickets rather than certain information. In a sense, one could argue that the presence of such an integrating agent makes a whole slew of end-states "complementary" that would not otherwise appear to have such a quality. Obviously, perfectly conventional rational choice theorists recognize that a chooser C could prefer X + Z to Y + Z even if he preferred Y to X outside the presence of Z if X and Z were in some sense complements (e.g., if X were a condiment that went especially well with some food Z even though it's not very tasty on its own). But we typically think of complementarity in consumption as a special, minor case, which we would expect to find when the goods were *used* together, in a physical sense, rather than *reconstrued*. Here, the 5 percent chance of learning that one is HIV+ is complementary to the prior 95 percent chance because, taken together, they permit hedonic adaptation, even though taken alone, the 5 percent chance of bad news is worse than the 5 percent chance of good news, while the 5 percent chance of good news or bad news, taken alone, merely creates anxiety.

However one explains the hedonic reaction to uncertainty reduction, findings like these suggest, counter to the traditional literature that certainty of punishment best increases deterrence, that uncertain but highly likely punishments may generate more disutility—and therefore deterrence punch—than fully certain punishments. The existing death penalty system—in which a subset of Death Row inmates is nearly, but never truly, certain that they will be executed, might, however inadvertently, both be the most punitive system we could establish if one wanted to increase the retributive punch of punishment and, to the degree that people pre-cognized this sort of punishment, might most thoroughly deter death-penalty eligible homicides. Similarly, auditing systems with long Statutes of Limitations might best deter certain forms of violation since they both make people feel pretty sure that they will be punished and anxious that they will, rather than allowing them to adapt to the reality that they will indeed be punished.

- *Duration neglect and peak/end reporting*

Fourth, and finally, H&B theorists posit that the duration of a bad or good event has far less impact on its *perceived* hedonic quality than one would expect. H&B-influenced researchers treat duration neglect as an unambiguous reporting or measurement error, grounded in simple attribution substitution. It is difficult to recall and sum all the pains and pleasures one felt over any substantial period, whether the period is as short as a colonoscopy or as long as a prison term. Thus, people typically substitute the average of the peak pain and the end-point pain for a cognitively unavailable true summation of their hedonic experience.

In the colonoscopy context, experimental subjects in Group A receive a regular half-hour colonoscopy, reporting, say, a peak pain of 8 on a 10-point scale and a final pain of 4 when the instrument is removed at the end of the procedure. For the next fifteen minutes, after the instrument is removed, the pain level is zero. They believe that the procedure as a whole produced a pain level of 6, the average of the peak and end pain levels. Those in Group B receive the same regular procedure but receive fifteen more minutes of moderate pain—the instrument is left in though it does not continue to probe. They report a peak pain level of 8 and a final pain level of 2, the pain level when the instrument is left in. Their peak/end report is that the procedure caused a pain level of only 5. Now, both people in groups A and those in group B experience identical experiences for the first half hour; those in Group B have a worse time of it for the next fifteen minutes (2, not 0-level pain). But those in group B report less pain *and* are more likely to show up for their next colonoscopy appointment.[47]

Kahneman is confident that this sort of duration neglect is a bias, a mere cognitive "reporting error." I have expressed my hesitations about that view in the past, but I do not think it is especially important for these purposes to decide whether "peak/end" reporters are mistaken as he believes. Those skeptical of the view that duration neglect is a reporting error believe that those judging events in terms of peaks and ends are expressing a more integrated view of life satisfaction and dissatisfaction, or engaged in construing their life-states by giving "meaning" to narrative events rather than thinking of themselves as dissolved mini-persons whose experience is the sum of the mini-people's experiences.[48] But what is important for now is how it might impact punishment policy if we believed subjects typically neglect the duration of bad feelings when they consider the hedonic quality of punishments.

The standard H&B-influenced story would go something like this: people will not think a ten-year prison term *was* actually worse than a six-year term merely by virtue of its length. To the degree that specific deterrence works through memory of the hedonic quality of past punishment, a criminal who was previously punished for ten years will be no more likely to be specifically deterred than one punished for six. At the same time, general deterrence effects will depend in part on the degree to which those who have been punished communicate to would-be violators how they experienced their punishment. Worse still, from the vantage point of those who believe they can deter more crime by increasing prison terms, doing so may be not only be unproductive but perversely *counterproductive*. If people indeed hedonically adapt to prison, those who serve longer terms will experience a more favorable "end" hedonic state than those who have served shorter sentences. Assuming their peak state is no worse—though this assumption may not be true if peak pain states are worse for those who enter prison anticipating a long and miserable term—their final, overall evaluation of prison will be *more* favorable if they evaluate by averaging the peak and end-state.[49] Our real experience, the amount of disutility we actually felt, might not be accessible; our judgment about how bad the experience was gets made by reference to an inaccurate, but more readily implemented, proxy.

- *Systematic errors in providing appropriate deterrence signals*

I will be especially brief, and merely suggestive, in noting that policymakers influenced by H&B theory tend to believe that the price signals the legal system often generates may reflect cognitive biases.

We can imagine, for instance, that actors are systematically overdeterred in situations in which we seek to punish only unreasonable behavior—whether the behavior is defined as unreasonable in wholly economic terms (i.e., it is unreasonable if and only if its expected costs outweigh its expected benefits), or other sorts of terms (e.g., it is not conventionally acceptable or the sort of behavior that people would engage in toward someone with whom they were strongly altruistically linked). They might be overdeterred if fact finders find it difficult, because of "hindsight bias," to put themselves back in the position that the actor was in *ex ante*. If they believe that when harms actually occur, the actor both took a higher *ex ante* risk than he actually took—one form of hindsight bias leads actors to believe that most everything that occurs was more inevitable or likely than it actually was—and that he *ought* to have foreseen whatever eventuated, then fact finders will typically find people were unreasonable whenever harm occurs.

To the extent that actors know that they will be found unreasonable whenever harm occurs because of this hindsight bias, they will take excessive precautions to avoid the harm in order to avoid facing *punitive* sanctions whenever harm occurs. For reasons familiar to those who study the choice between strict liability and negligence in tort law, the fact that they might be adjudged negligent and forced to pay *compensatory* damages in a tort suit even when they were not actually negligent will not induce them to take excessive precautions. Since hindsight bias merely makes the negligence system something closer to a strict liability system, and since a selfish putative defendant would take only cost-justified precautions in a strict liability system (since it is cheaper to pay the expected damages for accidents than to pay for precautions that will diminish accident costs by less than the costs of those precautions), hindsight bias does not inevitably lead to distorted incentives in a system that merely assesses compensatory, non-punitive damages.

Similarly, we may believe that legislatures will act as if they overestimate risks from readily available sources of morbidity, mortality, and injury relative to those sources that are actually more commonplace but less available. Regulation might well reflect the false belief, for instance, that airplanes are more dangerous per passenger mile than cars because plane crashes generally, or a small handful of salient ones, stick in memory. Legislatures may do so because the legislators themselves overestimate the risk of available negative outcomes or because they believe their constituents do, and that these constituents demand legislation responsive to the risks they care about. To the extent that is true, we may see rules that require "excessive" care in areas wrongly thought to be especially dangerous and unduly little regulation of risk taking in areas less available to memory. We may set high penalties that effectively deter conduct that contributes rather little to overall morbidity or mortality and low or no penalties to conduct that poses far more serious risks.

C. A BRIEF NOTE ON RETRIBUTIVE JUDGMENTS ABOUT JUST PUNISHMENT

Assume for argument's sake that while deterrence theorists should focus on the *expected* disutility that a would-be violator *perceives* he might endure, given the possibility that he will be apprehended and punished, a retributive policymaker interested in insuring that offenders experience an appropriate level of punishment for the offenses that they have committed will focus more on whether the offender, *ex post*, will have experienced the level of punishment that is commensurate with the offense. If this is the case, we must first figure out whether the retributivist policymaker thinks apt punishment levels are best measured by the best estimates of subjective disutility the offender (or typical offenders?) will experience given a particular nominal punishment or whether, instead, apt punishment involves a certain level of deprivation of significant capacities (e.g., liberty) without regard to the subjective hedonic experience of those deprivations. However, to the degree that the apt punishment is either entirely or partly set by reference to the disutility associated with the punishment, then we must decide if we can distinguish between "real" experienced disutility and reported disutility. If we can so distinguish, does a retributivist care how much the guilty party "really suffers" or does she care how much the offender believes she has suffered?

The first question—does a policymaker seeking retribution against wrongdoers care that the wrongdoers *suffer* or does she care about more objective sorts of deprivation?—resonates in debates that are far removed from the debates I am addressing in this book. What "end-state" should we care about distributing when we develop theories of distributive justice? *Very* broadly speaking, some have argued that we should care about distributing utility because anything else we might care about distributing is, at core, merely a *means* to utility, and it would be fetishistic to care about distributing anything that is a mere means to an end. Others believe we should care only about distributing concrete resources. They argue that differentiated subjective reactions to equal resource states are unimportant—neither anhedonic nor greedy people deserve more resources just because they need the resources to make them as happy as the easily pleased ascetic. Still others think we should distribute neither welfare nor particular resources but the capabilities or opportunities to flourish. For some individuals, it may take more resources to give them an equal chance to function; for example, people with mobility impairments might require more resources to have the same capacity to get around but may or may not be "happy" if they can get around or "unhappy" if they cannot.[50]

It is possible, in the punishment sphere, to believe that we ought to care less about whether prison "hurts" than that prison compromises a number of significant capacities (e.g., freedom of motion and freedom to try to realize a range of life plans, capacity to form certain sorts of relationships, capacity to live free from stigma). To the degree that is true, questions about whether or not people "feel" less or more badly than we might expect when imprisoned for certain periods of time, or in certain patterns, are simply beside the point because we are actually interested in our retributive mode solely in stripping people of these capacities.

To the extent, though, that a policymaker with a retributive bent believes levels of *suffering* matter, the literature I reviewed in the section on crime reduction is indeed germane. The policymaker may *not* believe that *individual* variation in suffering matters—one might believe a particular convicted offender does not deserve more time in prison becomes he is more stoic and less bothered by the bad situation—but may still believe that we should impose a punishment on each offender that would deliver a certain amount of pain to the *typical* person, with typical reactions to prison, and that the loss of "capacities" is important largely or only because the loss of capacities typically has bad hedonic effects.

Thus, to the degree that hedonic adaptation *generally* blunts the impact of longer terms, we may be punishing convicted criminals less severely than we think we are. If the "real" experience of an event is the mean of the peak and end of suffering, rather than that peak/end reporting reflects merely the inability to recall and report "real" suffering levels, then to the extent that we want to be more punitive, we might want to make sure that the time in prison ends relatively badly. We might do so, for instance, by manipulating the degree to which release dates remain uncertain for as long as possible, increasing anxiety relative to adaptation. We might also want to ensure that the worst times are especially bad, within whatever moral and legal constraints we think operative on making confinement especially bad.

We might also think that we underpunish career criminals by increasing their intrapsychic "immunity" to punishment when we first punish them quite moderately before aggravating punishment for recidivists. At the same time, we might overpunish many "moderate" offenders as well from a retributive vantage point. To the extent that the first periods in prison are radically worse in hedonic terms than later periods (e.g., because hedonic adaptation has not set in), we may be punishing people far more than we think or intend when we sentence them to short terms for minor offenses.

D. A BRIEF NOTE ON INCAPACITATION

Obviously, some policymakers believe that the primary, or at least a substantial, reason we ought to incarcerate at least some subset of offenders is that by doing so we can prevent them from offending, at least against the non-incarcerated population, while they are imprisoned. The question for policymakers interested in incapacitation is whether the criminal justice system can distinguish people based on how dangerous they are. Can we know how likely it is that a convicted defendant will offend, and for what period he is likely to offend if left free to do so?

F&F theorists are likely to believe that even if we are incapacitationists, we should use the conventional criminal law system to determine dangerousness levels. A single cue—did the defendant commit a certain form of offense that has been graded in terms of its severity?—should be sufficient to make adequate predictions of dangerousness. Any efforts by sentencing "experts" to predict dangerousness using multicue statistical methods are likely to be less accurate than decision rules grounded in one or a few cues. Thus, (pseudo)-sophisticated incapacitationists in a world unduly influenced by the lure of "rational choice" and statistical erudition might be tempted to use regression equations or similar tools that attempt to predict how likely a person would be to recidivate if set free given a range of variables that include, but are not exhausted by, the crime he is convicted of. We could imagine that F&F scholars would also be less prone to try to describe the crime in detail, to differentiate one instantiation of a typical criminal category from another. The regressions may include other factors, like job history, family background, scores on a variety of cognitive and affective psychological tests, an inventory of current relationships, drug or alcohol use/abuse, and so on. But these tools are (presumptively?) less accurate than the use of fast and frugal heuristics.

Of course, F&F theory does not establish meaningful, non-tautological boundary conditions to specify when these sorts of heuristics are particularly apt. Statements of the form, "the heuristics work especially well when there is a high correlation between the value of the single cue and the outcome variable of interest," are tautological, not useful for policymakers. So we are left with a general "predisposition"—best thought of in terms of the "sociology of knowledge"—among F&F theorists to believe in "less is more" effects.

Still, in studying bail-granting practices of English magistrates that surely resemble incapacitation-oriented sentencing decisions, F&F-influenced researchers indeed found that as a *descriptive* matter, the judges actually used fewer cues in deciding whether or not to grant conditional bail (involving curfews or some level of pre-trial detention) than they claimed they used when explicitly asked. The two cues they used were simple. They essentially "passed the buck" and looked to see, first, only if the prosecutors recommended conditional bail and, second, whether conditions had been placed on the prisoner in past cases. The descriptive finding is somewhat ambiguous because the judges might appear to follow prosecutor recommendations whenever they agree with prosecutor's assessments of otherwise unmeasured factors, though the prosecutor's recommendation is not *causal*. But leaving aside the descriptive ambiguity of the study, it is interesting to note that the judges did not assume or find that it was instrumentally *better* to use the few cues they seemed to employ, and, quite to the contrary, seemed to worry that the exclusion of further cues might compromise legitimate due process goals.

The case is complex, though, in terms of evaluating the social utility of fast and frugal heuristics. To the degree that any researcher, including one influenced by F&F scholarship, might find that this system "fails," it appears that it could be due more to a principal/agent problem than the intrinsic inadequacy of the heuristics. The magistrates might not really share the principals' goal—to make "just" bail decisions—but might instead seek a distinct selfish goal—to protect themselves from criticism. The "pass the buck" heuristic may indeed meet *that* goal quite efficaciously even if it does not meet the principals' goals.[51]

Those who think about how decision making may be *biased* are likely to worry that the attributes that make us think that a convicted offender—or, in preventive detention terms, a mere potential offender—is likely to be dangerous unless isolated are not enormously probative of true risk. Our perceptions of risk would be biased, largely in ways that would make us unduly punitive; thus, we would expect "clinical" judgments of risk, based directly on perceptions, to be especially troublesome.[52]

Those influenced by H&B theory would expect, first, that decision makers would systematically overpredict dangerousness. Past cases of false negative predictions—situations in which a dangerous person had been released and committed a crime, especially a brutal crime—would be highly salient and available. At the same time, false positives, in which people were needlessly isolated, even though they would not have committed a crime had they been free, are scarcely even recorded in memory, let alone made salient, by direct observation but are only identified at all through dry, statistical analysis. If it is true that we overestimate the objective probability of events that are readily recalled—in this case, the false negatives—we will tend to think we must perpetually increase detention rates because we have always been underestimating the dangerousness of those we release.

Similarly, it is likely the case that the perpetually dangerous criminal is more "representative" of violent convicts. Once more, we will overestimate the probability that representative traits are more common than is actually the case. Of course, predictions about how decision makers will assess the degree to which one instantiation of a category is more prototypical of the category are not especially well specified in H&B thought, but it appears at least plausible that an H&B-influenced criminal policymaker would worry that dangerousness would be systematically overstated for this reason as well.

Anchoring effects would cut in the same direction, at least in thinking about incapacitating convicted criminals rather than in thinking about purer preventive detention. What we know about a convicted criminal is that she did offend during the period just prior to our sentencing decision. Our baseline probability that she is someone who commits offenses is thus 100 percent. Whether we adequately adjust in predicting what she will do in the future from the anchored starting point—she is a dead certain offender—is dubious if the general studies on anchoring are correct. Again, "anchoring theory" is not so well specified that we can be sure that the anchor a decision maker will use is "the probability that the defendant offended recently," but it is hard to imagine another anchor as plausible as that for convicted criminals. (I think specifying the likely anchors in purer preventive detention cases would be considerably more difficult. I doubt that people would anchor to the global rate of offending, "uncorrected" for predispositions about the offense rates of individuals with distinct demographic markers.)

Finally, it may be the case that decision makers engage in the sort of base-rate neglect that H&B theorists frequently highlight when they try to figure out how likely a criminal is to commit a more serious crime than the one for which she was convicted. Imagine that we know that every single person who will kill in the next year has committed a crime in the past (i.e., murder is *never* a first offense). At the same time, we know that a number of offenders will not kill and that the base rate for murder is very low. Think of the parallel case I noted earlier. Virtually all people who are truly HIV+ will test positive for the presence of HIV, just as virtually all people who kill will "test positive" for having committed a crime. Imagine that the base rate for murder is, say, 1 in 10,000—just as the base rate for HIV infection in the low-risk population is that low. Far more than 1 in 10,000 people who will not murder—the group parallel to the 1 in 10,000 people who are actually HIV negative—will "test" positive (have committed crimes). Just as those who neglect base rates will falsely believe that a person who has received a positive HIV test is likely to be positive since all people who are positive test positive, so will people systematically tend to believe that all who have committed crimes are more likely to kill than they are, since all who kill have indeed committed crimes. Obviously, the false-positive rate for killing among criminals is actually quite high, but if that rate is overlooked in favor of a focus on the low false-negative rate among killers, then the actual aggregate risk of killing that criminals pose will be misunderstood.

E. CONCLUSION

F&F theorists, broadly speaking, believe that people make decisions—including decisions about whether or not to comply with legal regulations—by looking to a small number of decision-relevant cues, cues they are likely to process lexically. Theorists have not yet developed a precise picture of which cues agents process lexically in deciding how to behave in particular settings. Still, it would be instructive in understanding the conceptual scheme to imagine, for instance, that agents behave first according to habit (if they have faced the same decision in the past), then in accord with an internal code, then mimetically, and, finally, in accord with formal law. If this picture is right, we will not manipulate crime rates as well by tinkering with expected punishments or rewards (e.g., by increasing fines or imprisonment terms) as we will do by, for instance, engraining habits or conforming law to pre-existing social norms or altering the capacity of the putative violator to engage in unwanted conduct.

H&B theorists are more predisposed to believe that at least some would-be criminals *do* care at least some of the time about the expected value of a crime they are considering committing, but that they are likely both to misestimate the probability of being sanctioned and to evaluate sanctions in ways that are highly contextually sensitive. One can readily observe or construct sets of punishment practices, given these frame-sensitive evaluations and miscomputations of risk, which are remarkably inefficacious. The chances of punishment may often be underestimated, and both the experienced and remembered pain of the punishment that criminals actually suffer may be lower than one would expect given the widespread use of harsh sanctions and long incarceration terms.

Those interested in a correctional policy that is significantly or dominantly incapacitationist should also pay heed to the lessons of those who have thought about heuristics. The work of F&F scholars should lead us to be cautious about the wisdom of using multicue regression measures in predicting future dangerous rather than the simplest single cue—did the defendant commit an offense of a particular severity? H&B work should lead us to worry a good deal that we will systematically overestimate the dangerousness of criminals and be unduly prone to think tighter controls on release are necessary.

7

REGULATING MARKETS

A. HEURISTICS AND BIASES IN THE LEGAL ACADEMY: THE PATH TO "SOFT PATERNALISM"

The heuristics and biases (H&B) literature was so widely studied in the legal academy predominantly because it was thought to have profound implications for understanding the operation of markets and the appropriate scope of regulatory interventions in these markets. This is not to say that academics interested in legal policy did not find many other concrete policy implications in the vast literature, even beyond the implications for thinking about criminal punishment that I described, and attempted to extend, in Chapter Six. For instance, legal academics influenced by the H&B literature believed it had profound implications for thinking about the resolution of disputes. They were concerned, for instance, about the degree to which judges or juries could overcome "hindsight bias" in making a host of legal judgments. Would too many of the defendants who caused accidents be judged negligent? This may occur because they will be seen to have taken higher *ex ante* risks than might actually have been present—it sure might look that way to those predisposed to believe that all harms that occur were close to inevitable. It might also happen because fact finders will think the defendants should have been aware of these purportedly high *ex ante* risks—since those judging behavior from the *ex post* perspective will suppose that, all along, they themselves did know, and others should have known, whatever eventuated. Similarly, they wondered whether all inventions appear unduly obvious once invented so that too many patents will appear invalid when challenged.[1]

These scholars worried, too, about the political and regulatory process. What capacity did agencies or legislatures really have to make use of the sorts of contingent valuations generally needed to apply cost-benefit analysis to projects that degrade environmental amenities? If, as those influenced by H&B scholarship suspect, the valuations of these end-states are invariably markedly frame and elicitation sensitive, cost-benefit calculations will be held hostage to question form.[2] They also worried that voters and their representatives would systematically misunderstand many of the most critical public policy problems we face. If, for instance, global warming worsens as atmospheric "stocks" of carbon dioxide increase but people systematically believe that stocks will decrease as long as flows are decreasing, even though in fact stocks increase as long as flows are *positive*, then voters and representatives may mistakenly believe we are averting global warming whenever we *reduce* emissions and base policy on that misapprehension.[3]

They worried that whenever people must evaluate their hedonic reactions to disability, they will exhibit bias in making both personal decisions (e.g., choosing medical treatment options) and social decisions (e.g., devising medical care rationing schemes or determining how to award damages to those who suffered disabling injuries). In this regard, the academics were concerned that subjects would unduly devalue disability status because they would underestimate resilience and hedonic adaptation, and they would engage in undue focalism, ignoring the degree to which all of our lives continue to have *many* aspects after health status shifts.[4]

They postulated that default terms in contracts, and injunctions granted to resolve disputes, would be "stickier" than those who did not understand "endowment effects" would predict. To the extent that observation is correct, basing legal decisions on the supposition that parties would tailor outcomes to meet their particular tastes in situations in which *objective* transaction costs were low was significantly misguided. Default terms were far closer to substantive mandatory terms than some might intuit; injunctions were not merely a prelude to negotiations that decided little more than the distributive question of who would pay and who would be paid but something closer to a substantive declaration of appropriate equilibrium conduct.[5]

They tried to explain numerous "anomalies" in securities markets that suggested the possibility that greater intervention in those markets was needed. For instance, some postulated that stock prices would be prone to speculative bubbles or, more generally, be "inefficient"—that is, they would fail to correspond to the best estimates of underlying firm income stream values. This might be true in part because multiple investors would see similar "patterns" in random stock price movements and make investment decisions based on their overconfident reactions to the discerned patterns.[6] It might also be true because investors would overvalue certain positive or negative news about company performance that was deemed "representative" and then fail to adjust valuation estimates adequately when they learn relevant new information due to a form of anchoring or "conservatism" in judgment.[7] Some argued, too, that we could explain the equity premium puzzle—the spread between the return to equity and bonds exceeds, in some views, the premium needed to compensate equity holders for bearing greater risk given any plausible level of rational risk aversion—by reference to the ways in which standard expected utility theory was deficient. The gist of the argument is that if investors are simultaneously loss averse, as Kahneman and Tversky's prospect theory suggests, and evaluate their portfolios frequently, they will think that their stocks are doing badly unless they do *very* well.[8] It is worth noting, too, that another standard securities market anomaly generally referred to as the "dividend puzzle"—investors purportedly overvalue companies that pay out dividends even though as shareholders, they owned company assets, whether these were distributed or not and also could, if seeking cash, always sell some portion of their shares—has been "explained" by behavioral economists who are, not necessarily consciously, more directly influenced by the fast and frugal (F&F) modular tradition than by H&B research. These researchers argue that the dividend puzzle is at core a product of a significantly modularized mind that keeps separate mental accounts for "fund types" that can be expended and those that should be saved.[9]

But this list is nowhere close to exhaustive, nor is it intended to be. The literature has been such a fertile source of insight that it would be someone else's Herculean task to give even a modestly comprehensive summary of the uses of H&B writing in policy analysis. My main point, instead, is first to identify the most critical *conceptual* impacts the literature has had on policy and then, in a subsequent section, to attempt to identify the ways in which the use of H&B scholarship in thinking about the regulation of markets is most troublesome.

If one had to identify the single most vital "core" message that legal academics took away from studying the H&B school's work, it is that consumers will frequently misevaluate product quality and, more particularly still, misevaluate the risk of both product failure and product-based injury, as will workers misestimate on-the-job safety risks. To the degree that there is a secondary message—also related to protecting decision makers though not through the usual product or work safety regulatory mechanisms—it is that consumers will be unduly short-sighted. Thus, we must restrain various forms of impulsivity, including a tendency to consume too much in the current period relative to a "rational" lifetime consumption allocation plan or to make decisions with positive immediate payoffs and long-term costs, such as smoking, drug use, and physically or emotionally risky sex. In each case, though, we see the possibility of driving a wedge between protecting an abstract sort of "liberty" and concern with both enhancing "welfare" and promoting some versions of "autonomy." We may not be able to protect the ability of the consumer to do whatever she chooses without interference (liberty) while protecting the capacity of the consumer to meet her true, prudently assessed, considered ends (welfare and autonomy).

At the same time, I hope to identify the critical dilemma that confronts those attempting to root consumer or workplace market regulation in the most central insights of F&F theory. I will argue that each school's scholarship fails to do much to guide market regulation policy for the same reason, though each group of scholars arrives at the same problematic point through a different route. In each case, however, the heuristics scholars offer no real way to solve the problem that it is troublesome to mandate product features unless we believe, quite implausibly, that consumer tastes and circumstances are homogenous, but that efforts to "nudge" subjects to make choices distinct from those they might make in the "natural" decision-making environment cannot be judged as adequate or inadequate without paying almost exclusive attention to whether the "nudges" have induced substantively desirable choices. (It might also be the case, in some normative sense that I find extraordinarily difficult to evaluate, that it is perhaps even more important, as John Stuart Mills suggested in *On Liberty*, to allow people to exercise their faculties making something we could construct as relatively unfettered choices, even when these choices frequently fail to meet their considered ends, because doing so will develop their faculties, so that mandates are inadvisable for that reason alone.) It is a trickier question for me whether F&F theory has much to offer if, as policymakers, we believe that tastes are relatively homogenous but objective circumstances significantly differ. Just to make sure I make my basic paradigm case clear, I think it might be helpful to have readers imagine the following: Tastes are homogenous if all aspirin buyers with children under 5, aware of the actual risk of poisoning if they purchased bottles without child-proofing, would purchase child-proof bottles, even given the disutility that results from the fact that such bottles are more inconvenient to use or more costly. Circumstances would differ, though, if some, but not all, consumers rarely or never had young children in their households.

B. A BRIEF NOTE ON WHETHER THE HEURISTICS LITERATURE BEARS STRONGLY ON THE REGULATION OF MARKETS TO REDUCE DISCRIMINATION

It is difficult to assess whether the mainstream social psychological literature on prejudice and stereotyping also actually draws in significant ways on the H&B or the F&F literature. Obviously, to the extent that social phenomena as critically important as prejudice, based on race, gender, disability status, sexual orientation, and so on, could be significantly understood by reference to the heuristics literature, there is a third key message that policymakers studying both H&B and F&F theory should take home. We cannot either understand, or hope to counteract, the bigotry that impacts, for instance, employment and housing markets, until we see it as arising from familiar cognitive "errors," to put the point in H&B terms, or, to put it in more neutral terms that F&F scholars typically use, tendencies to use tools that typically fit but occasionally fail to fit the environments in which the tools are used.

At a basic formal level, one could surely describe stereotypes as heuristics, in the sense that H&B theorists generally use the term. Those who make use of them make complex judgments about a true target attribute (e.g., the productivity of the job applicant they confront, the "dangerousness" of the person they pass by on the street, the likelihood the person moving in next door will be "neighborly") based on a more readily processed substitute attribute (such as race, gender, sexual orientation, religion). There is certainly a substantial legal literature that draws to some considerable degree on this analogy.[10]

Prejudices could also be described in a fashion that relies more on the methodology of F&F theory. In this view, we should first search for some inclusive fitness advantage that our ancestors would have gained by dividing people into "groups" rather automatically. The most obvious candidate would be that our ancestors in the environment of evolutionary adaptation (EEA) needed to separate kin and allies from those unfamiliar to us, but obviousness hardly implies credibility. At the same time, one could readily construct a just-so EEA story that we automatically *distrust* or *dislike* immediately perceived outsiders because they were historically competitors, on the assumption that our ancestors traded and cooperated *within* groups and "duked" it out with those who were different. We would then look to identify some psychological mechanism or capacity that has evolved to permit us to perform this advantage-gaining task. The most obvious candidate would be something akin to "recognition" of familiar and unfamiliar individuals or "types." Recall, from Chapter Five, that Goldstein and Gigerenzer do indeed argue that one of the two main reasons we have developed recognition memory, alongside the need to recognize once-eaten food, revealed by past use as non-toxic, is to distinguish familiar from unfamiliar people.

When confronted by a person, automatically encoded as a group member, we then bring to bear strong positive or negative associations activated by retrieving relevant memories about other group members confronted in the past that determine, in the first instance current attitudes. (I assume, if just for the moment, that dislike of the unfamiliar is not itself automatic.) Theorists who are less prone to emphasize the difficulty or impossibility of overriding heuristics using compensatory processes or a greater opportunity to devote internal resources might tend to think that we have the capacity to sharpen or refine these initial judgments.[11]

It is open to question whether these generally adaptive prejudices are troublesome or not from the F&F perspective. This question is equally applicable to other sorts of fast and frugal heuristic decision-making devices that do not directly trigger disparate treatment of "outsiders" but have adverse impact on protected groups, for instance, hiring only those job-seekers known to incumbent workers because the cheapest and most reliable single cue to measure the quality of an applicant is that someone known to perform reasonably both vouches for the applicant and might realistically be expected to monitor and informally discipline him for bad performance. One will typically simply replicate the ethnic composition of the first-comer workforce if one follows this decision rule.[12] Some of the F&F-influenced theorists treat discrimination as an unwanted by-product of the general human tendency to use heuristics rather than defend its rationality,[13] and they even seem to do so without going through the conventional procedure F&F theorists use when "lamenting" the use of a heuristic (i.e., showing that it is now being used in a novel environment).[14]

The idea, increasingly accepted by many scholars in the legal academic world, that race and gender bias are implicit or unconscious also fits the picture of cognition that those who have studied heuristics in both schools typically proffer: The heuristics we use are typically not transparent to us.[15] At the same time, many of the standard suggested remedial responses to unconscious bias resonate in the familiar idea that the use of heuristics by individuals tends to be rather recalcitrant; if we wish to alter poor decision making, we have to change either the identity of the decision maker or the decision-making context. Thus, we see recommendations, for instance, that we should shift the decision-making environment by including diverse decision makers in organizations rather than trying to get individual "bigots" to change, through either reeducation or incentives.[16]

We might see commentators, such as Sturm and Reskin, as drawing a lesson *from* the heuristics literature; cognitive short-cuts are recalcitrant so it is wiser to circumvent them than to try to wipe them out. Alternatively, one might see them as anticipating what I called the sociologically influenced *critique* of the heuristics literature back in Chapter Four. This critique took the following form: People may make the actual decisions that matter collectively rather than individually (for instance, decisions about whom to hire or promote, how to share information with newcomer workers). This is especially true if they have discovered, through more reflective mechanisms, that the decisions they make that are not mediated through these collective mechanisms serve their long-term ends poorly. The collective decision-making processes, however, do not merely "sum" the decisions of the isolated individuals, beset by the limits and biases of cognition that we display as isolated individuals. Thus, in the context, say, of job discrimination, the firms that hire and promote may discover through forced systematic study—rather than intuition—that far fewer women advance within the organization than one would expect given initial hiring numbers and qualifications. This may result from the initially unfettered influence of unconscious biases, but it may not be corrected so much by "overcoming" the biases as by adopting collective mechanisms that alter decision making, and generate new information about ongoing problems and potential solutions.[17] Thus, for instance, a collective decision to force senior managers to write down and report on the assignments they have given to juniors, as Sturm reports firms that successfully limit subtle discrimination might do, may undo a huge barrier to the career advancement of women and minorities. The relevant barrier, the lack of quality opportunities both to receive training and to impress others, *arose* in part because of unconscious heuristic-like biases, but it can be overcome without making those biases *disappear*. (The same goes for the sorts of beneficial organizational decisions that Reskin highlights to remit decision-making authority to more diverse groups, to require greater reliance on objective performance measures, and to demand those making subjective judgments write detailed accounts of the basis of their judgments.)

On the whole, I am cautiously skeptical that the literature on the roots of and the appropriate concomitant responses to bigotry really owes all that much to the essentially parallel development of understandings of cognition that emphasized the widespread use of heuristics. Much of the literature on unconscious racism developed because of the *sociological* observation that overt animus-based racism had become socially unacceptable, while racist behavior persisted. While one *might* have chosen to explain even open animus as an outgrowth of essentially unavoidable heuristic based reasoning, such animus was more typically explained as a product of more-or-less conscious, perfectly deliberative motivation (e.g., economic competition, desires for "in-group" status production).[18] But if what some label as unconscious attitudes are merely motivated thoughts gone underground, it is not really a function of the automatic nature of categorization or prejudice that is doing the work in finding "unconscious racism."

Theories that relied more purely on bigotry as an outgrowth of cognitive processes, theories grounded in the inevitability of assigning people to categories, each of which has presumed attributes, tended to emerge as a *counter* to rational motivational theories. And, in fact, what is perhaps most interesting is that those who most sharply criticize the literature on unconscious or implicit racism argue that what is ostensibly unconscious racism is most typically not truly unconscious at all, but deliberately hidden, given social norms against expressing bigotry *openly*.[19] It is probably the case that resolving the thorny questions of whether "motivated" and self-conscious bigots actually either score differently on implicit bias tests and whether implicit bias (if it exists) has any behavioral bite in trying to explain the range of discriminatory behaviors we see will be vital to deciding how significant a role the heuristics literature will have in shaping discrimination policy. Even if unconscious, heuristic-based bias exists, it is probably less policy-relevant if it better explains flinching on the streets or eye-contact avoidance in the presence of young black males than it explains hiring decisions by multimember human resource staffs.

C. "SOFT PATERNALISM" AND THE H&B TRADITION

I am confident that the central contribution that the H&B literature has made to the legal academy is that it has radically expanded awareness of the problem of error. Whether or not one shares this judgment that this contribution is the indeed the school's most critical one, it seems more uncontroversial to say that the H&B literature is the primary source of the growing advocacy of "soft paternalism" (or "libertarian paternalism" or "asymmetric paternalism") in the law schools.[20]

Soft paternalists are paternalistic in the sense that actors motivated by soft paternalistic beliefs—state bureaucrats, agents, friends—are willing, or even duty bound, to override the manifest preferences of some other set of subjects. Their paternalism is supposedly "soft" because it is grounded not in the notion that the subjects have "false consciousness" or ill-considered *ends*, or ends that do not meet "duties" to themselves or others to become a certain sort of self, but in the belief that they are simply *incapable* of meeting their perfectly acceptable ends, *even given information* about the options they need to evaluate. Such paternalists could profitably also be thought of as asymmetric, first, in the sense that the interventions they favor are designed to interfere with the *liberty* of irrational people who fail to advance their own interests while not interfering with their *autonomy*. Alternatively, such paternalists may be thought of as asymmetric because while they will willingly interfere with the simple liberty interests of those acting irrationally, they try to shift decision-making environments in a fashion that will not interfere with *either* the liberty or autonomy of those making deliberate, rational decisions, whether across the board or in particular situations. In concrete policy-design terms, such asymmetric paternalists will tend to favor interventions that shift the behavior of those most likely to be "imprudent" in the relevant ways without imposing insuperable barriers to "deviant" actions by those who *are* prudent. Thus, for instance, we might think that a contractual default term will "stick" only for those who are least able to judge the terms they truly desire while those who have reflected on the "value" of the terms will contract around a default if they find it undesirable. If that were true, a default term would be asymmetric in the relevant sense in that it would have little impact on the prudent but protect the imprudent.

Again, one could write a book (this is not that book) that simply summarized all of the concrete "soft paternalist" recommendations that have been based on H&B work.[21] Here is an example, though, designed only to illustrate the *style* and *method* of argument. A theorist influenced by H&B scholarship might believe that even though consumers sign contracts mandating that disputes with sellers must be adjudicated by an arbitrator, rather than in court, they do not "truly" value whatever money they save by guaranteeing the seller that it will not be subject to expensive legal process or higher expected damages more than they value a "better" dispute resolution process. Instead, they evaluate the contract as a whole based on a few salient traits; this is consistent with partly lexical "elimination by aspects" *decision making* described by Tversky in his early work on decision making[22] that largely preceded the work on judgment upon which I have focused. Not only is the arbitration term not very salient, sellers might be able to lower price—and that *is* salient—if they can "make back the lost revenue" by minimizing future liability exposure and litigation costs. Given this, striking down the term is consistent with a desire to meet the consumer's real autonomous goals.[23] It is surely the case, too, that the sort of consumer F&F scholars model who makes noncompensatory Take-the-Best inferences about states of the world—and thinks, for instance, that something other than the mandatory arbitration term feature is the best signal of some external "state of the world" we could describe as product "desirability"—could be equally harmed by a contract with an undesirable term that simply has no impact on the purchasing decision. What typically distinguishes the F&F theorist from the H&B-influenced theorist in this regard is the general faith that the F&F theorist has that, by and large, people will use only ecologically rational methods, and the use of a heuristic that permitted sellers to so readily exploit buyers by lowering price and degrading quality would certainly not be one that met buyers' underlying needs.

Even a book that focused solely on interventions designed to undo the impacts of mistaken risk perception could be a pretty substantial one. Again, though, two illustrations should suffice to clarify the methodological point.

First, H&B-influenced legal academics believe not only that risk rates are *naturally* misperceived given our cognitive limits (e.g., relative mortality risks are misperceived because some causes of death are more salient than others) but that sellers will *exploit* buyers' use of heuristics to make their products appear safer than they really are. Moreover, any *honest* seller, presenting risk rates more "neutrally," would be driven out of the market by sellers who would mistakenly be perceived to purvey safer products. Unregulated sellers will take advantage of a variety of heuristics to degrade product quality and safety without facing a market penalty. Thus, for instance, sellers attempt to present a preliminary impression of the product that is both generally favorable and emphasizes its safety or low risk of malfunction. They will thereby take advantage of both anchoring effects and the tendency to overvalue evidence that confirms initial impressions. They will play on self-serving biases (closely related to optimism biases) that make it seem more plausible to consumers that product safety is in the control of the user himself, who perceives himself to be atypically skillful. They will recognize that risk perceptions will be driven by availability and flood potential buyers with easily memorable images of the product performing safely and efficaciously.[24]

Second, H&B-influenced legal scholars worry that subjects poorly assess the aggregate risks their choices actually entail because of framing problems and pseudo-certainty effects, and believe that they must be protected from the imprudent choices that arise from these irrational estimates. Here is the standard sort of experimental finding: one group of subjects is told that a disease will affect 20 percent of the population, and a vaccination is available that will reduce the risk of getting the disease in half. A second group is told that there are two strains of the same disease, and that each will affect 10 percent of the population but that a vaccination is available that will eliminate the risk of getting one strain entirely but have no effect on the other. It is certainly conventionally rational to frame the vaccinations as identical in effect; each will reduce one's risk of getting the disease from 20 to 10 percent. But many people spontaneously frame the second vaccine as eliminating a cognizable, separable risk with certainty and overvalue risks as they approach 0 or 100 percent (treating the additional imposition of risk as much worse when risk moves from 89 to 99 percent than from 40 to 50 percent and treating risk reduction as much more beneficial when a risk drops from 11 to 1 percent than when it drops from 50 to 40 percent). Given this effect, it is not surprising that 57 percent of people in group 2 said they would get vaccinated compared to only 40 percent in group 1.[25]

Not only does awareness of such pseudo-certainty effects give us pause in thinking about how, say, a public agency concerned with influencing risk-reducing behavior ought to present information about the impacts of behavioral change on risk, but it suggests the possibility that consumers may need to be protected from sellers who take advantage of these effects in framing the virtues of their products. Thus, Latin notes the possibility that people might pay more for an insurance policy offering complete protection against a subset of losses (e.g., from fire, but none for flood) rather than affording partial protection against the overall probability of property loss, even when the cover-all-fires-completely coverage was actually less extensive and less expensive for the insurer to provide.[26]

It is interesting to note that both legal theorists who have strongly associated themselves with H&B work in the past and those who have been more critical of the H&B-influenced idea that risk misperception is dominantly a function of cognitive error or cognitive limitations have been exploring the degree to which risks might be differentially perceived, and perhaps misperceived, for reasons not conventionally highlighted by H&B theory. For instance, perceptions of risk might vary because some people are either emotionally predisposed to accept a lower or higher risk estimate, or disposed to do so for ideological or cultural reasons. In each case, perception could be described as *motivationally biased* rather than cognitively misconstrued.

Thus, for instance, Sunstein, with (or perhaps despite) his strong roots in H&B theory, notes that people will systematically underestimate risks over which they have *control*. For instance, if someone is committed to smoking, she may underestimate the risks of smoking. At the same time, subjects may overestimate risks when they feel the risks are being imposed upon them, and they cannot control them. For instance, if the power company will build a nuclear power plant nearby, no matter what you try to do to stop it, you may overestimate the risks from the plant. While the first mistake might be thought to resonate in the optimism bias, the second seems only weakly related to that sort of cognitive error.[27]

And Kahan, looking to step completely outside the conventional H&B framework in which risk calculations are thought of as troublesome when performed by people using System One heuristics, has argued that people's estimates of *factual* risk express *normative* cultural commitments. Thus, for instance, experimental subjects estimate the risk that a not-imminently dangerous abusive husband will kill his wife as higher if they are "cultural" egalitarians likely to self-identify as feminists. At the same time, subjects estimate the risk that certain not-imminently threatening "thuggish" African-American youths will grievously injure a subway passenger toward whom they are ambiguously menacing as higher if they are more culturally authoritarian.[28]

H&B-influenced theorists often disagree among themselves about the likely extent of risk misperception; the ability of existing legal regulations that bar providing false information, rather than assuming that even true information will be misused, to manage actual problems; and the feasibility of proposed reforms. (For instance, is enterprise liability that nominally promises to force sellers to internalize the costs of all the injuries their products cause really feasible?)[29] But they are all working from a position that makes it attractive to investigate the possibility of soft paternalist interventions.

An interesting question in program design has also emerged in the H&B-influenced policy literature. Most of the prominent soft paternalists seem to favor a particular *form* of intervention, conditional on the desirability of intervention. Just as they are "soft" paternalists in the sense that they purportedly do not want to interfere with considered *ends* but only with *means*, they seem to prefer to interfere with target behavior in a "softer" way as well. They often extol "nudges" (like taxes, shifted decision contexts) rather than "mandates" (prohibitions, criminal penalties, direct physical coercion).[30] I recognize that it would be difficult to sustain the claim systematically that "soft paternalists" are typically wary of "more coercive" interventions. This is true both because it is very difficult to defend any scheme that categorized certain authors or articles as either within our outside the soft paternalist "school" and equally difficult to know what it would mean to show a preference for "nudges" rather than "coercion." Is any behavior really *prohibited* by law or would it be more accurate to say that the price of engaging in the behavior simply increases more and more as fines, taxes, or punishments increase? Have we "merely" changed choice context when we make the choice regulators disfavor truly difficult to make, or grotesquely unappealing?

All I want to note, though, is that to the degree that this connection between program method and program motive is "real," it is not *logically entailed*. One could disdain paternalism of any stripe entirely but believe that whenever one wanted to regulate behavior for what one considered permissible, non-paternalist reasons (e.g., that the target party's "natural" unregulated conduct would injure the legitimately protected rights and interests of others) it would best to try to shift that behavior by altering the environments in which the would-be rights violator decided how to act or by subsidizing "better" behavior rather than by engaging in something closer to overtly coercive prohibition or prevention of certain actions.

At the same time, those who suppose people made recalcitrant decisions that went counter to their considered judgment might believe that one should simply stop them from making these decisions, and that if "nudges" (however defined) fail, coercion (however defined) is permissible. In ways I will return to discuss, the choice between "nudges" and coercion seems to depend predominantly on whether the regulator is sure he knows precisely what the "right" form of conduct is for all regulated parties. It might be that soft paternalists are especially likely to be wary of their capacity to discern the regulated parties' stable interests, without regard to the behavioral feedback such wary and uncertain paternalists might value, believing, for instance, that if the regulated parties did not alter their choices even when "nudged" to do so, the "unregulated" choice might be a better one than the regulator initially suspected. (If fatty foods are taxed or made less attractive and eating patterns stay stable, people may like the fatty foods more than we suspected.) It might also be the case that soft paternalists are especially prone to believe that there is no *single* form of desirable target behavior, because something that might be described as deep, abiding, "true" underlying tastes or circumstances are divergent across regulated parties.

But regulators seeking to shift behavior that threatens to cause harms to third parties might also well worry in a somewhat parallel way that they are wrong in their preliminary judgment that the relative burdens to the regulated party are lower than the benefits to others of mandating any particular form of behavior. The fact that a regulated party is willing to persist in doing X though taxed for doing so or turns down a subsidy to do not-X might lead such a partially informed, rather than omniscient, regulator to reassess the costs of regulatory compliance.

Not only might the regulator of third-party harms be *wrong* about what behavior he should target, across the board, such regulators also face the problem of heterogeneous tastes and circumstances. The "optimal sanctions" literature in criminal law is based precisely on the assumption—albeit one I think is often unwarranted—that regulators need to learn when it is that certain violators value the behavior we choose to sanction in the general run of cases more than the costs that it imposes.[31] And to the degree that nudges are more prone to reduce, rather than eliminate, untoward effects on third parties, one can readily picture situations in which it would be helpful to know if merely *lowering* the level of some undesired impact were either sufficient or, to put it precisely the opposite way, of so little moment that further reductions seemed less credibly desirable.

Once more, one could write yet another book on whether the soft paternalist "program" is really analytically coherent. Is it feasible to distinguish between a subject's ends and the means to some set of fixed ends? Can't we always interpret the desire for any particular good or ostensible end-state as an imperfectly understood instrumental means to some further, more profound "higher order" end, whether we thought of that further end as something like "happiness" or "life satisfaction" or "self-realization?" Is it possible to select which of two or more preferences elicited through distinct means, or manifest in distinct choice contexts, should be respected without recourse to some "harder" form of paternalism, in which one judges whether the choice meets some set of interests that is not wholly defined by the agent herself?[32] Even if soft paternalism might be effective in some world in which regulating paternalists were better-than-human, are any regulating parties actually *more* competent than the agent herself to meet the agent's own ends, even if her judgment is indeed badly clouded by biases and her evaluations sensitive to framing and elicitation methods? Or, will all such "alternative" decision makers be even worse, suffering not only from the same judgment biases as the regulated party but from some mix of self-interest and indifference to the affected party's fate?[33] But this will not be that book either, though it will be to some extent the subject of the chapter's last substantive section, in which I argue that the heuristics literature has been, and is likely to be, of little use in resolving the most perplexing question about market regulation. When should we limit consumer options rather than try to "guide" choices among options?

D. INFORMATION REDUCTION, INFORMATION FORM, AND THE F&F SCHOOL

The F&F account of the problems that consumers and workers have in getting what they truly want in markets is, in many senses, a familiar, conventionally political conservative story highlighting *regulatory failure* rather than *market failure*.[34] It is decidedly *not* the case that scholars associated with the F&F school believe that unregulated markets will inexorably permit agents to assess their options in an ideal way, using the simple heuristics that typically "make us smart."[35] As I noted in Chapter One, for instance, Gigerenzer even worried that one of the most basic, and seemingly beloved, fast and frugal heuristics—the recognition heuristic—could be exploited by advertisers who would work to ensure that their product or brand name be merely recognized, understanding that consumers would often falsely infer that recognition correlated with product desirability. But, fundamentally, what F&F-influenced policymakers worry about is that the ostensibly protective regulatory state has swamped consumers with information that is meant to protect them against irrational decisions, but which actually interferes with their natural capacity to gather and use decision-improving information.

One aspect of this argument bears some substantial resemblance to conventional rational choice arguments that consumers may be "overloaded" with information in the sense that it is "costly" to process information and information should not be provided when its marginal value is lower than the costs of processing it.[36] Presumably, within the rational choice paradigm, the marginal value is the increase in the expected value of the choice made with, rather than without, the information.[37] But, of course, F&F theorists have, as I emphasized in Chapter Three, sharply criticized the idea that such "rational search" is plausible, that consumers have the capacity to assess the value of information that they have not yet received, so they are even more wary than the rational choice theorists that information mandates *ever* do any good.

What their argument shares with the conventional rational choice argument is the idea that if regulators simply mandate an unending *increase* in the information that consumers are exposed to, they will not inevitably improve the consumers' actual decision-making capacity. Some of the mandated information will be more expensive to process than it is worth in rational choice terms. And *most* or all will distract or pose barriers that impede subjects' efforts to locate the *best* piece of information, of the sort that "Take the Best" or "Mimic the Neighbor" lexical choosers that F&F theorists extol should seek. Markets would typically generate the single or small number of *useful* cues; meddling regulators are prone to obscure the best cue and induce people to ignore all the information and act as fully ignorant consumers. Perhaps, even worse, people flooded with mandated disclosures might make counterproductive efforts to combine multiple cues, making them vulnerable to the standard "sins" of compensatory decision makers (e.g., overfitting data, attempting to integrate incommensurable values, etc.) Not surprisingly, when Gigerenzer himself most directly addresses the problems that we would expect if regulators mandate the presentation of excess information, he highlights the fact that more information is not simply costly to process (the rational choice theorist's complaint) or likely to be ignored entirely, but that people will make *poorer* decisions when they do process it.[38]

Policy analysts influenced by F&F scholarship further emphasize a point that has also been made, though sometimes with considerably less rigor and enthusiasm, by H&B-influenced scholars. Regulators frequently fail to take adequate account of the *form* in which information is presented, blind to the fact that decision makers (whether consumers, jurors, or voters) are highly competent to process certain forms of information but may have a great deal of difficulty using information presented in other ways. The result of inattention to presentation form is more regulatory failure. At worse, consumers may be swamped with intractable information when, left to their own devices, they would elicit information in usable form. At best, regulators are simply not making things any better because they are mandating disclosure of what is effectively gibberish.

The canonical example, to which I referred in Chapter Four, is that F&F-influenced policymakers urge that most information about risks be presented in frequentist form rather than in percentage or probabilistic terms if we expect people to be able to process the risks they do and do not face.[39] While it appears quite clear from the experimental evidence that subjects simply *mistakenly* overestimate risks by neglecting base-rate information when given probabilistic, rather than frequentist, representations, it is often the case that the decisions made by those exposed to frequencies are different but not necessarily superior to those made by those exposed to probabilities. Thus, for instance, experienced forensic psychologists judge a patient more likely to commit an offense and are markedly less likely to recommend his release when told that "10 of every 100 patients like Mr. Jones are estimated to commit an act of violence" than if told "Patients like Mr. Jones are estimated to have a 10% chance of committing an act of violence."[40] And people—quite mistakenly—believe that a disease that "merely" kills 24.14 percent of the population is not as dangerous as one that kills 1,286 of every 10,000 persons,[41] though it is not clear they do so because they *overestimate* the risks presented in frequency terms or underestimate the risks presented in probabilistic terms. H&B theorists have noted the substantial possibility that exposure to frequencies leads to *overestimation* because of the affect heuristic: When given frequencies, they *picture* a number of actual people committing acts of violence in the first case or dying in the second while, when given probabilistic information, they picture a single person with a relatively low chance of committing an act of violence or dying. The negative affect associated with these images of violent acts and death trigger not clarity but a particularly cautious conduct frame.[42]

There is a host of other statistical inferential errors noted in both H&B and F&F-influenced legal reform literature that occur unless information is more carefully framed for decision makers: For instance, we must be careful to ensure that a judge not infer—easily, though incorrectly—that a particular child was overwhelmingly likely to have been abused when the judge learns that the child has nightmares, just because the judge learns that nearly all abused children have nightmares, unless the judge also is made to realize that most non-abused children have nightmares as well.[43]

In my view, much of the very best work done in the F&F tradition focuses not only on the benefits of frequentist presentation but on ways of increasing statistical literacy generally. Gigerenzer and his colleagues wrote an especially impressive piece on the ways in which patients misunderstand and doctors and pharmaceutical companies both misunderstand and misrepresent health-relevant data. At the same time, they carefully work through both cognitive and affective *reasons* that patients poorly process health data and recommend many shifts in data communication form that would reduce some of the illiteracy.[44] The most basic cognitive problem is the one I have already detailed—an undue reliance on single-event probabilistic presentation will befuddle subjects who are far better at manipulating other forms of data. The affective ones do not seem necessarily to grow from F&F insights. For instance, patients may not be motivated to be statistically literate because the patients trust the doctors as authority figures (of course, trust in authority may be a Take-the-Best heuristic); doctors may be committed to a model of the world in which their job is to understand causes, not chances; and patients may be comforted by certainty, even if it is illusory. Drug companies and, to a lesser extent, physicians, may also have conflicts of interest so that representing information in a fashion that maximizes the chances the patient will make use of their product or service is not necessarily done out of innocent misunderstanding.

But their recommendations for altering information presentation are by no means limited to, though they include, presenting more data in frequentist rather than single-event probabilistic form and in terms of natural frequencies rather than conditional probabilities. The authors also suggest using absolute rather than relative risk rates: Don't tell people that their cancer risk will double if exposed to X but, rather, that it will rise from 1 in 1,000 to 2 in 1,000.[45] They also strongly recommend using mortality rates instead of survival rates. The five-year cancer survival rate for a disease may be a function of how early diagnoses are made—including needless diagnoses in which the benefits of treatment are outweighed by the costs. Thus, for instance, five-year survival rates for prostate cancer increased dramatically when PSA (prostate specific antigen) screening became widespread, but the overall mortality rates for prostate cancer scarcely changed at all.[46] Survival rates are measured from "first diagnosis" and thus include in the pool many people who had non-progressive cancers that would not have killed them even if they had they not been diagnosed. Finally, the authors note that it would be prudent to use certain visual presentations that improve understanding of risk: The cues are generally pictograms that highlight natural frequencies within affected groups."[47]

It is also the case that regulators mandating substantial increases in disclosed information ignore the fact that when one increases the amount of information that must be disclosed (e.g., on a drug warning label), one will likely, however inadvertently, alter the *format* in which the information is presented. Assume manufacturers must, to fit it on a label, present vast quantities of negative information *in small-type laundry list form*. Product risks might be ignored not merely because it is *difficult* (i.e., to use rational choice language, *costly*) to read small print but because small print in and of itself *cues* insignificance for heuristic-using consumers. Such consumers have learned that laundry lists of warnings are of little consequence, in part because they typically contain warnings of events of such low probability that the events are best ignored.[48]

More globally, of course, F&F-influenced theorists are often skeptical that decisions will be guided by assessing the overall value of the decisions, grounded in consideration of information that would be used to help calculate value. Think back to the F&F-influenced arguments about crime reduction in Chapter Six. Just as it might in the eyes of F&F theorists be inefficacious to decrease crime by increasing expected penalties, it might be equally inefficacious to get people to use safer products, or to use them more safely, by increasing the availability of information, even in an effectively presented way, about the adverse impact of what the regulator sees as poorly considered risk taking. To make the analogy clearer, recognize that one can readily construct an argument that even a *well-designed* informational strategy to reduce speeding that presented readily processed, salient information about the shifts in accident risks as drivers sped up on the supposition that the decision about how fast to drive is basically mediated through expected utility analysis might well be ineffectual. It might do far less than a program that simply manipulated the cues that F&F theorists believe *really* impact driving speed, such as changes in road design and road markings that manipulated the perceived sense of how fast one was driving.

Similarly, there may be *no* information-based program that would lead people to take only those medications that are risk justified for them. It might be more sensible, if F&F theorists are right, to figure out broad groups of patient types who should mimic one another's behavior. But if information in the conventional sense is fundamentally irrelevant, it is incumbent upon policymakers to know what conduct is desirable, even in a world of heterogeneity. It is to that problem that I now turn.

E. HETEROGENEITY AND HOMOGENEITY OF TASTES AND CIRCUMSTANCES: HAS THE HEURISTICS LITERATURE CONTRIBUTED TO THE SOLUTION OF THE BASIC PROBLEM?

If consumers had identical tastes, and found themselves in identical circumstances, there would be no interesting problem of consumer choice. In the absence of regulation, there might be reasons that market competition broke down in such a way that consumers did not have the option of receiving the product that maximized net welfare gains (if the best technologically available product for the money could not be produced by an entity with market power). At the same time, it might sometimes be difficult for regulators to discern what the ideal choice would be, and it might also be the case that collective regulatory bodies would deliberately mandate that consumers select a non-ideal option because doing so would further the ends of a party that unduly influenced the regulator. But whatever else is the case, information would not have to be provided or used to permit consumers to make choices that were *locally* ideal. By definitional fiat, the local has been obliterated. So one must always entertain the possibility, at least absent regulatory capture, that it is easier and more straightforward in a world of homogeneity for centralized authorities simply to mandate the optimal product than to increase flows of information since such flows of information would only, at best, if properly processed, permit people to select the same globally optimal mix of product traits that could simply have been mandated.

At the same time, if consumers differ in tastes or circumstances, there will be no single ideal product. Vanilla ice cream is not *better* than chocolate; some people just like it more. Moreover, ice cream generally is not equally dangerous for all consumers, without regard to the consumer's weight, blood lipids, personal and family health history, exercise regimen, and so on. So the initial intuition is that heterogeneity should drive us toward an information-disclosing solution, whether one believes markets will generate optimal information or that information is disclosed in significant part because of regulatory mandates. Each person can then tailor her choices to match both her objective circumstances and subjective attitudes. But the simple dilemma the heuristics literature (of both stripes) has revealed, in quite different ways, is that it is very difficult for people to process information to make choices that permit them to serve their atypical desires or respond to their particular situation.

In the H&B world, this is true, above all, because people will poorly process the information that they are given. To some degree, this is true for reasons that closely echo the reasons that F&F theorists will emphasize: It is difficult to make decisions when one must weigh multiple good and bad traits to make a choice. In this regard, think of the "decision" rules like "elimination by aspects" in H&B theory, first discussed back in Chapter Two. These decision rules are distinct from the proxies for accurate judgment and perception, like availability, that help us form views of the probability of a bad or good outcome-aspect, *prior* to weighing how important the particular outcome-aspect is in evaluating a choice that bundles together a multiplicity of aspects. Most consumer decisions will involve choosing options with multiple attributes, and even if one could discern the expected utility of each attribute, it might be difficult to discern the expected utility of the option.

But what is more striking in H&B theory is that the decision maker will not even be able, even when "informed," to ascertain the expected value of option attributes or features. Even if some sub-set of consumers is especially risk averse or sensitive to a particular form of adverse reaction to a product, those consumers simply will not know what the global risks they face really are or whether they are dealing with a product that is unusually likely to trigger an untoward reaction. Moreover, the "value" of even those end-states that are certain to arise are sensitive to the ways in which the end-states are described and the contexts in which they are selected.

In the F&F world, information may not help those with distinct underlying product tastes because they will process very *little* information and find it difficult to pick out personally relevant information from large masses of information if it is made available. Thus, the consumer with atypical tastes or circumstances will generally not have any way to find out that something meets or fails to meet her special demands.

The H&B-influenced scholar will always be rightly tempted to believe that the choices he thinks are substantively likely to be wrong are a product of error, and he will have little way to discern whether he is confronting error or heterogeneous tastes. The consumer *may* be far more than typically willing to accept risk, but it is difficult to rule out the possibility that he simply does not perceive the risk inherent in the choice he is making. The consumer may *really* want to eat a healthier diet but may make food choices in contexts that unduly push him to eat "poorly," Or he may really love greasy food or rightly believe it poses a trivial risk to him. Will we ever know whether we have "nudged" the consumer *enough*—changed all of the situational, choice-affecting variables that we could and should—as long as he continues to make a choice we think is substantively indefensible? Does H&B theory define anything like boundary conditions to tell us when a choice context is as favorable to the "good" choice as we should expect? Does it define boundary conditions that tell us that the decision maker has truly both understood and translated from abstract knowledge to decision relevant knowledge all of the facts that he would need to be ideally informed?

H&B-influenced theorists have offered some modest suggestions to deal with these difficulties, but even those who have offered the suggestions seem reluctant to put a whole lot of stock in their power. Thus, for instance, Thaler and Sunstein argue that state regulators should not manipulate contexts in ways they would be unwilling to publicize or admit to,[49] but it is not at all clear that the publicity rule is justified. It might require more than regulators should have to do. What if unregulated decisions are a product of unrecognized influences? What if the "power" of the proposed contextual change is eliminated if the consumer is forced to be self-conscious about context? What if the *appropriate* context in which to make certain decisions requires that the person assimilate the decision to certain grotesque outcomes, but no one wants to say that they want to expose consumers to the grotesque? More important, I suspect, it is also not clear that a publicity requirement is especially efficacious in *limiting* the scope of regulation. How much guidance do we get from the publicity requirement in thinking about when we have "nudged" people to properly integrate privately held moral duties to their descendants in making private choices about driving by making gas more expensive or less available, or making driving less convenient?

Think, too, about "neutrality" principles that Thaler and Sunstein also briefly suggest but pretty much instantly disclaim. Such principles ostensibly call on the state to undo the influence of social forces that push in an undesirable direction. As they recognize, how can we imagine what our "neutrally" developed tastes for something like driving really would be? What is the apt level of facilitating driving to *reveal* some true underlying preference that balanced modestly immutable tastes for convenience with equally immutable tastes to "do the right thing?"[50]

The problem is especially acute, as I noted in Chapter Two, if we collectively believe that the consumer "misperceives" the value of end-states, but the problem is acute even in considering factual misperceptions. We could, at least in theory, though rarely in practice, test for the presence of mistaken factual perceptions, including risk perceptions if actual risk is known. The practical difficulty, though, of discerning whether we have adequately countered the problem of, say, misperceiving risk in a particular individual's case, so that we can be sure we are dealing with self-conscious distinctions in risk *proclivity*, seem insuperable. Take for instance, the problem of cigarette smoking. Consumers might be able to give very good information about global risks, and might even *say* that they understand the risks they personally face are identical to the global risks, but they may still suffer from various sorts of optimism bias that make them secretly underestimate personal risks and believe they are atypically immune. Or, conversely, they may overestimate cigarette risks because smoking deaths have been made so socially salient, or because non-smokers may want to believe that they have wiped out a cause of death that looms larger in the mortality risk world than it actually does by taking steps that they control. So in thinking through whether to regulate cigarette consumption by mandate—simply declare that virtually all smokers are misperceiving the cost-benefit ratio rather than manifesting distinct preferences for both the pleasures of smoking and risk tolerance—rather than trying to ensure that each consumer is properly processing information and making distinct choices because of heterogeneity, we will likely learn little on a consumer-by-consumer basis.

Moreover, the "theoretical" problems we noted in looking at how H&B theorists coped with the concept of "mistaken" evaluations—does regret really indicate *error*? can we condemn any evaluation unless it is logically self-contradictory?—recur when we think about policy formation. Once we know not only that consumers will misperceive the risk of, say, cigarette smoking (e.g., they may underestimate risks due to optimism bias or overestimate them due to availability) but also that the degree to which the perceived risk appears tolerably low may depend on whether one is implicitly comparing the risk to the risks that arise from one set of activities (e.g., thrill-seeking dangerous activities, binge drinking) rather than another (e.g., food toxicity), we come to recognize that the *taste* for the purported end-state is context dependent. Having seen that, we must always wonder whether we have presented the choice in the correct context as long as people continue to make a decision that we suspect is not in their "true" interests, as they might be defined by "hard" paternalists. Once more, it will be difficult to tell if we are dealing with genuine, acceptable heterogeneity or whether "underlying" preferences would converge once the decision were framed in the most "clarifying" manner possible.

The F&F scholar will be tempted to present only a single best piece of information that, when push comes to shove, is likely to nudge heavily toward a particular substantive choice or to establish other social cues that push a decision maker in a particular direction (e.g., cues that worked to guide decisions based on the heuristic proclivity for mimicry). Take the instructive work of Fong, Graham and Weil on transparency.[51] Consistent with F&F theory, and with aspects of H&B theory like "elimination by aspects," they noted that consumers were far more able to use information when presented with a single salient piece of information that either summarized other information or presented the most critical piece than when given a boatload of data.

Thus, for instance, rather than demand that a restaurant post a list of all the levels of pathogens discovered in the kitchen or in the food, or even a list of code violations, an effective regulator would demand that restaurants simply post a summary *grade* (e.g., A, B, or C) for "cleanliness." But the first problem is that we would be willing to assign a single grade only on the assumption that consumers are not differentially objectively situated. For example, a single grade could not possibly be appropriate if some patrons are vulnerable to one pathogen rather than another; if we assign a single grade, we presumably believe that consumer circumstances are fundamentally homogenous. Worse, though, *it is implausible that tastes really differ*. Who actually wants to patronize the dirty restaurant, even if the customers could save some amount of money if the restaurant "passed along" the money it saved by avoiding the need for cleanups? Moreover, wouldn't it be difficult to believe confidently that there is true taste heterogeneity even if consumers behaved differently or stated different views about the value of pathogen avoidance when they are given no real information about just how bad the health consequences of pathogens in restaurants really are? If, though, there is neither taste nor circumstantial heterogeneity, why are we using an information strategy at all rather than a more direct conduct-regulatory strategy (shutting down violators, or fining them directly rather than hoping the market will assess lost sales volume pseudo-fines)? The problem is more general. We can typically *select* a single best piece of information only if we know what people truly want or how they respond to distinct objective conditions, and if we can do that, we know what they should select.

If certain strong versions of F&F theory are correct, *additional* information designed to permit atypically situated individuals to tailor decisions to their own circumstances is simply impossible to process. "Additional" information is precisely the type of information that a lexical decision maker cannot use. (Recall Goldstein and Gigerenzer's view of the recognition heuristic, discussed in Chapter Five. In their view, a decision maker simply would not conclude that an unknown state capital is bigger than a recognized small town because recognition is a lexical cue that people will not compensate for.) Thus, if there is a single good cue—this restaurant is, broadly speaking, "dirty" and gets a cleanliness grade of "C" rather than "A"—the decision maker using a non-compensatory method simply would simply not process additional, more locally germane information in deciding whether the restaurant is "clean enough." He could not alter his decision by considering, for example, that the bad grade comes from the presence of a pathogen to which he has developed a certain degree of immunity through frequent prior exposure. Or, to use a more realistic example, if we describe some piece of machinery as "hazardous," the lexical decision maker simply lacks the cognitive capacity to account for the fact that he is a more than typically experienced user of similar machinery, or that he owns protective equipment, or that he uses it in settings in which it has not proven particularly dangerous. In fairness, Gigerenzer at times implies that some consumers will sometimes use not one but several pieces of information, and that consumers are more likely to use fully lexicographic decision making with stopping rules when flooded with information about a large number of product attributes than when asked to consider a small number of attributes.[52] In this discussion, however, I address the implications of F&F literature that expresses a more unambiguous commitment to lexical strategies.

Information provision—rather than mandates—seems viable only if at least one of two conditions obtains. First, people must have genuinely distinct tastes about the end-state that they all perceive using the lexical cue that can be processed, and the lexical cue must not so much trigger *behavior* (as, say, various mimetic heuristics would) as it triggers decision-relevant *perception*. This would permit heterogeneous consumers to act on their tastes. Second, if consumers can easily sort themselves into distinct groups of consumers in distinct circumstances, we could provide members of each group the critical bit of information tailored to their particular circumstance. For instance, there might be a best cue for households with and without young kids present, or a best cue for "experienced" and "inexperienced" users of a particular product.

It is doubtful that either of these conditions will frequently occur. The single best, easily processed cue to judge aspects of product acceptability will almost invariably be a cue that is both heavily normatively loaded and at core conclusory. Recall that we do not simply give a single measurement of one pathogen found in restaurants and hope that consumers use that cue to represent danger level: We give a *grade*. All consumers will react negatively to openly disparaging conclusions and affirmatively to positive ones; at the level of basic approach/avoid reaction to this sort of information, it is hard to see that there will be taste disparities. But they will not be given enough information (because they could not, if F&F theorists are right, process it anyway) to manifest their actual distinctions in taste (e.g., based on the intensity of their reactions to marginal distinctions in danger and to the secondary benefits of tolerating danger). Thus, we would typically see taste disparity where X is marginally more dangerous than Y but also marginally cheaper, and some, but not all consumers, will think that they will tolerate the *particular* increased exposure to risk if it permits them to get more goods generally. Accounting for this sort of taste disparity in making one's choices requires performing precisely the sort of expected value calculations that F&F theorists deny is possible, and that H&B theorists believe will usually be performed poorly. But I am dubious that there are other significant taste disparities in the arenas in which we worry about consumer or worker protection.

At the same time, it is difficult to imagine a world in which people would be *unable* to use compensatory processes to integrate many pieces of information to determine the costs and benefits of using a product but would be able to identify precisely what *sort* of user of a product they are, assuming circumstances differ across persons. This would seem clear except in situations in which there are very few, and very easily labeled and understood, sources of circumstantial heterogeneity. We definitely observe some such situations; for instance, we purvey both child-proof and. non-child-proof aspirin bottles on the assumption that the consumer knows which sort of household he or she heads. But strategies of this sort are grounded in the supposition that there are relatively few distinctions in circumstantial vulnerability across households, that risk from a certain cause is more binary than continuous. In fact, though, this notion is almost surely false on the bulk of occasions; consumers are typically distinctly situated along far more complex and continuous dimensions.

Think, for instance, of people trying to pick an "ideal" retirement savings portfolio. Not only is it difficult to represent any critical features of a fund with a single best cue, it would be difficult to find a single best cue for a discrete series of differentially situated consumers. Even ignoring what could be thought of as distinctions in "taste" for risk, consumers are differentially situated in a host of objective ways that are by no means dichotomous. They are not either vulnerable or invulnerable to liquidity crises but vary a good deal in subtle ways about what they might be unable to do if forced to sell assets that fluctuate in value, and what the likelihood of doing that at various points would be if their retirement savings happen to be held in distinct forms (bonds, bond funds, stocks, stock funds, CDs, etc.). They do not either care or not care about tax consequences when they ultimately distribute what they have invested, but will face, and might predict they will face, distinct, continuous marginal tax rates. Similarly, when people choose whether or not to annuitize past savings, they do not either have or lack private information about projected mortality relative to general mortality expectations; they have more or less such private information. But if they do not fall into a small and obvious set handful of salient categories, tailoring lexical informational strategies for sub-groups is simply not possible.

F. CONCLUSION

Policymakers influenced by the H&B school have almost surely been more sensitive to the problem of market failure than those rational choice theorists who believed that market actors would—unless atypically cognitively impaired or especially emotionally labile—be able to make self-regarding, prudent choices if information were available. In thinking about consumer decision making, they have worried both about problems of factual misperception—most particularly misperception of risk—and frame-dependent elicitation of preferences for end-states. At times, these arguments can merge to a considerable degree. When a consumer prefers some Action A that results in the near-elimination of one of two risks rather than some Action B that results in the reduction of both, even though she faces identical aggregate risk in each case, it is possible to believe that she has misperceived the aggregate risks of Actions A or B or that she "prefers" to eliminate sub-risks than to reduce aggregate risk. This may be the case even though the idea that one is "eliminating" a sub-risk is merely a way of framing the ends achieved through Action A, or eliciting preferences about those ends. At the same time, H&B-influenced policymakers believe that markets might fail in the sense that even informed actors will irrationally misevaluate the performance and virtues of members of "outsider" groups—discrimination will be stable even in competitive markets with full information—because stereotyping is a typical System One, cognitively easy method of drawing rough and ready factual conclusions. (In "fast and frugal" terms, both preferences for, and hasty and easy categorization of, "insiders" is adaptive, not just responsive to cognitive overload.)

H&B-influenced policymakers have tended to push programs that are described as "libertarian paternalist" or "asymmetrically paternalist." The interventions they recommend are meant to interfere with a subject's immediate "liberty" but not her autonomy, the manifestation of her considered second-order preferences. The interventions are also meant to permit subjects who have atypical tastes to manifest those tastes, in ways that mandates would not, while "nudging" those who have made a certain choice because it was contextually easy or a natural product of a particular sort of mistaken construal of facts to shift behavior. For a variety of reasons, I remain skeptical that H&B-influenced theorists have really resolved the question of whether we can distinguish those with atypical tastes from those who are merely mistaken, sorting them out through policy instruments that interfere with only the latter group. At some level, there is no good solution to the problem that those who believe a decision is "substantively bad" for more and more subjects will inevitably be skeptical that the decision has been made in an acceptable context, by people who are truly able to process available information about facts; such people will always want to "nudge" *more*.

Policymakers influenced by F&F theory have emphasized, to a much greater extent, that typical disclosure policies are misguided, if intended to permit subjects to meet their considered ends better. While it is both possible and desirable to improve the *form* in which information is presented—taking advantage of our natural capacities to deal with some sorts of information (e.g., risks represented in natural frequencies) while not subjecting us to information we are not naturally able to process (e.g., risks presented in terms of single-event probabilities), increasing the *amount* of information that consumers receive is generally counterproductive. This is true not mainly in the sense that rational choice theorists have highlighted—that we might get overloaded with information, and that it is never worthwhile for people to expend the time and psychic energy processing information unless the expected gains from processing it outweigh the costs. Instead, it is true because the extra information might worsen decision making. It might "crowd out" the search for a single best lexical cue that decision makers would ordinarily use or it might lead to efforts to incorporate the multicue menu, creating such problems as overfitting regressions or attempting to weigh together what should remain fundamentally incommensurable values.

However, the commitment to the notion that consumers are lexical thinkers poses a problem for F&F-influenced policymakers. If we know toward which lexical cue to direct consumers to use, why don't we just mandate the decision that those processing the single cue will make? Obviously, consumers *could* differ only in tastes, and evaluate the fact that the "best" cue directed them toward differently, but there are innumerable situations in which tastes won't be differentiated at the level of reactions to a single best cue but only in making trade-off judgments among multiple cues. Obviously, too, consumers could be in distinct *circumstances* (e.g., some have kids at home who need products that are harder to access, some are more experienced and safe users of machinery), and it would be apt to make different choices on that account alone. Once more, though, it is not clear that F&F-influenced policymakers have thought much about, or could solve, the question of whether the sorts of lexical decision makers they posit could "sort" themselves into apt groupings, each of which received its own, appropriate lexical cue. If, for instance, F&F heuristic users know to mimic some group 1 that is "more like them" than some group 2, are they making use of a non-heuristic capacity to assign themselves to an apt group, a capacity that relies on making judgments not especially dissimilar from those that rational choice theorists posit?

The problem, then, of "applying" basic conceptions about cognition to consumer regulation is not merely the problem we saw in thinking about criminal punishment in Chapter Six—that one cannot induce much about expected behavioral reactions to states of the world based solely on theory—but that neither theory about the nature of heuristic reasoning has yet done much to help solve the most basic problem in thinking about consumer "error." When can we trust that we can help consumers correct their "errors" and then make plural choices based on their inevitable diversity of circumstances and desires? And when do we worry that "deviant" choices remain a product of mistake, so that we despair of allowing consumers to choose, rather than mandating outcomes explicitly, or strongly directing them by disclosing only information that will strongly push consumers in a particular direction?

8

COGNITION AND VALUE INCOMMENSURABILITY

A. THE INCOMMENSURABILITY DEBATE: ITS BASIC CONTOURS AND BASIC CONNECTIONS TO THEORIES OF COGNITION

Determining what we mean when we say that values are incommensurable is no easy task.[1] Very broadly speaking, the value of two action-options or end-states could be deemed commensurable only if their values could be reduced (comfortably? practically?) to a single, exhaustive common measure. For example, if values were commensurable in this way, we might comprehensively evaluate each end-state in terms of the number of "utils" each outcome produces or in terms of the dollars we would pay to achieve the end-state, or have to be paid to forego it. Alternatively, the worth of distinct end-states could be deemed commensurable if their values, however measured, simply were *comparable*. Values would be deemed incomparable if and only if the bottom-line value of one option is not greater, lower, or the same as the value of the alternative option. Most, but not all, legal theorists who have addressed issues of incommensurability—both those who believe incommensurability is a genuine issue and those more dubious of that claim—have assumed that values are commensurable as long as they are comparable. Those who believe in value commensurability do not generally demand evaluation in terms of a single metric.[2]

Some argue that if options were commensurable in the first sense, we would always be able to make cardinal judgments about value while comparability requires only the capacity to make ordinal judgments. I am not convinced that is correct. It seems eminently possible that one could rank-order options along a single, determinative dimension without having the capacity to make cardinal judgments (e.g., one might rank-order which basketball player on a team of small, finite size is "better" in terms of a single metric, her capacity to increase the probability her team will win compared to how the team will do if she is missing) without purporting to know how *much* better a ballplayer is. The failure to make cardinal judgments need not arise from the barriers to combining "scores" across difficult-to-reduce dimensions (e.g., how important, in judging a basketball player's talent, should we consider grace, or the ability to do the spectacular, or the ability to avoid mistakes, or the capacity to maximize performance when game situations are most tense). It can simply come from the incapacity to establish a weighted, calibrated scale for a single virtue. While one can inevitably *infer* something quite like a cardinal scale if asked to make an ordinal ranking of a large or near-infinite number of cases, cardinal judgments are not guaranteed in the first instance.

Very broadly speaking, too, claims that we should recognize the incommensurability of values can be treated as either normative or descriptive. The basic *normative* argument is that any efforts by individuals and/or by collective decision makers either to comprehend the value of all options by reference to a single metric or to choose between options by "comparing their values" are, even if possible, destructive or harmful in some fashion. Such efforts might compromise our capacity to appreciate the true virtues of an end-state (e.g., appreciating the natural world with appropriate awe, preserving an important personal relationship). By reducing the process of considering the value of an end-state to assigning a single value number to its maintenance or sustenance—even if the "value" is merely the one that is no more than logically inherent if we demand comparability (i.e., "more worthy of being chosen, all things considered")—one may lose focus of its unique qualities and the particular end-specific modes one must use to appreciate and engage it.

Furthermore, efforts to make evaluative judgments by this method might also systematically distort the factors one brings to bear on bottom-line comparative judgments, even assuming such judgments must sometimes be made. For example, we might simply tend to omit certain positive or negative features of an action if we tried to express the virtues and flaws of the action in terms of its monetized costs and benefits. If asked, or forced, to quantify in this fashion, we might attend only to what is most easily quantified or to traits in which quantitative judgments are most readily explained or justified.[3]

The basic *descriptive* argument is that, as a matter of fact, people do not make at least some class of choices either by evaluating each option in term of some common metric or by comparing the "value" of options. Instead, they use some other method. Conventionally, philosophers who have emphasized either the ubiquity or importance of making judgments in situations in which values are incommensurable stress that people have the capacity to use "practical reason" when they need to make choices because they simply cannot achieve *all* of their goals. For example, they may choose in such a way that they express certain commitments or self-conceptions through their choice. Practical reason, though, appears to demand high-order cognition, even if it does not require high-order conventional expected value calculation.

The most central issue I want to consider throughout this chapter is whether we would be prone to both reformulate the traditional *descriptive* arguments about incommensurability, and perhaps find them more plausible, if we were convinced that the more modular views of cognition were correct. Such views are associated above all with the "massive modularity" (MM) school I discussed in Chapter Three but to a lesser extent with the "fast and frugal" (F&F) school more generally.[4] Scholars associated with the F&F school have definitely hinted, albeit briefly, that they strongly believe that values are incommensurable,[5] but they have not done much to specify the connections I draw between their views of cognition and the claim that values are incommensurable, in one or another sense.

As a preliminary approximation, the descriptive argument that modularists would be drawn to simply flips the conventional skepticism that rational choice scholars have expressed towards claims of incommensurability. In the final analysis, the rat-choice theorists' claim is that the value of end-state options *must* be comparable. We "know" this to be the case because we seem to be able to choose between options when we have to and can do so without merely flipping coins or feeling like we have behaved senselessly. Thus, they argue, we obviously *must* be able to compare the overall attractiveness of options.

What the modularists would say instead is that values *cannot possibly* be commensurable. Our responses to the cues that trigger judgment, emotion, and action are always incredibly localized, mandatory responses to delimited cues. They are not derived from any top-down calculating process in which we weigh all features of an action or end-state. Since the brain is not best seen as a general calculating machine but a collection of a large number of narrow problem-solving algorithms, we cannot act by deducing an evaluation from any sort of all-things-considered judgment of end-states or action-options. Instead, modularists would claim, our responses to inputs are domain specific, mandatory responses to the presence of some small number of particular cues.

Thus, for instance, we may well, given this sort of conception of cognition and judgment, determine what obligations we have to our friends in a distinct module from the module in which we figure out the precautions we believe we must take when we are at risk of being harmed. So if and when a rare clash arises between fulfilling a modularly perceived obligation to a friend and taking on problematic risk, we must inevitably be left with two wholly separate domain-specific reactions. Each is responsive to the small number of cues that trigger each reaction (e.g., to help the friend, to avoid the risk) that are generated through cognitive systems that are essentially separate. This will be true even if the responses generated by each "module" are actually incompatible on the particular occasion (i.e., we cannot, as a matter of fact, both help the friend and avoid the risk). The domain-specific module that tells us whether it is appropriate to help the friend is, in this view, informationally encapsulated and may simply not process information about risks that happen to be associated with meeting the demands of friendship, at least as long as trade-offs in these decision spaces are so uncommon that each "module" need not ordinarily process this type of generally extraneous information in generating an appropriate reaction.

Alternatively, one could argue, following the teachings of F&F theory more closely than those of the MM school, that in situations in which people face unavoidable choices in which some desired outcome must be sacrificed or some undesired outcome accepted, they may have the *capacity* to cognize factors relevant to the choice in a somewhat "generalist" brain. They may, though, nonetheless use a lexical decision-making rule that permits them to decide how to act by relying on a single discriminating cue rather than making an all-things-considered judgment of the comparative virtues and flaws of each option.

In this regard, there might be relatively little distance—descriptively—between F&F theory and Tversky's theory of "elimination by aspects" (EBA) that I discussed in Chapter Two. Two qualifications, though: First, Tversky emphasized the strong possibility that the use of an EBA procedure could be irrational, could preclude the decision maker from reaching the best judgment, while F&F theorists typically emphasize the *virtues* of lexical decision making. Second, as I noted in Chapter Two, I am not at all convinced that decision makers in fact regularly use EBA or any other lexical method. I also suspect that the domains in which EBA will be used are themselves established by a prior non-lexical cognitive process in which the subject determines, given particular facts about the particular options he is selecting among, whether a cue is likely or not be a cue that discriminates adequately in terms of expected utility.

To get back to the many ways in which these points, or variants of them, play out in thinking about incommensurability, I must trace some of the conventional depictions of the nature of value incommensurability. Along the way, I try to indicate the significant ways in which adopting either more modular or more lexical views of cognition might impact our understanding of each sort of claim, and, to a lesser extent, explain why the skepticism I have generally exhibited toward these views of cognition might make us suspicious of this revisionist view of incommensurability. Finally, I try to come to terms with a distinction that has attracted little attention in the existing literature: Is it best to think of values as incommensurable when decision makers *subjectively experience* choices as ungrounded in any kind of conventional rat-choice form of evaluation and comparison? Or, is it better to think of incommensurability as an *objective* feature of the *interaction* between environment and brain? Think in this regard of describing a sub-atomic particle as "invisible." It is profitably thought of as invisible in the sense that, given its objective size, our eyes and brains lack the visual perception equipment to see it. In the same way, it might be apt to describe a decision to do X rather than Y as requiring us to compare incommensurable options if the environmental cues that would trigger X are processed separately from the environmental cues that trigger Y and the means of resolving the clash in situations in which both X and Y are triggered is *not* by a mental mechanism that translates the value of each option into some third action-triggering cue (e.g., X generates more utility, X is "better.")

B. COMMENSURABILITY AS REDUCTIONISM TO SINGLE METRICS

Values would most obviously be commensurable if we evaluated all end-states in terms of a single metric; most obviously, but not necessarily, the single metric would be something like the "utility" the end-state generated. We might, if values are commensurable, gain or lose things like utility when we achieved distinct end-states for radically different *reasons*. The reasons we evaluate a massage as a positive experience might be readily differentiable from the reasons we judge working through a difficult text or giving blood as positive, and we might even describe distinct forms of "pleasure" or "satisfaction" in different ways. Still, in the final analysis, we could readily compare the experiences because our ultimate judgment about the experience would be both felt and expressed in a single term, its contribution to utility.

In my view, the most telling of the many traditional arguments that not all values are descriptively commensurable in this way is that we experience some, but not all, choices as "tragic." Choices subjectively "feel" tragic in the sense that there are times in which we feel an irreducible sense of loss when we have to choose some Option X over some Option Y, even if we think the bottom-line decision correct or justifiable.[6] If all choices were really experienced in terms of the degree to which they contributed or detracted from the achievement of a one-dimensional goal, there would be no such sense of irreducible loss from abandoning Y because all action courses would simply involve the ambition to maximize the achievement of a single end.

Think about choices in which gains and losses *are* clearly thought of one-dimensionally (e.g., choices in which we evaluate outcomes solely in terms of how much money they generate). If we put $1 in a slot machine and the gamble turns out to pay out $100, the decision (a plainly good one, looked at *ex post*) does not give rise to an experience of loss of the dollar we stuck into the machine. We do not think we irreducibly lost something to get something else. We simply *made* $99, net, on balance. The example does not, I think, turn on the truncated temporal frame. If we are evaluating jobs solely in terms of how much income they generate and we give up job Y to take some higher paying job X, we will not feel a sense of loss about abandoning job Y.

If we simply toted up how many "utils" we lost when we sacrificed time with our family compared to the amount we might gain to achieve the utility that we derived from the respect of our peers if we worked longer hours on a common project, we would not feel a sense of irreducible loss from losing time with the family *as long as maximizing utility were our one-dimensional, sole goal.*[7] Instead, if the choice were "correct," we would simply think we had gained some amount of utility, on balance, from taking the overall course of action that we took. The subjective sense that making a "better choice" does not obliterate the losses associated with renouncing the untaken path reflects the fact that the losses are of their own particular sort and are not precisely counterbalanced by gains of a different type. So, in this view, one of the paradigmatically tragic aspects of "Sophie's Choice" is that no matter how much one might "gain" by saving one child, rather than losing both, the loss of the child one chooses to sacrifice cannot be "counterbalanced." The gains are not just weightier versions of the same, negated kinds of outcomes as the losses.

Could we better understand the domain of this variety of incommensurability by, first, attempting to identify choices in which this feeling of "irreducible loss" is present? If it is present whenever we seek goods and avoid "bads" that are not best described as wholly instrumental to further, as-yet unspecified ends, then perhaps the sense of "irreducible loss" comes as much from lingering uncertainty about our ability to evaluate well as it comes from the infelicity of using a single evaluative metric. In this view, the reason we so readily net out money gains and losses is simply that we are for most practical purposes *certain* that having more money is better than having less, and certain whether we have indeed wound up with more. But we are rarely certain that we have gained more "utility"—even if that were the only metric we used to evaluate our experiences—when we achieve certain non-instrumental goals (e.g., we are safer but less stimulated).

In this view, then, we would expect the feeling of irreducible loss to occur most typically, and perhaps even exclusively, when we made "hard calls" rather than simply when we made trade-offs "across domains." Thus, we might not feel the sense of irreducible loss from losing time with the family if we lost rather little time, and the family members seemed to care rather little about our absence because they were all busy too, and the income or prestige gains from work seemed quite high. In this view, then, the sense of "lingering irreducible loss" simply masks rumination over the wisdom of close-call choices, not the fact that the undesirability of losing time with family is processed as a distinct form of undesirable experience.[8]

If, however, this feeling of loss is not merely the way in which we manifest ongoing uncertainty, it would be helpful to understand more about the domains in which the relevant sense of loss persists whenever we sacrifice or trade off achievement of a goal we feel we should seek. Are they, in a cognitive sense, domains that seem more plausibly the subjects of more domain-specific processing? That is, would we expect judgments made about appropriate or obligatory action in the domains in which we experience an irreducible sense of loss when we decide we must sacrifice one goal to meet another to be those judgments that would need to be made relatively quickly and "economically" in a recurring fashion in order to solve commonplace "survival" problems? Are they the problems we would expect to be solved using relatively delimited cue sets to make the judgments? Do we feel an irreducible sense of loss because we have had to act counterheuristically or counterintuitively, given the presence of the delimited cues we would typically use to trigger the action response that we were unable to take in these tragic, necessary trade-off situations?

As dubious as I am generally about domain-specific accounts of cognition, I am more dubious still that subjective feelings of irreducible loss are most typically or strongly felt in relationship to the subset of problems we should believe are most plausibly solved domain specifically. The domains in which those who have written about incommensurability most clearly identify these sorts of irreducible loss reactions hardly seem to be domains in which the "basic choices" are likely to be remitted to plausible domain-specific cognitive modules. This seems to be the case whether they involve choices which lead us to think we have betrayed an important *commitment* to reach another goal (friendship for family, family time for money, religious or patriotic principle for loyalty to a cherished individual) or those that force us to give up one important *selfish life goal* to achieve another (security for adventure, meaningful work for money).

It is hard to imagine the delimited set of cues that we might use to tell us precisely what kinds of acts and feelings of loyalty to friends are demanded in the wide array of situations in which loyalty issues arise, even if we believe that the capacity to develop some more generic "sense of loyalty" played a useful evolutionary role in facilitating exchange or cooperation. It is hard to see that a "loyalty-demanding module" (let alone one that processed delimited cues to direct that one "seeks adventure or novelty" or "meaningful work") would arise in the same way that we might develop more economical, heuristic, quasi-modular mechanisms that trigger recalcitrant fears or phobias when we confront certain limited cues that ordinarily signal danger or toxicity.

Still, it would almost surely be the case that we would more plausibly experience this sort of incommensurability if certain commitments or reactions were "automatic" (mandatory and encapsulated) given the presence of particular cues. The sense of irreducible loss, the feeling that gains in one sphere were somehow orthogoanl to losses in another, would best be described as neither "right" nor "wrong" but merely as inevitable as a reflex reaction, the most paradigmatic instances of modularized processing.

At the same time, it might also help us see some of the difficulties in believing that goods would be commensurable in the sense that people have the capacity to evaluate all options in relationship to a single metric were we to reflect on the fact that single metric reductions often seem pragmatically pointless, almost perversely inane. In this view, recognizing that it would be terribly uninteresting and pointless to compare many end-states across any single dimension reflects the fact that end-states are not naturally or ordinarily reduced to such a single dimension. Thus, the exercise of figuring out whether Michelangelo is a "better artist" than Bach seems like a sophomoric parlor game. It is not a useful or interesting—and hence appropriate—way of thinking about each person's qualities. If this is true, we should look at single metric reductionism merely as one evaluative technique among many that may or may not help achieve some goal. That seems persuasive whether the goal is making interesting, rather than foolish, lists or making certain sorts of choices between action-options that are incompatible.

What is critical to note, however, is that this critique of the descriptive reality of "reductionism" resonates a good deal more in the idea that practical reason is an even richer, more multidimensional cognitive process than the process imagined by the rational choice theorists, who tend to see the preliminary reduction of ends to utility judgments as relatively effortless and choice between evaluated options as easy and mechanical once these preliminary values are assigned. Manipulating *expected* values under conditions of factual uncertainty may be difficult and effortful—hence, in the H&B tradition, frequently performed through simplifying attribute substitution—but judging the attractiveness of known outcomes is usually thought by the rat-choice people to call on easily accessible judgments. Even for the H&B people, who are more prone to think end-state judgments are frame sensitive, there is little sense that the judgments of "utility" of a single aspect of a decision are effortful, given the frame in which they have been presented.[9]

Those who argue that people can use practical reason without being reductionist imply, though, that people will rely even less on modular simplification and softly or massively encapsulated decision making. Making choices that are consistent with our underlying personal commitments or that respect the intrinsic demands of maintaining social practices of a particular form in the ways that Anderson or Raz suggest that we do[10] and should is plainly high-order cognitive work. Finding out thought was more modular, then, would hardly bolster the case that we can choose in the face of incomparable options using this sort of pragmatic, practical reason.

C. TRUMPING RULES

Some writers who describe two values as incommensurable seem to mean simply that subjects either *do* not in a descriptive sense, or sometimes *should* not in a normative one, trade off *any* loss of end-state X for any gain in alternative end-state Y. Any loss of some good or interest X trumps any gain in Y.[11] There is, thus, a lexical decision-making rule. As soon as we determine that X has been compromised by taking some action A, we reject A without attending to any further positive consequences Y that taking step A might produce.

Those who take this position may believe it is, or ought to be, "qualified" in "extraordinary" or "emergency" situations in which foregone gains of Y are truly momentous. Thus, for instance, strong deontological rights theorists who treat respect for individual rights as incommensurate in this way with social welfare gains may argue that rights should be "suspended" in situations in which the refusal to sacrifice individual rights would have truly calamitous results. Hypothetically, then, if the police could avert millions of deaths by engaging in torture that violated the rights of an innocent who possesses "ticking bomb" information—or, to be less dramatic, if a warrantless search of a house might do so—then it might be both factually commonplace and morally permissible to reject the lexical priority of respecting the individual's rights.

This account of incommensurability is fundamentally skew to the basic accounts I offered of the phenomenon at the beginning of the chapter. In this view, it would seem that options X and Y really are wholly comparable and choosing X, or as much X as one can, is simply always *better*. Options could, in fact, be incommensurable in this way, at least in theory, even were they not merely comparable but evaluated in terms of a single metric. However, this type of lexical decision-making process seems less plausible if end-states are evaluated in terms of a quasi-utilitarian metric, given that the marginal utility of additional units of each good is likely to decline. Thus, for instance, it is unlikely that preserving the marginal tree in a virgin growth forest, given a lexical commitment to forest preservation, would generate more utility than gaining the utility derived from the first unit of health care sacrificed by the refusal to sell the tree and spend the money on medicine. *Any* incremental gains along dimension X simply outweigh any gains along dimension Y if this conception is true.[12]

What is most striking, in terms of the alternative accounts of cognition that I have explored throughout the book, is that, for F&F theorists, incommensurability of this sort would be the norm rather than the exception. Thus, we need not seek out the handful of domains socially constructed as "sacred," nor look for domains in which there is some strong ideological commitment to treating the achievement of or respect for a goal as a side constraint[13] in order to find domains in which the achievement of a single goal trumped all other gains.

Instead, we should assume, in F&F theory, that lexical decision making is routine. *Most* binary choices get made by "Taking the Best" reason to choose one action *rather* than another. If we lack the cognitive wherewithal to figure out the gains and losses from each marginal shift in achievement of a goal, we will not typically engage in trade-offs. Action A is chosen over action B simply because it differs in achieving the single most important objective. For instance, a decision set in which one chooses the course of action that leads to complete forest preservation precludes us from assessing the impact of each more localized choice on jobs or housing construction costs. Similarly, the fact that one choice better manifests loyalty to a friend is all we need to know if the others do not do so, even though the paths not chosen may have a host of other virtues.

In this sense, then, the F&F theorists, contrary to their usual claims (and contrary to massive modularists), do not so much present a picture of cognition that would be expected to *create* the *feeling* of incommensurability as they present one that would *eliminate* it. The *subjective feeling* of incommensurability grows out of the inability to make decisions easily or to ignore the cognitions and emotions that were triggered by environmental cues that were superseded by cues that led to the chosen action.

For both the subjects described by massive modularists and those described by rational choice theory, decision makers cannot merely react to the most salient cue and *ignore* all the rest. If using "practical reason" of one form or another, one needs to figure out something far more profound and conventionally deliberative about the meaning of all that is gained and lost when one makes a decision. Anderson's tormented rational decision maker—who has to judge whether she expresses rationally supportable intentions in behaving in particular ways—is anything but a single-cue decision maker. She does not simply trade off risky work for higher wages, because a single dominant fairly generic, easily perceived cue (what must I do to pass my gene line along by making sure I can feed my youngsters?) swamps all other cues. (She also does not ask, like the conventional rat-choice subject, "How much risk am I willing to take on to get each item that we actually get with my extra income?") Instead, she determines that she is obliged to take on certain risks to express her obligation to discharge responsibilities, like family responsibilities.[14] The "massively modularized" thinker does not express "commitments," but she is stuck with a residue of tragically unfulfilled urges, each triggered by the presence of urge-creating domain-specific cues.

At the same time, the granularity problem rears its ugly, and ubiquitous, head once more for those of us skeptical of lexical theories of cognition. We may well have cheated in our example by characterizing the choice as a choice between A (save the trees) and B (increase jobs or build more houses). Even if we really do frequently "Take the Best" and ignore all further cues that must be evaluated and weighed by a generally calculating mind, we still need to *characterize* the options among which we choose. It is hardly clear that there are "natural" bounds to the options.

So if we *first* conceive of the choice as a choice between sacrificing 25 percent of one particular forest, posing a mere 0.000001 percent risk of the substantial deforestation, species extinction, or destruction of habitat for all other life forms in the area and characterize the other choice in any number of glowing ways (e.g., in terms of employment opportunities for an impoverished group that will not have to disperse and lose their culture in order to seek jobs in nearby cities), then the "Best" decision-impelling cue may be quite different than it would appear to be if the choice was between "showing respect for nature" and "mere material goods." We can imagine that a single cue—will any living being immediately perish as a result of my action if I do B rather than A?—is the best single cue to sort out whether action A or B is compulsory in a world in which demands to "respect nature" have lexical priority over "seeking material goods." But even that cue would be useless in calculating how to solve the problem if trade-offs were built into the problem's initial formulation.

More generally, it is often difficult to tell whether theorists who claim to be devoted to incommensurability maintain this devotion only by utilizing seemingly lexical decision rules whose precise parameters are extraordinarily sensitive to the characterization of the problem. I focused on this same problem in the discussion in Chapter Six on criminal punishment, noting the extent to which the notion that the use of fast and frugal heuristics (like "Take the Best," like "Imitate Thy Neighbor") may *seem* to preclude the need for either metrics or complex comparability judgments but does so only by picking one of many plausible characterizations of the choice situation.

But look at a decidedly non-heuristic view of how people should resolve choices between "incomparable" options. Anderson suggests we do and ought to use a certain sort of pragmatic reasoning. I think we see in her work the same problem of manipulating choice characterization, albeit in a slightly different form, that we see in F&F theory. Anderson, I think, often eliminates seeming conflicts by taking advantage of the inexorable flexibility we have in describing the virtues and vices of seemingly incompatible options. She does this in much the same way as F&F theorists, who find a single best cue to resolve choices by artificially characterizing the problem in a fashion that allows us to distinguish two options along a salient dimension when the problems could be as readily seen in a way that does not allow them to be differentiated along that dimension. (To put this point in one of its most extreme forms, most choices first painted as involving choices between, say, safety and material goods could readily be reframed as choices between two methods of increasing mortality and morbidity outcomes, since saving health-protecting resources in domain X always permits the resources to be deployed to protect health in some domain Y. Or lexical rules to choose safety over all else can be seen as artifacts of forcing binary choice frames that are never applied across the board to all consumption domains, even though there is a safety dimension to almost all consumption choices.)

Here is how it plays out in Anderson's work. Anderson describes a person seemingly unable to compare her obligations to keep a promise to see a friend when she discovers she needs to break the date to see her sick mother. Such a person may, following Anderson, simply obliterate the enduring sense of conflict and uncertainty. She may do so by deciding (at least in one hypothetical version of how Anderson's practical reasoners resolve the conflict) that there is no real friendship obligation since a "true" non-neurotic friend would not really expect you to put a mere date ahead of a powerful family obligation. Alternatively, she may decide that the time or resources spent with the dying parent would be worthless or self-indulgent.[15]

In a sense, ostensible lexicality (or to put it in Anderson's terms, a hierarchical set of commitments that are triggered once one understands what values one expresses by making one choice rather than another)[16] is preserved by characterizing the dominant cue in a fashion that masks the tragic trade-offs. At the same time, pragmatic practical reason can seemingly dispense with comparisons by altering the operative depiction of the seemingly outweighed option, embedding its negative features in its basic description in such a way that it need not really be rejected or outweighed, rather than dismissed as utterly without virtues. I am dubious that we have true trumping rules if we seem to achieve the capacity to use them only on the assumption that when we confront cues that would cause us to think there is true conflict in our goals, we simply cannot process those discordant cues. Similarly, I am skeptical that we have true trumping rules or considered hierarchical commitments if all the allegedly trumped options are first reformulated or re-depicted as intrinsically unappealing (rather than seen as appealing but outweighed or compared unfavorably to chosen options) whenever achieving them in fact compromises some superior interest.

D. INCOMPARABILITY: OPTIONS ARE NEITHER EQUAL NOR UNEQUAL IN VALUE

- *Raz's basic arguments and its problems*

If it were the case that one option was not superior to, inferior to, or the same as another, it would seem that they must be skew to one another, to be deeply incomparable. Raz offered a forceful argument that such incomparable option sets are widespread. There are many situations, he claims, in which it is unclear whether an option with a certain set of virtues (e.g., a job as a lawyer that guarantees a certain sort of security, income, etc.) is better or worse than an option with very different sorts of virtues (e.g., a job as a concert musician, which is insecure but more expressive and exciting). Yet the fact that neither option seems better than the other does not seem to make them equal in value. If, Raz says, they were truly equal in value, an improvement in one option (e.g., the same job as a lawyer with a 10 percent raise in salary) would plainly make that option superior since the lawyer-job-with-a-raise would demonstrably be better than the initial lawyer job, which was already purportedly tied with the musician job.[17]

Like many other commentators, I ultimately find this argument unpersuasive and a bit puzzling. The situation he accurately describes seems a product of epistemological uncertainty rather than value incommensurability. Imagine that I am comparing two persons across what is unambiguously a single, measurable, transparently commensurable metric; I am trying to assess which one is heavier. Imagine, too, that I do not have much information about each person's precise weight. (There is no scale onhand, so I am just eyeballing.) I might say that, as best as I can discern, X is not heavier than Y, nor is Y heavier than X. At the same time, I am by no means sure they are equal in weight. If I were told the next day that X had gained four pounds overnight and Y's weight was unchanged, I *still* wouldn't be able to say that X is heavier. Obviously, if I had been *sure* they were equal in weight on day one, I would be sure X was heavier on the second day.[18] And just as I *might* be willing to say that X is heavier if told he had gained 100 pounds, I might be able to say that the supposedly incomparable jobs of lawyer and musician were now readily compared if the lawyer's salary jumped not by 10 percent but by 500 percent.[19]

Chang argues that two options may simply be roughly "on a par" with one another.[20] To put this point in terms that make the factual uncertainty analogy more salient, the value of each option is best thought of as a blurry value where one's best guess of value is surrounded by a broad confidence interval, just as eyeball estimates of weight are not truly pinpoint numbers but rough estimates surrounded by a confidence interval. If options are "on a par" in this way, all we must do when we learn that the value of only one of the options has improved is think it more likely that we would prefer it than we did before, not that we must now prefer it with certainty when we had previously been in the broad range of equipoise. Unless there are different sorts of reasons to move out of ignorance-based equipoise when one learns that X has gained a bit of weight than there are to move out of ignorance-based equipoise when one learns that the value of an option has improved slightly, then it does not seem that value incomparability is doing any work here in helping us understand how options can be neither unequal nor equal.

- *Incomparable reactions and their relationship to valuation*

So claims about incomparability must ultimately involve a different sort of assertion about how we make choices when the positive and negative reactions we have to outcomes seem difficult to compare, because each reaction resonates in a wholly distinct "conception" of the good and the bad. ("Conception" is in scare quotes precisely because it is possible for modularists to reinterpret the "sensation" of this sort of incomparability not in terms of distinct *ideas*, derived from high-order cognition, about the meaning of distinct good and bad outcomes, but as simply distinct action-impelling reactions triggered in the relevant portion of the brain by a delimited set of input cues.)

It seems helpful in this regard to begin by considering the evaluation of options that are not the object of choice. There are many abstract comparisons, outside the domain of forced choices between options, in which we would seem confused or puzzled were we to call an item or outcome or virtue better, worse, or equal to another. It seems hopeless to say, for instance, that Danielle's bravery is "better" than Emma's perseverance or Fiona's wit or Gail's kindness.

But it might well be that those who claim values are comparable merely mean that when it is *useful* to compare them—when one has to pursue one end rather than another, reward one party rather than another—one has a *basis* to do so. For this purpose, the basis cannot be an arbitrary device like coin flipping or even what Raz refers to as an exercise of "the will."[21] One must make the choice using a method that at core draws on making an overall judgment of the quality of outcomes, even if the quality judgment is multifaceted and cannot be reduced to a single dimension. If we are doing this, it suggests that all virtues have some traits of commodities, even if they need not be bought or sold for material goods or money. We trade off losses in one space for gains in another. There would appear to me to be at least three ways of criticizing this form of comparability claim, the third of which draws most heavily on the view that cognition is substantially modularized.

- *Criticizing comparability: trading devalues or destroys the traded good*

The first criticism of the idea that all "virtues" can be evaluated relative to other virtues, and thus rationally traded, strikes me as powerful but quite limited in scope. It is derived from a broader claim—closer to the next claim, one I explore in more depth—that asserts that one will, in essence, obliterate an end (or to put it less melodramatically, radically alter the meaning of the end or the social practice of valuing it in a particular way) if we think of it as comparable in terms of overall quality to some other end. My view is that there are a small handful of cases in which the idea that we could compare two states, and then trade them off for one another, selecting the higher valued end, sacrificing a lower loss of value, would simply be impossible given existing social practices.

Thus, for instance, it may well be paradoxical to say that you could be paid to believe an argument that you found unconvincing, even if you could readily be paid to *act* as if you had been convinced. Given our understanding of what it means to be convinced by an argument, one cannot "choose" to be convinced simply because the value of remaining unconvinced is lower than the value of some other good one could gain if one could be convinced. We cannot trade away state X (remaining unconvinced) for state Y (more money) because what it would mean to trade away the state of being unconvinced (one can only truly stop being unconvinced by becoming convinced) would destroy the good (being convinced) that the buyer had ostensibly acquired. Were we to compare the value of having more money with the value of believing only those things we were actually convinced were true, it would not help us select an option course because in trying to do so we would destroy the meaning of one of the options. We could no longer maintain, given trades, the practice of really "being convinced."

Naturally, people differ about the institutions or end-states that could not survive being "chosen" or "rejected" on the basis of this kind of comparative evaluation. But it is commonplace to believe that the set of such states is not empty. Many would argue, for instance, that one cannot be truly in love, as love is understood in our culture, simply because one gets something else that is valuable by so being, whether that something is money, security, or power.

- *Criticizing comparability: The fragility of the non-commodity form*

There is an analytically separate, but closely related, set of arguments, most strongly associated in the legal academy with Radin's claims that treating *instances* of action-outcomes as commodities will destroy non-commodity relationships with the outcome because the non-commodity relationship is "fragile."[22] Thus, in this regard, one could imagine that while it is *possible* to trade sex for money, doing so will compromise the long-term ability to have a non-instrumental relationship to sexuality.

This "fragility" argument and arguments that certain goods cannot be traded and maintain their identity or integrity are hardly identical but bear some strong resemblance. They are similar in the sense that the prelude to trading sex for money is to compare the value of the money with the disvalue of the otherwise-unwanted sex, and doing that may alter the meaning of sex. The claim that the two arguments are identical would go something like this. Sex—like love or being convinced—is something that belongs in the category of goods that simply cannot be traded. What one trades for money is not "really" sex but certain physical acts that resemble sexual acts, just as what one trades for money is not "really" being convinced but acting convinced. Radin is making an *additional* argument here, though, about why such trades are bothersome. Even if one *could* trade something that could reasonably be described as "real" sex for money or, conversely, even if the sex that was traded for money were not "real," that would not be her main concern. Her main concern would be that sex that was *not* explicitly traded for money would be changed by the fact that such trades occurred.

(She is presumably interested both in the non-exchange sex that those, like prostitutes, have when not doing sex work, and the sex that those who never exchange sex explicitly have in the course of their relationships, being aware of the existence of sexual trades that others make.)

It appears to be an empirical argument—not surprisingly, one not especially informed by empirical data—whether and where attitudes about particular end-states are fragile in the feared way. Many argue that selling babies or sex will alter our ability to relate to children or sexuality in a certain way; few argue that the existence of professional sports will destroy either the professional athlete's intrinsic appreciation of playing or the appreciation that non-professionals have for playing sports.[23] Radin's argument, on balance, appears more like what I referred to as a normative argument against *choosing* commensurability—one *should* not compare the value of money with the "disvalue" of otherwise-unwanted sex—rather than a descriptive argument that the attempt to do so is incompatible with maintaining the choice set in its initially proposed form. Thus, normatively, it might be *bad* to act as if one were convinced if paid to do so (e.g., because it would lead us to change our practices of actually being convinced in undesirable ways), but what I take to be the more powerful descriptive argument is that one simply *cannot* actually be convinced because one has been paid to. To restore parity between the arguments, one must believe that sold sex is simply different than unsold sex, and that one really cannot sell the distinctive end-state of unsold sex. That argument might seem even more plausible in relationship to love.

- *Criticizing comparability: tyranny and inapt reasons*

Walzer argued in *Spheres of Justice* that many socially significant goods *should* be distributed only on the basis of appropriate reasons. The essence of tyranny, in Walzer's view, is that those who possess some socially valued virtue or good attempt to gain dominance outside the sphere in which it is apt that they achieve dominance given their possession of the good or trait. Someone possessing one good or virtue G tries to convert it to get some good H though having G is not the apt basis for getting H. For instance, the proper basis for distributing political power is not birth or money but the capacity to represent and lead; the apt basis for distributing medical care is medical need, not money or political power, or the virtues that appropriately give rise to political power.[24]

Arguments like those made by Walzer have been roundly criticized as unduly nominalistic. As Nozick noted, even if one affirmed the notion that the appropriate reason to distribute "doctoring" services was to meet medical needs, why couldn't one become a "schmoctor" whose goal was to distribute not simply to the sick but to those sick people who could pay for her services?[25] If making a judgment that the pleasures of taking money for providing health care services outweighs the satisfaction of meeting medical need destroys *one* understanding of what it is to be a doctor, so be it: It simply instantiates a new relationship to the concrete actions (performing surgery, doing a medical exam) in which people engage.

The standard Walzerian response to the nominalism critique is that *within a culture*, there *are* apt reasons to make particular decisions and firm understandings of particular practices. As a matter of cultural practice, there cannot be trade-offs across all domains. The problem with this response is that it generally strips Walzer's argument of critical bite. It is difficult to say that we ever *improperly* make trades across domains if we are *able* to do so, because if we are, it appears compatible with the available cultural understandings of what goods are comparable and can be traded off. In a sense, what is striking then about the impossibility of "being paid to be convinced" is that when trade-offs simply *cannot* be made within the culture, as in this case, there need be no normative or critical argument to extend the domain of incommensurability. Instead, incommensurability is self-enforcing. But where social practice makes trade-offs *possible*, the argument that they are *impermissible*—that our culture somehow separates the spheres to such an extent that we cannot envision the maintenance of an option once it is subject to trade-off—seems to fade away.

It is hard for me to tell if there is a "cognitive" argument that modularists would make that would echo the "cultural" argument in Walzer. Are there domains so separate that efforts to think about comparisons across the domains renders thought within and about one conventional domain incoherent or infeasible? Would we, for instance, no longer be thinking about "friendship," using the cognitive resources that process friendship-related cues, once we suppressed the cue-triggered demands of friendship to meet some other goal? And, for the modularist, what "module" (non-generalist part of the mind) might suppress the "demands" of friendship in the presence of some competing, more urgent action demand?

- *Commitment, not comparison*

The second, broad argument that options may be incomparable is that the mechanisms we use to make choices in what amount to forced-choice situations—situations in which we simply cannot achieve all the ends we would want to achieve—do not involve choosing based on relative valuation as much as they express commitments to a particular life plan or view of the end-states that we must embrace or defer. An end-state is not less *valuable*, in this sense, simply because seeking an alternative is more urgent, pressing, or necessary to pursue in order to maintain one's integrity of viewpoint, to take action that meets one's rationally considered intentions. It is simply the case that pursuing it is less consistent with becoming the self one wants to be or with demonstrating some particular understanding of the meaning of all the feasible alternatives.[26]

This view of incommensurability is based on a particular account of reason and cognition. For those adopting this perspective, there is a fairly bright line, at least conceptually, between unreflective mere appetites and value judgments that are grounded in attitudes developed by reflecting on whether the value judgment is one we would rationally endorse. Appetites or raw tastes, such as the "desire" to smoke, are both impervious to reasoned reflection (e.g., data on the dangers of tobacco) and, perhaps more important for these purposes, both weighted in intensity and ultimately prone to be maximized.[27] Value judgments are not only the outcome of a reflective, critical process but tend to be distributed rather than maximized. Thus, for example, we accord respect, admiration, or love to those who are appropriately respected, admired, or loved, given our reflections about the right bases for according these value judgments, but we do not seek to maximize the amount of respect we give, or think that giving more in one appropriate setting leaves less available for others.[28]

I find it extraordinarily difficult to work through the degree to which these expressive theories of choice are intended at least in part as arguments against an idea on which rational choice theorists fixate: It is irrational to change one's trade-off structure in situations in which trade-offs are explicit in certain ways (that make the expressive consequences of choice transparent) rather than implicit (so that the choice "expresses" nothing, because the "choice" is invisible). For conventional rational choice theorists, it is the height of irrationality that we readily trade off both the certain loss of statistical lives of others and increases in risk of premature death for ourselves for modest increases in access to material goods, but put a much higher value on saving known lives. One might even argue that we sometimes put a near infinite value on saving identifiably jeopardized individuals, in the sense that we may spend until incremental spending does no good. In this sense, we express a "commitment" to the incomparable value of life, but only when have framed a problem as involving explicit trade-offs.[29]

More generally, I suspect, but cannot demonstrate, that it would be possible for H&B researchers to treat many conventional instances of subjectively experienced incommensurability as arising in situations in which one action-course is readily evaluated and the other is not. That is, there is some easy way of assessing the probabilities of various outcomes associated with one possible action, whether that easy way is conventionally rational or grounded in an attribute-substituting heuristic and the evaluative frame for these feasible outcomes are readily established and stabilized. At the same time, the second action-possibility is one in which probabilities are hard to assess, or even approximate using heuristics, and the evaluative frames for the outcome are not readily stabilized. In this sense, what makes it so hard to compare some set of actions to the standard list of "incommensurable" actions (such as actions taken out of loyalty or actions taken to preserve friendships or sustain the natural world) is that we have no causal stories in mind to tell us what happens, with what probability, if we do or do not take certain steps that sustain personal relationships or cherish the natural world. Similarly, we have no tools that permit us to assess broad counterfactuals about basic life decisions (how will we feel if we gave up adventure for security?).

It is quite clear that scholars in the F&F tradition have embraced the idea of incommensurability. I thus feel modestly confident trying to expand on why and how they might embrace it. But there is, as best as I can tell, no writing from an H&B perspective, however undeveloped, pushing the idea that what makes us "feel" on occasion as if we are dealing with incommensurable options is that we sometimes face a particular type of difficulty making comparisons in a certain range of practical cases. It is not the case that the feeling arises when comparisons across domains are either intrinsically impossible or objectionable.

Assume, though, that the certain death of named persons and material gain are subjectively felt to be incommensurable. Assume, too, that at the same time, statistical deaths and material goods are felt to be far more commensurable. How could this be sensible? How do we resolve the first "forced choice" between material goods and life-saving resources devoted to a named person? According to those embracing the view that we make decisions between incommensurables not by comparing end-states but by manifesting commitments, the action-course is not chosen by comparing the value of lives with the value of goods. We do not say the lives we have certainly saved are more valuable than the goods we could receive if we let the people die; instead, we decide whether a certain choice does or does not demonstrate and express a certain sort of life-affirming identity, an evaluative attitude toward life preservation that we would rationally affirm. But that says nothing about whether we need to resolve the second forced choice (evaluating decreased statistical death and increased access to material goods) by looking to see what identity-affirming option we are drawn to. It is perfectly possible we resolve *that* choice like we resolve the choice between vanilla and strawberry ice cream, by simply comparing values because making the choice does not force us to reveal, examine, or express *any* set of intentions or judgments.

As I mentioned before, Anderson's reflective, commitment-expressing decision maker is nothing like a person a modularist would recognize. She lives a well-examined life, replete with meta-preferences. Nor is she a fast and frugal decision maker who "Takes the Best" rather than trying either to weigh decision attributes as a rational choice theorist might suggest she would and should or to reflect on the meaning of the choices she makes.

She might, however, be something like the person that H&B scholars envision we are, creatures who use both "intuition" and "higher-order reason" to resolve problems.

(I do not mean to suggest that Anderson would like or embrace this account of the pragmatic rationalist, but I am hoping it is an interesting gloss on her view.) The decision maker's initial System One reactions may be heuristic and modularized—the feeling that she is facing an insoluble problem in which the virtues of distinct options seem incomparable comes from the fact that each domain-specific reaction is associated with its own motivating set of emotions. But the System Two big-picture thinker is able to make more complex judgments about the agent's more particular ends, interests, and self-conceptions, rather than merely making more general survival-appropriate hasty judgments. (This view of the System One/System Two distinction comes out especially strongly in Stanovich's work.)[30]

- *Modular thought revisited: parallel processing as the root of incomparability*

The final broad argument that options are incomparable is simply that people essentially engage in parallel processing of domain-specific inputs. There is no "central planner" in the brain that compares the value of action-options, each of which is initially evaluated by its own domain-specific modules that move quickly and automatically from perceived cue(s) to motivating emotion to action. I have referred to variants of this argument frequently throughout the chapter, so for now I merely want to highlight the critical question that this picture of cognition raises, a question I have left hanging. How does such a brain resolve apparent conflicts, choose some mandatory action X over some equally mandatory action Y when it is simply impossible to do both X and Y?

Gigerenzer seems to believe that such conflicts are avoided because, in some fashion, the brain is organized "hierarchically."[31] Certain "modules" are in some sense more "basic." They may have evolved *first*,[32] or it may simply be an evolved feature of the brain that simultaneously evolved faculties are organized hierarchically. What it means, I take it, for a particular module to be more basic or "higher" in the hierarchy is that information relevant to making choices in a particular domain is processed sooner or faster than information in less basic domains *given the presence of some cue that determines which module should be activated first*. That is, there is some set of sequential triggering algorithms.[33]

More plausibly, perhaps, the implicit claim may be that one effect of "triggering" a more "basic" module is to inhibit (at least partly) certain responses that would otherwise occur in "less basic" modules. This second suggestion is more mine than Gigerenzer's. It is grounded in my more general desire to figure out what biological processes might underlie a "modular" brain.

It is not entirely clear to me that Gigerenzer thinks that problems of incommensurability—in which conflicting emotional, action-impelling reactions could get, or do in fact get, triggered by distinct environmental cues—do not preclude choice or action because the signals are processed in a sequential hierarchy. One might think that one would never subjectively experience emotional conflict if the less basic module never got "activated," so that the subjective incommensurability *problem* must *not* involve situations in which there is such sequential processing.

At any rate, Gigerenzer certainly describes the hierarchical model of the brain in relationship to a rather different set of problems than the incommensurability problem. He describes it as part of an effort to figure out how people know which of many modules to activate in a world where there is imperfect information about the "type" of situation one is confronting, not as part of an effort to figure out which activated module to "respond" to. Thus, for instance, he hypothesizes a sequence in which a person confronts a murky object in the dark forest and first ascertains whether it is living or inanimate—assuming there are modules to deal with each distinct class of object—before deciding whether it is human or non-human and before deciding whether it is an enemy or would-be cooperator.

Presumably, as I said, the "incommensurability" problems occur because multiple systems have been activated that dictate distinct choices in situations in which something must give. But even if this creates the subjective experience of irreconcilable conflict in goals, because subjects remain "conscious" of the actions that feel compulsory but cannot be undertaken, the experience of facing such incommensurable choices need not be action defeating if some modules have some sort of lexical priority over the others. What needs to be explained more clearly though is what cues trigger the priority of one particular module. (To parrot one of Fodor's critiques of massive modularism, first raised in Chapter Three, it is not clear whether there is a module that decodes cues to assign priorities to modules, and if so, how it might work.)

Again, it strikes me as mildly more plausible to assert that one effect of some brain activity is to inhibit some sub-set of reactions that one would have in the absence of that activity. A straightforward non-cognitive biological analogy might help. When muscles move one eye so that it is looking to the right, movement of the other eye in the opposite direction is inhibited.

It is also possible that Gigerenzer believes instead that what triggers the use of lexical decision-making F&F heuristics is the experience of irreducible conflict that arises because distinct modules make irreconcilable emotional demands given the presence of multiple environmental cues activating multiple modules. Again, choice and action are possible, but not through compensatory weighing of the virtues and flaws of each possible cue-responsive option that has triggered its own "valuation emotion." Instead, there is some decision-triggering cue that is present (e.g., a "best" cue that triggers a "Take the Best" choice).

"Take the Best" strategies are most plausible, though, if the task is to make some factual determination, and there is a single best cue that the organism has learned (experientially? through social learning or mimicry? because responding to that cue automatically gave an evolutionary advantage?) correlates well enough with the fact to be determined. Thus, it is plausible that there *is* a single best cue that will determine with pretty good accuracy, given time constraints in making judgments, if food is toxic or even which of two cities is larger. But it is unclear what it might *mean* to say that there is a best cue to determine which of two choices that trigger distinct action-motivating reactions is actually the best cue or the best reaction. The fact that the outcomes are incommensurable makes it hard to judge *ex ante* or *ex post* whether one had made the "best" choice between incommensurables.

It is possible that Gigerenzer believes he can avoid this problem as massive modularists do by arguing that the "best" cue is simply the one that induces gene-survival maximizing action. This might seem modestly plausible if the "dominant" domains were always defined fairly simply (e.g., helping kin trumps helping friends trumps helping strangers). But this will not always be true in the very examples that Gigerenzer is drawn to in deriding rat-choice theorists who ignore incommensurability.

Certain sorts of rights violations may always seem unacceptable or may sometimes seem acceptable. We can imagine that sometimes a domain that trumps the rights-respecting domain has been activated, that the rights-respecting domain "merely" evolved to permit social exchange, and that this is a lower-priority evolutionary need than some other set of domains. But violating rights or failing to violate them even when it feels compelling to do so can still give rise to an irreducible sense of tragic loss, even if either step is taken in the service of kin. When the novelist E.M. Forster remarked that he would hope he would have the strength to betray his country rather than his friends if put to the test, what resonates most in the comment is not that he spotted the biologically appropriate imperative but that he spotted a tough issue. (And he spotted one on which it is rather unlikely that we would get the sort of cross-individual consistency we would expect if the response were dictated by evolutionary pressure.) If Gigerenzer does not believe this, though, I am skeptical that one can account for choice-in-the-face-of-incommensurability by relying on the purported tendency to "Take the Best" cue.

E. CONCLUSION

Values could be incommensurable in a number of distinct ways. At times, theorists seem to conflate a variety of situations that others have treated as quite separable. Actions seem truly incommensurable only in situations in which the ends we seek are truly incomparable: We cannot figure out whether an end is better, worse, or equally valued compared to another end. But at times people describe ends as incommensurable when we are simply unable to make trade-offs because one end has lexical priority over other possible ends. Some also describe ends as incommensurable when the value of the ends cannot be expressed in some single reduced form (e.g., "utils" or dollars), and some who emphasize that form of incommensurability do so largely because they worry that decision makers, especially public decision makers, who try to reduce the value of all ends to a single metric, will overvalue ends that can most readily be evaluated in terms of the metric.

It may be *preferable* normatively that we treat the value of two options as incomparable, let alone as incapable of being expressed in terms of a single metric. It might also be true descriptively that we frequently do not make choices between two possible courses of actions by deciding which one is preferable, all things considered. To the extent that it is simply descriptively the case that we do not choose between courses of action by comparing the value of the options, it is possible that this gives rise to a subjective feeling that the ends we would achieve by pursuing one or the other course of action are incommensurable with other ends. It is also possible that we make choices without recognizing that we might have been torn between two possible courses of action, so we never subjectively recognize that our ends are incommensurable.

Both MM theory and the aspects of F&F theory that emphasize that decisions are made lexically, rather than by balancing the virtues and flaws of each option, have interesting implications for the debates over the plausibility of theories that choices are incommensurable in the relevant way. Unlike theorists, most obviously Anderson, who believe we resolve choices between incomparable ends by reflecting more deeply on how choosing one or the other end would best express deep existential commitments, both MM and F&F theorists argue that incommensurable choices are made by a brain that obliterates conflict, either by remitting decisions to a dominant module or by following lexical heuristic decision-making processes.

It would appear to be the case that MM theorists could to some modest extent explain why people subjectively *feel* that certain ends are incommensurable, because the intuition to take actions one ultimately does not take, because they cannot be taken if one is to take a more "urgent" action, is not obliterated, but "lives on" in its own module. At the same time, F&F scholars would seem to have a good model of "pseudo-incommensurability"—the use of trumping rules that categorically forbid making trade-offs—because they believe that *most* cognition involves similar trumping rules. It is easy to imagine thinking about a mind that treats "rights" as side constraints if the mind is supposed to treat "recognition" of one of two cities as trumping all other information about the size of the two cities. The F&F theorists, though, would also assume that if people could make choices between incomparable options by following a lexical decision-making rule of the form, "if actions A and B are distinguishable in terms of impact on helping kin, go new further and pick the option that helps kin," they should not subjectively experience the incommensurability of, say, the desire to help kin and the desire to live in a nicer house. They would simply never have processed information about whether option A or B would have resulted in living in a nicer house.

It is far harder to ascertain what position H&B-influenced scholars would take on the debates over incommensurability, though Tversky's account of decision making through EBA suggests a process, much like "Take the Best," in which second-order interests never become salient. My suspicion—and it is really no more than a suspicion—is that they would be sympathetic, in the first instance, to the idea that people describe or subjectively experience ends as incommensurable largely because they are *uncertain* of the relevant value of each option. Ends are most typically deemed incommensurable, in this view, when the value of one option is markedly more readily ascertained than the value of the other. At the same time, biased processing of cues may mislead people into being unduly confident of their capacity to ascertain value or unduly skeptical of that same capacity.

9

CLASSICAL ORTHODOXY AND LEGAL REALIST RESPONSES THROUGH THE LENS OF THE HEURISTICS DEBATE

A. INTRODUCTION

There are many things I will *not* try to do in this chapter. I will not even attempt to give a definitive account of the nature of Classical Orthodoxy, the variant of late nineteenth-century American legal formalism associated with Christopher Langdell, or of any, much less all, of the many variants of twentieth-century American legal realism, whether those associated with Oliver Wendell Holmes, those associated with sociological jurisprudence, those associated with descriptive empiricism and/or policy analysis, or those associated with the idea that legal decisions are best understood as situation-tailored responses to very narrow factual problem types. Not only will my accounts be highly partial, they will be deliberately insensitive to quite significant *disputes* about the proper way of characterizing the internal analytical structure, historical or political implications, and social and intellectual origins of the various schools of modern American legal thought. This chapter is definitely not, nor is it meant to be, a contribution to the more general debates among intellectual historians on these important subjects.

Instead, I hope to present a highly stylized but moderately extensive account of Langdell's understanding of law and legal method, a stylized but more succinct explanation of certain views associated with early critics of the Langdellian synthesis, especially Holmes, and finally an even briefer summary of the quite tentative tendency among certain mid-twentieth-century Realists to believe that legal rules might best be understood as responsive to recurring narrow fact patterns, generally emerging in particular industries or sectors of the economy (e.g., disputes involving interactions between railroads and automobiles) or involving other recurring specific problems (e.g., "slip and fall" tort cases). My accounts draw predominantly on the work of

Thomas Grey, in large part because I find his depictions both thoughtful and fundamentally persuasive and also because I think I can best avoid the appearance that I am even trying to do synthetic intellectual history work if I largely restate a particular view of the theorists upon whom I am commenting, without doing more than briefly acknowledging the existence of many counterinterpretations.[1]

At the same time as I attempt to set out what I will treat as the defining, central views associated with these distinct schools of thought, I hope to show that our understanding of these various positions can be sharpened by imagining that each school adopted programs for thinking about *systematic, legal* decision making that would mirror one of the particular views of how *individuals* either do or should make decisions more generally that I have examined to this point in this book. My claim is decidedly *not* that Langdell believed what he believed about legal decision making because he thought that individual decision making or cognition was best described by some precursor of the "fast and frugal" (F&F) school, or even that he anticipated, however imperfectly, that understanding of cognition and incorporated it into his legal theory. Rather, my claim is that there are interesting homologies between Langdell's understanding of legal decision making and Gigerenzer's conception of human decision making more generally, and that we will better understand Langdell, and more fully appreciate both the strengths and weaknesses of his views, if we consider the F&F approach to cognition. At core, Langdellians share with F&F scholars both the idea that people use lexical decision-making processes (rules) rather than balancing a host of factors (standards) and that they can derive "local" rules from a small number of higher order principles that resemble an adaptive toolbox of basic cognitive capacities. Moreover, Langdell's preference for adjudication over legislation is homologous with the disdain that F&F scholars show for efforts to incorporate all seemingly relevant data when making a decision; only courts try to solve problems by discovering a small number of robust principles rather than trying to overanalyze a particular social problem.

To a lesser extent, but otherwise similarly, I think we can also better understand some aspects of early Realist critiques of the Classical Orthodoxy, especially those associated with Holmes, by thinking about homologies with the "heuristics and biases" (H&B) school. Holmes's views on the relationship between habitual thought and reflective reconsideration bear an interesting resemblance to System One/System Two theory in H&B literature; his views on the need to establish conceptual order in law solely to help lawyers learn their field look a lot like H&B ideas that heuristics are an aid to cognitively limited agents.

Finally, we can also better understand why "fact-type" Realism (arguably Arnold, Corbin, Llewellyn, and Green were all influenced by this tendency) has had so little impact by recognizing that these theories share many of the quite severe problems that massive modularists face in thinking about human cognition more generally.

B. LANGDELL'S CLASSICAL SYNTHESIS

- *The nature of a formal legal system*

In describing Langdell's thought as embodying one variant of legal formalism, I realize that there are many distinct accounts of what formalism is, as well as distinct accounts of the virtues and flaws of formalist reasoning. For purposes of this exposition, however, I will generally assume, with Grey, that we can define whether a legal system is formal in relationship to five issues: comprehensiveness, completeness, two varieties of formality (permitting decisions to be deduced readily at both the base level (i.e., in relationship to each particular dispute) and the higher level (i.e., in terms of facilitating our capacity to derive precise rules to deal with novel disputes), conceptual order, and the significance of acceptability.

Legal systems are comprehensive to the extent, first, that they purport to resolve all disputes. The resolution may of course simply be that the complaining would-be plaintiff has no cause of action. They are comprehensive as well if and only if the institutional body appropriate to the ultimate resolution of each controversy is clearly specified. One key to a system's comprehensiveness is that jurisdiction over a dispute does not overlap or if more than one body is entitled to resolve a dispute, at least preliminarily, there is a clearly specified body that has the final call either to make a *de novo* substantive judgment or to decide which of the preliminary decision makers had actual determinative authority if these initial decision makers diverged in their judgment. It is critical as well that a comprehensive system cannot generate contradictory answers to the same legal question.

Could a legal system fail to be comprehensive unless competing decision makers purported to have the ultimate authority to resolve the same dispute? In some sense, the answer might appear to be "no" because we could analytically characterize the refusal of a decision maker to adjudicate some class of disputes as a form of resolution. Analytically, the argument would be that it could be characterized as a ruling in favor of preserving the status quo at the time a suit is commenced. But formalists, among others, clearly believe that a legal system fails to be comprehensive not only if there are competing, potentially contradictory dispute resolution loci with no rules to explain which decision trumps the other or institution to resolve contradiction definitively but also if adjudicators refuse to resolve disputes simply because they cannot locate a clear rule that covers the subject matter at hand. Thus, formalists believe it might be appropriate to *decide* that the status quo at the time of suit should be maintained, but that must be the product of a decision that resembles other decisions the authority makes, not a product of the inability to find a basis for decision.

Most non-formalists agree that comprehensiveness is an important virtue—some think the key virtue—of a legal system. Disputes must be resolvable, lest we regularly fall into brutish state of nature conflicts, and it must be clear who resolves them. As we will see, though, non-formalists tend to draw the implication from the fact that authorities must resolve every case they confront that many decisions are likely to be unprincipled or of little value as precedents. Since courts—the typical dispute settler—are, above all, obliged to resolve each dispute that comes their way, whether they have good reasons to resolve it one way rather than the other, they will have no choice but to generate results whether or not these results are systematically patterned or well-reasoned. On grounds I soon attend to, though, formalists do not draw that implication, though they gladly acknowledge that the *first* feature of a formal legal system is that jurisdiction over disputes is complete and fully specified.

The relationship between comprehensiveness and distinct views of individual decision making is, however, attenuated and uninteresting. All those who think about cognition recognize that in making whatever judgments and decisions the subject makes, she herself will be the exclusive authority and will be unable to evade decision-making authority simply because she despairs she has insufficient grounds to reach a decision.

A legal system is not merely comprehensive but complete if there is a not just an answer but a *right* answer to the question of whose interests should prevail in each dispute. Legal systems are complete to some extent simply because they are comprehensive—a complete legal system cannot have any gaps or cases in which the decision maker just throws up her hands because she is unable to locate a governing rule. But they are incomplete, as well, if outcomes are inconsistent or if the decision maker cannot see a *good* reason not to simply favor one party over the other *arbitrarily*. Formalists believe that legal systems are and should be complete in this way. But non-formalists—most prominently Ronald Dworkin—who believe that there is a best principled answer to all legal disputes also believe the legal system is and should be complete in this sense.[2]

Along this dimension, Langdellian formalists, believing in the virtues of non-arbitrary completeness, depart in an interesting fashion from the F&F theorists they otherwise often resemble. (In this respect, they depart from H&B scholars in precisely the same way.) One of the key features of heuristic cognition is that the subjects who use heuristics often can neither know they are using them nor justify their use. As I have noted, F&F and H&B theorists do indeed contemplate the *possibility* that people adopt heuristics as conscious rules of thumb. Recall that I noted in Chapter Three that in their work on decision making by emergency room doctors considering whether a patient needs to be placed in the coronary care unit, F&F theorists often *urge* people to make more use of heuristics, something that would be senseless if such heuristics could not be consciously adopted.

In this sense, both schools differ significantly from massive modularity (MM) theory, which assumes the modularized cognitive responses are both mandatory and opaque, immune to reflection. Still, one must recognize that F&F theory, with its substantial debt to MM theory, is grounded, above all, in the notion that people have developed, for adaptive reasons, cognitive capacities that are *automatic* and unreflective. Automatic and unconscious judgments may in the minds of F&F theorists still be *patterned* even if the pattern is opaque to those making the judgments. The inner logic is that they consistently meet adaptive ends, however, not that they are *formally consistent*.

Third, formalists generally, and Langdell more particularly, believed in the importance of formality at two distinct levels of the legal system. First, in resolving particular disputes, the decision maker ought to rely on "rules" rather than "standards." What this means is simply that the proper resolution of a particular dispute should be mechanically dictated once one discerns a tractably small number of readily perceived facts. Thus, at this "base" case-by-case decision level, it would be preferable to follow a rule that stated that "18-year-olds can vote" rather than a standard fundamentally merely stating the purpose behind establishing a practice to distinguish voters from non-voters for which the rule that 18 is the age of political majority is a tractable proxy. A standard such as "politically mature persons with a strong material or ideological interest in the outcome of public disputes can vote" should be avoided. Similarly, a rule like "a will must have two witnesses to be valid" is preferable to a standard like "a will must be adequately attested."

It is vital to note that the preference for base-level rules could profitably be seen as a preference for the conscious adoption of fast and frugal heuristics. Decisions made lexically on the basis of one or a few observable features are ideal. The F&F school's preference for using rules in law doubtless arises in part from recognition of the classical political virtues associated with rules, such as discretion reduction, but it is of course supposed to be bolstered by the argument that using rules *fits* our basic cognitive styles and capacities. What legal decision makers are cognitively capable of is making rule-bound, fast and frugal heuristic decisions.[3]

At the same time, it is imperative to recognize that such case-by-case base-level formalism—which might well increase predictability for particular litigants, would-be litigants, and parties engaged in planning their affairs—could be achieved without any higher order formalism. Such higher order formalism requires the capacity to fill gaps in a legal system by reference to general principles that give as determinative an answer to the question of what rule should be created to cover a situation that had never before been confronted as a base-level rule gives to the question of how to resolve a concrete, particular dispute. Base-level formalism could be created by an ever-expanding legislative code, or by unprincipled courts that simply makes up new base-level rules each time a novel situation arises.[4]

It is possible to believe one can generate "completeness" (no contradictory or arbitrary results) without higher order formalism. Dworkin, for instance, argues that "balanced" principles, rather than mechanically applicable ones, can do so. Still, one is far more likely to believe that completeness can be generated if high-order formalism dictates results at the base. The notion that balancing tests will generate fully consistent results or results that seem fully non-arbitrary to the decision makers has hardly been an easy idea to sell, and Langdellians certainly rejected it.

It is important to realize that Realist critics of Classical Orthodox formalism believed that formalism at the base level was both almost certainly incompatible with higher order formalism *and* that the virtues of base-level formalism were no more than virtues, to be prudentially balance against the *flaws* that inevitably accompany the use of mechanically applicable rules. Thus, they argued, it is doubtless true that there are virtues associated with the use of mechanically applicable rules (e.g., two adult witnesses to a will are necessary and sufficient) in terms of reducing official discretion to reject or accept wills or in terms of permitting will writers to know what they must do to write a valid instrument. It is inconceivable, though, that an arbitrary rule of that form could be mechanically derived from *any* abstract principle, for instance, one that requires "adequate" evidence that a will forces genuine or adequate reflection on the document by the drafter.

The Realist critics also recognized that the genuine virtues of rules—discretion reduction, predictability, litigation reduction, clarity about obligations, horizontal equity[5]—were simply virtues to be weighed against the obvious flaws of rules. Thus, they often emphasized these flaws: injustice in particular cases due to the inevitable over and underinclusiveness of rules, false sense of predictability and certainty, and so on.[6] But what is critical to understand is that the classically orthodox formalists like Langdell both reject the argument that base and high-order formalism are incompatible and extol the use of mechanically applicable base-level rules (i.e., the lexical use of proxy features) in all circumstances.

Fourth, Langdellian formalists believe that they can achieve completeness because of high-order formalism, and that high-order formalism comes from the fact that the legal system does and should have a great measure of *conceptual order*. In this view, there are a small number of highly abstract first principles that determine base-level legal decisions. Pre-classical "Grand Style" judges also believed there were a small number of abstract principles but saw these principles as nothing more than loose guides that would point the judge in the direction of sound decision making. What distinguished Langdell and other proponents of classical orthodoxy was the idea that this small set of abstract principles *dictated* results in particular cases. (One sees this same view in much modern libertarian and quasi-libertarian legal theory.)[7] There could not be completeness (i.e., consistency and no feeling of arbitrariness when new base-level rules were created) if the high-order principles were themselves vague.

The principles Langdell aspired to locate were substantive and prescriptive; they did more than supply mere organizational concepts useful in ordering the legal universe. Thus, for instance, Langdell believed in substantive principles such as "a valid contract requires mutual consideration—something given by each side" or "people are responsible in tort only for those injuries that are proximately caused by their conduct." He was not referring merely to descriptive organizational principles without prescriptive bite, such as "there is a distinction between torts which establish duties owed to legal strangers from contracts which involve duties created by explicit or implied agreement."

Here, the ties to the F&F school are again both quite strong and instructive. The small menu of abstract principles from which concrete base decisions should derive are strongly homologous with the basic heuristics or adaptive toolbox of cognitive mechanisms that get used both in the settings in which they were initially employed and in novel situations. Obviously, their origin is not the same—in ways I return to discuss in a moment, Langdell does not seem to think our knowledge of these principles is "intuitive" or that it naturally evolves—but they play much the same *role*. Each permits the subject to avoid the need to make complex situationally sensitive judgments because she can rely, instead, on using a more basic simple decision-making rubric.

What was the source of the first principles in Classical Orthodoxy? Ideally, all existing case law would fit into the conceptual order. This was the sense in which Langdell saw reported cases as the laboratory experimental results that legal scientists would study; these legal scientists would simply *describe* existing patterns of cases, as parsimoniously as possible, and observed patterns would constitute the set of first principles. But Langdellian classicism had a mild critical bite as well. *Some* existing cases could be seen as "inconsistent" with the first principles, though cases generally are the sole source of these principles.

Naturally, Realists raised a host of questions about how cases could both be the source of principles and yet sometimes be inconsistent with principles and questions about whether Langdell had jumbled the factual with the normative. Why is the pattern of existing case law, even if there is one, the source of principle to be used as a guide to future behavior? Obviously, the question of how one can derive normative from factual propositions is a vital one in looking at work influenced by F&F theory more generally. Langdell cannot even rely on the standard answers that F&F-influenced theorists often employ: that the heuristics in the toolbox are adaptive and gene replication is the highest (only?) value and/or that talking about normative superiority or inferiority is pointless because our evolved traits are the only ones we are *capable* of manifesting.

At the same time, Realists argued that deriving principles from settled practice, even if such practice could be observed, would render the law unduly static. Can the law make progress or deal with novel social situations, in which the balance of real interests in a "dispute type" may have changed, if past case law generates immutable higher order rules? Again, this critique harkens back to a standard critique of both MM theory and aspects of F&F theory that builds on MM theory in this regard. Highly domain specific responses are insufficiently flexible to cope with a world that changes both because the external environment naturally alters over time and because malign agents exploit one's rigid domain-specific responses by making the world *appear* to have traits that trigger a response that the malign agents prefer you to have, rather than one that is truly in your own interest.

In the standard biological domain, think of having an unduly domain-specific mechanism to detect trustworthiness, triggered by the presence of a cue that the sneaky could ultimately mimic. More important for our purposes, think, too, in this regard of one of the prototypical arguments against using rules in a legal system: not only are rules "naturally" over and underinclusive, given the state of the world we would observe if no agents knew the rules, but selfish agents will learn to shape their behavior into forms that meet the demands of mechanically applied rules, but not their purposes, in order to receive the favorable treatment they desire.

Imagine, for instance, the tax law permits employees "required" to live on their employer's premises for work not to include in taxable income the market value of those premises on the generally true supposition that the taxpayer does not value housing he is forced to live in at its market price. In the "natural" world, this assumption will obviously be inaccurate for *some* taxpayers no matter what. Some sub-set of employees required to occupy housing on the employer's premises *would* purchase that housing at its market value with cash or a housing voucher and have thus been enriched by this housing as much as they would have been enriched had they received cash to spend on anything, including housing. But what is worse is that once the rule is announced, the rule will *become* overinclusive more and more often. People who know that they will pay less in taxes if they foreswear cash income will negotiate with their employers to be "required" or "forced" to live on premises that they do not in fact undervalue.[8]

Ultimately, what may be hardest to fathom is the answer to a very basic question about why Langdellian principles are worthy of weight. In what sense, if any, would the pattern of case law describe something about the real world worth addressing, in the same way that Euclid's axiomatic first principles seemed, at least to the pre-non-Euclidian geometricians of Langdell's time, to describe real space? I return to this question when I discuss, in a moment, the place of "acceptability" in Classical Orthodoxy.

Finally, then, formalists had a particular view about the role that a rule's substantive acceptability should play. Should we care about a rule's fit with the ideals of the governed, whether these ideals are generated by intuitive good sense or well-reasoned policy analysis? For Langdell, substantive acceptability was utterly irrelevant in thinking about base-level rules. This view is the source of the typical Realist accusation that Langdell cared more about the aesthetics of form than instrumentally good outcomes. However, it did play some part in thinking about the higher order principles, which would, could and should make sense.

- *Normativity in Langdell's orthodox thought*

Langdell thought the higher order principles would, as a matter of descriptive fact, make sense both because the mere existence of *some* conceptually ordered legal system meets "rule of law" policy ideals such as discretion reduction and predictability *and* because the principles that emerged would likely have been subject to long-term collective scrutiny. There are few hints in Classical Orthodoxy that principles might be naturally selected by a vaguely Darwinian process of a form that Priest made explicit nearly a century later in arguing that the common law would move toward efficiency because inefficient holdings would tend to be re-litigated.[9] Similarly, there are no more than a few hints, somewhat reminiscent of attacks by Hayek on the desirability of centralized economic planning, that the principles that emerge from case law are "wiser" than those that even the smartest individual could work out on his or her own because they take advantage of the accumulation of local knowledge.[10]

Once more, analogies with the teachings of the F&F school are both apparent and edifying. Higher order principles—the basic tools in the adaptive toolbox—are substantively acceptable. They are acceptable in the F&F world, though, because they are adaptive. The criteria for acceptability in Langdell's world are, as I soon note, more ambiguous. At the same time, Langdell believed though, that base-level *applications* of higher order principles are not subject to substantive critique, in part because we are incapable of making such localized, context-rich judgments and also because the virtues of completeness and conceptual order require adhering to high order principles even when they generate bad local outcomes. In F&F thought, the base-level applications—the selection of a "tool" from the adaptive toolbox—may be *subject* to critique; F&F theorists do consider heuristics that misfire in particular settings. But there is neither a presumption of the sort Langdell makes that such applications are "acceptable" or well-defined criteria for judging acceptability. While the H&B theorists readily recognize some errors (e.g., illogical or counterfactual judgments), F&F theorists merely state, in a far more circular manner, that a judgment reveals the relevant sort of error if it fails to help the organism meet its proximal goals but does not help us figure out how we would know if it succeeded or failed in this fashion.

In fact, it seems that functional arguments for learning from the common law are more likely to be seen in the more ambivalent Realist paeans to precedent and *stare decisis* than in Classical writing. In the final analysis, the truth is that there is little in the Classical formalist formulation that tells us why we should think that the principles that emerge from case law, even if we can find them, are entitled to much deference. Langdell seems to reject rather plainly two promising possibilities for validating existing holdings: that we will see that the cases are correctly decided because they appeal to our universal moral sense or that they are right because they inevitably demonstrate a detailed knowledge of local custom and local morality (and what we mean when we call a decision "morally right" is no more than that it conforms with a given community's developed sensibilities).

But either answer promises the possibility of making acceptability judgments about particular cases, and Langdell wants to restrict these judgments to the bigger principles.[11] Moreover, any answer that relies on the existence of a natural, intuitive moral sense will not do for the Classical thinkers because deriving these higher order principles is *not* intuitive for people generally but merely *becomes* the trained intuition of the educated professional lawyer. And the second answer seems to imply that the source of legitimate law is history. Good law is a mere path-dependent accident; good law is highly localized. But Langdell was a conceptualist, not a historicist.

It is interesting to note that F&F theorists have offered an additional argument that Langdellian method will lead to "good law." The argument is posed as an argument in favor of adjudication and against legislation.[12] Of course, while Langdell made few explicit or principled arguments against the authority, legitimacy, or wisdom of legislatures, he clearly never thought of statutory (or even constitutional law) as "real law," because it was ungrounded in broad general principles. (Not surprisingly, the Langdellian law school curriculum actively disdained public law, legislation, and administration.)[13] An argument that F&F-influenced theorists make, which I think might better express a nascent intuition in Langdell, is not simply that legislatures are untrustworthy because readily corrupted (see public choice theory) or unduly moved to respond to isolated, unduly psychologically salient crises rather than long-term problems (see H&B theory). More generally, in the F&F view, the fact that legislatures do not have to announce rules in the relatively broad heuristic form that courts use, because doing so permits judicial decisions to act as precedents for new cases, leads them to make the errors that Gigerenzer generally associates with efforts to overanalyze particular problems rather than to rely on fast and frugal simple responses to a wider range of problems. Legislatures, like any decision maker not committed to using heuristics, will overfit a solution to a particular crisis in the same way that formally rational decision makers will overfit regression equations to a particular data set. They will believe temporarily relevant factors must be attended to though these factors will be of no ongoing moment, unlike the small number of stable factors that are accounted for by the user of a heuristic.

- *An illustration: the mailbox rule*

It might be instructive to review some of the points I have made about Classical Orthodoxy generally, and its relationship to the F&F school, by looking at one of the best known Langdellian analyses of a particular legal controversy. Langdell is widely known, at least in narrow circles, for his rejection of the "mailbox rule," a rule that held that a contract was formed as soon as the offeree had mailed his acceptance of the contract, even before the initial offeror had received it. It follows from the demand that a legal system be comprehensive that a court with determinate jurisdiction to decide any controversy between a party who believes a contract was formed and one who claims to remain unbound must indeed ultimately decide whether the contract was formed before the offeror had received an acceptance. This is true whether or not there is settled law on that question or especially strong arguments that it should be resolved one way rather than the other. What more uniquely characterizes Langdell's view of the case is that he believes one can mechanically derive a *correct* answer to the case (completeness), and that one should do so without making reference to the acceptability in policy terms of the rule as a resolution to the particular controversy. Rather, the appropriate rule can be derived from some higher order principle; in this case, the principle that all contracts require mutual consideration.

Here is a quick summary of Langdell's deliberately quasi-geometric, deductive reasoning about this case. If we look at case law, we discover a general principle that contracts require bargained-for consideration to be binding. Consideration can be performance or a promise to perform. Since the offeree in these cases has obviously not performed, she can bind the initial offeror only when she herself has made a promise. The nature of a promise, however, is that it must be communicated to the promisee, who, in this case, is the initial offeror. Until the initial offeror receives the acceptance, then, there is no promise, and hence no consideration and no contract.

The base-level rule that Langdell ultimately defends—the acceptance must be *received*—is itself "formal" and rule-like, compared, for example, to a vaguer standard of the form, "the acceptance must be received *and understood* by the initial offeror to constitute a promise." It appears, at this step, that an undefended preference for the use of rules at the base level affects ostensibly syllogistic reasoning. If one were really committed to the idea that there is no promise until the party to whom the promise is made "receives" the promise, it is hardly clear that she "receives" it until she understands it.

At the same time, the *mere* preference for base-level rules—borne, for instance, out of a desire for predictability—could just as well dictate the mailbox rule that Langdell rejects. Courts could readily implement a rule that the contract is complete as soon as the initial offeree sends out his acceptance of the offer. This was indeed the mailbox rule that predominated in actual court cases at the time Langdell wrote.

Moreover, of course, the preference for base-level rules is not itself obviously justified in the face of competing considerations. As a matter of fact, courts have rejected *both* the mailbox rule and Langdell's preferred rule that the offeror must receive the acceptance before we can find a binding contract. They have done so in cases in which the result would lead to manifest injustice and pose no problem for the putatively bound party because, for instance, the party was in the business of routinely "accepting" offers before it communicated the fact that it would accept them. Thus, courts have found, for instance, that life insurance companies must pay out on a policy when the putatively insured party dies even before the insurance company's home office mailed out its acceptance. The fact that the company had not even prepared a letter notifying the would-be insured that the company had accepted that party's offer to purchase the life insurance that the company sells through branch agents has not barred recovery, given that insurance companies are in the business of rubber-stamping the "offers" from customers that effectively respond to their solicitations.[14]

What is clear is that Langdell was uninterested in acceptability arguments for or against the base-level mailbox rule. He simply deemed them irrelevant. Think in this regard about lexical, noncompensatory decision making in F&F theory: No factors other than the presence or absence of consideration need be taken into account. It is even clear that Langdell tolerated rules derived from the broad principle that contracts require mutual consideration when he was quite certain that deriving the "required" base-level rule from that principle results in a manifestly unjust and unacceptable result in the particular case. For instance, if X says he will give a reward if Y climbs a flagpole, and revokes the offer when Y is 90 percent of the way up, Langdell said there is no contract because Y has neither performed nor made a promise, though he recognized this result is unjust.

What is perhaps more puzzling is that Langdell simply assumed that the consideration "principle" itself has governing force, even though its normative pedigree is highly ambiguous. To the extent that one might argue that it *must* have at least some practical wisdom behind it because it is universal (think about telling an adaptationist story about traits that all systems or members of a species must possess), one is faced with the fact that it is plainly *not* universal. And Langdell knew perfectly well that requiring consideration is not universal. He noted that in the Anglo-American system, promises made under seal did not require consideration, and European legal systems dispense with consideration requirements as well. So Langdell was left with an observation that, even if true, was of puzzling relevance. It appeared to him merely to be settled American judicial practice to demand consideration.

But, of course, we then face the familiar granularity problem we saw in looking at all partly or fully modularized theories of cognition in Chapter Three. It might seem like there is a settled judicial practice if we think that the right category of thinking about "practice" is, "Do we demand consideration to enforce contracts most of the time?" If that is the question, then the answer might well be yes. If, instead, we should be employing a narrower grain to describe settled practice—do we demand consideration when parties who deny that their putative contracting partner has given consideration are dealing with parties who both intended to make a promise and took steps to communicate that promise?—then the answer is more obviously no. As Langdell noted, most of the few courts that faced the "mailbox rule" question resolved it in favor of finding a binding contract as soon as the acceptance was mailed.

Langdell seems to be making a secondary claim about the apt level of granularity. One should not only abjure a narrower-grained view of practice but also not look to find a broader-grained covering principle that would be derived more explicitly from acceptability considerations looking at the cases (e.g., "enforce contracts each party found in his self-interest to commit to unless the party who is held responsible has good reason to be surprised to find that he is bound to perform as a result of what he has already said or done"). To do so would be to strip the "high level" principles of formal determinacy. This second claim appears troublesome both because it overstates the determinacy of the principles that he does discover and because it fails to explain why maintaining conceptual order is a lexical commitment that trumps all other competing concerns.

In terms of determinacy, one group of Realists reveled in pointing out the almost total failure of those post-Langdellians who set out to do the Restatements of various fields of the law to locate the small number of principles that governed each field that Langdell expected to derive. Others pointed out that any extremely short list of generally quasi-libertarian principles, parallel to Epstein's "simple rules," were actually quite indeterminate. Thus, for instance, one could not void coercive contracts and accept some other class of non-coercive contracts because coercion, of one form or another, was ubiquitous.[15] One could not determine the appropriate amount of information sharing that is needed by reference to a principle that contracts should be voided for "fraud" but accepted in its absence; one could not establish prima facie rules against harming strangers both because unidirectional causal judgments were senseless[16] and because many harms were plainly legally privileged (e.g., injury to business competitors, blocking view, many kinds of infliction of emotional distress).

C. HOLMES'S PROTO-REALISM

The potential to discover interesting homologies between aspects of legal realism and the H&B school increases dramatically if we focus on a Realist who was not completely committed to the idea that all law was instrumental to the achievement of certain well-defined policy goals, and that the means for achieving these goals would be revealed through careful empirical study and policy analytic work (e.g., the early Pound, many of the New Deal Realists). Such confident views of law-as-technocracy resonate more in the rational choice tradition that H&B researchers treat as significantly premised on misunderstandings of actual human capacities and observable decision-making processes. Grey gives us an intelligible reading of the jurisprudence of Oliver Wendell Holmes that permits us to see some of the same sorts of ambivalent reactions among Legal Realists to technocratic instrumentalism in law that the H&B scholars show toward rational choice theories of cognition.[17]

In this view, what makes Holmes's variety of Realist thought most interesting is the way in which he combines historicist and analytical/instrumentalist views of law. Like the historicists, he sees law as path dependent, as responsive to particular local customs, traditions, and habits. Like the Benthamite instrumentalists, he nonetheless sees law as ultimately goal directed, as designed to meet some set of aims. He was certainly sympathetic to the notion that lawmakers of any stripe do and should seek to meet some set of ends. At the same time, he was considerably more skeptical than Bentham that the aims could be reduced to a simple metric: maximization of "utility." He viewed "utility" as significantly underdefined and immune to measurement.

Note in this regard the degree to which Holmes anticipated the skepticism that H&B researchers have displayed toward the mainstream account of utility associated with preference utilitarianism and neo-classical microeconomic theory. In these mainstream views, people achieve higher states of utility to the degree that they get what they prefer. H&B theorists were especially adept at pointing out that preferences—which are, at core, merely predictions of future hedonic states—were frequently mistaken, not merely, as economists recognized, because of externally imposed shortfalls of information but because of the very sort of *internal* deficits of processing ability that those associated with H&B always emphasize. (It is not so much that people lack information as that they misprocess the information that they get.) Hedonic forecasting is poor for the same reasons that most factual judgments are in error—for example, attribute substitution, reason-based decision making, inability to account for the extent to which preferences are sensitive both to the situation in which they are formed and the manner in which they are elicited.[18]

At the same time, however, it is worth noting that Daniel Kahneman, one of the key figures in developing the H&B school generally, came to believe in the possibility of revitalizing the direct Benthamite measures of pleasure and pain that Holmes thought infeasible by measuring spontaneous approach/avoidance reactions to events. Kahneman contrasted these truer measures of "objective happiness" with both the inaccurate predictions that might be made by those whose preferences were satisfied and the distorted memories displayed by those asked to give overall, long-term summaries of their hedonic states.[19]

But, at the same time as he saw both the law and human activity more generally as directed toward the satisfaction of ends, Holmes was skeptical of conventional distinctions between means and ends. I will come back to this issue, though I think, in this regard, Holmes's views anticipate some of the *difficulties* that H&B theorists have faced in giving content to the idea of "biased" or mistaken judgments, rather than reflecting the affirmative program of the H&B school.

Holmes came to this more integrated view of historicism and instrumentalism, in part, because of his more general post-Darwinian view of the nature of thought. The external world, post-Darwin, was not observed by an ephemeral, disembodied mind (the Cartesian dualist view): The mind itself was plainly embodied. The mind, like any other product of evolutionary pressure, served a purpose—to develop plans to meet organism needs. Thought is not geared toward achieving accuracy or logic in the abstract or for its own sake; it is geared toward being useful. Recall the quite parallel F&F view explored in Chapter Three that we can best understand cognition as directed toward ecological, rather than logical, rationality.

Both biological and, for Holmes, more pointedly, cultural evolution have fixed certain "habits of mind." These habitual reactions, which strongly resemble heuristics, are *always* the starting place in solving any problem, including legal ones, but they can be shaken or "irritated" when "good results" fail to follow if we adhere to settled belief. Holmes is more interested in the degree to which situated reactions are historically dictated, rather than dictated by evolutionary pressure. Methodologically, the Holmes view is thus more collectivist and sociological than the H&B school which is fundamentally individualistic and psychological. Still, the situated collective path-dependent cultural products end up playing a role in Holmes's thought that is strongly homologous to the role that effortless System One reactions play in the H&B literature. So while, like the historicists, he assumes that our presuppositions are simply *given* by the mix of local custom and, to a lesser extent, species evolution, he insists that, as a matter of description, people *will* discard their habits when following them misfires. Think in this regard about the hesitation that H&B theorists share with conventional rational choice theorists that judgments are reached through lexical methods, in the fashion that F&F scholars maintain. Think too of the H&B belief in the possibility of System Two "overrides" of System One reactions. At the same time, Holmes also believes that unconscious habit and slowly evolved custom have no strong, trumping normative priority. Continuity is best seen as a necessity, but not a duty.[20]

It is true that Holmes recognized the familiar functional argument that a presumptive preference to follow settled doctrine might make sense if we are modest about our capacity as individuals to see things that a large number of others who have dealt with a similar problem might have missed. Recall, in this regard, the preference shown by both F&F and H&B theorists to argue that individuals, no matter how motivated or trained to avoid whatever intuitive errors they make, may often be unable to do so; instead, it might frequently be preferable to overcome error by altering the institutional setting in which decisions are made. Arguably, developing case law over time, with distinct individuals evaluating arguments made by advocates interested in exposing the limits of an intuitive reaction, is such a superior institutional setting. Still, for Holmes, the capacity to engage in self-conscious reflection and innovative reason are as much aspects of the human mind as is the capacity to adhere to tradition, and the human power to innovate appropriately must not be dismissed.

One sees this mixture of historicism and instrumentalism—which I take to be homologous to the mixture of System One and Two thought—most clearly, perhaps, in Holmes's brief explication of one of his most famous anti-formalist aphorisms: "the life of the law is not logic but experience."[21] Holmes's account of experience blends the idea that we inevitably approach a problem given situated starting points but that these (intuitive? heuristic? System One?) responses that arise given these presuppositions are inevitably incomplete sources of decision. Instead, they are inexorably combined in some fashion with transcendent instrumentalist analysis. Thus, he notes that law is situated in the sense that it draws on the "felt necessities of the time," unconscious intuitions, the prejudices that judges share with others. At the same time, it is a product of instrumental reasoning; it responds to *avowed* intuitions of public policy and moral and political *theories*.

It is also interesting to consider the degree to which Holmes, in much of his detailed writing, was a stickler for conceptualist and formal distinctions at the same time as he disavowed a conceptualist method for resolving novel cases. Thus, Holmes abjured what I referred to as the Classical Orthodox commitment to conceptual ordering as a method of filling gaps in "base level" legal doctrine. His view of "higher order" principles, in the first instance, more closely resembled the views of the antebellum "Grand Style" jurists. Principles were rules of thumbs and guidelines that pointed the judge in a direction when he started to consider a case, but they were by no means lexical stopping points. Moreover, he was one of the first Realists to emphasize the point that to the degree to which one sought base-level formality, one could do so only by adopting innumerable arbitrary rules that he was certain could not be deduced from higher order principles.

Conceptualization itself, then, had to be built on a set of familiar or habitual concepts but have an instrumental aim, just as all thought did. Its aim, though, was *not* to generate completeness as it was for the Langdellians but merely to act as an aid to those attempting to learn the law. Think in this regard about heuristics as a form of mnemonic devices. This view of their use is not especially close to the views adopted by either F&F or H&B scholars, though it arguably comes marginally closer to drawing on the "attribute substitution" view of problem solving adopted in H&B thought.

Holmes was extremely skeptical that we could imagine a stable set of narrow-category legal rules. Think in this regard of the granularity problem I emphasized as bedeviling both MM and F&F theory. It is hard to imagine why the mind would form any particular narrow category rather than a broader or still narrower one.

Not only was Holmes convinced that those who purported to describe a pattern of judicial decisions in terms of fine-grained categories were likely to be descriptively inapt, he was surer still that these narrow categories would be useless in helping lawyers master their discipline. It would not aid the learning process to try to learn all the cases about telegraphs, but thinking about the general features of torts, even at the risk of simplifying key traits and overstating distinctions, *would* serve a pedagogic role, and the pedagogic role was hardly trivial, given our limited learning power. Note that this view of the degree of appropriate generalization or granularity purports to give an answer to the question of why we pick a certain level of generality and at least purports to provide a limited normative evaluative mechanism when we consider whether we are using the appropriate level. If it helps people learn how to operate as lawyers, or judges, it is "right." If it confuses them, or does not reduce the cognitive load in being able to anticipate what courts typically do, it is "wrong." Conceptualizers must be judged by their capacity to teach to the test.

Once more, emphasizing the limited learning power that Holmes posits in extolling the need for conceptual reductionism is strongly reminiscent of emphasizing the limits on *internal* computational resources that H&B theorists believe drive the use of generally accurate heuristics. At the same time, in their work specifically focused on law, it has been F&F theorists who emphasize the need to establish legal rules that are readily learned by people accustomed to thinking that a few rules or concepts will resolve most of the problems we confront.[22]

Finally, it is interesting to note that Holmes's commitment to any form of instrumentalism—to the idea that in the final analysis our thoughts, habits, and rules are ultimately directed at meeting goals, no matter how situated, habitual, stuck, and potentially counterpurposive they might be in the first instance—was interestingly incomplete. For Holmes, the distinction between means and ends was a blurry one. It might be the case that humans have developed the capacity to think and to establish products of thought like legal rules in order to meet the sorts of gene-replicating survival ends that Darwinians of his time, and F&F theorists today, would each assert drive the development of thought.

But Holmes, though often wary of the ungrounded spiritualism of some of the pragmatists of his era such as William James, clearly found the notion that humans were mere survival-maximizing machines a little too philistine. As he said, "thinking is an instrument of adjustment to the conditions of life—but it becomes an end in itself."[23] He was moved by the intrinsic pleasures of craft, moved by the idea that we might pursue knowledge or adventure or novelty even at the expense of survival.[24] "A man begins a pursuit as a means of keeping alive—he ends up following it at the cost of his life."[25] The process of legal rulemaking, like any process of thought, that begins as an effort to solve instrumental, survival-like problems takes on a life of its own. Law cannot then be purely instrumental because we develop an aesthetic ideal of how law ought to be articulated. And we can imagine these aesthetic ideals having both good and ill effects if we were thorough-going instrumentalists.

This view that means and ends converge departs quite clearly from the evolutionary psychological roots of F&F theory but resonates, albeit only partially, in two strands of H&B work. To the degree that H&B theorists are simply classical rational choice theorists skeptical of the descriptive plausibility that people can engage in fully rational choice, they will not question the conceptual sharpness of the means/ends distinction. But it is worth noting that some depart quite sharply from the notion that ends are readily understood or dictated by inclusive fitness imperatives. Some H&B scholars are especially inclined to look at "System Two" as the part of the brain that handles the development and fulfillment of non-survival-related tasks. In this view, System Two *develops* in order to cope with survival tasks in a changing and unpredictable environment, challenges that cannot be handled by more modularized System One mechanisms responding to predictable, recurring survival problems. But, in much the same way that Holmes argues that people get entranced by exercising the ability to think, some H&B theorists argue that the flexibly *responsive* System Two also develops flexible, more individualized *goals*.[26]

Second, Holmes's skepticism about the sharpness of the divide between means and ends is reflected in the hesitation that many H&B scholars have shown in evaluating whether particular judgments are "mistaken." From the vantage point of MM and F&F theory, the notion of "mistake" has a relatively clear meaning, even if it is difficult to operationalize. Decisions are mistaken only to the degree that they are made in settings that resemble, but do not adequately match, the settings in which they evolved. If used in their apt settings, one might either say that they meet normative ends because the sole normative end is inclusive fitness or argue that it is simply meaningless to think about whether evolved capacities are normatively desirable or not: They are simply the capacities that we have. But from the vantage point of H&B

theorists, it is difficult to judge whether a judgment is mistaken unless it is illogical or factually incorrect. It always seems plausible that the subject is not so much failing to meet an end that we attribute to him as meeting an alternative end.

D. NARROWER CATEGORIES

It is especially difficult to comprehend what might be described as the branch of Realist thought, or a tendency among Realists with broader agendas, dedicated to one particular form of anti-conceptualism. This "school" of Realists advanced the proposition that we can best understand patterns in the disposition of disputes not by imagining that the facts of the dispute are first abstractly represented as instances of broad legal categories but by imagining that certain dispositions recur when we look at the more precise response adjudicators have had to the concrete, narrower fact patterns. Thus, for instance, consistent with this view, Arnold argued that there is no general category of "attempt law," in which we initially try to represent the actions that the defendant took in terms of some general preparation versus attempt line[27] or try to represent his mental state in terms of his "specific intention" to commit the consummated offense. Instead, there are recurring patterns of actions that might or might not be adjudged attempts to commit particular crimes, taken through particular means, which generate concrete decisions. Whether these concrete decisions are generated by some alternative informal principle (e.g., a decision on these issues might be generated by making a conscious judgment about whether it is worthwhile extending the scope of the substantive prohibition regulated by the law proscribing the consummated offense) or whether the fact types generate reactions that are grounded either in the very localized practices of the disputants or intuition may be less than clear.[28]

One can easily find Realists writers making general, ironically abstract pleas for the use of "narrower" concrete and fact-specific categories and readily find a handful of casebooks written by Realists that purport to track not the broad conceptual elements of a field (e.g., no generalizations about offer and acceptance or generalizations about proximate cause) but to examine particular case types (contracts in particular industries, particular harmful interactions.) It is not clear, however, that anyone really ever believed that one could predict case results better by looking only at holdings from the same narrow field of cases rather than cases that others would argue were more similar in terms of the broad conceptual categories. Nor is it clear that anyone believed that it would be normatively preferable to trust fact-specific reactions, either because fact-specific customs had emerged or because cognitive intuitions tended to come to be responsive to narrow stimuli rather than derived logically and abstractly from "principles."

Take, first, general statements of the sort made by Llewellyn, who described one of the tenets of Realism as, "The belief in the worthwhileness of grouping cases and legal situations into narrower categories than has been the practice in the past. This is connected with the distrust of verbally simple rules—which so often cover dissimilar and non-simple fact situations (dissimilarity being tested partly by the way cases come out, and partly by the observer's judgment as to how they ought to come out . . .)."[29] It is important to note, first, that the argument that the attraction to narrower categories is somehow connected to a distrust of rules may be an artifact of Llewellyn's unsurprising fixation on critiquing Langdellian classicism. He may be un-self-consciously associating the case for "rules" (at what I called the "base level" in describing formalist Classical Orthodoxy) with the case for Langdellian conceptual ordering (high-level rules that would dictate the content of base-level rules). But as I noted, these can be wholly dissociated: It is perfectly conceivable that the law is filled with mechanically applicable rules that are each quite specific to a narrow fact type. In this sense, narrow categories are perfectly compatible with rules. It is also possible that there are higher order standards that govern case decisions at the base level but that the application of the higher order standards to the base-level decisions is impervious to the narrow fact type we are confronting. For example, we might use the same non-rule-like *principle* to govern all attempt cases—convict when and only when one is sure, beyond a reasonable doubt, looking at action alone that the defendant would have consummated the offense but for factors outside her control—and apply that across factual case types. In that sense, standards are completely compatible with *ignoring* narrow case types.

But what is more important for my purposes at this point is that the "argument" that narrow fact types dictate results, both normatively and descriptively, never gets worked out in particular detail and may actually encompass a host of quite distinct points. The claim may simply be, for instance, that the way in which general principles are framed is openly sensitive to the pre-existing norms that govern distinct factual settings and that, as a result, the precise outcomes of cases vary with factual setting. For instance, one could believe in what some might see as a quite general rule that incomplete, unspecified terms of contracts are and should be filled in by well-established commercial practice. If that were the case, the precise terms that would be filled in would obviously be distinct if the commercial practices in two industries differed. (For example, if there were a standard practice about when it was legitimate to reject shipments of raw cotton to cloth manufacturers that differed from the practice about accepting distinct types of diamonds among diamond merchants, one *could* argue that cases about "imperfect tender" were industry specific.) But it is not clear that the cases would aptly be described as adjudicated according to distinct "principles" or that the results could best be understood as directly responsive to a fact type, rather than derivative of a principle.

Alternatively, the argument may be, as Arnold implies in referring to the "feelings" that distinct attempt-like situations evoke, that we have strong intuitions about the just resolution of particular kinds of disputes, and that the nature of the dispute we think we confront is not "derived" from thinking about how broader policies are implicated in a setting but by simply reacting to what the mind perceives as a "natural kind" of controversy. It is this view that seems most closely associated with the ideas of MM and, to a lesser degree, F&F theorists. Our minds are built to compute non-theorized responses to factual problems; responses are triggered by the perception of a small number of localized cues. In this sense, the narrow legal categories are like the distinct tasks with which modularists think the brain is designed to cope. Just as the modularist believes the process of choosing a mate is wholly distinct from the process of choosing safe food, which is distinct from the task of taking precautions against predators and detecting defectors from cooperative games, so too by implication is the task of figuring out the adaptive solution to each narrow form of social conflict.

The problem with this view, of course, simply restates the basic conceptual problem with MM theory I reviewed in Chapter Three. There is no decent solution to the granularity quandary. Maybe all aspects of mate selection are done by the "same module." Whatever that might mean in neurobiological terms, it is plainly meant to be the case that there are a small number of cues relevant to mate selection that determine, in a mandatory and opaque fashion, at least initial intuitive responses without additional information coming into play. But perhaps at least some aspects of "mate selection" are better thought of as "cheater detection" tasks (do women judge men who will have sex and bolt without caring for the children using the same "module" as they use in judging other defectors from "contracts" or not?)

We see the same problem in "case type" legal realism. Maybe it is correct to think that the "natural" category for parsing disputes is to analyze, say, contracts related to the family, but maybe that category is either too broad or too narrow. And do we simply perceive apt narrow categories because they appear to us as natural kinds or do we develop some fact-based categories over time because we first self-consciously apply broader, vague principles to cases, and then economize to some degree on the costly process of applying principles to each new case by assuming that "similar" cases will raise "similar" substantive issues?

So assume, for instance, that we have developed a *practice* that plaintiffs will not receive damages to compensate them for emotional losses when the defendant breaches a contract to build a home. The practice might have evolved by applying principles, in a deductive, non-intuitive way to a class of factually similar cases in which we believe, for instance, that damage measurement is especially difficult, in which we believe that inefficient breach will be adequately deterred by non-emotional damages, in which we believe that plaintiffs would be unwilling as a group to purchase the implicit insurance contract that a default damage remedy implies. That does not mean that "building contracts" are a natural kind of social conflict or dispute to which we have any intuitive reaction. Nor does it foreclose the possibility that there will be some future building contract in which the application of these same principles would suggest that we *should* assess damages for emotional suffering, assuming it is also seemingly "worth" the litigation and administrative costs inherent in doing more case-by-case analysis of consequences.

Think too, for instance, about Green's work on torts in thinking about the seeming futility of the "narrow category" reform project. If one looks at the table of contents of his casebook,[30] one might think it was a precursor to the famous Borges meditation on the almost absurd plasticity of categorization schemes.[31] The section on physical harms—arguably too narrow a category already from a deductive/instrumentalist viewpoint—is divided into sections on "Threats, Insults, Blows, Attacks, Wounds, Fights, Restraints Etc.," "Surgical Operations," "Keeping of Animals," "Occupancy, Ownership, Development of Land," "Manufacturers, Dealers," "Builders, Contractors, Workmen," "Power, Telephone and Telegraph, Water, and Gas Companies," "Counties, Towns, Cities, Boards," and "Traffic and Transportation." The case-type scheme gets considerably more surreal. Not only are transportation and traffic injuries seemingly sharply distinguished from injuries caused by those who keep animals, transportation injuries are differentiated depending upon whether they involve "Highway and Railway Traffic," "Waterway Traffic," "Passenger Transportation," or "Freight Transportation."

The problem is not merely that there is no text in the casebook that gives us a clear sense of why Green thinks the results in cases actually do or should turn in any significant way on whether they involve waterways or railways. After all, the custom of the time was for casebooks to contain little or no commentary, so this is hardly revealing. The more puzzling problem is that when one reads Green's law review essays on torts, they invariably invoke conventional policy-driven Realist interpretations of the conventional broad categories and thoroughly eschew the narrower categories.[32]

As difficult as it might be to defend the MM belief that *individuals* solve problems that come in pre-boxed narrow packages, unable to apply more general principles to solving them even when local conditions shift, there are at least explanations lodged in time pressure, limited cognitive resources, and information-processing limits to suggest that some variant of the claim is plausible. It is far less credible that collective decision makers, processing arguments on both sides of an issue offered by counsel representing parties with distinct interests, unconstrained by time pressure, should react with strong intuitions to case types or why, even at the individual biological level, there would be any reason to expect intuitions to correspond to the narrow contingent dispute categories of modern life rather than far broader dispute categories (that centered on avoiding, compensating, and blaming intentional and accidental harm to strangers, creating and maintaining the conditions for mutual cooperation and agreements). Narrow category realism has all the granularity problem flaws of massive modularism and no adaptationist story with built-in cognitive limits to make the development of the relevant localized narrow-grained intuitions even vaguely plausible. Its ongoing lack of influence in the legal academy should come as no surprise.

E. CONCLUSION

Neither Langdell nor Holmes self-consciously addressed the nature of human cognition in defending, respectively, the Classical synthesis about law or a more pragmatic Realist approach. It is instructive, nonetheless, to see some of Langdell's beliefs as homologous with F&F conceptions and to see some parallels between Holmes's thought and H&B theory.

Ultimately, Langdell's arguments for base-level rules resonates in the idea that cognition is lexical; instead of trying to consider all the factors and balance them using an uncertain set of weights, we resolve issues by noting the presence or absence of some critical, readily discerned feature. More subtly, though, his arguments for deducing a small set of principles that permit judges to fill gaps in the law, to criticize existing decisions, and to establish a normatively acceptable system, without appealing to policy in particular disputes, resonate in F&F views of cognition. The principles that he believes can be deduced by careful study of existing case law are not natural or intuitive in the way that basic tools are in F&F theory, but the principles otherwise strongly resemble the basic cognitive tools in the adaptive toolbox that can be utilized in novel situations. Finally, F&F arguments about the possible superiority of adjudication over legislation and administration—judges try to find a few apt generalizations rather than looking for situation-specific solutions by trying to discern and manipulate the multifaceted roots of a particular problem—bear a resemblance to Langdell's views about what constitutes "real law."

Holmes believed that our problem-solving "intuitions" developed historically and collectively to a greater extent than they derived from individually adaptive cognitive algorithms. But like H&B theorists who describe the relationship between System One and System Two thinking, Holmes believed that such intuitions exist to meet functional ends, and that following them will often do so, but that we have the capacity to override them. He also, like H&B scholars, believed that internal limits in our cognitive processing capacity dictated the problem-solving techniques that we employ; for Holmes, legal categories are useful almost entirely because they permit us to learn how to resolve cases consistently, despite our limited cognitive powers, rather than because they establish guiding principles that best meet our goals.

There was a group of mid-twentieth century Legal Realists who were loosely committed to the idea that we should repudiate broad conceptual categories more thoroughly and look to see how we respond to very fine-grained dispute-types. Their views seem strongly homologous with the views of MM (and to a lesser degree F&F) scholars who reject the idea that the mind has general computational abilities, rather than the capacity to respond in adaptive ways to extremely delimited cues. This view has had little influence on the legal academy for many of the same reasons that MM theory is suspect; it is not at all clear that any of the fine-grained categories of disputes that people ostensibly respond to in a unique way is appropriately broad, narrow, or otherwise apt.

PART FOUR
Final Thoughts

10

CONCLUSION

It is debatable whether there is a "heuristics debate" at all. In many ways, proponents of the two schools of thought that I have reviewed—the "heuristics and biases" (H&B) school and the "fast and frugal heuristics" school (F&F)—use similar methods in investigating human judgment and decision making, and at some very high level of generality, they can be seen to have a similar picture of what heuristics are and how people use them.

Methodologically, heuristics researchers draw on the work of many other psychologists. Those psychologists who studied memory treated accurate memory as a dependent variable and investigated the conditions in which accuracy increased or decreased as a way to comprehend and model basic memory processes, and those who studied visual perception looked to consider what parameters of an object produce a particular visual illusion or permit an object to be seen. Similarly, researchers who study the use of heuristics from both schools use a fundamentally similar method. They treat accuracy in judgment as the dependent variable and manipulate the choice-making environment to see what inputs produce both erroneous and proper judgments in order to understand judgment and decision making more generally.

Substantively, researchers working in both traditions define heuristics in a fairly similar way, if we look at the most general definitions; subjects are using heuristics whenever they make a judgment or reach a decision without making use of some potentially germane information or some computational abilities that at least some people possess. They agree, too, that using these strategies is sometimes absolutely necessary and often "functional" in the sense that subjects who use them reach results that are satisfactory to meet their ends and would, at a bare minimum, not improve performance enough to justify the use of other more time- and attention-intensive methods. The strategies developed because they were adaptive to or adequate for the bulk of situations in which they arose.

Researchers from each school agree as well that heuristics may also be used in situations in which their use is dysfunctional. F&F researchers are more prone to emphasize that the use of heuristics is not invariably functional because heuristics may have evolved in an environment that has changed while H&B researchers may emphasize to a greater degree that using heuristics, like using any proxy or generalization, will inevitably be inapt in some situations. Scholars associated with each school also recognize that those who would exploit others have the capacity to manipulate an environment so it has, or appears to have, traits that trigger a particular judgment or decision, inducing behavior that the manipulator desires rather than the behavior that the agent would engage in if he either used a wider range of informational cues or if he encountered the single or simple cues that he would have encountered absent the manipulation.

Both H&B and F&F scholars agree that it is often difficult to alter how individuals process fixed cues, whether by offering incentives or giving instructions. Thus, if we are worried about "bad decisions," it is usually preferable to change the cues the decision maker confronts or to delegate decisions from a badly positioned to a well-positioned decision maker.

But while noting these similarities is important, it should not blind us to the genuine distinctions between the research programs of the two schools. The distinctions are not just significant if our goal is to understand how each group of scholars pictures cognition, but they are also important if we want to understand the implications of modeling cognition in different ways for thinking about law and policy formation.

There are many ways of thinking about the substantive distinctions between the schools. Here is the most basic set of distinctions I would draw: *H&B scholars believe that subjects typically make decisions by assessing the probability that certain outcomes will occur if they follow each particular course of action they contemplate taking and by evaluating each of these possible outcomes. Because people have limited computational capacity, they do not always make accurate judgments about what will happen even if they have perfect information. Impediments to accuracy are not simply those external barriers that rational choice theorists emphasize; internal processing deficits often preclude people from reaching ideal factual judgments. Instead of processing all information, people often make a judgment based on a substitute attribute. Most frequently, using the easily processed substituted or proxy attribute permits accurate judgment, but it sometimes does not. Moreover, evaluations of known consequences are far more labile than rational choice theorists presume; they are frame and elicitation sensitive.*

How, then, should we conceive of the F&F school? In what ways is the basic description of cognition different? *F&F scholars do not believe that the dominant source of the use of heuristics is our computational incapacity or that the use of heuristics simply permits us to make a "good enough" approximation on most occasions of the judgments we would make were we to process more information. The mind is not best pictured as a general computing machine; it is better pictured as having developed a number of adaptive tools to solve practical problems that present themselves in the real world, making use of environmentally available cues to meet actual organism ends. These tools are readily employed in the contexts in which they initially evolved and can also be profitably "hijacked" when we face novel problems that can be aptly solved using them. Even when judgment appears to fall short of meeting the demands of classical rational choice theory, the judgments may be ecologically, if not logically, rational in the sense that they meet our actual proximal goals. Heuristics are best seen as one of the most critical sources of our practical intelligence, not as a reflection of our limited intelligence. While rational choice theorists extol multifactor judgment and decision-making processes in which general purpose minds weigh cues and factors, and H&B theorists believe our incapacity to perform such multifactor balancing may often lead us astray, F&F theorists believe, descriptively, that we typically use lexical decision-making processes and, normatively, that doing so typically leads us to make better judgments.*

Given these basic disputes, we would expect that partisans of each school would have genuine hesitations about the scholarship associated with the other school. Although some of the nastier bickering that I observe as an outsider to the field occasionally feels as though it might have as much to do with scholars trying either to stake or to resist claims to novelty or to reflect what seem like feuds over slights of murky origin, there are real disagreements as well.

Even if one is drawn fairly strongly to the H&B research program, I think there is a great deal to be learned by reflecting on the basic critiques that F&F scholars have articulated of that program. F&F theorists criticize H&B research for two reasons. First, and most important, they argue that subjects *seem* to perform sub-optimally in H&B experiments only because they are given problems in these experimental settings that do not accurately mimic problems that they would confront in natural environments. Second, they argue that the H&B theorists neither explain why people use the precise heuristic problem-solving techniques that they purportedly use nor, even more important, *define* the mechanisms in adequate detail. Because they do not tell us when people will use any given technique whose precise contours can be specified, H&B scholars make far too few predictions that can be either falsified or verified.

Within the F&F paradigm, the gap between performance on real-world problems and H&B laboratory problems is caused by the fact that the mental capacities that evolved are the capacities to solve recurring problems that increase inclusive fitness, not the more diffuse capacity to be an abstractly better calculator. If this is right, what goes wrong in H&B research is that the H&B experimenters test people's capacity to solve formal problems and then misinterpret formal failures on these problems as functional failures of cognition.

Whatever its *genesis*, the gap between good real-world performance and bad lab performance occurs, according to F&F researchers, because H&B experiments are misleading or poorly constructed in four distinct ways. F&F theorists argue, first, that H&B researchers often present problems in a cognitively intractable *form*; subjects would do better if data were presented in the way it is more typically confronted in naturalistic settings. Second, they claim that H&B theorists often present problems that precisely correspond mathematically to problems people have learned to solve contextually, not mathematically or formally, when it would meet their goals to do so. The H&B researchers then express what F&F scholars see as unjustifiable surprise that people cannot solve the formal equivalents of these practical, real-world problems. Third, they present problems with payoffs that differ from the payoffs in real-world decision-making situations; the laboratory games strongly remind subjects of the decision-making situations that they have confronted in the natural environment, and they respond to the payoffs that are familiar from that environment. Once more, the F&F scholars think that H&B experimenters convey unmerited surprise when the lab subjects play the lab games by the rules of the real-world game that the lab games most closely mimic rather than playing them by the rules they first confronted when they showed up to be experimental subjects. Fourth and finally, H&B researchers wrongly believe that their subjects make mistakes when they reinterpret the experimenter's instructions in a fashion that makes their responses reasonable, even when their reinterpretations display the subjects' conversational competence and the experimenter's inability to read sub-text as well as text.

Just as those fundamentally drawn to H&B work would almost surely profit from gaining a sympathetic understanding of the F&F school, so it would seem that F&F scholars could sharpen their work if they were less adversarial in responding to criticisms of their approach, more willing to construct and try to incorporate to the degree possible the best conceivable version of the critiques. This may not always be possible. Both rational choice theorists and H&B theorists fairly flatly reject both the descriptive proposition that people use lexical, rather than compensatory, judgment and decision-making processes and the even more puzzling normative claim that it is almost invariably good that they do so. While one could imagine that this is merely a dispute about *how often* they use compensatory rather than lexical strategies and how often the lexical process outperforms other methods, the actual gap on this critical issue is probably impossible to bridge. A commitment to lexicality (or "soft encapsulation") is, in my view, what most defines the F&F school, even though those in the policy world who are aware of the F&F research at all are more likely to think that it is centrally defined by its relative optimism or cheeriness about judgment and decision making.

But other critiques of F&F scholarship seem to permit a far greater opportunity for interchange and adjustment of ideas. H&B theorists might be right that F&F researchers are unduly prone to posit idealized cognitive capacities that would serve to resolve real or imagined adaptive problems rather than to describe these capacities in adequately nuanced form. Even if they are right on this count, though, F&F theory would remain almost wholly intact. It would not seem, for instance, that we would by any means need to reject, say, the existence of some sort of recognition heuristic—even if one rejected both the proposition that it was typically used lexically and the claim that its use was optimal across any domain range that could be specified non-tautologically—if we revised the particular F&F account of familiarity memory, the cognitive capacity that recognition heuristic users purportedly employ.

Similarly, I don't think it is seriously damaging to the F&F program to acknowledge the problem that it has not yet developed anything close to an adequate theory of how people know it is appropriate to use any heuristic at all, or which one to employ in a particular setting. It is hard enough to know precisely what triggers dedicated modules in massive modularity (MM) theory; it is far harder still to figure out how tools from the F&F theorists' adaptive toolbox get utilized in settings outside the ones for which they were ostensibly specifically adapted. But H&B theorists, after all, have survived though they do little more to specify when System One "intuitions" will or will not be "overridden" by more conscious System Two processes, except to the limited degree that they posit that subjects are more prone to do so when they have more resources (time, lower cognitive load, etc.). And rational choice theorists' idea that people use more informationally impoverished rules of thumb only when the costs of acquiring and processing more information outweigh the gains from the additional information depends on imagining some wholly underspecified meta-cognitive skill to evaluate the gains and costs of information that one does not yet even possess.

Not only do I suppose that those predisposed to think that people make decisions following the dictates of rational choice theory, those who believe that the H&B scholars have best identified the key troublesome features of judgment and decision making, and those drawn to the F&F program could all benefit if they took one another's work more seriously, I suspect as well that many people who read these literatures from an outsider's perspective may think that various sorts of mixing and matching are attractive. Plainly, I do not feel I am even remotely qualified or prepared to offer anything resembling a general theory of judgment and decision making, but it is worth mentioning the sorts of theories to which I am drawn, merely to illustrate how one might be influenced by, but not embrace, any of the schools.

Like rational choice theorists, I presume people use compensatory methods in making judgments and decisions. Even if they first approach a problem expecting to look at only a single or small number of cues, they will not stick with that predisposition when they notice something in the environment that makes it clear that they should account for more. Thus, for example, in terms of making factual assessments, they will not merely look to recognition in making judgments of city size when there is easily processed information available that would allow them to infer that recognition is not the best predictor of size. This is true when they are making decisions as well. They may generally drive at the speed of traffic, mimicking those around them, but stop doing so if everyone is speeding and they see a police car around the bend. They may be able to use a cue lexically in some settings and know not to use it in that way in settings that might at first blush seem "similar;" no one in Palo Alto drives two hours just to go to an inexpensive ethnic restaurant (i.e., proximity is a first discriminator in an elimination by aspects approach), but they may drive that far for a fancy meal yet still *account* for distance in making a decision about where to go for the fancy meal.

Like H&B theorists, I believe that people may systematically overvalue how probative easily processed cues may be, especially if using these cues rarely causes problems. I suppose, for instance, that even though subjects do not use recognition information exclusively when judging the relative size of two cities, they overestimate how probative it is relative to other cues, even when they have noticed that they must attend to some other cues. (And I also think, like F&F scholars, that they use either just one or a small number of cues radically more frequently than rat-choice theorists would presume they would.) Rational choice theorists surely understate both the problem of processing error and the utility of making judgments and decisions based on a small number of inputs.

I trust, too, that rat-choice theorists overestimate the degree to which people can make evaluative choices without regard to the ways in which tastes are elicited or framed, but they also conclude that H&B theorist have traditionally drastically overstated the degree to which tastes are context dependent. I am convinced that preferences are labile in shallow ways, but not so much in deep ways. It might be far easier to get someone to select one model of camera by placing it as the intermediate priced camera or by placing it alongside a similar camera that it clearly dominates than it is to get someone uninterested in photography to become interested by manipulating context, let alone to get people to act radically more altruistically or to be less impulsive. H&B theory can be used, too loosely and metaphorically, to imply that we can readily re-socialize people to be rather different people, and I think the evidence for the capacity to alter important tastes by manipulating a tractable set of situational mediators is not very strong.

Finally, I think F&F scholars are right to remind us that we may make many judgments and decisions directly, rather than deductively. There might be many situations in which cues generate apt responses, and we need not figure out in any sense why the response will meet our needs. This is not just true in situations in which it is most obviously the case—when, for instance, we remove our hand from a very hot object, we don't calculate the expected value of keeping it in place—but is also surely true in situations that might look, at first blush, as though they might require elaborate cost-benefit calculation. It is only partly ironic to say that life may be a bit easier than it looks, and that if it weren't, we would mess up a whole lot more. We would indeed be far less intelligent, far less capable of meeting our ends, if we actually had to *figure out* how we should act each time we had options. We may in some part just do what we are taught, habitually, and take advantage of the more explicit formal rationality of others who have come before us, but it is likely that we find many useful responses either especially easy to learn or instinctive.

While I do not ultimately think that the F&F and H&B schools are best distinguished in terms of their faith in human judgment and decision making, there is no doubt that some of the important implications for policy we can draw from reflecting on the heuristics debate do indeed come from considering how optimistic the scholars are about the use of heuristics. In this regard, it is instructive to think about some very basic attitudes or predispositions that rational choice theory, H&B theory, and F&F theory display, given their beliefs about the relative virtues and perils of heuristic reasoning.

Table 10.1 might be helpful in this regard:

What is most important to consider in looking at Table 10.1 is not just the bottom-line conclusions; it is that F&F theory and rational choice theory diverge in so many important respects. This is especially noteworthy because F&F theory has been used in the law and policymaking communities, to the degree it has been attended to at all, largely to bolster rational choice theorists' negative reaction to H&B theory's skepticism about the self-governing capacity of consumers and voters. The message of F&F has generally been reduced to the message, "People make choices pretty darn well, and there goes the case for increased levels of paternalism." And it is worth noting as well that even in terms of manifesting a disposition toward Pollyanna-ish reactions to unregulated markets, F&F scholars are notably less sanguine about the rationality of discrimination than most rat-choice theorists. They are more inclined to emphasize the possibility that both in-group favoritism and out-group animus are atavistic remnants of kin favoritism that was far more rational in the environment of evolutionary adaptation than in a modern economy than that discrimination is an information-cost reducing strategy, adopted by rational actors only when getting individualized information about the relevant traits of would-be employees and customers is unduly costly.

Table 10.1

Issue	H&B School	F&F School	Rational Choice Theory
Overall quality of human judgment	Good for typical situations but fallible and subject to manipulation by malign outsiders	Excellent	Superhuman; only external impediments (like information) limit capacity to reach accurate judgments
Need for expert judgment	High because more prone to use System Two to override "intuition"	Low; experts prone to overfit data and to try to "balance" rather than seek a single best goal	High because they have more information
Need for paternalistic regulation	High	Low	Low
Need to increase information flow	Relatively low	Low; focus on few critical pieces	Moderately high (though information is costly to process)
Cost-benefit analysis desirable?	Useful analytical tool	Generally misguided, due both to incommensurability of values and need to process and combine too much information	The ideal mechanism for both individual and collective choice
Rules versus standards	Depends: rules may be faulty heuristics	Strong preference for rules	Each has virtues and flaws that can be assessed through cost-benefit analysis
Nature of status-based discrimination	Troublesome: Based on typical heuristic over-generalizations	May be troublesome if grounded in in-group preferences that are less important outside the EEA	Likely to be based on information cost reduction if manifest in markets or on political power

It is indeed important to emphasize that rat-choice and F&F scholars have a radically distinct picture of cognition; the F&F scholars find the rat-choice claim most strongly associated with Stigler that people acquire more information as long as the expected benefit from information acquisition outweighs the cost of acquisition to be one of the most preposterous claims about decision making ever made. But it is at least as vital to recognize that they have very different views about policy that grow out of their distinct views about what people are capable of and how people make decisions that best serve their ends. Rat-choice scholars believe that agencies making collective decisions ought to utilize technical expertise to make decisions based on cost-benefit analysis. F&F scholars distrust technical expertise because they suspect that experts will overfit the particular multifactor data sets they analyze rather than work to identify more enduring rules of thumb about how the world really works. They also disdain all-things-considered cost-benefit analysis, not only because both benefits and costs may often be, in their view, incommensurable but because maximizing along a single critical dimension (or small handful of dimensions) is almost always going to achieve proximal goals better than trying to attend to a multitude of factors.

Rational choice theorists generally believe as well that decision makers will do better if given more information, though they recognize both the possibility that one can give people information whose incremental value is lower than the cost of processing it and that people can be so flooded with information that their decision-making prowess decreases. But for F&F theorists, there is no similar presumption that increased information is valuable; quite to the contrary, decision makers will typically do best when given one piece, or a small handful of pieces, of the most critical information that they need to make the relevant decision. Moreover, F&F scholars have been uniquely devoted to considering carefully how matching information presentation methods to our native information processing capacities is of far greater importance to creating informed choosers than simply piling on information. My strong sense is that if you want patients to give *meaningful* informed consent, you would be much better off consulting with an F&F-influenced psychologist than either a rat-choice proponent or someone trained by H&B scholars to note defects in judgment.

Finally, rational choice theorists believe one can evaluate the choice between employing rules and standards using conventional cost-benefit methods; one simply compares the value of the gains in accuracy that one achieves using standards with the administrative costs borne by officials and the costs that citizens bear due to increased unpredictability that arises if one disdains mechanically applicable rules. F&F theorists, on the other hand, believe that the legal system is almost invariably best off using rules, both because actors in the system are cognitively capable of applying them while they cannot comfortably apply standards and because properly selected rules, which force decision makers to attend only to a small number of critical features of a situation in which they need to pick a course of action, will outperform decision-making rubrics that direct attention to a multitude of factors.

The contrasts between both rat-choice theory and F&F theory on the one hand and H&B theory on the other are probably more predictable for those who are attuned above all to the H&B school's more jaundiced view of decision making capability. Those trying to incorporate H&B insights are far more likely to see market failure arising from the ubiquitous use of inaccurate generalizations (thus, seeing a higher need for both paternalist interventions in markets and antidiscrimination law). They are more skeptical that information alone improves either individual or collective decision making, so that disclosure mandates may be inadequate in market settings and experts do better not so much because they know more as because they make decisions in settings in which they deliberate more. Those incorporating H&B scholarship are warier of rules, believing that many may be heuristics that are often, but not invariably, accurate mechanisms for resolving problems.

What is least transparent in the law and policymaking academy are the implications for both legal policy and legal theory of adopting, in both normative and descriptive terms, the more "softly encapsulated" lexical judgment and decision-making theories associated with F&F scholarship rather than theories postulating that people use compensatory methods, strongly associated with rational choice theory and more weakly associated with H&B theory. (H&B theorists see lexicality as less prevalent, descriptively, than F&F experimenters do, though they see it as more commonplace than rat-choice theorists do; normatively, they share with rat-choice theorists considerable skepticism that lexical methods outperform compensatory methods though they may be somewhat more apt to think they are good, mentally "cheap" options on a larger number of occasions.)

If people indeed use lexical methods, reducing crime by manipulating the expected net benefits of committing crime is a hopeless strategy. The problem is not simply, as H&B scholars would suggest, that there is likely to be a mismatch between changes in actual expected punishment levels (or even punishment levels about which there was information) and *perceived* punishment levels, nor is the problem that those who might commit crimes are atypically unlikely to calculate these levels. Instead, if F&F scholars are right, people don't even attempt to calculate whether committing a crime has a positive expected value. Instead, they decide to obey or disobey legal commands based on the presence or absence of hierarchically arranged single cues that generally have little to do with the crime's expected value. A successful crime-fighting strategy is not one that makes punishment more certain or harsh (or even, echoing H&B theory, a strategy that makes people *process* any given set of expected punishments as more likely or more harsh), but rather one that establishes an environment in which putative offenders confront cues that direct them toward obedience, such as habit or mimicry.

If people use lexical methods, we need to provide just one or a few pieces of information to consumers, sorted out (if possible) so that each receives only information relevant to his or her own case given the possibility of sorting by taste or by situation. The H&B strategy of trying both to give more information but to present it in a manner that allows us to guard against its being badly processed (e.g., because some is more easily available or representative) is, in this view, hopeless.

If F&F theorists are right that people typically use lexical processes, they may experience many "conflicts" as involving incommensurable values. Actions seem truly incommensurable only in situations in which the ends we seek are truly incomparable; that is, we cannot figure out whether an end is better, worse, or equally valued compared to another end. But ends are often described as incommensurable when we are committed to the idea that we ought not to make trade-offs because one end has lexical priority over other possible ends. To the extent that it is simply descriptively the case that we do not choose between courses of action by comparing the value of the options, it is possible that this gives rise to a subjective feeling that the ends we would achieve by pursuing one or the other course of action are incommensurable with other ends. It is also possible that we make choices without recognizing that we might have been torn between two possible courses of action, so we never have the subjective sensation that our ends are incommensurable.

What F&F theorists contribute to the long-standing debate on whether values are incommensurable is the claim that choices generally are made by a brain that obliterates conflict, either by remitting various types of decisions to distinct modules, one of which is the dominant module in terms of generating action responses, or by following lexical heuristic decision-making processes; incommensurability is then no longer an exceptional case that is basically quite hard to conceptualize, but instead, the ordinary case. Incommensurability is, of course, almost tautologically inconceivable within rat-choice theory; the fact that we can ultimately choose an action course implies commensurability for rat-choice scholars. While MM theorists could to some degree explain why people subjectively *feel* that certain ends are incommensurable, because the intuition to take actions one ultimately does not take "lives on" in its own "trumped" module, F&F scholars would seem merely to have a good model of "pseudo-incommensurability." What this means, fundamentally, is that they anticipate the regular use of trumping rules that categorically forbid making trade-offs; it is hardly a problem to picture a mind that treats "rights" as absolute side constraints if the mind is supposed to treat "recognition" of one of two cities as trumping all other information about the size of the two cities. But if F&F theorists are right that we think lexically in this way, we ought not subjectively experience the incommensurability of two "conflicting" desires. If option A entailed the sacrifice of a lexically prior goal, we would always choose some option B that did not; the fact that A had some other virtues would simply never come to mind, because we do not evaluate A against B along that second dimension if they differ along the first.

Surprisingly, perhaps, the commitment to the claim that people do and should make decisions lexically, using a handful of straightforward decision-making algorithms, is also homologous with, though not causally related to, many of the ideas associated with Classical legal orthodoxy. Langdell's arguments for using base-level *rules* to resolve the disputes that courts face resonates in the thought that cognition is lexical; instead of trying to consider "all the factors" and "balance" them, we do and should resolve controversies simply by determining whether some critical, easily discerned feature is present or not. More subtly, Langdell's arguments for deducing a small set of *principles* that permit judges to fill in and evaluate existing law also sound in F&F views of cognition. The principles that the Classical thinkers believe can be deduced by careful study of existing case law are not natural or intuitive in the way that basic cognitive tools are in F&F theory, but the principles otherwise strongly resemble the cognitive tools in the adaptive toolbox that can be utilized as the unique basis for reaching decisions in novel situations.

Interestingly, critics of the Classical synthesis, like Holmes, abjured the belief in noncompensatory decision making in much the same way that H&B scholars rejected the F&F commitment to the idea that we use lexical or near-lexical processes exclusively. Holmes believed that our intuitions about how to resolve conflicts arose historically and collectively, not from individually adaptive cognitive algorithms. But like H&B theorists exploring the ways in which self-conscious, reflective System Two cognitive processes may override less deliberative System One reactions, Holmes believed that such intuitions exist to meet our needs and that following them will often do so, but that we have the capacity to supersede them.

Ultimately, I am not sure what anyone can really make of the "mood" of either F&F or H&B theory. I barely know what it means to have overarching priors about whether we are "good"(not "bad") decision makers or whether the fact that we use heuristics makes us smarter or reveals that we may not be as smart as we think. Such moods and predispositions seem to me to fall on a continuum; it must be the case that people do well *sometimes*, and do even better because we use simpler methods sometimes. But it must also be true that we mess up sometimes and sometimes do so because generally useful judgment and decision making proxies sometimes go astray. Expressing any strong prior commitment to whether the term "sometimes" means something more like "occasionally" or something more like "plenty, and plenty enough to worry about," seems an odd errand.

On the other hand, if F&F theorists were right that we very rarely do anything resembling expected value calculation—albeit expected value calculation beset by a host of problems in assessing both facts and values of the sort that H&B theorists highlight so capably—then we would have to revise considerably our views of how law can and should operate. It is not only the case that we would need to revise comprehensively our conception of what it meant to inform a decision maker more completely about the options she was considering if it were true that we cannot trade off virtues we learn exist in one domain for flaws we learn exist in another. Even more strikingly, we would think that virtually all of the social control mechanisms that relied on shifting the expected gains from engaging in one activity rather than another were irrelevant; all of the positive and negative incentives that characterize the typical tools that we employ to channel behavior would simply be of no moment, except to the limited extent that such mechanisms induced certain behavioral changes that in turn cued apt behavior for some target population. These would be truly enormous changes. Fortunately, in my view, for those who are loathe to rethink *everything*, the F&F school's devotion to the idea that people cannot integrate additional probative cues in reaching judgments and making decisions is no more convincing than the school's unpersuasive claim that it is virtually invariably a good thing that people ignore probative data.

Views that blend the critical insights from each school seem most promising for legal thinkers and policymakers. People may well calculate expected values (as rat-choice theorists believe), at least sometimes. But they may often have better methods of reaching helpful judgments (as F&F theorist insist) and they may (as H&B theorists emphasize) overestimate how well their quick and dirty rules of thumb work, particularly in a world in which cues are manipulated by those with agendas. Keep all those thoughts in mind, recognizing that none has lexical priority, and one's policy prescriptions are considerably less likely to go astray.

NOTES

Chapter 1

1. See Gerd Gigerenzer and Reinhard Selten, "Rethinking Rationality" in *Bounded Rationality: The Adaptive Toolbox* 1, 7 (G. Gigerenzer and R. Selten eds., Cambridge, MA: MIT Press, 2002). Computer-driven robots are programmed to catch fly balls by mimicking the heuristic rule that people seem to use. Those in the fast and frugal heuristics "school" note, more generally, that the term "heuristics" first gained prominence when used by mathematicians to refer to informal and inductive methods of solving intractable problems. See especially George Polya, *How to Solve It: A New Aspect of Mathematical Method* (Princeton, NJ: Princeton University Press, 1954). This usage was also the one typically made by computer scientists who thought of heuristics as computationally efficient solutions to problems that have a high probability of reaching an effective solution, even if the solution is not optimal.

2. For an example from the "fast and frugal" (F&F) school focusing on the capacity of manipulative advertisers to "take advantage" of buyers' use of heuristics, see, e.g., Daniel G. Goldstein and Gerd Gigerenzer, "Models of Ecological Rationality: The Recognition Heuristic," 109 *Psychol. Rev.* 75, 86–87:

   ... a firm may opt to manipulate the product's name recognition through advertising instead of investing in the research and development necessary to improve the product's quality. Advertising manipulates recognition rates directly and is one way in which institutions exploit recognition-based inference ... [A]dvertisers pay great sums of money for a place in the recognition memory of the general public ... on the principle that if we do not recognize them, then we will not favor them ...

   The distrust of profit-seekers exploiting consumers who make inaccurate heuristic-based inferences is likely even more pronounced among theorists working in the heuristics and biases (H&B) tradition: For examples, see Russell Korobkin, "The Problem with Heuristics for Law," in *Heuristics and the Law* 44, 49–50 (G. Gigerenzer and C. Engel eds., Cambridge, MA: MIT Press 2006); Jon D. Hanson and Douglas A. Kysar, "Taking Behaviorism Seriously: The Problem of Market Manipulation," 74 *N.Y.U. L. Rev.* 630, 724–33 (1999); Melissa L. Finucane, Ali Alhakami, Paul Slovic and Stephen M. Johnson, "The Affect Heuristic in Judgments of Risk and Benefits," 13 *J. Behav. Decision Making* 1 (2000).
   For an example from the F&F school of the fear of manipulative attorneys, see, e.g., Callia Piperides et al., "Group Report: What Is the Role of Heuristics in Litigation?" in *Heuristics and the Law*, supra note 2 at 344, 364:

   Difficulties arise because lawyers, knowing that juries will rely on heuristic reasoning, strive to acquire witnesses who give the appearance of expertise and neutrality ... When the reliability of opposing witnesses is crafted and manipulated by lawyers, as is often the case with opposing scientific experts, the ecological rationality of the cues, and thereby of Take the Best may decrease . . . If there were no lawyers involved, it is plausible that the most memorable . . . evidence would be the most reliable and probative. However, lawyers manipulate evidence to make the most useful facts and inferences for their side . . . the most memorable . . . The recognition heuristic can be fooled, and the previously anonymous can inherit the appearance of being skilled, famous, important or powerful.

3. In Chapter Four, I discuss more explicitly both the possibility that people are more prone to understand the likelihood they are HIV+ if they tested positive if the information is presented in "frequentist" rather than probabilistic as well as some alternative explanations for this finding. Here is the basic finding, though. Most people have a great deal of trouble processing information conveyed in the following "probabilistic" form that H&B researchers studying "base rate neglect" had presented it in: "99.8% of those who are HIV-positive test positive. Only 0.01% of those who are not HIV-positive test positive. The base rate for the disease among heterosexual men with few risk factors is 0.01%. How likely is it that a particular low-risk factor heterosexual man is HIV-positive if he tests positive?"
On the other hand, most people find it relatively easy to comprehend properly the same information presented in the following frequentist way:

Think about 10,000 heterosexual men with few risk factors for acquiring HIV. One is infected, and he will almost certainly test positive. Of the remaining 9999 uninfected men, one will also test positive. Thus, we'd expect two of the ten thousand men will test positive and only one of them has HIV. So what are the chances that a person who tests positive is infected?

4. For a terrific summary of work in this tradition, see *Heuristics and Biases* (T. Gilovich, D. Griffin and D. Kahneman eds., Cambridge, UK; New York: Cambridge University Press, 2002).
5. It is perfectly plausible to me that from the perspective of an "insider"—someone whose dominant interest was in cognitive psychology rather than the relationship between pictures of cognition and policy formation— the two distinct schools I contrast in the book are not really distinct "schools" at all to the degree that they use fundamentally similar methodological approaches. Instead, they might be described as researchers working within the same tradition who have produced some research studies with distinct findings.
6. Excellent summaries of the key insights of the literature, with special attention to legal and policy applications, can be found in *Heuristics and the Law*, supra note 2. One might get a better sense still of the methodology and key tenets of the school by looking at *Bounded Rationality* and *Simple Heuristics That Make Us Smart* (G. Gigerenzer, P. M. Todd and the ABC Research Group, New York: Oxford University Press 1999).
There is a good deal of conceptual overlap between the work of Gigerenzer and his associates and the work of Payne, Bettman and Johnson though there are important distinctions as well that I do not address. See John W. Payne, James R. Bettman and Eric J. Johnson *The Adaptive Decision Maker* (New York: Cambridge University Press, 1993). I exclusively discuss the F&F school, in significant part because authors in this tradition, like authors in the H&B tradition, have explicitly addressed the connection between heuristics and the law.

7. A decision maker has lexical preferences if she decides that X is better than Y when it is better along the "most important" dimension (or if tied on the most important trait, that it is better along the second most important dimension etc.). When we make judgments about the relative size of two numbers, our judgments are lexical in precisely that sense: We know that 510 is bigger than 498 because the "five" in the hundreds column is bigger than the "4." We don't look at the tens column unless there is a tie in the hundreds column, nor do we look at the ones column unless there is a tie in both the hundreds and the tens.
8. Understanding the "gaze heuristic" I briefly described at the beginning of the chapter might indeed help a programmer who wanted to program a robot to catch fly balls, but in role as lawyers, we don't build a lot of fly-catching robots.
9. Of course, the further hope is that as an academic lawyer, it is easier to see the implications of these works for legal policy and legal theory. But that defense of the project goes more to Part III, in truth, than to Part II.
10. There are innumerable interesting issues—worthy of considerable sustained attention, though it will receive none at all in this book—about how non-expert policymakers can ever hope to use expert knowledge, especially when experts disagree. Writing this book raises a pretty trivial version of this nontrivial problem.

   I have had to deal for many years with the issue of whether, and when, it is appropriate as an outsider to intervene in disputes that I acknowledge are outside my discipline in confronting work I have been suspicious of. This has been true in reacting both to work done by both H&B theorists and to work done by theorists associated with the F&F school.

   Here are two of the basic stories. Many—though not all—H&B theorists reacted in a way that I would describe as quite ferociously negative to the first circulated draft of a piece I co-wrote arguing that one aspect of the literature on "hindsight bias" was highly misleading. For those interested in a more detailed account of what we ultimately argued, see Mark Kelman, David E. Fallas and Hilary Folger, "Decomposing Hindsight Bias," 16 *J. Risk & Uncertainty* 251 (1999). We had argued that what we called "primary bias"—the tendency to believe that outcomes that actually occurred were more probable, *ex ante*, than they actually were—was largely a function not of a recalcitrant judgment bias (or irrational substitution of a proxy variable—outcome—for the real target variable—prior probability) but of inadequate information about *ex ante* probabilities. We argued, in the same vein, that where such prior probabilities *could* be known or readily computed, outcomes did not affect judgment of these probabilities. The bulk of H&B-influenced readers basically made two particular claims, each directed at demonstrating the overarching idea that we were incompetent interlopers: First, some claimed that we simply did not understand the hindsight bias literature. More specifically, they claimed—or in my mind, clearly *misclaimed*, given both the explicit statements and experimental prompts in Fischoff's seminal work on hindsight bias—that the literature addressed *only* what we had called secondary and tertiary bias—the tendency to believe that one knew all along or that others should have known all along prior probabilities that one did not in fact know. Second almost all of the hostile readers claimed that we did not properly appreciate or understand that "hindsight bias" was merely a "heuristic" and that such heuristics are used only when non-heuristic computations are otherwise difficult. Of course, from our viewpoint, it was unclear why it would be classified as a "bias" if it is used only when it is the best feasible technique available to calculate probabilities. While it would be possible to demonstrate that result-information is over-valued in estimating *ex ante* probabilities even if it does not invariably *substitute* for other ways of judging *ex ante* probabilities, it remains the case, in my view, that none of the research on hindsight bias has actually demonstrated that theoretically plausible point. We viewed our piece as pressing hindsight bias researchers to come to terms with the question of how to think about conditions in which over-weighting would occur, and the degree to which it would occur. For another example of a situation in which I found myself unconvinced by the experimental work of H&B scholars with drastically more experimental psychology experience than I have, see Mark Kelman, "Problematic Perhaps, but Not Irrational," 54 *Stan. L. Rev.* 101 (2002) (criticizing work that assumes that the person whose judgment of the "badness" of an event changes depending on the context in which she makes her judgment—is the defendant's action morally deplorable compared to other actions pretty much like the defendant's or bad compared to all actions that all defendants engage in?—has, in some sense, committed a cognitive error or "been irrational" in precisely the same way that the person who thinks two identical circles are different in size depending on the backdrop circles in the field is mistaken).

The second story relates to the study of the recognition heuristic. F&F-influenced psychologists have reacted with similar contemptuous disdain towards the portion of the work that I have done on the recognition heuristic (with Nicholas Richman Kelman), which I summarize in fair detail in Chapter Five. Once more, we face the parallel accusation that we misapprehended what those we were criticizing (in this case, Goldstein and Gigerenzer) actually claimed in their work on the recognition heuristic: The basic claims are that we are wrong to think that Goldstein and Gigerenzer actually believed, as we assert, that their subjects make binary judgments that are grounded in binary familiarity memory, of whether they "recognize" one city in a pair of cities whose sizes they will then be asked to compare; that we are wrong to believe they have any view on whether people given additional information about unrecognized cities rather than information that recognized cities might be smaller than they might at first suspect will use that information; or that there is anything in their writing that suggests that they cannot explain why subjects recognize proper names in context (Roosevelt as a president but not as a town) given their accounts of the adaptive tool that recognition heuristic rely upon. Once more, in ways Idetail, in Chapter Five, I am convinced that our critics are wrong, but understand that a reasonable reader's prior would likely be that the experts are right and we interlopers confused.

11. Here is a quick account of the contrast between "traditional" views of cognition and domain-specific theories:

> According to a long predominant view, human beings are endowed with a general set of reasoning abilities that they bring to bear on any cognitive task, whatever its specific content... In contrast to this view, a growing number of researchers have concluded that many cognitive abilities are specialized to handle specific types of information. In short, much of human cognition is domain-specific.

Lawrence A. Hirschfeld and Susan A. Gelman, "Toward a Topography of Mind: An Introduction to Domain Specificity," in *Mapping the Mind: Domain Specificity in Cognition and Culture*: 3 (L.A. Hirschfeld and S.A. Gelman eds., Cambridge, UK; New York: Cambridge University Press, 1994). A cognitive system that is characterized as highly domain-specific will have some technique for partitioning the cues we confront in the world, so that, for instance, we "naturally" link together animals, rather than confronting cats and robins as "things weighing less than fifty pounds" and some more-or-less mandatory accounts of the important features shared by category members. A domain-specific capacity is also likely to be universal with relatively few distinctions in individual performance among functional adults, and domain-specific minds make many judgments that are inaccessible to the will and consciousness because a sub-system dedicated to particular tasks does not make use of inputs outside the triggering mechanism to make the domain-specific judgment.

12. Leda Cosmides and John Tooby, "Evolutionary Psychology, Moral Heuristics, and the Law," in *Heuristics and the Law*, supra note 2 at 175, 185–89. It is neither here nor there for my purposes whether the studies purporting to show that rent control dampens housing construction and increases homelessness are right or wrong.

13. See Keith E. Stanovich, *Who is Rational? Studies of Individual Differences in Reasoning* 250 (Mahwah, NJ: Lawrence Erlbaum Associates, 1999). Throughout the book, Stanovich (echoing the theme generally emphasized more in F&F literature) also emphasizes ways in which our ancestral intuitions are ill-suited to the modern world. His examples almost invariably invoke the possibility that we have become vulnerable to the sorts of exploitation and short-sighted illiberal decision-making that conventional political liberals typically worry about. See, e.g., id. at 217 (cognitive errors account for global warming, depletion of fishing stocks and animal extinction, neglect of preventive vaccination) and 207, 226–27 (use of heuristics increase consumer vulnerability to misleading advertising and misleading presentation of price information by auto dealers).

Chapter 2

1. Kahneman and Tversky were pretty explicit about this interpretation of the foundational works of H&B in their response to some of Gigerenzer's early attacks on H&B. "... the study of systematic error can illuminate the psychological processes that underlie perception and judgment... The main goal of this research was to understand the cognitive processes that produce both valid and invalid judgments." Daniel Kahneman and Amos Tversky, "On the Reality of Cognitive Illusions," 103 *Psychol. Rev.* 582 (1996). They have reiterated this point on other occasions: See, for instance, Amos Tversky and Daniel Kahneman, "Extensional Versus Intuitive Reasoning: The Conjunction Fallacy in Probability Judgment," in *Heuristics and Biases* 19, 47 (T. Gilovich, D. Griffin and D. Kahneman eds., Cambridge, UK; New York: Cambridge University Press, 2002).

2. The classic source is Daniel Kahneman and Amos Tversky, "Prospect Theory: An Analysis of Decision Under Risk," 47 *Econometrica* 263 (1979).

3. For the basic initial formulation of the priority heuristic, see Eduard Brandstatter, Gerd Gigerenzer and Ralph Hertwig, "The Priority Heuristic: Making Choices Without Trade-Offs," 113 *Psychol. Rev.* 409 (2006). At core, subjects using the priority heuristic to make choices involving risk look first to find a no-conflict solution. That is, they try to find an option that differs from another option only along a single dimension and select the option that is clearly superior to the other along that dimension. Failing that, and finding conflicts between higher returns with probabilities less than 1 and lower returns with higher probabilities, they do not weigh and sum (as expected value, expected utility, and prospect theorists each expect they do, albeit in a different fashion) but instead establish sequentially acted-upon fast and frugal rules to distinguish the choices. They stop and reach a decision when the difference along the next sequentially chosen reason is "large enough."

I am not certain the precise formulation of sequential rules that they suggest people use is truly adequately motivated in the paper, but, for completeness sake, I will note what the sequential "rules" are: In comparing some lottery X with some lottery Y, the subject will select a lottery if one-tenth of the maximum payoff from either lottery is greater than the difference between the lowest payoffs one can earn from the other lottery. (My sense is that the one-tenth is chosen because computations are performed on the numbers we "naturally" scale in a base ten system, but I am not at all sure that I am interpreting them correctly in that regard.) If that "test" does not discriminate between the lotteries, one would select a lottery L if the probability of the *worst* outcome, plus one-tenth (0.1) were less than the probability of the worst outcome under the alternative lottery L.' Finally, if that second "test" still did not discriminate between the lotteries, one would choose the lottery with a higher probability for the best outcome.

There are critiques of the claim that people typically make choices using the priority heuristic. Critics argue, essentially, that (1) its domain is more seriously limited than its advocates acknowledge, and/or (2) its advocates have selectively "mined" existing experiments on risky choices in claiming that it provides a good description of decision making, not recognizing that existing experiments were designed to distinguish between expected utility theory and prospect theory in a narrow range of circumstances in which their predictions differ, and/or (3) that even if subjects behave "as-if" they are using the heuristic, there is little reason to believe they are actually using these decision techniques, and/or (4) that the "theory" is filled with ad hoc adjustments which do not fit the idea that those using it are using a fast and frugal heuristic. Critics emphasize that the fact that people usually make—but can be manipulated not to make—choices in which one option stochastically dominates another depends on their paying heed not just to the best and worst possible outcomes of a gamble but to "middle terms" as well and the F&F approach here suggests they ignore these "middle terms." They further emphasize that people don't use the priority heuristic, by its advocates' own admission, when the expected value of one option is more than double the value of another but argue that this observation contradicts the notion that people use heuristics *rather* than calculating expected values. For good summaries of such critiques, see Marc Oliver Rieger and Mei Wang, "What Is Behind the Priority Heuristic? A Mathematical Analysis and Comment on Brandstatter, Gigerenzer, and Hertwig (2006)," 115 *Psychol. Rev.* 274 (2008), and Michael H. Birnbaum, "Evaluation of the Priority Heuristic as a Descriptive Model of Risky Decision Making: Comment on Brandstatter, Gigerenzer, and Hertwig (2006)," 115 *Psychol. Rev.* 253 (2008).

The authors who initially formulated the priority heuristic reply to their critics in Eduard Brandstatter, Gerd Gigerenzer and Ralph Hertwig, "Risky Choice with Heuristics: Reply to Birnbaum (2008), Johnson, Schulte-Mecklenbeck and Willemsen (2008) and Rieger and Wang (2008)," 115 *Psychol. Rev.* 281 (2008).

4. For a discussion of this point, see part e., infra. The critical articles are Amos Tversky, "Elimination by Aspects: A Theory of Choice," 79 *Psychol. Rev.* 289 (1972), and Amos Tversky and S. Sattath, "Preference Trees," 86 *Psychol. Rev.* 542 (1978).

5. For a general discussion of these two sorts of research, and the relatively recent development of the second research method, see Daniel Kahneman and Shane Frederick, "Representativeness Revisited," in *Heuristics and Biases*, supra note 1 at 49, 60. The particular experiment is reported at 61.

6. See Amos Tversky and Daniel Kahneman, "Availability: A Heuristic for Judging Frequency and Probability," 5 *Cogn. Psychol.* 207, 208 (1973). For a very good review essay on the pioneering work on availability, see S.E. Taylor, "The Availability Bias in Social Perception and Interaction," in *Judgment Under Uncertainty: Heuristics and Biases* 190 (D. Kahneman, P. Slovic and A. Tversky eds., Cambridge, UK; New York: Cambridge University Press, 1982).

7. For a fuller discussion, arguing that ease of recall is the mechanism that dominates when subjects make "trivial" judgments and pseudo-sampling is the mechanism they use in making highly personally salient judgments, see Norbert Schwarz and Leigh Ann Vaughan, "The Availability Heuristic Revisited: Ease of Recall and Content of Recall as Distinct Sources of Information," in *Heuristics and Biases*, supra note 1 at 103.

8. See, e.g., Peter Sedlmeir, Ralph Hertwig and Gerd Gigerenzer, "Are Judgments of the Positional Frequencies of Letters Systematically Biased Due to Availability?" 24 *J. Exp. Psych: Learning, Mem. & Cogn.* 754 (1998) (arguing that if we define "ease of recall" either as the amount of time it takes to recall the first instance of a category or as the number of items in the category one can recall in a fixed time, then ease of recall does not correlate with probability estimates of words that have "r" as a first rather than third letter).

9. In Chapter Five, I note a counter-critique of the F&F work by H&B-influenced researchers. Many such researchers seem to believe that F&F researchers often simply re-label and take credit for discovering heuristics that H&B researchers had already discovered. It is not entirely clear that the "recognition heuristic" that I mentioned in Chapter One and that a co-author and I discuss at length in Chapter Five is truly distinct from the availability heuristic. One reason that F&F researchers believe it is distinct is that they think its mechanisms are more precisely specified and its evolutionary roots clearer. To the extent neither of those claims is true, its uniqueness fades. It is also distinct insofar as one believes, as F&F theorists do, that it is best conceptualized as a source of better-than-rational judgment rather than a useful short-cut that is generally as accurate as rational choice but may sometimes misfire. Once again, H&B scholars dispute the claim that its use is typically (let alone inexorably) better-than-rational.

10. See, e.g., Douglas A. Kysar et. al., "Group Report: Are Heuristics a Problem or a Solution?" in *Heuristics and the Law* 103, 113–14 (G. Gigerenzer and C. Engel eds., Cambridge, MA; MIT Press, 2006); Gerd Gigerenzer, *Adaptive Thinking* 259–61, 290–91 (Oxford, UK; New York: Oxford University Press, 2000).

11. Tversky and Kahneman, "Extensional Versus Intuitive Reasoning: The Conjunction Fallacy in Probability Judgment," in *Heuristics and Biases*, supra note 1 at 19, 22, 23.

12. See Amos Tversky and Daniel Kahneman, "Judgment Under Uncertainty: Heuristics and Biases," 185 *Science* 1124, 1128 (1974).

13. See Gretchen B. Chapman and Eric J. Johnson, "Incorporating the Irrelevant: Anchors in Judgments of Belief and Value," in *Heuristics and Biases*, supra note 1 at 120, 121.

14. See, e.g., Gretchen B. Chapman and Brian H. Bornstein, "The More You Ask For the More You Get: Anchoring in Personal Injury Verdicts," 10 *Appl. Cogn. Psychol.* 519 (1996).

15. This general point is highlighted in Daniel Kahneman and Shane Frederick, "Representativeness Revisited: Attribute Substitution in Intuitive Judgment," in *Heuristics and Biases*, supra note 1 at 49, 81 (emphasizing the degree to which errors made by people making judgments under uncertainty now appear more like sub-sets of broader classes of errors, even though the initial H&B research program was rather blind to that).

16. See Manjit S. Yadav, "How Buyers Evaluate Product Bundles: A Model of Anchoring and Adjustment," 21 *J. Consumer Res.* 342 (1994).
17. This is true even setting aside the possibility that those who succeed initial promisors would demand more to do Y or forebear from doing so because they are able to "hold up" covenantees who have taken steps in reliance on ongoing performance of the covenant.
18. See, for instance, Nicholas Epley and Thomas Gilovich, "The Anchoring-and-Adjustment Heuristic," 17 *Psychol. Sci.* 311 (2006) (in situations in which people do adjust from initial anchors, generally when anchors are self-generated, they fail to adjust adequately because adjusting is effortful and does not seem worthwhile as soon as they have reached a plausible answer); Fritz Strack and Thomas Mussweiler, "Explaining the Enigmatic Anchoring Effect: Mechanisms of Selective Accessibility," 73 *J. Personality & Soc. Psychol.* 437 (1997) (when third parties generate initial anchors, anchoring effects are produced not so much by inadequate adjustment as by the enhanced availability of anchor-consistent information). If one adopts the view that the tendency to select a preliminary value for the target close to the anchor's value is a technique that would be used by limited minds most readily able to retrieve only the most easily retrieved information from short-term memory and the tendency to adjust inadequately away from that preliminary anchor arises from the fact that adjustment is effortful, one would predict that increasing cognitive load would decrease the amount of adjustment, but the experimental design that suggests this might in fact be the case does not perfectly match traditional anchoring and adjustment studies. See Daniel T. Gilbert, Douglas S. Krull and Brett W. Pelham, "Of Thoughts Unspoken: Social Inference and the Self-Regulation of Behavior," 55 *J. Personality & Soc. Psychol.* 685 (1988). Moreover, there is little evidence that providing incentives increases adjustment, see Timothy D. Wilson, Christopher E. Houston, Kathryn M. Etling and Nancy Brekke, "A New Look at Anchoring Effects: Basic Anchoring and Its Antecedents," 125 *J. Exp. Psychol.: Gen.* 387 (1996). This is true even though providing rewards would seemingly overcome the tendency to expend little effort. Thus, Busemeyer and Goldstein *predicted* that incentives would diminish the degree to which target judgments would resemble anchors, believing that effortful adjustment would overcome the effect. Jerome B. Busemeyer and William M. Goldstein, "Linking Together Different Measures of Preference: A Dynamic Model of Matching Derived from Decision Field Theory," 52 *Organizational Behav. & Hum. Decision Processes* 370 (1992).
19. For a very similar example, albeit one that has been experimentally confirmed for between-subject groups (i.e., in situations in which one group of subjects is given one event whose probability the group members must estimate and another, distinct group of subjects is given the other event), as well as a number of other instances of the conjunction fallacy, see Tversky and Kahneman, "Extensional Versus Intuitive Reasoning: The Conjunction Fallacy in Probability Judgment," in *Heuristics and Biases*, supra note 1 at 19, 39.

    One could directly demonstrate *incoherence* only in within-subject experiments, of course (i.e., experiments in which each subject is asked to estimate the probability of each event). But it is odd to assume, as Gigerenzer seems to, that the between-subjects designs don't measure the mistakes in coherent judgment that each subject would be making in real judgment situations, at least as long as the subject is not given direct extensional cues that alert him to the fact that he is judging the probability of both a set and a sub-set.
20. Tversky and Kahneman, "Extensional Versus Intuitive Reasoning," supra note 1 at 27–28. Not surprisingly, the F&F researchers are skeptical that the H&B people have demonstrated a conjunction *fallacy* in this case, and their objections in this instance will help us understand

some of their more general objections to H&B methodology generally. These are some of the objections which I revisit, in more detail, in Chapter Four. Think about whether it is irrational as a juror to think that a defendant was more likely to kill the victim with some particular motive than to think that he killed him at all, with no motive given. It may well violate abstract norms of rationality to believe it less likely that X occurs than that X and Y co-occur. One can therefore design a trial-like *experiment* in which we can depict experimental subjects as making a *mistake*. It may, however, help meet one's actual ends (in this case, to ascertain guilt or innocence accurately) if one commits the logical fallacy in the realistic ecological context evoked by the unnaturally formalized experiment. Serving as an actual juror, it may be right to say that if one hears evidence that X killed but hears no motive, he *is* less likely to have killed. Jurors following something that could be called a heuristic ("show extreme reluctance to convict without a motive" or "think it improbable that the defendant killed unless there is a motive for his having killed") may judge guilt more accurately than those who think they can readily establish whether the defendant killed solely on the basis of other cues. If that is right, then the behavior serves a rational end—accuracy in fact finding—better than behavior that under the strict conditions of the experiment (in which the fact that the experimenter offers no motive has none of its conventional conversational/situational implications) violates the conjunction rule, an abstract canon of rationality.

21. More radical subjectivists would deny the possibility of random sampling. In assessing how many green balls will be drawn, we are merely making subjective estimates that *include* our estimates of how close to (conventionally) unbiased or random the ball-drawing process will be.

22. See, e.g., L. Jonathan Cohen, "Can Human Irrationality Be Experimentally Demonstrated?" 4 *Behav. & Brain Sci.* 317 (1981).

23. In a between-subjects test, one group is asked to estimate the probability of one event and another group asked to estimate the possibility of another event. To draw on an example from the text, one group might be asked how likely it is that 1,000 people will die in a California earthquake and another asked how likely it is that 1,000 will die in a natural disaster west of the Rockies. If a single subject were asked each question, his answer could be formally irrational if he said the former were more likely. (I return in Chapter Four to discuss why Gigerenzer does not think this formally irrational response is actually irrational.) The narrower point of interest now is that since each member of each of the two separate groups is, from the vantage point of the subjectivists, merely expressing a subjective bet about likelihood, the estimates cannot be inconsistent or irrational.

24. See Gerd Gigerenzer, "Why the Distinction Between Single-Event Probabilities and Frequencies Is Important for Psychology (and Vice Versa)," in *Subjective Probability* 129 (G. Wright and P. Ayton eds., Chichester, UK; New York: Wiley, 1994).

25. Steven A. Sloman and David E. Over, "Probability Judgment From the Inside and Out," in *Evolution and the Psychology of Thinking* 145, 159 (D.E. Over ed., Hove, East Sussex, UK; New York: Psychology Press, 2003).

26. Gilovich and Griffin, "Introduction—Heuristics and Biases: Then and Now," in *Heuristics and Biases*, supra note 1 at 1, 13.

27. Daniel Kahneman and Amos Tversky, "Choices, Values, and Frames," in *Choices, Values, and Frames* 1, 5–6 (D. Kahneman and A. Tversky eds., New York: Russell Sage Foundation; Cambridge, UK: Cambridge University Press, 2000).
Lichtenstein and Slovic demonstrated intransitive preferences surrounding bets: 87 percent of subjects who chose the "P" bet (an 11/12 chance to win 12 chips valued at a quarter a piece

and a 1/12 chance to lose 24 chips) over the "S" bet (a 2/12 chance to win 79 chips and a 10/12 chance to lose 5 chips) demanded more to sell the S bet. They hypothesized that subjects select gambles as more or less attractive largely by focusing on probabilities of winning or losing but set prices for gambles largely by focusing on the amounts that can be won or lost, but this means that they might select gamble A over B and B over C, but pay more for C than A. See Sarah Lichtenstein and Paul Slovic, "Reversals of Preference Between Bids and Choices in Gambling Decisions," 89 *J. Exp. Psychol.* 46 (1971), and Sarah Lichtenstein and Paul Slovic, "Response-Induced Reversals of Preferences In Gambling: An Extended Replication in Las Vegas," 101 *J. Exp. Psychol.* 16 (1973).

28. The problem was originally presented in Amos Tversky and Daniel Kahneman, "The Framing of Decisions and the Psychology of Choice," 211 *Sci.* 453 (1981). Not atypically, or surprisingly, critics of this H&B finding emphasize the possibility that subjects pick up on subtle conversational cues, and interpret the scenarios differently than the experimenters intended them to. I return to this point in Chapter 4. For an early presentation of this critique, see Anton Kuhberger, "The Framing of Decisions: A New Look at Old Problems," 62 *Organizational Behav. & Hum. Decision Processes* 230 (1995).

29. It is by no means clear *why* subjects' judgments of the value of options are sensitive to these contrast effects. Evaluative contrast effects might readily be *analogized* to perceptual contrast effects. Here is an example of a typical perceptual contrast effect: People asked to judge the relative size of two identical circles will judge the circle placed against a backdrop of smaller circles as larger in size. It is not clear, though, that the analogy is anything more than illustrative or pedagogic.

I have always been drawn to the "explanation" that evaluative contrast effects are created as follows: Subjects "solve" *easy* problems first (is the Mark Cross pen better than the cruddy pen?) and then get *anchored* to the judgment that the Mark Cross pen is the *preferred option* and move away from that conclusion only when it is rather compelling to do so. This view of the mechanism might help explain another puzzling bias: Assume that subjects are asked to express whether something "feels" like a better prospect, rather than being asked to compute the numeric probability of winning each of two gambles, so that they are drawing on "unconsidered" heuristic judgments. In one situation, they are given 15 lottery tickets while other participants in the same lottery are given 10, 11, 7, 9, 7, 8, and 8 tickets respectively; in the other, the other seven participants receive 39, 3, 1, 7, 5, 2, and 3 tickets. In each case, the surveyed party has 20 percent of the tickets but a substantial majority of participants feel better about their chances of winning in the first case. My sense is that they feel relatively bad about the second lottery because they first identify another individual with a much better chance of winning than they have and, having most immediately done so, feel like they are unlikely to win; they never adequately "correct" for this anchored evaluative judgment. See Paul D. Windschtitl and Michael E. Young, "The Influence of Alternative Outcomes on Gut-Level Perception of Certainty," 85 *Organizational & Hum. Decision Processes* 109 (2001). It is an interesting question whether this "bias" affects choices people make as consumers or voters about the likelihood certain events will occur: The findings seem to imply that judgments of certainty will once more be affected by the form of elicitation. If "alternatives" to a focal outcome are bundled together, so that some "alternative" appears more likely, the focal alternative may seem less likely than if the alternatives were all presented separately. Imagine in this regard comparing the favorable health outcome from a procedure with a series of discrete bad outcomes rather than a set of bad outcomes that are bundled together in a category.

30. See Mark Kelman, Yuval Rottenstreich and Amos Tversky, "Context-Dependence in Legal Decision Making," 25 *J. Legal Stud.* 287 (1996). The article merely provides concrete legal applications of more general H&B literature on contrast effects. See, especially, Itamar Simonson and Amos Tversky, "Choice in Context: Tradeoff Contrast and Extremeness Aversion," 29 *J. Marketing Res.* 281 (1992), and Amos Tversky and Itamar Simonson, "Context-Dependent Preferences," 39 *Mgmt. Sci.* 1179 (1993).
31. See Eldar Shafir, "Choosing Versus Rejecting: Why Some Options Are Both Better and Worse Than Others," 21 *Mem. & Cogn.* 546 (1993).
32. Imagine a subject asked to choose between some Vacation Plan A and Vacation Plan B. He may be asked, in one elicitation condition, whether he would like to cancel Plan A, without financial penalty, and substitute Plan B. Or he may be asked to cancel Plan B and substitute A. Or he may be asked to book one or the other vacation assuming he has made no plans. If Plan A has many markedly bad and many markedly good traits, while B is "blander," he is prone to cancel A under the first condition (seemingly showing a preference for B) and yet book it under the third (revealing a preference for A). He will not typically cancel B under the second condition (once more "revealing" a preference for B). See, e.g., Eldar Shafir, Itamar Simonson and Amos Tversky, "Reason-Based Choice," 49 *Cognition* 11 (1993).
33. For a typical H&B finding that heuristic-based decisions may be regretted, see Paul Slovic, Melissa Finucane, Ellen Peters and Donald G. MacGregor, "The Affect Heuristic," in *Heuristics and Biases*, supra note 1 at 397, 416–19 (reviewing evidence that people employing an "affect heuristic" in decision making—favoring or disfavoring options based on their initial automatic feelings—may at times make choices that they come to regret).
34. See Daniel Kahneman, Peter P. Wakker and Rakesh Sarin, "Back to Bentham? Explorations of Experienced Utility," 112 *Q. J. Econ.* 375 (1997).
35. It is an upper bound if one assumes that the marginal value of saving more members of the species declines. Of course, the marginal value could increase, in theory, if saving just a few is not worthwhile, and until one gets to a large number, one has not reached a critical mass.
36. See W.H. Desvousges, F. Johnson, R. Dunford, S. Hudson, K. Wilson and K. Boyle, "Measuring Resource Damages with Contingent Valuations: Tests of Validity and Reliability," in *Contingent Valuation: A Critical Assessment* (New York: Elsevier, 1993).
37. It is worth mentioning that this is another instance where representativeness impacts not just probability judgments but judgments of the value of end-states.
38. See Daniel Kahneman, "Objective Happiness," in *Well-Being: The Foundations of Hedonic Psychology* 3, 21–22 (D. Kahneman, E. Diener and N. Schwarz eds., New York: Russell Sage Foundation, 1999).
39. Two of the foundational works are Stephen Sloman, "The Empirical Case for Two Systems of Reasoning," 119 *Psychol. Bull.* 3 (1996), and Jonathan St. B.T. Evans and David E. Over, *Rationality and Reasoning* (Hove, East Sussex, UK: Psychology Press, 1996).
    Many H&B writers cite this "two system"/dual process literature favorably. See, e.g., Thomas Gilovich and Dale Griffin, "Introduction: Heuristics and Biases, Then and Now," in *Heuristics and Biases*, supra note 1 at 1, 16; Daniel Kahneman and Shane Frederick, "Representativeness Revisited: Attribute Substitution in Intuitive Judgment," in *Heuristics and Biases*, supra note 1 at 49, 51–52 57–60, 68–70. Others argue, for instance, that *some* heuristics—predominantly those associated with judgment rather than decision making—are System One heuristics, while decision-making heuristics are consciously System Two chosen *strategies*. In this view, when using System Two strategies, agents consider the advantages and limitations

of using an informationally impoverished technique. See Shane Frederick, "Automated Choice Heuristics," in *Heuristics and Biases*, supra note 1 at 548 (noting the existence of a handful of "automatic" decision-making heuristics but endorsing the idea that it is judgment heuristics that are generally "automatic").

40. See, e.g., Keith E. Stanovich and Richard F. West, "Individual Differences in Reasoning: Implications for the Rationality Debate," in *Heuristics and Biases*, supra note 1 at 421, 436–39. Stanovich and West are especially drawn to a rather idiosyncratic account of the distinct roles of Systems One and Two. In their view, System One serves basic adaptationist ends, maximizing the replication of genes, while System Two meets the utility-seeking ends of persons, the "vehicles" that house the replicating genes. See Keith E. Stanovich and Richard F. West, "Evolutionary versus Instrumental Goals: How Evolutionary Psychology Misconceives Human Rationality," in *Evolution and the Psychology of Thinking*, supra note 25 at 171, 186 (". . . System 1 instantiates short-leashed genetic goals, whereas System 2 instantiates a flexible goal hierarchy that is oriented towards maximizing goal satisfaction at the level of the whole organism").

Here is their basic picture: People develop System 2 capacity to deal with a world that shifts too fast to rely solely on modular responses to recurring, familiar problems. But when System 2 is given the very sort of generalized functions it is given—to figure out what is best to do to meet very general gene-replicating ends like sexual reproduction and survival—it is possible that "organism" and "gene" goals will diverge. So if there were simply a System One mating protocol that accurately pre-identified the circumstances in which one should desire sexual relations, one could follow it. (And many evolutionary psychologists of sex think we essentially do follow such a protocol.) But if System Two works with far more general instructions ("have sex when pleasurable, figure out when that is") there is room for a gap between the gene-replicating goals and the utility-seeking goals: The System 2-driven organism may find pleasure when there is no gene-replicating advantage. Id. at 191–92. Of course, the evolutionary psychologists of sexual desire would agree that the modular rules they posit do not always serve to insure reproductive sex—informationally encapsulated systems won't account for the additional cues that might make the subject realize that behavior that is generally adaptive is non-adaptive in the particular instance—so that they would hardly be surprised to find out that men will have sex with nubile women knowing full well they are using birth control devices, even if "nobility" was a cue *because* it typically signaled fertility. Desires for plainly non-procreative sex are sometimes explained as adaptive by-products, sometimes as serving other social bonding roles. See generally David M. Buss, *The Evolution of Desire* (New York: Basic Books, rev. ed. 2003) for the mainstream evolutionary psychologists' views of sexual desire.

41. See, e.g., Slovic et al., "The Affect Heuristic," in *Heuristics and Biases*, supra note 1 at 397, 416 ("like other heuristics that provide efficient and generally adaptive responses but occasionally lead us astray, reliance on affect can also deceive us. Indeed, if it was always optimal to follow our affective and experiential instincts, there would have been no need for the rational/analytic system to have evolved and become so prominent in human affairs.").

42. See A.R. Luria, *Cognitive Development: Its Cultural and Social Foundations* (Cambridge, MA: Harvard University Press, 1976). Luria's work is cited extensively by Keith Stanovich. See, e.g., Keith Stanovich, *Who Is Rational? Studies of Individual Differences in Reasoning* 171, 193–94 (Mahwah, NJ: Lawrence Erlbaum Associates, 1999).

43. For an atypically detailed account of "correction" in a dual process model, see Daniel T. Gilbert, "Inferential Correction," in *Heuristics and Biases*, supra note 1 at 167. But the correction "metaphor" shows up repeatedly in the H&B literature. See, e.g., Kahneman and Frederick, "Representativeness Revisited," in *Heuristics and Biases*, supra note 1 at 49, 52, 57–60; Stanovich and West, "Individual Differences in Reasoning," in *Heuristics and Biases*, supra note 1 at 421, 439.
44. See, e.g., Kahneman and Frederick, "Representativeness Revisited," in *Heuristics and Biases*, supra note 1 at 49, 59–60.
45. See, e.g., Franca Agnoli, "Development of Judgmental Heuristics and Logical Reasoning: Training Counteracts the Representativeness Heuristic," 6 *Cogn. Dev.* 195 (1991); Franca Agnoli and David H. Krantz, "Suppressing Natural Heuristics by Formal Instruction: The Case of the Conjunction Fallacy," 21 *Cogn. Psychol.* 515 (1989).
46. See especially Stanovich, *Who Is Rational?* supra note 42 at 32–52, 98–141.
47. Somewhat fewer fall prey to the conjunction fallacy when the test is put in frequentist rather than probabilistic terms. In the probabilistic presentation, one asks how likely it is that Linda holds each particular job. In the frequentist form, one asks subjects something like the following: "Assume there are a hundred people with descriptions just like Linda's. How many of the 100 are bank tellers? Feminist bank tellers?" I return to discuss the significance of frequentist versus probabilistic presentations in Chapter Four, because F&F theorists believe that H&B theorists generate seemingly irrational behavior by asking subjects to perform a task—manipulation of probabilities—that they are not adapted to perform rather than frequency manipulation, which they are adapted to perform.
48. See Stanovich and West, "Individual Differences," supra note 40 at 433–34. The distinction between frequentist and probabilistic presentations was discussed, among other places, in note 47 supra. The distinction between within-subject and between-subject tests was discussed in note 23 supra.
49. For instance, subjects who give the same answer to the canonical H&B question of whether they would recommend the same medical program whether or not the program is "framed" in terms of the lives it would save or the number that died are significantly higher in cognitive ability, as measured by the SAT, than those subject to the framing effect. Id. at 432–33.
Those with higher SAT scores are also less likely to avoid engaging in the sort of probability-matching I will discuss in some detail in Chapter Four. Briefly, a subject who engages in probability matching will, if told that there are seventy red and thirty green balls in an urn, and asked to select which color balls will be drawn in the next ten drawings, with replacement, knowing she will get a prize for each correct choice, still select seven red and three green even though one would select ten reds if maximizing expected value. See Richard F. West and Keith E. Stanovich, "Is Probability Matching Smart? Associations Between Probabilistic Choices and Cognitive Ability," 31 *Mem. & Cogn.* 243 (2003). In Chapter Four, I discuss the claim made by F&F scholars that those who use "probability matching" might well be "rational" even though they fail to maximize expected value in the experimental setting.
50. For a discussion of the evidence, see Stanovich, *Who Is Rational?* supra note 42 at 153–89, 213, 221–23.
51. Consider in this regard one aspect of hindsight "bias," which I and two co-authors dubbed "primary hindsight bias:" the tendency to believe that whatever turned out to happen (ex post) had a high prior (ex ante) probability of occurring. (Set aside the aspects of the bias

which leads people to believe either that they knew all along what turned out to occur—what we called secondary bias—or that others should have foreseen events that eventuated even though there was little reason to believe that they had information, ex ante, to indicate what outcome would occur—what we called tertiary bias.)

People exhibit far less primary bias when actual ex ante probabilities are readily computed. Thus, it may well be that judging ex ante probabilities by reference to what occurred is simply the *easiest* strategy (when computations of prior probabilities are difficult), not that it is an *automatic* strategy that must sometimes be overridden.

Thus, in our experiments, people demonstrated primary hindsight bias when they had to assess the prior probability of rolling either a "13" or "14" when rolling three dice (given outcome information) but exhibited no such bias when assessing the prior probability of rolling a "2" on one die. This is true though the actual probability—one in six—is the same in each case. We did not explore this possibility in our experiments, but it is perfectly plausible that people with very good math-in-your-head computational skills who could quickly calculate that the odds of rolling a "13"or "14" in the three-die setting are identical to the odds of rolling a single number in the one-die setting would not rightly be said to *overcome* a heuristic-based System One tendency to believe that the odds of rolling a "13" or "14" must be pretty high because that is what was actually rolled. They would merely compute those odds the same way that virtually all of us compute the odds of rolling a single number given one die and *ignore*, rather than overcome, whatever tendency might exist to reason through outcome information that gives rise to "hindsight bias." In neither case, though, would it be apt to say that some System Two "corrects" System One: Each person simply uses the best technique available to calculate prior probabilities consistent with her computational abilities and only a sub-set of people are able to use the better, albeit harder, calculating technique.

For a discussion of this view of hindsight bias, see Mark Kelman, David E. Fallas and Hilary Folger, "Decomposing Hindsight Bias," 16 *J. Risk & Uncertainty* 251, 252–53 (1998).

52. Stanovich and West, "Individual Differences," supra note 40 at 427–28.
53. See Lee Ross, David Greene and Pamela House, "The 'False Consensus Effect': An Egocentric Bias in Social Perception and Attribution Processes," 13 *J. Exp. Soc. Psychol.* 279 (1977)
54. See Stanovich, *Who Is Rational?* supra note 42 at 74–78 (for both empirical findings that SAT scores do not predict "vulnerability" to the "false consensus effect" and an explanation of the rationality of the inference).
55. See Paul Slovic and Amos Tversky, "Who Accepts Savage's Axiom?" 19 *Behav. Sci.* 308 (1974) (arguing that if more reflective and engaged subjects are more likely to affirm the "rational choice" model, the gap between initial performance and rationality was more likely due to lack of ability or effort). See also Stanovich and West, "Individual Differences in Reasoning," supra note 40 at 425–27.
56. See, e.g., L.L. Lopes and G.G. Oden, "The Rationality of Intelligence," in *Probability and Rationality: Studies on Jonathan Cohen's Philosophy of Science* 199, 209 (E. Eells and T. Maruszewski eds., Amsterdam; Atlanta, GA: Rodopi, 1991). Similarly, a number of theorists broadly in the F&F camp have assumed that more intelligent people do *not* do better on the tasks that H&B theorists have posited are performed poorly as a result of infirmities of reasoning, and that this "fact" bolsters their argument that the supposed reasoning defects are not in fact defects. For a critical discussion of the work of these theorists, see Stanovich, *Who Is Rational?* supra note 42 at 65–66.

57. Se Gerd Gigerenzer, "On Narrow Norms and Vague Heuristics: A Reply to Kahneman and Tversky (1996)," 103 *Psychol. Rev.* 592, 593 (1996).
58. See Shane Frederick, "Automated Choice Heuristics," in *Heuristics and Biases*, supra note 1 at 548, 548–59. In some ways, the EBA decision "heuristic" that Tversky describes resembles the take-the-best F&F heuristic, but as Gigerenzer has noted, EBA deals with the formation of *preferences* for actions while take-the-best, like the other H&B heuristics I have discussed in this chapter, fundamentally deals with *inferences*. Moreover, a cue is a "best" cue, in F&F terms, when it is "valid" (i.e., correlates with the fact one is trying to infer), while a choice maker may select any *first* aspect with few constraints (she must merely choose an aspect that distinguishes between her options; so, for instance, no aspect shared by all options can be used). For a brief discussion of EBA from the perspective of F&F theory, see Gerd Gigerenzer, Jean Czerlinski and Laura Martignon, "How Good Are Fast and Frugal Heuristics?" in *Heuristics and Biases*, supra note 1 at 559, 565.
59. See Amos Tversky, "Elimination by Aspects: A Theory of Choice," 79 *Psychol. Rev.* 281 (1972).
60. Id. at 296.
61. Id. at 298.
62. The conceptual line between principals and agents is inevitably blurry in ways that need not concern us much here. The fact that principals are not asked to follow explicit rules does not mean that they are not influenced by external constraints. And since some of these external constraints will be deliberately chosen rules, designed to change the incentives the principal would otherwise face, every purported principal is in part some rulemaking policymaker's agent. The driver picking an appropriate level of precaution is a principal in the sense that we expect her to make judgments about how much she cares about getting some place quickly (or spending money on safer brakes, or risking injury to herself or to others), but the cost structure she will face is plainly in part a product of a liability rule structure intended to influence her behavior. At the extreme, imagine that the penalties for driving over 70 MPH are so high, and the probability of detection so high, that hardly anyone would ever choose to do so: She could then be readily seen as an agent implementing a policymaker's desire to control the speed of the cars on the road.

    At the same time, we recognize that people expected to act as other's agents may well have interests of their own. Thus, at least in descriptive terms, it may be hard to understand the behavior of those dominantly conceived of as agents without understanding that they may be acting, in at least some substantial part, as principals. Thus, we may not be able to understand how jurors behave unless we understand that they may be more interested in going home quickly than following complex instructions; legislators may be more interested—alternatively—in advancing the ends of only those constituents who can help them fulfill their own interests in reelection or in meeting their private ideological goals than in meeting the ends of the voters generally; managers may be more interested in protecting their own non-diversifiable human capital in the firm than in maximizing share values.
63. Mark Kelman, Yuval Rottenstreich and Amos Tversky, "Context-Dependence in Legal Decision Making," 25 *J. Legal Stud.* 287 (1996).

Chapter 3

1. See, e.g., Gerd Gigerenzer, "Heuristics," in *Heuristics and the Law* (G. Gigerenzer and C. Engel eds., Cambridge, MA: MIT Press, 2006) 17, 18–19.

2. See e.g., Gerd Gigerenzer, "The Adaptive Toolbox," in *Bounded Rationality: The Adaptive Toolbox* 37, 38 (G. Gigerenzer & R. Selten eds., Cambridge, MA: MIT Press, 2002) ("*Unbounded rationality* encompasses decision-making strategies that have little or no regard for the constraints in time, knowledge, and computational capacities that real humans face. For example, models that seek to maximize expected utility or perform Bayesian calculations often must assume demonic strength to tackle real-world problems."). See also Gerd Gigerenzer, *Adaptive Thinking: Rationality in the Real World* 167 (Oxford, UK; New York: Oxford University Press, 2000).

3. See, e.g., Gerd Gigerenzer, "The Adaptive Toolbox," supra note 2 at 38. ("The goal of this program is to understand how humans . . . make decisions, as opposed to heavenly beings equipped with practically unlimited time, knowledge, memory, and other infinite resources.")

4. This classic economic view of bounded rationality is set out especially clearly in Thomas J. Sargent, *Bounded Rationality in Macroeconomics* (Oxford, UK: Clarendon Press; Oxford, UK; New York: Oxford University Press, 1993). The idea that people stop searching for more information when the costs of search outweigh the expected benefits was first made explicit in George J. Stigler, "The Economics of Information," 69 *J. Pol. Econ.* 213 (1961).

5. See, e.g., Gerd Gigerenzer & Reinhard Selten, "Rethinking Rationality," in *Bounded Rationality*, supra note 2 at 1, 5 ("Stigler . . . used the example of a person who wants to buy a used car, and stops searching when the costs of further search would exceed the benefit of further search . . . The problems with this form of optimization as a model of cognitive processes are well known. First, reliable estimates of benefits and costs, such as opportunity costs, can demand large degrees of knowledge; second, there is an infinite regression problem (the cost-benefit computations themselves are costly, and demand a meta-level cost-benefit computation, and so on); and finally, the knowledge and the computations involved can be so massive that one is forced to assume that ordinary people have the computational capabilities and statistical software of econometricians . . . All in all, this attempt to model limited search leads to the paradoxical result that the models become even less psychologically plausible.").

6. At a broad level of generality, both conventional rational choice theorists and H&B theorists would agree that the use of heuristics (or rules of thumb) saves time and energy, and that the value of the saved time and energy might well exceed the value of improved accuracy. And obviously, it is more plausible that the costs of using more information-intensive methods would outweigh the gains if they produced little shift in accuracy of judgment. So, in part, the distinction among theorists is a non-trivial distinction in *degree*. The F&F people spend a lot of time modeling what they take as common situations in which a heuristic-based decision rule discriminates as well or better than alternative methods. H&B researchers, on the other hand, have spent more time on problems that the F&F people would describe as abstract laboratory problems deliberately or inadvertently designed to be solved only by the use of rational choice methods that people solve rather poorly using heuristics.

But there is a conceptual—or perhaps merely terminological—distinction as well as a distinction in degree. H&B theorists contend that it is not always worthwhile to make a rational choice, while F&F theorists believe that a decision *is* rational if it is the proper decision to make given trade-offs among speed, accuracy, and ease.

7. The phrase appears at least four times in *Heuristics and the Law*, supra note 1. See pages, 4, 5, 129, and 452. It appears at least five times in Gerd Gigerenzer, *Adaptive Thinking: Rationality*

in the Real World (2000) (126, 127 174, 179, and 184) and three times in *Bounded Rationality*, supra note 2 (57, 63, 178).

   One of the reasons it seems like a mantra rather than a helpful observation to me is that it is used across situations in which its meaning diverges a good deal. We discuss in Chapter Five how it has been used in the context of extolling the recognition heuristic. The argument—which is ultimately quite misleading in the "less is more" form it is conventionally put—is that relatively ignorant people will outperform those who know more because they can make use of heuristics that people with more information cannot. More specifically, those who would recognize fewer cities (e.g., Germans rather than Americans looking at a list of American cities) are more likely to select which of two cities in a pair is larger because they alone are more prone to recognize but one of the two cities, and recognition correlates with city size closely, while semantic knowledge of relative city size is weak (including knowledge of other cues that more weakly correlate with city size). But it is misleading to say that the Americans actually have *more* information than the Germans: Most important, they don't have easy access to information about which city is more typically recognized. (The Germans do because each recognizes himself as a member of the sample of those who recognize but one of two cities and can infer readily that what he or she recognizes is what is more typically recognized.) Americans could be said to have *more* information only if they had all the information the Germans have plus additional pieces of information; otherwise, they simply have *different* information. Imagine that "rational choosers" get that one more piece of information as well about which of two cities is more typically recognized by foreigners (in addition to all sorts of cues that help them determine when recognition does not correlate with city size): Less-informed Germans might well do worse than the more-informed rational choosers. One can say that the Germans know less (so that being less knowledgeable leads to better performance) only by restricting domains of knowledge to those bits of knowledge that facilitate acquisition (but are not the only conceivable source) of information about how recognized the two cities typically are.

8. See Gerd Gigerenzer, "Heuristics," supra note 1 at 19.
9. For an excellent summary of the limits of theories that assume incommensurability of values, see Richard Craswell, "Incommensurability, Welfare Economics, and the Law," 146 U. Pa. L. Rev. 1419 (1998). For a discussion of the transformation of ordinal rankings into a welfare function with pay-offs, see, e.g., James Griffin, *Well-Being: Its Meaning, Measurement and Moral Importance* (Oxford, UK: Clarendon Press, 1986).
10. I go into these issues considerably more in Chapter Eight, but assume, for the moment, that the value of preserving a friendship and the value of receiving certain goods to betray a friend are "incommensurable" in the sense that human beings compute the value of friendship in a different portion of the brain than they compute the value of the goods, and that these distinct portions of the brain cannot "communicate" with one another (or supply information to some third portion of the brain that could tote them up). Even then, we would seemingly describe incommensurability as a feature of the human decision makers, not of the friends and the goods.
11. See Kim Sterelny and Paul E. Griffiths, *Sex and Death: An Introduction to Philosophy of Biology* 329 (Chicago: University of Chicago Press, 1999) ("Evolutionary psychologists . . . should be cautious about accepting a modular theory of mind. For specialized mechanisms have a downside: they are vulnerable to exploitation in a malign world . . . A rigid, modular language acquisition device is unlikely to be exploited by other agents to prevent someone

12. See Gerd Gigerenzer, "The Adaptive Toolbox," supra note 2 at 47–48.
13. Gigerenzer describes the overfitting problem in some detail on many occasions. See, e.g., Gerd Gigerenzer, "Heuristics," supra note 1 at 21. See also Laura Martignon, "Comparing Fast and Frugal Heuristics and Optimal Models," in *Bounded Rationality* supra note 2 at 147, 166.
14. See David E. Rumelheart et al., *Parallel Distributed Processing: Explorations in the Microstructure of Cognition* (Vols. 1 and 2) (Cambridge, MA: MIT Press, 1986), and Robert M. Nosofsky and Thomas J. Palmeri, "An Exemplar-Based Random Walk Model of Speeded Classification," 104 *Psychol. Rev.* 266 (1997).
15. See, e.g., Gerd Gigerenzer, *Adaptive Thinking* supra note 2 at 233 ("... the means and ends of social intelligence are broader than consistency (coherence) and accuracy—the accepted norms of logic and statistics. Social intelligence can involve being inconsistent (e.g., adaptive unpredictability may be optimal in competitive situations: the opponent will be unable to predict one's behavior), taking high risk in trying to come out first (that is, options with low probabilities rather than those that maximize expected value), responding quickly rather than accurately (e.g., to make too long a pause in a conversation in order to think of the best answer can be embarrassing and seen as impolite) and making decisions that one can justify and defend afterward."). See also Gerd Gigerenzer, "The Adaptive Toolbox," supra note 2 at 41 ("From a functional view ... consistency in choice and judgment is not a general norm to follow blindly, but rather a tool for achieving certain proximal goals.").
16. Bruce D. Burns, (2004). "Heuristics as Beliefs and as Behaviors: The Adaptiveness of the 'Hot Hand,'" 48 *Cogn. Psych* 295 (2004).
17. For the initial account of this finding, see Thomas Gilovich, Robert Vallone and Amos Tversky, "The Hot Hand in Basketball: On the Misperception of Random Sequences" 17 *Cogn. Psychol.* 295 (1985).
18. See, e.g., Gerd Gigerenzer, "Heuristics," supra note 1 at 18.
19. See, e.g., Gerd Gigerenzer and Reinhard Selten, "Rethinking Rationality," supra note 5 at 8.
20. Gigerenzer more explicitly models the recognition heuristic in this way in *Adaptive Thinking*, supra note 2 at 170–71, in which what I am calling the recognition search cue is treated as prior to, but otherwise parallel to, a "Step One search" for cues that differentiate already recognized objects. Whether or not Gigerenzer says that the cue value of the recognized city is positive at Step Zero in a fashion that is distinct from a differentiating cue at Step One, the judgment process is plainly identical. Recognition is a positive differentiating cue value that allows the person making a judgment to stop looking for further information/differentiating cues and draw a conclusion. If there is a reason to differentiate the "Take the Best" from the recognition heuristic—in which recognition is simply the first, best cue—it is one of little moment to policymakers thinking about how people make judgments, though it might plausibly be of interest to cognitive psychologists. As I note in the text, one could argue that the recognition heuristic's domain is narrower than the domain of "Take the Best," referring only to those judgments made exclusively through memory-based inferences. I confess having difficulty seeing this distinction is anything but definitional or tautological, even within psychology, but gladly concede this might reflect my underlying outsider's naiveté about the significance of distinct modes of cognitive inference.

It is worth noting too that Gigerenzer's associates have often treated the recognition heuristic as the simplest and most basic "Take the Best" heuristic. Thus, for instance, Laura

Martignon wrote, "When recognition is correlated with the criterion, it is the very first building block of both Take the Best and Minimalist." ("Comparing Fast and Frugal Heuristics," supra note 13 at 149.)

21. Naturally, "searching" memory to determine whether an object is familiar or recognized is not precisely the same sort of cognitive task as searching to see whether two objects of inquiry, each of which the subject remembers, are distinguished along some critical dimension. Presumably, it is for that reason that Gigerenzer describes the recognition heuristic as operating *prior* to the search/stop/decide process, but from our vantage point as policy analysts interested in whether decision makers can make a judgment about some important feature of objects they are comparing solely on the basis of a single factor, the distinction seems of no moment.

22. In the MM picture, particular cues are typically cognized in an informationally encapsulated way, but the presumptive relationship between a particular cognition and *action* may nonetheless be mediated by mental processes outside the module: Take the standard evolutionary psychologists' picture of male sexual desire and behavior. A handful of fertility marking cues (e.g., facial symmetry, lustrous skin, and youth) create sexual lust through a lust-creating module whose inclusive fitness goal is to maximize the chances of mating with someone both fertile and healthy enough to raise the young. Lust is mandatory, opaque, and informationally encapsulated in the sense that information that the object of lust is infertile does not act within the lust-creating module. But action (e.g., seeking to mate consensually or to engage in predatory sexual violence) need not occur in response to lust. Outside-the-module cues (the person who is lusted after is married, sexual violence is morally problematic and/or punished) may still influence conduct. See, e.g., Owen D. Jones, "Sex, Culture, and the Biology of Rape: Toward Explanation and Prevention," 87 *Cal. L. Rev.* 827 (1999) (noting that it is not inevitable that men will act on sexual desires, even if the desires are deeply biologically programmed). Obviously, in a fully MM view, one must cognize these other cues in other modules, for there is no other way of thinking, but that is not the point for now.

23. See, e.g., Thorsten Pachur and Ralph Hertwig, "On the Psychology of the Recognition Heuristic: Retrieval Primacy as a Key Determinant of Its Use." 32 *J. Exp. Psychol.: Learning, Mem. & Cogn.* 983 (2006). Similarly, Volz et al. argue that recognition heuristic decisional processes involve an "assessment" about the applicability of the heuristic. Kirsten G. Volz, Lael J. Schooler, Ricarda L. Schubotz, Markus Raab, Gerd Gigerenzer and D. Yves von Cramon, "Why You Think Milan is Larger than Modena: Neural Correlates of the Recognition Heuristic," 18 *J. Cogn. Neurosci.* 1924 (2006).

24. See Pachur and Hertwig, "On the Psychology of the Recognition Heuristic," supra note 23.

25. See Volz, "Why You Think Milan is Larger than Modena," supra note 23. I discuss this point further in Chapter Five.

26. It is possible to interpret at least some F&F theorists as believing something like the following, though: Once one decides to use a heuristic, or decides which capacity from the adaptive toolbox to use in a certain setting, following the search, stopping, and decision rules that the heuristic dictates is effortless and rather automatic. But the heuristic-selection process is *not* nearly so automatic. One can see an argument to this effect in Christoph Engel, "Social Dilemmas Revisited from a Heuristics Perspective," in *Heuristics and the Law*, supra note 1 at 61, 66–68.

27. See Gigerenzer, "Heuristics," supra note 1 at 24–28.

28. Recall that a sub-set of H&B researchers have thought of availability in this way: See supra, Chapter Two, note 7. Thought of this way, there is not a whole lot of distance between the availability and recognition heuristics, though there is no effort to lodge the "capacity to recall an item easily" in a particular adaptive story.
29. In this chapter, I discuss a view of modularization most associated with Fodor—who is both the source of the revitalization of the idea that certain cognitive functions are significantly modularized *and* the view that the brain cannot possibly be massively modularized. I do so because it is this view of modularity that best helps clarify the F&F project. See Jerry A. Fodor, *The Modularity of Mind* (Cambridge, MA: MIT Press, 1983), and Jerry Fodor, *The Mind Doesn't Work that Way* (Cambridge, MA: MIT Press, 2000). But most "neo-modularists" would disclaim the view that the modularized mind has all the features that Fodor attributed to it, arguing instead that those who believe in "modularity" merely believe in a variety of forms of functional specialization of cognitive functions. For a good account of the "neo-modularist" view, see H. Clark Barrett and Robert Kurzban, "Modularity in Cognition: Framing the Debate," 113 *Psychol. Rev.* 628 (2006).
30. See Leda Cosmides and John Tooby, "Consider the Source: The Evolution of Adaptations for Decoupling and Metarepresentations," in *Metarepresentations: A Multidisciplinary Perspective* (D. Sperber ed., Oxford, UK; New York: Oxford University Press, 2000).
31. Broadly speaking, the EEA is the hunter-gatherer savannah environment in which people lived for such a high proportion of our evolutionary history that we would expect that most of our traits evolved to maximize gene-replicating success given the constraints and challenges that existed in such a setting.
32. For a fuller discussion of this distinction, see Fodor, *The Mind Doesn't Work that Way* supra note 29 at 58–61.
33. Leda Cosmides and John Tooby, "Origins of domain specificity: The evolution of functional organization," in *Mapping the Mind: Domain Specificity in Cognition and Culture* 85, 89–90 (L.A. Hirschfeld and S.A. Gelman eds., Cambridge, UK; New York: Cambridge University Press, 1994).
34. See Sterelny and Griffiths, *Sex and Death* supra note 11 at 322–23, 328, 352 for a lucid statement of the grain problem.
35. There are questions about how the cues would be perceived or combined by a modular brain: The mate selection cues that men are supposed to use in the standard evolutionary psychology picture are at least the sort of delimited cues associated with informationally encapsulated heuristic *perception* (complexion, hip-to-waist ratio) but the "cues" women are supposed to process (social power and resources, dependability, and fidelity) are not nearly so obviously delimited in ways that are consistent with processing by a massively modularized brain. It is possible to *see* a particular hip-to-waist ratio; the determination that one is dealing with a male with social power may well rely on having made a far more complex judgment, grounded in innumerable separate cues that themselves need to be weighed.
36. See, e.g., Cosmides and Tooby, "Origins of Domain Specificity," supra note 33 at 103. ("The world is full of long-enduring structure—social, biological, physical, ecological, and psychological—and the mind appears to be full of corresponding mechanisms that use these stable structural features to solve a diverse array of adaptive problems. Like a key in a lock, the functional organization of each cognitive adaptation should match the evolutionarily recurrent structural features of its particular problem-domain.") Typically, MM theorists posit

something like a signal detection process to identify where to "send" environmental cues. See, e.g., Gary L. Brase, "The Allocation System: Using Signal Detection Processes to Regulate Representations in a Multimodular Mind," in *Evolution and the Psychology of Thinking* 11 (D. E. Over ed., Hove, UK; New York: Psychology Press, 2003).

37. "Suppose . . . a cognitive scientist is impressed by Cosmides and Tooby's arguments for an encapsulated, domain-specific Cheater Detection Module . . . (CDM) . . . Well, one of the things that's supposed to make the Cheater Detection Module modular is that it operates only in situations that are (taken to be) social exchanges. Its operation is thus said to invoke inferential capacities that are not available to the mind when it is thinking about situations that it does not take to be social exchanges . . . So, then, the CDM computes over mental objects that are marked as social exchange representations; and its function is to sort them into disjoint piles, some of which represent social exchanges in which cheating is going on and others of which do not. But . . . this story requires postulating a prior mechanism that responds to situations at large . . . and maps them onto representations some of which represent the situations as social exchanges and some of which do not. This mechanism is patently less domain specific than the CDM. Query: does it nonetheless still count as a module? And, if it does, what about the mechanism whose outputs turn this social exchange module on? To what domain is it specific? . . . (There is) a related worry that is less principled but arguably more pressing. We've been assuming that there's something in the input to the CDM that turns it on: some property of its input representations to which it is selectively sensitive and that 'carries the information' that the current distal array constitutes a social exchange. Question: What feature could this be? . . . [Y]ou presumably do not believe that social exchanges have proprietary sensory telltales. So you presumably do not believe, for example, that the distinction between social exchanges and everything else is somehow implicit in the sensory transducer outputs that they evoke. After all, it's not as though some Lurking Benevolence paints social exchanges a proprietary color. Figuring out whether something is a social exchange and, if it is, whether it's the kind of social exchange in which cheating can be an issue (not all of them are, of course) involves the detection of what behaviorists used to call Very Subtle Clues. Which is to say that nobody has *any idea* what kind of cerebration is required for figuring out which distal stimulations are social exchanges . . ." Fodor, *The Mind Doesn't Work That Way*, supra note 29 at 74–76.

38. One of many clear statements of this problem can be seen in Ben R. Newell, "Re-visions of Rationality?" 9 *Trends in Cogn. Sci.* 11 (2005).

39. Gerd Gigerenzer, Ulrich Hoffrage and Daniel CG. Goldstein, "Fast and Frugal Heuristics Are Plausible Models of Cognition: Reply to Dougherty, Franco-Watkins, and Thomas (2008)," 115 *Psychol. Rev.* 230, 238 (2008).

40. Id. at 232.

41. See Fodor, *The Mind Doesn't Work That Way*, supra note 29 at 69.

42. Id. at 12.

43. Id. at 12–19.

44. "'The frame problem' is a name for one aspect of the question of how to reconcile a local notion of mental computation with the apparent holism of rational inference; in particular, with the fact that information that is relevant to the optimal solution of an abductive problem can, in principle, come from anywhere in the network of one's prior epistemic commitments." Id. at 42.

45. Id. at 63–64.

46. Not only are those influenced by rational choice theory skeptical of the claim that judgment and decision-making processes, rather than input detectors, are generally speaking encapsulated, there are conceptual reasons to find the *idea* of encapsulation difficult to fathom in relationship to certain forms of thought processes. At core, modular thought is context-independent (if one depends on a theory of the causal role of a particular mental representation, rather than its abstracted syntactic representation, one is not thinking modularly). But it is hard to figure out why certain inputs in their wholly syntactically represented forms might possibly have the same meaning, regardless of their causal relationship to a decision: Learning that "it will not be at all windy tomorrow" has the same formal structure whether one is processing the fact to determine whether it will be possible to sail down Lake Michigan to Chicago or whether one is driving, but it might radically simplify the process of deciding whether to sail (might even be a lexical cue if it will not be windy at all!) but generate needless complexity if it is used as an input into the driving decision. And, once more, there is no heuristic shortcut to tell you *whether* to exclude or include the information unless (and this is sure plausible!) there are separate modules to make decisions about water-borne transport and motor-driven transport issues. A brain that *had* to exclude information about the wind from some significant *class* of decisions if it were to exclude it from others is very hard to fathom. If that is right, though, the idea that the brain is *massively* modularized—that we can do most of the things we need to do with highly specific modules dedicated to the solution of truly repetitive problems that aptly tailor all information-optimal output relationships, seems extraordinarily hard to fathom.

47. They are more likely still, in thinking about law, to eschew reform: We needn't correct people's decision making very often, and internal legal system rules (from laws of evidence to the simple rules of contract and tort that Epstein has long-extolled) have typically evolved in ways that map up to the useful fast and frugal heuristics people already use. Epstein gives an F&F interpretation of his long-standing, if occasionally qualified, faith in the majestic simplicity of common law libertarian rules in Richard A. Epstein, "The Optimal Complexity of Legal Rules," in *Heuristics and the Law*, supra note 1 at 141. For a fuller version of his arguments against conscious utilitarian deliberation, with less reference, either direct or indirect, to F&F theory, see Richard A. Epstein, *Simple Rules for a Complex World* (Cambridge, MA: Harvard University Press, 1995).

48. See Christoph Engel and Gerd Gigerenzer, "Law and Heuristics: An Interdisciplinary Venture," in *Heuristics and the Law*, supra note 1 at 1, 6. My weakly held suspicion is that this is the sort of "credit-grabbing"/pointless renaming by F&F scholars that often irks H&B people. H&B authors paid a great deal of attention to the stickiness of default rules, given endowment effects, for decades before we first saw mention of the scarcely distinguishable "don't change the status quo" fast and frugal heuristic.

49. For an illustration of this sort of argument, see Douglas A. Kysar, Peter Ayton, Robert H. Frank, Bruno S. Frey, Gerd Gigerenzer, Paul W. Glimcher, Russell Korobkin, Donald C. Langevoort and Stefan Magen, "Group Report: Are Heuristics a Problem or a Solution?" in *Heuristics and the Law*, supra note 1 at 103, 132–33.

Chapter 4

1. Gerd Gigerenzer *Adaptive Thinking: Rationality in the Real World* 233 (Oxford; New York: Oxford University Press, 2000).

2. Gerd Gigerenzer "The Adaptive Toolbox," in *Bounded Rationality: The Adaptive Toolbox* 37, 41 (G. Gigerenzer and R. Selten eds., Cambridge, MA: MIT Press, 2002).
3. There is obviously an enormous literature trying to describe how it is that people acting collectively in organizations come to make decisions. Typical in its effort to find some microfoundations in individual capacities for the decisions that organizations make and also typical in its efforts to move dialectically between initial (isolated) individual inputs and group decisions and how having been exposed to the group process alters the individual's subsequent perceptions is S.T. Allison and D.M. Messick, "From individual Inputs to Group Outputs and Back Again: Group Process and Inferences About Members," in *Review of Personality and Social Psychology* Vol. 8 (C. Hendricks ed., Newbury Park, CA: Sage Publications, 1990). The debate over whether organizations or groups can do "better" than the best individuals in the group can do is an old one as well. For some very good summaries and contributions, see Norbert L. Kerr, Robert J. MacCoun and Geoffrey P. Kramer, "Bias in Judgment: Comparing Individuals and Groups," 103 *Psychol. Rev.* 687 (1996) (noting that groups sometimes amplify, and sometimes mute, the biases that the individuals that comprise them would manifest, if acting on their own, depending in part on group size, the nature of the initial judgments, the magnitude and type of initial bias, and, above all, the nature of the group judgment process); Norbert Kerr and R. Scott Tinsdale, "Group Performance and Decision Making," 55 *Ann. Rev. Psychol.* 623 (2004). Much of the older lab-based literature frequently found that the "upper bound" of performance for the group was the performance of the most competent members, but researchers have also found in "field studies" that "real groups" outperform their most competent members in more than 95 percent of cases. For a summary of these controversies, see, for instance, Larry K. Michaelsen, Warren E. Watson and Robert H. Blank, "A Realistic Test of Individual Versus Group Consensus Decision Making," 74 *J. Appl. Psychol.* 834 (1989).

There have been many efforts to *model* the circumstances in which groups of decision makers who are themselves using heuristics will be more and less prone to error. An interesting one grounded in an F&F view of the general utility of heuristics is Torsten Reimer and Ulrich Hoffrage, "The Ecological Rationality of Simple Group Heuristics: Effects of Group Member Strategies on Decision Accuracy," 60 *Theory & Decision* 403 (2006).

There has obviously also been a long-standing debate about whether the existence of the quite pervasive collective institution of multibuyer markets results in consumers' receiving the product quality/price mix that they would receive if they were less subject as individuals to biased judgment. The literature is very capably summarized in an article dubious of the claim that markets "correct" individual error. See Colin Camerer, "Do Markets Correct Biases in Probability Judgments? Evidence from Market Experiments," in *Advances in Behavioral Economics* Vol. 2, 126 (L. Green and J.A. Kogel eds., Norwood, NJ: Ablex Publishing Corp., 1990).
4. Psychologists have in fact explicitly studied the distinction in behavior of juries and jurors, generally attending not so much to the sorts of judgment biases studied by H&B theory but more conventional "biases" (e.g., racial bias, bias created by attorney behavior, and personality). See, for instance, Norbert L. Kerr, Keith E. Niedermeier and Martin F. Kaplan, "Bias in Jurors v. Juries: New Evidence from the SDS Perspective," 80 *Organizational Behav. & Hum. Decision Processes* 70 (1999) (finding that juries are less biased than jurors in "extreme" cases—in which the base rate for conviction among individual jurors is very high or very low—but more biased in "moderate" cases). For one of the pioneer pieces raising this issue,

see Martin F. Kaplan and Lynn E. Miller, "Reducing the Effects of Juror Bias," 36 *J. Personality & Soc. Psychol.* 1443 (1978).

5. For examples beyond those mentioned in the previous two footnotes, see the discussions of inter-jury unreliability and bias in the award of punitive damages, which is thought to exceed the bias and variability across individuals, in Verlin B. Hinsz and Kristin E. Indahl, "Assimilation to Anchors for Damage Awards in a Mock Civil Trial," 25 *J. Appl. Soc. Psychol.* 991 (1995), and Cass R. Sunstein, Reid Hastie, John W. Payne, David A. Schkade and W. Kip Viscusi, *Punitive Damages: How Juries Decide* (Chicago: University of Chicago Press, 2002).

6. For purposes of the discussion in the text, I counterfactually assume that psychologists uniformly accept that base rate neglect is both widespread and problematic. Koehler, among others, famously largely rejects this argument, noting that evidence of true base rate neglect is often exaggerated and noting more particularly that people may reject only those base rates that are artificially stated to be true base rates in lab instructions. They do so, he claims, in significant part because they are suspicious that the base rate information they are getting is truly accurate for the population they are making judgments about. For one of many good summaries of his work, see Jonathan J. Koehler, "The Base Rate Fallacy Reconsidered: Descriptive, Normative and Methodological Challenges," 19 *Behav. & Brain Sci.* 1 (1996).

We do know that Gigerenzer believes that patients are misled and overestimate the likelihood that they are HIV+ in these cases, though. He has devoted lots of attention in his most "applied" work to teaching doctors how to explain such tests to patients in a way that they will understand them better, in order to alleviate both needless anxiety and excessive medical intervention. He is interested not only in verbal reformulations of the mathematical relations—using frequencies rather than probabilities—but in using pictograms to illustrate how likely one is to be infected. For examples of various practical methods designed by F&F scholars to improve patient numeracy, see Elke Kurz-Milcke, Gerd Gigerenzer and Laura Martignon, "Transparency in Risk Communication: Graphical and Analog Tools," 1128 *N.Y. Acad. Sci.* 18 (2008); Gerd Gigerenzer, Wolfgang Guissmaier, Elke Kurz-Milcke, Lisa M. Schwartz and Steven Wolosbin, "Helping Doctors and Patients Make Sense of Health Statistics," 8 *Psychol. Sci. in the Pub. Interest* 53, 58–60, 83(2008); Gigerenzer, *Adaptive Thinking*, supra note 1 at 252–54.

7. See Gigerenzer, *Adaptive Thinking*, supra note 1 at 77–91.

8. See Ralph Hertwig, "Do Legal Rules Rule Behavior?" in *Heuristics and the Law* 391, 403–06 (G. Gigerenzer and C. Engel eds., Cambridge, MA: MIT Press, 2006).

9. It is an interesting question whether subjects intuitively ignore population size more generally and attend too much to probabilities of salient single events in judging what outcomes follow from what actions or what outcomes are predictable given certain information. Agencies that regulate risk frequently focus solely on the degree to which the most at-risk individual's chances of dying will increase if a particular hazard is left unregulated, ignoring the question of whether some other hazard might expose a far larger group to increased (albeit lower) mortality risk if another hazard were unregulated, though that would be irrational if the agency's goal was to minimize the number of excess deaths caused by hazards. For a far fuller discussion of this and some related issues, see Matthew D. Adler, "Against 'Individual Risk': A Sympathetic Critique of Risk Assessment," 153 *U. Pa. L. Rev.* 1121 (2005).

10. For the classic exposition, see Amos Tvesrky and Daniel Kahneman, "Evidential impact of base rates," in *Judgment Under Uncertainty: Heuristics and Biases* 153 (D. Kahneman, P. Slovic, and A. Tversky eds. Cambridge, UK; New York: Cambridge University Press, 1982).

11. See Gerd Gigerenzer, *Adaptive Thinking*, supra note 1 at 92–123, and also Leda Cosmides and John Tooby, "Are Humans Good Intuitive Statisticians After All? Rethinking Some Conclusions from the Literature on Judgment Under Uncertainty," 58 *Cognition* 1 (1996).
12. At times, the F&F theorists highlight the contrast between frequentism—keeping counts of past events—and probabilistic estimates of single events that have yet to occur. In this view, single events either occur or do not; they do not *occur* probabilistically. Some event X and the event not-X can occur with different frequencies if and only if there have been repeated trials in which one or the other might occur. In this view, subjects' reluctance or inability to give probabilistic estimates of future events (e.g., to repeat an example from Chapter Two, to refuse to give estimates of how likely is it that Linda is a bank teller *or* a feminist bank teller) simply reflects their proper resistance to the notion that there are meaningful probabilities for single events (Linda either is or isn't a feminist bank teller). As I noted in Chapter Two, this attack on the "reality" of single-event probabilistic thinking (a restatement of the subjectivist critique of probability theory) seems beside the point: The way in which we likely induce probabilities for single (future, uncertain) events is simply to infer from past frequencies, observed or inferred, for like events. Thus, it is indeed true that it will either rain or not rain given the current cloud cover tomorrow, but we infer the probability that it will from past observations of rainy and non-rainy days that followed similar cloud covers.

    That is not the fundamental basis of H&B skepticism toward this set of F&F findings. What is far more telling is that some H&B theorists claim that frequency presentation does not itself markedly improve performance, and they implicitly disbelieve the adaptationist story about how we learned to observe natural frequencies when we were foraging or hunting or figuring out which people around us were dying from particular causes or after displaying particular symptoms. While I largely want to emphasize the degree to which those in the H&B school resist the claim that one can invariably significantly reduce a particular bias—base-rate neglect—simply by using any old sort of frequentist presentation of a problem in which subjects have manifest this infirmity of judgment, it is important to note, more generally, that those in the H&B school note that many of the biases they have historically demonstrated occur in settings in which subjects are asked to estimate not probabilities but frequencies. For instance, those purportedly making judgments based on "availability" rather than accurate actual sampling do so not only when they make probability estimates ("how likely is one to die in a plane crash relative to a slip in the bath tub?") but when making frequentist judgments as well ("how many words begin with "r" compared to the number whose third letter is r?"). For a brief review, by H&B researchers, of such claims that bias has been frequently manifest by subjects asked to manipulate frequencies, see, e.g., Thomas Gilovich and Dale Griffin, "Introduction—Heuristics and Biases: Then and Now," in *Heuristics and Biases* 1, 14–15 (T. Gilovich, D. Griffin and D. Kahneman eds., Cambridge, UK; New York: Cambridge University Press, 2002). ("Evolutionary psychologists . . . maintain that success in our ancestral environment required only a talent for working with frequencies, not probabilities . . . The evidence for heuristics and biases, it is claimed, 'disappears' when stimuli are presented and questions are asked in terms of frequencies . . . This was a bold argument when first introduced and it is even bolder to maintain now . . . when a score of studies have indicated that it simply does not hold up empirically. In fact, presenting frequencies rather than probabilities sometimes makes judgments distinctly worse. . . . sometimes makes judgments distinctly better. . . . and quite often leaves the quality of judgments unchanged . . ."). In much the same vein, see Daniel Kahneman and Amos Tversky, "On the Reality of Cognitive Illusions," 103 *Psychol. Rev.* 582 (1996).

Moreover, H&B scholars often argue that F&F scholars are simply wrong to claim that those whose performance is improved by an alternative mode of presenting the data to be manipulated do better because they are dealing with data presented in terms of frequencies. They argue, instead, that the particular experimental frequentist presentations that Cosmides and Tooby used in "disproving" the claim that base-rate neglect was a "bias" or demonstrated infirmity of judgment is misleading to the extent that their prompts cue a simple mental model of set inclusion by focusing every statistic on a group of the same number of people. In this view, people barely do better in accounting for base rates when presented frequentist information in a form that does not cue set inclusion.

Thus, assume we give experimental subjects data of the following form: "Assume about one in ten thousand men are HIV positive and further assume that 1000 of 10,000,000 men will test positive even if they are not HIV positive, what are the chances that a man who tests positive is actually positive if nine hundred and ninety nine out of a thousand men who are HIV positive test positive?" H&B theorists like Evans (and colleagues) note that though such data is presented in *frequentist* form, subjects barely do better in assessing the odds of being sick conditional on a positive test result in this experimental condition than they do when the experimental prompt is presented in probabilistic form. The claim is that they can figure out how likely an individual is to have one trait rather than another only when comparing frequencies of each trait within the precise same set. See Jonathan St. B.T. Evans, Simon J. Handley, Nick Perham, David E. Over and Valerie A. Thompson, "Frequency Versus Probability Formats in Statistical Word Problems," 77 *Cognition* 197 (2000).

Arguably, Evans et al. have done no more than re-name or refine the "natural setting" in which subjects think best about conditional probabilities. It is not exactly a setting in which there are frequentist presentations, it is a setting in which the presentations cue set inclusion. If that is all they have done, though, their point seems rather thin unless they also mean to claim that there is little or no reason to believe that people will naturally observe and count up false positives and negatives within the same set in out-of-laboratory settings. I am not sure if they mean to imply this.

But the critical F&F point would remain that distinct environments induce distinct forms of performance, and that some performances are superior to others, at least if we are willing to assume that the subject's goal is to make a veridical judgment about the likelihood that he will need medication. In this sense, the F&F theorists are plainly right to *emphasize* points that H&B theorists may at least arguably be prone to make only in passing. The degree of irrationality that subjects may display may be highly context-specific, and figuring out how prevalent the contexts in which irrationality is most apt to be manifest really are in solving actual problems is plainly important.

13. See Gerd Gigerenzer, "The Bounded Rationality of Probabilistic Mental Models," in *Rationality: Psychological and Philosophical Perspectives* 284 (K. Mankteh and D. Over eds., London; New York: Routledge, 1993).

14. See Amos Tversky and Daniel Kahneman, "Extensional versus Intuitive Reasoning: The Conjunction Fallacy in Probability Judgment," 90 *Psychol. Rev.* 293 (1983). Once more, I suspect H&B theorists would simply note that the simplest versions of the conjunction fallacy are simply wiped out by problems with strong set inclusion cues. I share the views of most H&B scholars on this score; I am skeptical of the claim that "natural" problems of estimation

of events in natural environments inexorably signal set inclusion, even if people ("naturally") used frequencies (X out of Y) rather than percentages/probabilities (5 percent chance.)

It is also worth noting what is once again no more than a very weak outsider's intuition on my part that a number of scholars associated with the H&B school were especially miffed by Gigerenzer's failure to note that H&B experimenters had anticipated the very manipulation whose absence he criticized them for failing to make.

15. For a general discussion of this task, see P.C. Wason, "On the Failure to Eliminate Hypotheses in a Conceptual Task," 12 *Q. J. Exp. Psychol.* 129 (1960).

16. Consider the following finding by Gigerenzer and Hug. Some experimental subjects are asked to take the perspective of an employer when asked to figure out what cards to turn over in seeing whether there have been violations of the rule, "If an employee gets a pension, then that employee must have worked for the firm for at least ten years." These subjects are more prone to turn over the card with an employee working less than ten years to see if he's gotten a pension nonetheless than those subjects asked to take the perspective of an employee; these subjects are more likely to check whether the employer has cheated (to check whether everyone who has worked more than ten years has a pension). But whether this distinction in performance is grounded in motivation or in the use of dedicated cognitive mechanisms with a particular form is less clear. See G. Gigerenzer and K. Hug, "Domain-Specific Reasoning: Social Contracts, Cheating and Perspective Change," 42 *Cognition* 127 (1992).

17. See R.S. Nickerson, "Hempel's Paradox and Wason's Selection Task: Logical and Psychological Puzzles of Confirmation," 2 *Thinking & Reasoning* 1 (1995).

18. Assume it is true, as H&B researchers such as Stanovich and West find, that more conventionally "intelligent" people do markedly better on versions of the non-deontic Wason selection task (like the four-card selection task) than do less "intelligent" people, though differences on the "does a person follow a particular type of obligatory rule?" version are small. See Keith E. Stanovich and Richard F. West, "Individual Differences in Framing and Conjunction Effects," 4 *Thinking & Reasoning* 434–36 (1998). (One might assume, further, that once the four-card task is explained to people, they acknowledge they need to turn over both P and not-Q cards, though I have found no experimental findings to that effect.) Would either finding imply that the "non-normative" response is or is not the ecologically rational one? The key problem in answering this question is determining what the experimental version of the task is most like in the natural world. Does this mean that ecologically rational people are in the habit of ignoring not-Qs in these sorts of rule-verification tasks, or that they are in the habit of ignoring them only when they are confronting problems more like the raven problem than a four-card problem? Are the "smart" people not only more formally rational but more rational in the F&F sense because they are better able to identify what sort of problem they are solving? If we need some sort of non-domain-specific cognition to assign a problem to a particular domain-specific module (if such modules exist), is the capacity to make apt assignments what characterizes "smart" people? Or, alternatively, do Stanovich and West find that "smarter" people do better on this task because, as folk wisdom often suggests, abstract book smart people aren't street smart and they really are doing something that is dysfunctional in the real world—reducing concrete problems to general abstract forms before they solve them—but happen to be doing it "right" in the unreal lab conditions?

19. See David E. Over, "From Massive Modularity to Metarepresentation: The Evolution of Higher Cognition," in *Evolution and the Psychology of Thinking* 121 (D.E. Over ed., Hove, UK; New York: Psychology Press, 2003).

20. Ledaa Cosmides and John Tooby, "Cognitive Adaptations for Social Exchange" in *The Adapted Mind: Evolutionary Psychology and the Generation of Culture* 163, 205 (J.H. Barkow, L. Cosmides and J. Tooby eds., New York: Oxford University Press, 1992). It is also plausible to respond, following Gigerenzer's general methodology, that the cheater-detection capacity is the basic evolved ability and that it is hijacked or co-opted over time for use in novel situations in which it is helpful to do so, given the environment in which decisions must be made.

21. See Valerie E. Stone, Leda Cosmides, John Tooby, Neal Kroll and Robert T. Knight, "Selective Impairment of Reasoning About Social Exchange in a Patient with Bilateral Limbic System Damage," 99 *Proc. Nat'l Acad. Sci., USA* 11531 (2002). Of course, while I am once again reluctant to venture into neuroscience, I believe the conventional picture would be that it is possible that the lesion compromised the subject's capacity to perform a task that sub-serves reasoning about precautions, not that a precaution-reasoning *module* was destroyed by the brain injury.

22. For a fuller account, see K.I. Manktelow, N. Fairley, S.G. Kilpatrick and D.E. Over, "Pragmatics and Strategies for Practical Reasoning," in *Deductive Reasoning and Strategies* 111 (G. De Vooght, G. D'Ydewalle, W. Schaeken and A. Vandierendonck eds., Hoboken, NJ: Taylor & Francis, 1999).

23. See, e.g., Morris P. Fiorina, "A Note on Probability Matching and Rational Choice," 16 *Behav. Sci.* 158 (1971); William S. Cooper and Robert H. Kaplan, "Adaptive Coin-Flipping: A Decision-Theoretic Examination of Natural Selection for Random Individual Variation," 94 *J. Theoretical Biol.* 135 (1982); Catrin Rode, Leda Cosmides, Wolfgang Hell and John Tooby, "When and Why Do People Avoid Unknown Probabilities in Decisions under Uncertainty? Testing Some Predictions from Optimal Foraging Theory," 72 *Cognition* 269 (1999).

24. Richard F. West and Keith Stanovich, "Is Probability Matching Smart? Associations Between Probabilistic Choices and Cognitive Ability," 31 *Mem. & Cogn.* 243 (2003).

25. H. Paul Grice, "Logic and Conversation," in *Syntax and Semantics* Vol. 3, 41 (P. Cole and L. Morgan eds., 1975). Those committed to cooperative conversation should also be guided by considerations of quantity—conversational offerings should be as informative as is necessary to communicate action-relevant data, but no more so; quality—one should only say what one believes to be true and what one has adequate evidence to believe; and manner—one should avoid ambiguity, obscurity, long-windedness, and disorderliness. As I note in the test, in thinking about the "Linda problem" relevance and quantity are most significant.

26. For examples of this criticism, see, e.g., Jonathan E. Adler, "An Optimist's Pessimism; Conversation and Conjunctions," in *Probability and Rationality: Studies on L. Jonathan Cohen's Philosophy of Science* 251 (E. Eells and T. Maruszewski eds., Amsterdam; Atlanta, GA: Rodopi, 1991); D.E. Dulaney and D.J. Hilton, "Conversational Implicature, Conscious Representation, and the Conjunction Fallacy," 9 *Soc. Cognition* 85 (1991); Guy Politzer and Ira A. Noveck, "Are Conjunction Rule Violations the Result of Conversational Rule Violations?" 20 *J. Psycholinguistic Res.* 83 (1991).

27. See Ralph Hertwig and Gerd Gigerenzer, "The 'Conjunction Fallacy' Revisited: How Intelligence Looks Like Reasoning Errors," 12 *J. Behav. Dec. Mak.* 275 (1999), and Gerd Gigerenzer, "On Narrow Norms and Vague Heuristics: A Reply to Kahneman and Tversky (1996)," 103 *Psychol. Rev.* 592, 593 (1996). Gigerenzer further notes that subjects may have reinterpreted the question in yet another way. Experimental subjects may think that when the experimenter asks whether it is more "probable" that Linda is a feminist bank teller than a

bank teller, they believe that something is more "probable" if it is more plausible given the interlocutor's prior comments. Frankly, I find this interpretation too hard to comprehend to comment upon.
28. See Stanovich and West, "Individual," supra note 18 at 289. See also Daniel Kahneman and Amos Tversky, "On the Reality of Cognitive Illusions," supra note 12 at 586.
29. See Anton Kuhberger, "The Framing of Decisions: A New Look at Old Problems," 62 *Organizational Behav. & Hum. Decision Processes* 230 (1995).
30. See, e.g., Peter R. Sedlmeir, Ralph Hertwig and Gerd Gigerenzer, "Are Judgments of the Positional Frequencies of Letters Systematically Biased Due to Availability?" 24 *J. Exp. Psych: Learning, Mem. & Cogn.* 754 (1998) (finding that if we define "ease of recall" either as the amount of time it takes to recall the first instance of a category or as the number of items in the category one can recall in a fixed time, then ease of recall does not correlate with probability estimates of words that have "r" as a first rather than third letter, as H&B theorists had predicted.)
31. See Peter Ayton and Ilan Fischer, "The Hot-Hand Fallacy and the Gambler's Fallacy: Two Faces of Subjective Randomness," 32 *Mem. & Cogn.* 1369 (2004). What Ayton and Fischer find is that subjects simultaneously exhibit negative recency in relationship to patterns generated by an inanimate object—if the roulette wheel has been generating reds, they (falsely) believe it is more likely to self-correct with a black on the next trial—while exhibiting positive recency with regard to what they perceive as exercises of skill—if they have predicted accurately how the roulette wheel will land on several trials, they unduly believe they will continue to do so. I must confess I remain a bit puzzled by the claim that it is adaptive to believe that the skilled will ever manifest skill *beyond their average global performance level* unless there really are atypical *runs* of skill. It may well be that the hot-hand "fallacy" arises from our short memories and leads us to treat the limited amount we recall as an adequate sample. If people cannot readily remember if X is a globally better shooter than Y, but can remember if he's made more of his last ten shots, *and* accurately perceive that X is more likely to have shot well lately if he's a globally better shooter, then the "fallacy" is nothing more than a reflection of a sampling problem that arises from weak memory and inadequate access to semantic knowledge.
32. See Harold A. Latin, "'Good' Warnings, Bad Products, and Cognitive Limitations," 41 *UCLA L. Rev.* 1193 (1994).
33. See Alan Schwartz and Louis L. Wilde, "Imperfect Information in Markets for Contract Terms: The Examples Of Warranties and Security Interests," 69 *Va. L. Rev.* 1387 (1983).
34. See Douglas A. Kysar et al., "Group Report: Are Heuristics the Problem or the Solution?" in *Heuristics and the Law* 103, 121 (G. Gigerenzer and C. Engel eds., 2006).
35. See Lee Green and David R. Mehr, "What Alters Physicians' Decisions to Admit to the Coronary Care Unit?" 45 *J. Fam. Pract.* 219 (1997). The heuristic technique is enthusiastically endorsed in Gerd Gigerenzer, "Heuristics," in *Heuristics and the Law*, supra note 8 at 17, 24–27.

Chapter 5

1. Perhaps the most systematic critiques of F&F that resemble in significant ways the critiques that we articulate in this chapter—arguably informed in some part by H&B work—come

from Professor Newell. For a readily accessible summary, see Ben R. Newell, "*Re*-visions of Rationality?" 9 *Trends in Cognitive Sciences* 11 (2005). For examples of pieces by Newell focusing on one of the most critical themes in this chapter—skepticism about the F&F claim that subjects invariably use fundamentally lexical, non-compensatory methods, see Ben R. Newell and David R. Shanks, "Take the Best or Look at the Rest? Factors Influencing 'One-Reason' Decision Making" 29 *J. Exp. Psychol. Learning, Mem. & Cogn.* 53 (2003), Ben R. Newell et al., "Empirical Tests of a Fast and Frugal Heuristic: Not Everyone Takes-the-Best," 91 *Organizational Behav. & Hum. Decision Processes* 82 (2003). There is a relatively rich literature criticizing the claim made by F&F scholars that subjects use lexical, non-compensatory decision-making processes. We return to the literature suggesting that people use additional information rather than merely relying on recognition later in the chapter, but there are many other studies questioning the veracity of claims that subjects more generally "Take the Best." See, for instance, Arndt Broder, "Assessing the empirical validity of the 'Take-the-Best' heuristic as a model of human probabilistic inference," 26 *J. Exp. Psychol.: Learning, Mem. & Cogn.* 1332 (2000); Peter Juslin et al., "Cue Abstraction and Exemplar Memory in Categorization," 29 *J. Exp. Psychol.: Learning, Mem. & Cogn.* 611 (2003). Obviously, too, Kahneman and Tversky, the pioneering researchers in the H&B tradition, did explicitly address some of the critiques of their work that Gigerenzer had leveled over the years, though there is little in the piece explicitly criticizing the fast and frugal countertheory. See Daniel Kahneman and Amos Tversky, "On the Reality of Cognitive Illusions," 103 *Psychol. Rev.* 582 (1996).

A quite separate line of criticism—which we neither elaborate nor embrace—comes from those who claim that that the plausibility of fast and frugal heuristic decision making rests on the capacity of subjects to "learn" from "probabilistic mental models" that were created and updated through some sort of automatic frequency counter that people in fact do not possess. This critique is articulated in Michael R. Dougherty, Ana M. Franco-Watkins and Rick Thomas, "Psychological Plausibility of the Theory of Probabilistic Mental Models and the Fast and Frugal Heuristics," 115 *Psychol. Rev.* 199 (2008).

2. For a fuller discussion of this standard criticism, see, for instance, Kim Sterelny and Paul Griffiths, *Sex and Death: An Introduction to the Philosophy of Biology* 341–42 (Chicago: University of Chicago Press, 1999).
3. See, e.g., Mark Kelman, "Thinking About Sexual Consent," 58 *Stan. L. Rev.* 935, 942–43, 960–61 (2005).
4. See, e.g., Deborah Blum, *Sex on the Brain* 224 (New York: Viking, 1997).
5. See, e.g., Alan Wertheimer, *Consent to Sexual Relations* 76, 81 (Cambridge, UK; New York: Cambridge University Press, 2003).
6. See, e.g., Diana Sculley, *Understanding Sexual Violence* 71–72 (Boston: Urwin Hyman, 1990) (reporting that 89 percent of rapists, compared to 91 percent of non-rapists, had engaged in consensual sex at least twice a week before entering prison; 42 percent of rapists compared to 37 percent of rapists had consensual sex daily; 49 percent of rapists had lived with three or more women and 62 percent had already fathered children); Kok Peng Gwee et al., "The Sexual Profile of Rapists in Singapore," 42 *Med. Sci. & L.* 51, 53 (2002) (60 percent of rapists, compared to 44 percent of non-rapists had had more than ten consensual sexual partners in their lifetime).
7. Not surprisingly, most rapists commit an enormous amount of nonsexual crimes and show across-the-board antisocial dispositions. Moreover, rape rates typically correspond to more general rates of violent crime, both across time and across communities. See Martin

L. Lalumiere et al., *The Causes of Rape* 62, 72–76 (Washington, DC: American Psychological Association, 2005).

Similarly, while it might be *plausible* that EP theorists are right that the adaptive *role* that female rape aversion plays is to insure that women can be picky in having sex with only men likely to assist them in raising children to the point where the children themselves can bear children, the purportedly observed behavioral correlate—that women who might be fertile are both markedly more rape-averse than those who are older or younger and that they are especially averse to sexual coercion that risks pregnancy (vaginal rape)—cannot actually be adduced from the data. The proposition was most forcefully advanced and defended in Nancy Wilmsen Thornhill and Randy Thornhill, "An Evolutionary Analysis of Psychological Pain Following Rape: I. The Effect of Victim's Age and Marital Status," 11 *Ethology & Sociobiology* 155 (1990), and Randy Thornhill and Craig T. Palmer, "Rape and Evolution: A Reply to Our Critics," 4 *Psychol., Evolution & Gender* 283 (2002).

Critiques of the empirical claim are legion: Post-menopausal women seem in fact to be just as rape averse as fertile women, and reactions to anal rape appear as negative as reactions to vaginal rape. The critiques are articulated in Jerry A. Coyne and Andrew Berry, "Rape as an Adaptation: Is This Contentious Hypothesis Advocacy, Not Science?," 404 *Nature* 121 (2000) and explored further in Mark Kelman, "Thinking About Sexual Consent," 58 *Stan. L. Rev.* 935, 960–61 (2005). See also Thomas W. McCahill et al., *The Aftermath of Rape* 66 (Lexington, MA: Lexington Books, 1979) (anal rape is as traumatic and aversive as vaginal rape.).

I should note that I think that the *best* evidence for the proposition that rape revulsion is driven most powerfully by the adaptive desire to avoid unwanted pregnancy is that fertile women's resistance to rape may well be higher during the portions of their menstrual cycle when they are most likely to get pregnant. See Sandra M. Petralia and Gordon G. Gallup Jr., "Effects of a Sexual Assault Scenario on Handgrip Strength Across the Menstrual Cycle," 23 *Evolution & Hum. Behav.* 3 (2002) (finding that women in the ovulatory phase of the menstrual cycle showed a marked increase in handgrip strength after reading an essay depicting a woman walking to her car pursued by a strange man, but handgrip strength did not increase for women in any other phase of the menstrual cycle who read this essay, nor for ovulating women who read an essay in which a woman was walking to her car with many other people around).

8. Another instance in which H&B researchers are making this same fundamental critique was noted in note 12 to Chapter Four. H&B theorists like Evans say that F&F scholars have badly misidentified the relevant capacity needed to overcome base-rate neglect, precisely because they assume that the capacity *must* be whatever it *should* be to solve some (real or theorist-constructed) adaptive problems.

9. The key studies in the "performance variability" tradition were those done by Stanovich and West. See, e.g., Keith E. Stanovich, *Who Is Rational? Studies of Individual Differences in Reasoning* (Mahwah, NJ: Lawrence Erlbaum Associates, 1999); Keith E. Stanovich and Richard F. West, "Individual Differences in Reasoning: Implications for the Rationality Debate," in *Heuristics and Biases* 421 (T. Gilovich, D. Griffin and D. Kahneman eds., Cambridge, UK; New York; Cambridge University Press, 2002); Keith E. Stanovich and Richard F. West, "Individual Differences in Reasoning: Implications for the Rationality Debate," 23 *Brain & Behav. Sci.* 645 (2000). But the variability issue has certainly been raised by other researchers responding to F&F work. See, e.g., Eric. J. Johnson, Michael Schulte-Mecklenbeck and Martijn C. Willemsen, "Process Models Deserve Process Data: Comment on Bradstatter,

Gigerenzer, and Hertwig (2006)," 115 *Psychol. Rev.* 263 (2008) (finding that experimental subjects differ in the ways in which they make selections among lotteries, sometimes using something like the F&F "priority heuristic" and sometimes using other methods).

10. Daniel C. Goldstein and Gerd Gigerenzer, "Models of Ecological Rationality: The Recognition Heuristic." 109 *Psychol. Rev.* 75 (2002).

11. San Antonio and San Diego are essentially identical in population. In fact, San Antonio is now larger than San Diego so presumably all of the Germans in the initial study would now get the answer to the question wrong, not right, but at the time it was asked, in the late 1990s, Germans indeed correctly identified the city that was less than 1 percent larger.

12. The most accessible summary of their views about how subjects come to use a heuristic or not to use one can be seen in Gerd Gigerenzer, Ulrich Hoffrage and Daniel C. Goldstein, "Fast and Frugal Heuristics Are Plausible Models of Cognition: Reply to Dougherty, Franco-Watkins, and Thomas (2008)," 115 *Psychol. Rev.* 230 (2008). Broadly speaking, they argue that subjects may use heuristics when there are direct evolutionary/adaptive pressures that make their use mandatory (this is closest to the massive modularity picture set out in Chapter Three, though it applies to only a sub-set of the heuristics), may use them when they are mimicking those around them (so the "imitation heuristic" becomes the meta-heuristic that dictates the use of other heuristics), or when, as individuals, they learn that the use of the heuristic meets their proximal goals. The last strategy (individual learning by feedback) is modeled by F&F theorists in Jorg Rieskamp and Phillip E. Otto, "A Theory of How People Learn to Select Strategies," 135 *J. Exp. Psychol.: Gen.* 207 (2006).

13. Tobias Richter and Pamela Spath, "Recognition Is Used as One Cue Among Others in Judgment and Decision Making," 7 *J. Exp. Psychol.: Learning, Mem. & Cogn.* 150 (2006).

14. Thorsten Pachur and Ralph Hertwig, "On the Psychology of the Recognition Heuristic: Retrieval Primacy as a Key Determinant of Its Use," 32 *J. Exp. Psychol.: Learning, Mem. & Cogn.* 983 (2006).

15. Kirsten G. Volz et al., "Why You Think Milan Is Larger Than Modena: Neural Correlates of the Recognition Heuristic," 18 *J. Cogn. Neurosci.* 1924 (2006).

16. I generally follow Goldstein and Gigerenzer's terminology by asking whether subjects "recognize" a city or "recognize" photos. This idiosyncratic characterization may be misleading to those used to more conventional descriptions of memory. Most memory researchers would say that those who identify the photos they have seen as previously encountered find the photos "familiar" and that those who know that San Antonio is a city "recollect" not only its proper name but background contextual facts about the proper name. In mainstream memory research "recognition depends upon two kinds of memory: recollection and familiarity." See, e.g., Andrew P. Yonelinas, "The Nature of Recollection and Familiarity: A Review of 30 Years of Research," 46. *J. Mem. & Lang.* 441 (2002); Daniela Montaldi, Tom J. Spencer, Neil Roberts and Andrew R. Mayes, "The Neural System That Mediates Familiarity Memory," 16 *Hippocampus* 504 (2006). I return to this point in considerable detail later in the text.

17. For a representative sample of this work, see Ben R. Newell & David R. Shanks, "On the Role of Recognition in Decision Making," 30 *J. Exp. Psychol.: Learning, Mem. & Cogn.* 923 (2004); Daniel M. Oppenheimer, "Not So Fast! (and Not So Frugal!): Rethinking the Recognition Heuristic," 90 *Cognition* B1-B9 (2003). Rudiger F. Pohl, "Empirical Tests of the Recognition Heuristic," 19 *J. Behav. Decision Making* 251 (2006); Richter and Spath, "Recognition Is Used as One Cue," supra note 13.

18. The new material on the recognition heuristic draws on research done by Mark Kelman and Nicholas Richman Kelman. A fuller account, of both methods and findings, can be seen online in "Revisiting the City Recognition Heuristic" (2010).
19. Here are the critical passages supporting that this was how Goldstein and Gigerenzer viewed the recognition heuristic when they first formulated it. First, at the most general level, they described the fast and frugal program as designed to test computational models of heuristics that are "founded in evolved psychological capacities like memory...." Goldstein and Gigerenzer, "Models of Ecological Rationality: The Recognition Heuristic," supra note 10 at 75.

More important, in describing what it means for a subject to recognize a city in a fashion that permits him or her to use the recognition heuristic, Goldstein and Gigerenzer describe Germans comparing the sizes of San Diego and San Antonio in the following way: "All of the Germans tested had heard of San Diego; about half of them did not recognize San Antonio." Id. at 76.

How, though, in the authors' view, do they make a fast and frugal judgment that they "have heard of" a city?

The mechanism for distinguishing between the novel and recognized seems to be specialized and robust. For instance, recognition memory remains when other types of memory become impaired ... Laboratory research has demonstrated that memory for mere recognition encodes information even in divided-attention learning. *Because recognition continues to operate even under adverse circumstances, and it can be impaired independently from the rest of memory, we view it as a primordial psychological mechanism* ... (our emphasis). Id. at 76–77.

They further demonstrate their commitment to the idea that the heuristic is grounded in a particular form of memory by stating, "Experiments that use nonwords or never-before-seen photographs [rather than those that rely on the subjects' capacity to know which known word they saw on a particular list] capture the distinction of interest here; that between the truly novel and the previously experienced." Id. at. 75. Such experiments, are, of course, experiments about familiarity, not recollection.

Never-encountered and encountered *items* are logically binary and dichotomous (if one *ever* encountered San Antonio, it should be "recognized" in the relevant sense if recognition *memory* were capacious, unfailing, and itself dichotomous). Goldstein and Gigerenzer commit to the idea that item-recognition memory is as binary as the actual experience of encountering itself is. (As we argue in the text, this view is a view of memory that few memory researchers share): "[T]he recognition heuristic does not address comparisons between items in memory, *but rather the difference between items in and out of memory* ... The recognition heuristic treats recognition as a binary, all-or-nothing distinction ..." (our emphasis). Id. at 77.

The authors also explicitly lodge the (purported) existence of binary recognition memory in the adaptive advantages of such memory and the use of such a heuristic. They explain, in essence, why it is a tool in the adaptive toolbox in the following terms: "What is the origin of the recognition heuristic as a strategy? In the case of avoiding food poisoning, organisms seem as if they are genetically prepared to act in accordance with the recognition heuristic. Wild Norway rats do not need to be taught to prefer recognized foods over novel ones; food

neophobia is instinctual." Id. at 85. They purport to show other advantages for what they treat as similar forms of recognition in social bonding and making alliances. Id. at 87.
20. For a (re)vision of the heuristic that backs away from the claim that it relies on any particular account of, or form of, memory—whether one for which there is a simple evolutionary adaptation story or not, see Gerd Gigerenzer, Ulrich Hoffrage and Daniel C. Goldstein, "Fast and Frugal Heuristics Are Plausible Models of Cognition: Reply to Dougherty, Franco-Watkins, And Thomas (2008)," 115 *Psychol. Rev.* 230, 234. ("The recognition heuristic is not a model of memory processes, rather it models how inferences are made on the basis of the output of memory processes . . . It draws on all-or-none recognition *judgment*, which . . . 'is counter to the literature on recognition memory.' . . . However, one needs to distinguish between continuous trace activation and a binary recognition judgment . . . For instance, Schooler and Hertwig . . . assumed that activation of a memory record (the continuous underlying value) cannot be accessed directly. However, its activation does govern sensations of which people can be aware, namely yes-no recognition judgments . . . The assumption of being able to arrive at yes-no recognition judgments is intuitively plausible; we classify people as recognized or unrecognized with ease and hesitate only rarely.") (emphasis added). As we note in the text, this revision does not really solve the problem that most of the experimental subjects *can* recognize widely known cities in the forced-choice condition (or that subjects making such forced choices don't make yes-no judgments "with ease"). But the main point, for now, is not whether this reformulation is satisfactory, it is that given this reformulation, we cannot really either tell what precisely delineated evolved capacity subjects are using (it's certainly not the recognition of non-words or once-confronted photographs that they highlight in the initial article), nor is it nearly so clear that the capacity plays a simple adaptive role.
21. See footnote 19 for text in the seminal article supporting this view that they believed they were describing familiarity memory only, and compared what people comparing city size did to what people who recognized non-words and once-confronted photographs did.
22. Goldstein and Gigerenzer, supra note 10 at 77 (emphasis added).
23. The relevant part of the instruction in the forced-recognition condition is: "We have listed the names of 32 towns and cities below . . . Sixteen are real German cities and towns; the other sixteen are simply made up. Please circle the sixteen names that you think are real. Please don't circle more than sixteen; please don't circle fewer than sixteen. Don't worry that you may be guessing (occasionally, frequently, or always . . .)."
24. What we did in analyzing the actual experiments is to compare the number of persons who recognize a city in the forced-choice condition, having not recognized it initially, with the number who would have picked the city by chance, given how many cities they had to guess about. Thus, for instance, imagine that Subject 1 had recognized eleven of the sixteen real cities listed in Part Two when he responded to Part One: When answering Part Two, if he randomly guessed there would be a five in twenty-one chance that he would select any city that he did not consciously recognize in Part One. So fifteen subjects did not recognize Leipzig in the first test; if each of them had circled eleven cities on part one, each would have had a five in twenty-one chance of merely guessing Leipzig were real. If that were the case, we'd expect that Leipzig would be circled 75/21 times. In our data analysis, we compared the number of actual times "famous," "modestly known," "modestly unknown," "unknown," and "made up" cities are circled in the forced-recognition condition compared to the expected number. The ability of subjects in the forced-choice condition to recognize a city that they

ostensibly do not recognize in the circle-a-recognized-city condition essentially varies in a linear fashion with their probable actual exposure to the city, measured by the proportion of respondents who consciously recognize the city. If subjects were simply unfamiliar in a dichotomous way with all the cities they purportedly do not recognize, they would be no more prone to pick out the cities others generally consciously knew at greater than chance or "guessing" rates

25. It is not surprising that Goldstein and Gigerenzer eventually disclaimed their initial claim that recognition itself, rather than judgments based on memory, are binary because the mainstream work on familiarity is unambiguous that familiarity judgments are *not* binary. We know, behaviorally, that subjects have more or less confidence that an item is familiar or not and that their confidence judgments are related to their accuracy in identifying actually confronted items: See John C. Dunn, "Remember-Know: A Matter of Confidence," 111 *Psychol. Rev.* 524 (2004), and Yonelinas, "The Nature of Recollection and Familiarity," supra note 16.

There is considerable neurobiological evidence as well that items are more or less familiar, that memory strength is on a continuum: Single-cell recordings show experience-based changes in perirhinal neuronal firing patterns consistent with item recognition—firing rates decrease in response to stimuli that has been previously encountered more relative to more novel stimuli. See J.Z. Xiang and M.W. Brown, "Differential Neuronal Encoding of Novelty, Familiarity and Recency in Regions of the Anterior Temporal Lobe," 37 *Neuropharmacol.* 657 (1998). Similarly, fMRI studies reveal that there is more limited neural activity in the medial temporal cortex when humans recognize faces that were previously encountered relative to faces that are novel and that the magnitude of the repetition reduction both varies in a continuous fashion and is associated with greater levels of confidence in item recognition. See Brian D. Gonsalves et al., "Memory Strength and Repetition Suppression: Multimodal Imaging of Medial Temporal Cortical Contributions to Recognition," 47 *Neuron* 751 (2005), and R.N.A. Henson, S. Cansino, J.E. Herron, W.G. Robb and M.D. Rugg, "A Familiarity Signal in Human Anterior Medial Temporal Cortex?" 13 *Hippocampus* 301 (2003).

26. This same capacity to distinguish a formally "unrecognized" city that is in fact relatively well-known generally—formally recognized by high proportions of other respondents—from either made-up cities or cities that are infrequently recognized by others, so that it is more likely that the respondent has genuinely never confronted the city, is demonstrated repeatedly in other surveys we administered as well.

For instance, eleven of twenty Stanford subjects responding to one of the questionnaires don't circle Mesa, Arizona as recognized, but all nine of those eleven who circled one of the two when asked to pick a more prominent city believe it is more prominent than the moderately large city Nampa, Idaho, which only one recognized. Six of twenty Stanford students responding to this questionnaire did not recognize Arlington, Texas; none recognized the made-up city of New Booth, Michigan. All five of the six who circled one of the two when asked to name the more prominent city identified Arlington as more prominent, though they ostensibly had, in Goldstein and Gigerenzer's sense, never heard of it.

27. This is of course the procedure used in Lionel Standing, "Learning 10,000 Pictures," 25 *Q. J. Exp. Psychol.* 207 (1973), that is one of the key articles on "recognition memory" that Goldstein and Gigerenzer cite and rely upon. Subjects are not asked whether a picture they have seen briefly is familiar or not, they are asked which of a pair of pictures is familiar, where one had actually been shown to them and one is novel.

28. Lael J. Schooler and Ralph Hertwig, "How forgetting aids heuristic inference," 112 *Psychol. Rev.* 610 (2005).
29. In a sense, the forced-recognition versus simple recognition tests implicitly present distinct "shame/pride payoffs" for each sort of error: Presumably, people are embarrassed to say that they recognize a city when they are not sure that they have but are not embarrassed to circle a city they are unsure they have heard of when they have been directed to circle sixteen cities as real.

    Perhaps it would further clarify the point we were interested in to think about the following hypothetical experiment. (We searched to see if anyone had run an experiment just like this in reality, but could not locate one.) Assume that one group of 100 people are exposed to, say, 1,000 pictures for some brief period. They then are asked five days later to make forced-choice judgments in pair comparisons between the 1,000 pictures they have confronted and 1,000 novel pictures. Assume on average they get 900 judgments right, and there is little variance among subjects. Imagine another group of 100 people exposed to the same 1,000 pictures each of whom is then exposed to those pictures five days later and asked which are familiar. Assume we are right, first, that the average subject would label far fewer than 900 "familiar." (Of course, we might be wrong. As I said, we found no experiments like this.) The distinction in "recognition" rates would be grounded in the distinct implicit psychological payoffs for false positives in the two settings: In the forced-choice setting, the experimenter has essentially told you that false positives are of no moment. Assume too, again, perhaps incorrectly, that there is wider variance in the number of pictures recognized by this group than in the group that "force recognized" pictures: This could be due to the fact that subjects impose differential "payoff" structures for distinct sorts of errors (as well as distinctions in memory capacity). It takes a good deal of work to figure out how the recognition heuristic works quickly and frugally if individuals impose such distinct implicit payoff structures on false positives and negatives in making these distinct sorts of recognition judgments.
30. Yonelinas, "The Nature of Recollection and Familiarity," supra note 16; Michael D. Rugg and Andrew P. Yonelinas, "Human Recognition Memory: A Cognitive Neuroscience Approach," 7 *Trends in Cogn. Neurosci.* 313 (2003); Daniela Montaldi et al., "The Neural System That Mediates Familiarity Memory," 16 *Hippocampus* 504 (2006).

    Conventional memory researchers would also distinguish repetition priming (or priming)—a change in the processing of a stimulus due to prior exposure to the same or related stimulus—from both recall and familiarity. It appears that priming survives in amnesiac patients whose declarative memory is impaired. (For a review, see J.D.E. Gabrieli, "Cognitive Neuroscience of Human Memory," 49 *Ann. Rev. Psychol.* 87 (1998).) It does not appear that Goldstein and Gigerenzer believe that the sort of recognition that grounds the recognition heuristic is merely priming.
31. Montaldi et al., "The Neural System," supra note 30, review this evidence.
32. See Lila Davachi, Jason P. Mitchell and Anthony D. Wagner, "Multiple Routes to Memory: Distinct Medial Temporal Lobe Processes Build Item and Source Memories," 100 *Proc. Nat'l Acad. Sci.* 2157 (2003).
33. Most conventional memory researchers have indeed rejected the proposition, advanced for instance by Donaldson, and by Dunn, that recall is merely an especially strong form of familiarity (unitary strength accounts). See, e.g., W. Donaldson, "The role of Decision Processes in Remembering and Knowing," 24 *Mem. & Cogn.* 523 (1996); Dunn, "Remember-Know," supra note 24. However, it is simply not the case that researchers can yet reject the possibility

that familiarity is a necessary condition for recall, though recall requires additional recollection-specific mechanisms. In that sense, the capacity to make familiarity judgments is not exclusively (and maybe not dominantly) a directly selected independent module so much as it at least partly sub-serves recollection functions. At the same time, it remains possible that the two processes are wholly independent. The strongest lesion-based physiological evidence for the proposition that the processes are wholly independent, as Goldstein and Gigerenzer seem simply to assume, would be finding that the two were doubly dissociated (i.e., finding not only that familiarity can exist without recall but finding some patients had intact recall despite impaired familiarity) but lesion studies reveal only single dissociations (intact familiarity despite impaired recall) See Rugg and Yonelinas, "Human Recognition Memory," supra note 30. This is true, though, in part because MTL lesions are so rare (See Montaldi et al., "The Neural System," supra note 30.) The strongest neurobiological evidence that the processes are independent comes from fMRI studies that show activation of the hippocampus predicts recall but not familiarity judgments and activation in perirhinal cortex predicts episodic item recognition but not source recollection. See Davachi, Mitchell and Wagner, "Multiple Routes," supra note 32.

While the MTL may not typically be associated with episodic recall, it may well be associated with recall that occurs when there is longer-term exposure to cues. One must attend, in this regard, to models that rely more on the physiological structure of the relevant brain regions that may make our judgments of what is "recall" and what is "item recognition" more complex. See, e.g., Randall C. O'Reilly and Kenneth A. Norman, "Hippocampal and Neocortical Contributions to Memory: Advances in the Complementary Learning Systems Framework," 6 *Trends in Cogn. Sci.* 505 (2002). In this view, the hippocampus makes fast, non-overlapping representations to encode the details of specific events while the neocortex (including the perirhinal regions) has a slow learning rate and uses overlapping distributed representations to extract the general statistical structure of the environment. Think, in this regard, of two distinct *functional* memory tasks: In one case, you need to remember precisely where you parked your car this morning (single-episode recall memory), in another you need to extract information from experience to figure out what part of the parking structure you usually park in is most likely to be empty at a particular time of the day. To master the first task, you need not only to be familiar with having confronted some parking space but to recall detailed contextual information matching the car, the space, and a particular arrival time. This is likely to be done by a part of the brain (the hippocampus) that makes non-overlapping representations of events. The second *task* is likely to be done by a part of the brain (the neocortex) that makes slower, more general judgments that permit the development of rules. In this view, making *familiarity* judgments is not the dominant functional goal of the neocortex (extracting rules is) but one will nonetheless be able to generally perform item recognition making use of neocortical resources only, because, say, the details of the garage spaces will be submerged, in lieu of a general feeling that you have seen different parts of the garage before, which is all you needed to make the relevant sorts of generalizations. At the same time, if confronted with cues over a longer period of time, the neocortex can slowly evolve recollection: In this sense, acquisition of semantic knowledge can give rise to recollection.

If this fairly conventional picture is correct, not only are the learning systems significantly complementary but the distinction is not entirely accurately understood as a distinction in "item recognition" and "recall." Thus, if this view is correct, we would expect hippocampus damage to compromise the capacity to perform a *sub-set* of item recognition tasks: We would expect such damage to compromise these judgments in cases in which the subject had to recall whether he had confronted the precise item he had confronted or a very similar item, generally referred to as a "lure" (e.g., he had seen the word "cat" but not the word "cats") because he'd recognize the distinction between actually confronted item and lure only if he were able to make sharply distinct non-overlapping representations. For empirical findings to that effect see O'Reilly and Norman, id. Thus, in this view, even if we characterized the "city recognition" task, as Goldstein and Gigerenzer do, as an item recognition task, it is almost surely an item recognition task in which subjects must often deal with the presence of such "lures" (do I know the proper city name Roosevelt or the proper presidential name Roosevelt?). Thus, the idea that it is necessarily dominantly a neocortical episodic memory task, closely related to the face recognition tasks they posit as identical, would be called into question.

34. There are many ways to understand how it is that people learn to differentiate a recognized proper name (Roosevelt) from a recognized city (Roosevelt, New York). It may be, for instance, that our learning systems are complementary: A fast-learning system acquires new information (familiarity with a name) but also serves as an input into a slower-learning system that acquires semantic knowledge (facts about names). See, for instance, James L. McClelland, Bruce L. McNaughton and Randall C. O'Reilly, "Why There Are Complementary Learning Systems in the Hippocampus and Neocortex: Insights from the Successes and Failures of Connectionist Models of Learning and Memory," 102 *Psychol. Rev.* 419 (1995).

35. Goldstein and Gigerenzer imply, but do not clearly state, that familiarity judgments are performed by something like an isolated "recognition module" that works largely as an isolated, simple mental faculty. (It is hard to know what it would mean to co-opt this evolved capacity to solve the city size problem unless it were such a capacity.) Once more, it seems this view is derived more from their disposition to induce from adaptive function, rather than describe, capacities. Certainly, the conventional position is that there is good reason to believe that familiarity judgments are not made by some isolated part of the brain that simply handles all familiarity problems—that is, stores and retrieves all items as confronted, correlatively capable of declaring objects as previously not confronted as well—in the same way, without input from any cognitive processes not readily described as relying on unadorned familiarity judgments.

The capacity to demonstrate familiarity with certain sorts of cues is significantly dissociated from the capacity to demonstrate familiarity with other cues. To the degree that they imply that the findings that they cite that people can identify faces when they recall nothing about the faces they identify tell us that we have the same item recognition capacity in relationship to proper names, their account would conventionally be described as *insufficiently modular*: People may, for instance, maintain the capacity to identify faces they have seen while finding it difficult to recall tools or animals or names. See, e.g., Hanna Damasio, Thomas J. Grabowski, Daniel Tranel, Richard D. Hichwa and Antonio R. Damasio, "A Neural Basis for Lexical Retrieval," 380 *Nature* 499 (1996); Elizabeth K. Warrington and T. Shallice, "Category Specific Semantic Impairments," 107 *Brain* 829 (1984); Elizabeth K. Warrington and Rosaleen McCarthy, "Category-Specific Access Dysphasia," 106 *Brain* 859 (1983). It appears, then, that item recognition is not performed by a single portion of the brain, though there is considerable controversy in how to account for distinctions in the capacity to recall and identify distinct "sorts" of items. Putting the debate in *very* broad terms, some believe that the "modularity" of identification tasks by category is best understood in terms of adaptive functional differentiation (i.e., we have one class of reasons to identify faces and another to identify tools and their uses so that face-identifying capacities therefore evolved separately from tool-recognizing ones). Others believe that the portions of the brain that are most active in identifying faces are not best understood as functionally evolved "face-identifying" modules, but merely portions of the brain that help us make more discerning, non-overlapping visual representations—which we care about making with faces but not, say, animals or tools. See, e.g., Martha J. Farah, Katherine M. Hammond, Zayih Mehta and Graham Ratcliff, "Category-Specificity and Modality-Specificity in Semantic Memory," 27 *Neuropsychologia* 193 (1989); Alice J. O'Toole, Fang Jiang, Herve Abdi and James V. Haxby, "Partially Distributed Representations of Objects and Faces in Ventral Temporal Cortex," 17 *J. Cogn. Neurosci.* 580 (2005); James L. McClelland and Timothy T. Rogers, "The Parallel Distributed Processing Approach to Semantic Cognition." 4 *Nature Reviews/Neurosci. I* 310 (2003); Alex Martin and Linda L. Chao. "Semantic Memory and the Brain: Structure and Processes," 11 *Curr. Opin. in Neurobiol.* 194 (2001).

At the same time, the idea that any item can be as readily identified as familiar without regard to any cognitive processes besides a simple recognition process is belied by a number of conventional findings. These findings suggest that the F&F account of memory is not only insufficiently modular at times but also *excessively modular*. For instance, when subjects are forced to identify which of a pair of non-words they have been exposed to in the past, they are correct more often when the non-words are made up of familiar English phonemes that they can more readily read and cognize than of Finnish non-words that they are unable to "sound out." See C. Papagano, T. Valentine and A.D. Baddeley, "Phonological Short-Term Memory and Foreign Language Vocabulary Learning," 30 *J. Mem. & Lang.* 331 (1991).

The item recognition task is not a task best described as encoding and retrieving a random or meaningless set of shapes or letters: The phonological articulatory component of the phonological system appears to play a central role in the encoding of novel words into long-term memory. See also Dav Clark & Anthony D. Wagner, "Assembling and Encoding Word Representations: fMRI Subsequent Memory Effects Implicate a Role for Phonological Control," 41 *Neuropsychologica* 304 (2003), for confirming fMRI evidence. Furthermore, patients with acquired prosopagnosia maintain covert recognition as long as they are provided with the *names* of the ostensibly forgotten faces they are exposed to, though other information (e.g., on party affiliation of politicians or nationality) does not facilitate covert recognition. See Jason J.S. Barton, Mariya Cherkasova and Margaret O'Connor, "Covert Recognition in Acquired and Developmental Prosopagnosia,"57 *Neurol.* 1161 (2001). Similarly, subjects generally do better on forced-item-recognition tests when exposed to pictures rather than words; the "dual code hypothesis" is the commonplace explanation for this "picture superiority effect"—picture encoding includes the visual form as well as associated lexical/semantic knowledge, whereas words are only encoded in a lexical/semantic manner. For the classic discussion, see Allan Paivio, *Mental Representations: A Dual-Coding Approach*. (New York: Oxford University Press, 1986). Once more, then, picturing item recognition as a simple, isolated cognitive process appears highly misleading.

36. For a parallel argument that rational choice theorists would presume that "recognition" information would be used when it was the only sort of available information, see. Newell and Shanks, "On the Role of Recognition in Decision Making," supra note 17.
37. These are the studies we cited supra note 17.

38. See, e.g., Newell & Shanks, "On the Role of Recognition in Decision Making," supra note 17.
39. There are surely methodological difficulties in ascertaining when a subject is or is not using recognition as the sole cue in solving the size-assessment task. *Some* people who answer, for instance, that Kitty Hawk is bigger than Kannapolis do so, as F&F theory posits, because they are using only the single recognition cue. Others may be assessing multiple cues carefully and simply coming to the incorrect conclusion that Kannapolis is smaller. We know this to be the case because a small number of subjects voluntarily reported their thought process to the experimenters when they handed in their surveys. One Stanford subject, for instance, stated, "Well, I knew Kitty Hawk was small when the Wright Brothers flew there, but I know it is near the Carolina coast so I figured it's a beach boom town now. And since you didn't say the minor league teams were AAA or AA teams, I figured some of them might be in really small places."
40. Goldstein and Gigerenzer should have noticed, in reviewing their own data, that *all* of their German subjects assumed that San Diego was more populous than San Antonio even though roughly half *recognized* San Antonio: This must have been on the basis of a prominence judgment that shares little with item recognition. We would hypothesize that making the cognitively complex relative prominence judgments for these two cities would be more difficult for American subjects: Germans would not likely know that San Antonio has a professional basketball franchise while San Diego does not; that San Antonio is the site the Alamo, a major American historical site, while little of great historical note occurred in San Diego, that each is plainly not the largest city within its large state, that neither has an extraordinarily large or developed urban center but each sprawls over a wide geographic area.
41. See Stanovich, *Who Is Rational*, supra note 9, and Stanovich and West, "Individual Differences," supra note 9.
42. Plainly, the lack of semantic knowledge about the size of the small cities cannot be entirely driving their bad performance. This is transparently true because in the double cue recognition tasks in which the unrecognized city is a state capital, the small towns whose size they are comparing to unrecognized towns are almost always the same small local towns (Atherton, La Honda, Los Altos Hills) since so few recognize out-of-state small towns like Wounded Knee. If they merely failed to know these towns were small, they would *never* decide that an unrecognized town is larger.
43. Our "rational choice" account of subjects who would sometimes, but not always, make use of a single cue is not entirely dissimilar from a more general account of evidence-accrual-based cognition offered in Michael D. Lee and Tarrant D.R. Cummins, "Evidence Accumulation in the Decision Making: Unifying the 'Take-the-Best' and the 'Rational' Models," 11 *Psychol. Bull. Rev.* 343 (2004). Interestingly, Lee and Cummins also find individual variability in the use of compensatory decision-making processes.

Chapter 6

1. Deterrence theorists typically focus on state-influenced, price-based movements along a fixed curve. They study the degree to which the amount of crime will decline if expected punishment rises given any level of background taste for both the positive results of crime (how much the defendant "enjoys" vandalizing or assaulting or values the goods he steals) and the negative ones (how bad is any particular fine or term of imprisonment or guilt pangs).

Naturally, though, it is also possible to focus on the social and legal forces that shape the relevant tastes. For instance, exposure to pornography may diminish the guilt that sexual assaulters feel—they will be more prone to believe that women are not truly harmed by the sorts of assaults they have seen in pornography; exposure to TV or video-game violence may similarly lower guilt or increase the pleasure of assaults; lack of alternative economic opportunities may make the economic return to crime relative to the return to other activities rise. For a discussion of this point, and references to some of the relevant literature on pornography, exposure to media violence, and unemployment, see Markus D. Dubber and Mark G. Kelman, *American Criminal Law* 20 (New York: Foundation Press, 2d ed. 2008). Further, it is possible to focus on changes in the expected costs and benefits of crime that occur because of private action rather than state punishment, e.g., private counter-violence or anti-theft devices. Id. at 19.

2. For a very thoughtful, analytically balanced account of these sorts of hesitations about the "realism" of deterrence theory, see Paul H. Robinson and John M. Darley, "Does Criminal Law Deter? A Behavioural Science Investigation," 24 *Oxford J. Leg. Stud.* 173, 179–80, 194 (2004).

3. The idea that many actors contemplating crimes neither know anything about the content of the law nor about apprehension and prosecution practices is raised by Robinson and Darley. Id. at 175–78

4. For a brief discussion of distinct forms of "imitation" heuristics, focused on how they might operate in the context of making decisions about law compliance, see Ralph Hertwig, "Do Legal Rules Rule Behavior?" in *Heuristics and the Law* 390, 398 (G. Gigerenzer and C. Engel eds., Cambridge, MA: MIT Press, 2006).

5. For a depiction of this sort of process in the context of persons trying to figure out whether to download music without paying, see Daniel C. Goldstein et al., "Group Report: How Do Heuristics Mediate the Impact of Law on Behavior?" in *Heuristics and the Law*, supra note 4 at 439, 444–45

6. Id. at 451.

7. Id. at 452.

8. Id. citing long-standing work on conformity and imitation.

9. For a discussion of these rules, see Dubber and Kelman, supra note 1 at 356–57. There are certain qualifications to the rules. For instance, there may be constitutional Due Process limits that preclude punishment of those who are not at least proven to be negligent in being unaware of the governing law when the law the defendant is charged with violating is not one that we would expect most citizens to be aware of. Furthermore, legislatures can specifically require awareness of the governing norm as a precondition for conviction. Id. at 346–81.

10. The distinction between the propositions that knowledge of the law is not an offense element and the proposition that ignorance of the law is no excuse is of no real moment for this discussion. I should note, though, that if it served as an excuse, the defendant could constitutionally bear the burden of proof (he would have to satisfy the fact finder that he was either ignorant or perhaps not culpably ignorant). If, on the other hand, awareness of the law is an offense element, the state must prove beyond a reasonable doubt that the defendant knew the law (if the requisite mental state for the offense element were knowledge) or, say, that the defendant was negligent in not knowing the law (if negligence is the requisite mental state).

11. For a good summary of John Mikhail's work, arguing that most of our moral knowledge is not learned, but rather that we have the modularized capacity to learn and follow only certain

sorts of moral rules, and that we know these rules even before we could have learned them through ordinary learning methods, in the same way that we know grammatical rules without having been able to generate them by generalizing from phrases and sentences we have been exposed to, see, e.g., John Mikhail, "Moral Heuristics or Moral Competence? Reflections on Sunstein," 28 *Behav. & Brain Sci.* 557 (2005); John Mikhail, "Universal moral grammar: theory, evidence and the future," 11 *Trends in Cogn. Sci.* 143 (2007); Marc Hauser, Fiery Cushman, Liane Young, R. Kang-Xing Jin, and John Mikhail, "A Dissociation Between Moral Judgments and Justifications," 22 *Mind & Language* 1 (2007). Mikhail's arguments are echoed in arguments made by the psychologist Marc Hauser. For a good overview of Hauser's views on "moral realism" see Marc D. Hauser, *Moral Minds* (New York: Ecco, 2006).

12. For a discussion of such "cultural defense" cases, see Dubber & Kelman, supra note 1 at 370–74.
13. Goldstein, supra note 5 at 455–56.
14. Id. at 457–58.
15. Id. at 461–62.
16. Recall from Chapter Five the proposition that it might be faster and simpler, on some occasions, to rely on semantic memory in making judgments of the relative size of two cities (the subject simply *knows* New York City is bigger than Oakland) than to rely on any "substitute" judgments (e.g., the subject recognizes one and not the other, believes that one city is more "prominent" than the other, or knows that one city has infrastructure features typical of big cities).
17. For empirical evidence that convicted criminals have and had at the time of offending little idea of the precise punishment imposed for particular crimes, see, e.g., David Anderson, "The Deterrence Hypothesis and Picking Pockets at the Pickpocket's Hanging," 4 *Amer. L. & Econ. Rev.* 295 (2002).
18. See John M. Darley, Kevin M. Carlsmith and Paul H. Robinson, "The Ex Ante Function of the Criminal Law," 35 *Law & Soc. Rev.* 165 (2001).
19. The finding that there are sharp drops in crime at the age of majority was highlighted in Steven Leavitt, "Juvenile Crime and Punishment," 106 *J. Pol. Econ.* 1156 (1998). Even those generally skeptical of the deterrence impact of crime *reform* or doctrinal reformulation accept the significance of this sort of deterrent effect. See, e.g., Robinson and Darley, supra note 2 at 177.

    F&F theorists would likely argue that while the punishment of violators upon reaching the age of majority may initially alter the behavior of some late adolescents through its impact on the expected punishment they face, *most* juveniles we now observe who decide to stop committing crimes when they reach the age at which they are punished stop not so much because they calculate that as the wise decision but because they imitate the behavior of others within their criminal sub-culture who stop committing at least certain crimes at that point in time. I am skeptical that the persuasiveness of these alternative explanations can be evaluated empirically.
20. Robinson and Darley, supra note 2 at 184, citing behavioral economics work by Zeckhauser and Viscusi on the overestimation of low-probability events.
21. Dana argues that for would-be offenders generally, and especially for those who have never before committed a crime, both availability and optimism bias cut strongly in the direction of underestimating the actual likelihood of punishment. David A. Dana, "Rethinking the Puzzle of Escalating Penalties for Repeat Offenders," 110 *Yale L.J.* 733, 733–35 (2001). He relies

on the H&B literature in thinking about the existence and impact of optimism bias—defined rather capaciously as a tendency to underestimate the possibility of bad outcomes and to overestimate one's own skills. (The union of these phenomena is that people will be particularly likely to believe that they will avoid bad consequences if there is some skill involved in avoiding them; if would-be criminals each believe they are "above average" at avoiding detection, they will be especially optimistic.) He especially relies on Neil D. Weinstein, "Unrealistic Optimism about Susceptibility to Health Problems: Conclusions from a Community-Wide Sample," 10 *J. Behav. Med.* 481 (1987), but also looks to Lynn A. Baker & Robert E. Emery, "When Every Relationship Is Above Average: Perceptions and Expectations of Divorce at the Time of Marriage," 17 *Law & Hum. Behav.* 439 (1993), and Ola Svenson, "Are We All Less Risky and More Skillful than Our Fellow Drivers?" 47 *Acta Psychologica* 143 (1981).

22. The paragraph in the text illustrates some of the difficulties of deriving "policy" from theory. Psychological theory may suggest reasons that persons both over and underestimate objective risks, and that they both ignore and focus to an undue extent in making decisions on certain sorts of risks that are perceived to be low. But the "theory" is not nearly so well-specified that we know the boundary conditions in which each observation is thought to govern, so that "predicting" behavior from theory is simply not possible.

23. See Robinson and Darley, supra note 2 at 183.

24. Id.

25. For the classic discussion of the gambler's fallacy, ordinarily manifest in something like the false belief that one is less likely to toss a heads, even using a fair coin, if the coin had shown several heads in a row, see Amos Tversky and Daniel Kahneman, "Judgment Under Uncertainty: Heuristics and Biases," 185 *Science* 1124 (1974). In the next chapter, I return to the earlier discussion of the F&F understanding of the gambler's fallacy in the context of optimal provision of consumer information. I should note, though, that F&F theorists would be skeptical of the claim that recently released criminals would be swayed by the gambler's fallacy rather than the (opposite) "hot-hand fallacy" (that would lead them to *overestimate* the probability of detection if they had been detected in the past). F&F scholars argue that it is adaptive, and therefore commonplace, to believe intentional actors will exhibit "positive recency" (i.e., to believe that they will repeat what they have been doing). In this case, the law enforcement community, a group of intentional actors who would be expected to keep doing what they have done, would be responsible for apprehending them.

26. See Dana, "Rethinking the Puzzle of Escalating Penalties," supra note 21 at 742–53.

27. Id. at 759–64, 769.

28. For suggestions very much like these, see Christine Jolls, Cass R. Sunstein and Richard H. Thaler, "A Behavioral Approach to Law and Economics," in *Behavioral Law and Economics* 13, 45–46 (Cass R. Sunstein ed., Cambridge, UK; New York: Cambridge University Press, 2000).

29. See Samuel M. McClure, David J. Laibson, George Loewenstein and Jonathan D. Cohen, "Separate Neural Systems Value Immediate and Delayed Monetary Rewards," 306 *Science* 503 (2004), and S.M. McClure, K.M. Ericson, D.J. Laibson, G. Loewenstein and J.D. Cohen, "Time Discounting for Primary Rewards" 27 *J. Neurosci.* 5796 (2007).

30. For a discussion of some of the traditional literature on irrational impulsivity among the "crime-prone" (creating discontinuities in the evaluation of events separated by a year depending on whether they are a year in the future or five v. six years in the future), see Bradley Wright, et al., "Does the Perceived Risk of Punishment Deter Criminally Prone

Individuals? Rational Choice, Self-Control, and Crime," 41 *J. Res. in Crime & Delinquency* 41(2004). For a standard discussion of hyperbolic discounting more generally, see David Laibson, "Golden Eggs and Hyperbolic Discounting" 62 *Q. J. Econ.* 443 (1997). For an early formulation of a similar point, see R.H. Strotz, "Myopia and Inconsistency in Dynamic Utility Maximization," 23 *Rev. Econ. Stud.* 165 (1955).
31. See Mark Kelman, Yuval Rottenstreich and Amos Tversky, "Context-Dependence in Legal Decision Making," 25 *J. Leg. Stud.* 287, 290–95 (1996).
32. Id. at 295–97.
33. It is not entirely clear—in ways that I touch on in the text—that it is even sensible to talk about misperception or distorted memory of hedonic states. The question to which I return is whether one can reasonably say that someone has been unhappy or in pain without knowing it or recalling it. I suspect that giving a decent answer to that question requires both complex philosophical inquiry and a great deal of neurobiological sophistication about how pain and pleasure are processed.
34. See Philip Brickman, Dan Coates and Ronnie Janoff-Bulman, "Lottery Winners and Accident Victims: Is Happiness Relative?" 36 *J. Personality & Soc. Psychol.* 917 (1978). The piece is subject not just to the deep methodological critiques, noted in the text, that Kahneman makes—above all, that accident victims misreport their actual level of unhappiness. It is also subject to the critique that there are, in the author's own studies, rather large distinctions in the happiness levels reported by lottery winners and accident victims, even if they are not as large as the authors believe the lay public would "expect."
35. See Shane Frederick and George Loewenstein, "Hedonic Adaptation," in *Well-Being: The Foundations of Hedonic Psychology* 302, 303 (D. Kahneman, E. Diener and N. Schwarz eds., New York: Russell Sage Foundation, 1999) ("Because the persistence of an aversive state is an indication that it cannot be changed, hedonic adaptation may prevent the continued expenditure of energy in futile attempts to change the unchangeable and redirect motivation to changes that can be made").
36. See, e.g., Robinson and Darley, supra note 2 at 187–89.
37. Id. at 186–86, emphasizing this point. See also Frederick and Loewenstein, supra note 35 at 304–05.
38. See Fritz Strack, Leonard L. Martin and Norbert Schwarz, "Priming and Communication: Social Determinants of Information Use in Judgments of Life Satisfaction," 18 *European J. Soc. Psychol.* 429 (1988).
39. There are a number of discussions of this sort of transparent misreporting. For a summary, with references to the primary literature, see Mark Kelman, "Hedonic Psychology, Political Theory, and Law: Is Welfarism Possible?" 52 *Buff. L. Rev.* 1, 19–27 (2004).
40. Note that this schema is of little use in figuring out whether patients who have been administered "hypnotic" or "memory-reducing" anesthetics are "really" in pain.
41. See Lindsay M. Hayes, "'And Darkness Closes In': A National Study of Jail Suicides," 10 *Criminal Just. & Behav.* 461 (1983).
42. See Daniel Kahneman, "Objective Happiness," in *Well-Being*, supra note 33 at 3, 5–6, 11–15. See also John T. Cacioppo and Gary G. Berntson, "Relationships Between Attitudes and Evaluative Space: A Critical Review with Emphasis on the Separability of Positive and Negative Substrates," 115 *Psychol. Bull.* 401 (1994).
43. Frederick and Loewenstein, supra note 35.
44. See Edward Krupat, "Context as a Determinant of Perceived Threat: The Role of Prior Experience," 29 *J. Personality & Soc. Psychol.* 731 (1974). See also Reuven Dar, Dan Ariely and

Hanan Frank, "The Effect of Past-Injury on Pain Threshold and Tolerance," 60 *Pain* 189 (1995) (veterans who had suffered more serious injuries in the past both waited longer before *reporting* severe pain when exposed to 48-degree Celsius water, and, *behaviorally*, terminated the test by withdrawing their hands from the water later). But there is contrary evidence as well: See, e.g., Paul Paulus et al., "A Note on the Use of Prisons as Environments for Investigations of Crowding," 6 *Bull. Psychonomic Soc'y* 427 (1973).

45. For a far fuller account of this "durability bias"—including experimental studies that both demonstrate its general existence and attempt to demonstrate which of the causal explanations for the tendency to discount the "return to equilibrium" are most invariably operative—see Daniel T. Gilbert, Elizabeth C. Pinel, Timothy D. Wilson, Stephen J. Blumberg and Thalia P. Wheatley, "Immune Neglect: A Source of Durability Bias in Affective Forecasting," 75 *J. Personality & Soc. Psychol.* 617 (1998).

46. See Jason Brandt et al., "Presymptomatic Diagnosis of Delayed-Onset Disease with Linked DNA Markers: The Experience in Huntington's Disease," 261 *J. Am. Med. Ass'n* 3108 (1989), and Jeffrey M. Moulton et al., "Results of a One Year Longitudinal Study of HIV Notification from the San Francisco General Hospital Cohort," 4 *J. Acquired Immunity Deficiency Syndromes* 787 (1991).

47. See Daniel A. Redelmeier and Daniel Kahneman, "Patients' Memories of Painful Medical Treatments: Real Time and Retrospective Evaluations of Two Minimally Invasive Procedures," 66 *Pain* 3 (1996). For confirming results, see, e.g., Daniel Kahneman, Barbara L. Frederickson, Charles A. Schreiber and Donald A. Redelmeier, "When More Pain Is Preferred to Less: Adding a Better End," 4 *Psychol. Sci.* 401 (1993). For similar findings about duration neglect, see Carol Varcy and Daniel Kahneman, "Experiences Extended Over Time: Evaluation of Moments and Episodes," 5 *J. Behav. Decisionmaking* 169 (1992); Barbara L. Fredrickson and Daniel Kahneman, "Duration Neglect in Retrospective Evaluations of Affective Episodes," 65 *J. Personality & Soc. Psychol.* 45 (1993).

48. I express some of my hesitations in Mark Kelman, "Hedonic Psychology and the Ambiguities of "Welfare," 33 *Phil. & Pub. Aff.* 391, 406–11 (2005). For a fuller account, see Kelman "Hedonic Psychology, Political Theory, and Law" supra note 39 at 26–27, 38–55. I draw inspiration in my arguments from Barbara L. Frederickson, "Extracting Meaning from Past Affective Experiences: The Importance of Peaks, Ends, and Specific Emotions," 14 *Cognition & Emotion* 14 (2000).

49. This picture of the counterproductive impact of longer terms is suggested in Robinson and Darley, supra note 2 at 189–93.

50. Here are some of the many interesting readings that raise these issues: Amartya Sen, *Inequality Reexamined* ix–xi, 26–29, 31, 38, 41–42, 107–16 (Bologna: Il Mulino, 1994); G.A. Cohen, "Equality of What? On Welfare, Goods and Capabilities" in *The Quality of Life* 9–28 (Martha C. Nussbaum and Amartya Sen eds., New York: Oxford University Press, 1993); Elizabeth S. Anderson, "What Is the Point of Equality?" 109 *Ethics* 287 (1999).

51. For a fuller discussion, see Gerd Gigerenzer, "Heuristics," in *Heuristics and the Law* supra note 4 at 17, 28–30, 40. One sees the "predisposition" to assume that "less is more" especially clearly in Hertwig, supra note 4 at 407 ("Although [the magistrate's] approach deviates from the ideal of due process, it is impossible to find out how accurate the decision tree is. Judging from the good performance of other 'fast and frugal' decision-making heuristics, however, it may not result in less accurate judgments than due process.").

52. For a fuller account, influenced by H&B theory, of the infirmities of clinical judgments, relative to actuarial judgments, in a host of distinct settings in which predictions must be made (e.g., survival rates for patients, dangerousness, judgment about whether symptoms have a psychiatric or medical root), see Robyn M. Dawes, David Faust and Paul E. Meehl, "Clinical Versus Actuarial Judgment," in *Heuristics and Biases* 715 (T. Gilovich, D. Griffin and D. Kahneman eds., Cambridge, UK; New York: Cambridge University Press, 2002)

Chapter 7

1. For discussions that highlight both the problems that hindsight bias is likely to pose for legal decision makers, and the ways in which the legal system has adapted to minimize its adverse effects, see Kim A. Kamin and Jeffrey J. Rachlinski, "Ex Post ≠ Ex Ante: Determining Liability in Hindsight," 19 *Law & Hum. Behav.* 89 (1995), and Jeffrey J. Rachlinski, "A Positive Psychological Theory of Judging in Hindsight," 65 *U. Chi. L. Rev.* 571 (1998).

    For a critique of the standard claims by H&B-influenced theorists that their experiments actually demonstrate that experimental jurors are demonstrating hindsight bias rather than engaging in either rational Bayesian updating or reinterpreting the tasks they are being asked to perform, see Mark Kelman, David E. Fallas and Hilary Folger, "Decomposing Hindsight Bias," 16 *J. Risk & Uncertainty* 251 (1998).

2. Contingent valuations may be frame sensitive in a variety of ways. I discussed scope neglect in Chapter Two: The value that people put on saving ten birds from an oil spill may scarcely differ from the value they put on saving orders of magnitude more birds. It is also worth noting that H&B-influenced theorists may believe that contingent valuations are affected by context in yet another sense. People may purport to value some environmental end-state highly when it is evaluated alongside other more trivial end-states but far less highly when it is considered alongside more serious harms. See Cass R. Sunstein, Daniel Kahneman, David Schkade and Liana Ritov, "Predictably Incoherent Judgments," 54 *Stan. L. Rev.* 1153 (2002).

3. See John D. Sterman and Linda Booth Sweeny, "Understanding Public Complacency About Climate Change: Adults' Mental Models of Climate Change Violate Conservation Of Matter," 80 *Climactic Change* 213 (2007). The worry about how voters will process concerns about climate change is grounded in experiments demonstrating that even statistically sophisticated subjects have a great deal of trouble understanding that stocks will increase as long as flow is positive, even if it is diminishing. See, e.g., John D. Sterman and Linda Booth Sweeny, "Bathtub Dynamics: Initial Results of a Systems Thinking Inventory," 16 *Syst. Dyn. Rev.* 249 (2000). For elaborations, confirmations, and some rather desultory efforts at explaining the phenomenon, see Matthew A. Cronin and Cleotilde Gonzalez, "Understanding the Building Blocks of Dynamic Systems," 23 *Syst. Dyn. Rev.* 1 (2007).

4. See, e.g., Samuel Bagenstos and Margo Schlanger, "Hedonic Damages, Hedonic Adaptation, and Disability," 60 *Vand. L. Rev.* 745 (2007).

5. For representative exemplars of this approach, see Russell B. Korobkin, "Inertia and Preference in Contract Negotiation: The Psychological Power of Default Rules and Form Terms," 51 *Vand. L. Rev*, 1083 (1998) and Russell Korobkin, "The Endowment Effect and Legal Analysis," 97 *Nw. U. L. Rev.* 1227 (2003).

6. An excellent account can be found in Kent Daniel, David Hirshleifer and Avanidhar Subramanyan, "Investor Pricing and Security Market Under- and Overreactions," 53 *J. Fin.* 1839 (1998).

7. The standard account is in Nicholas Barberis, Andrei Shleifer and Robert W. Vishney, "A Model of Investor Sentiment," 46 *J. Fin. Econ.* 307 (1998). Note, as well, that a variant of hindsight bias might also lead to "bubbles." If people are unable to assess, *ex ante*, the future performance of a company whose stock price has been rising, but merely assume that whatever has happened (the past price rise) signals a persistent state (ever-rising profits)—just as they take any outcome as reflective of a state rather than a probability distribution—then prices, once rising, may simply continue to rise.

8. Consider a problem posed in the early 1960s by Paul Samuelson. He asked a colleague whether he would take a bet with a 50 percent chance of gaining $200 and a 50 percent chance of losing $100 (a bet with a positive expected value of $50.) The colleague turned it down, implying strong loss aversion. (The loss aversion was not merely implied, it was *overt*. The colleague *said* the loss of $100 would hurt much more than the gain of $200 would feel good.) At the same time, though, the colleague stated he would take 100 such bets, implying (to some) that if he did not *account* for any particular bet, and determine in some separated mental account that he had *lost* a particular bet, he would not have to experience the adverse consequences of losses.

So imagine an investor who must choose between a risky asset that pays an expected 8 percent annually with a standard deviation of 20 percent (like stocks) and a safe asset which pays a sure 1 percent. The attractiveness of the risky asset will depend on the time horizon of the investor. The longer the investor will hold the asset, and the less frequently he "evaluates" its performance, the less likely he is to "feel" losses. Investors would, according to this H&B-influenced theory of relative asset pricing, be indifferent between the historical return on stocks and the historical return on bonds if they evaluate returns annually and show the sort of loss aversion that prospect theory predicts. See Shlomo Benartzi and Richard H. Thaler, "Myopic Loss Aversion and the Equity Premium Puzzle," 110 *Q. J. Econ.* 73 (1995).

9. See Hersh M. Shefrin and Meir Statman, "Explaining Investor Preferences for Cash Dividends," 32 *J. Fin. Econ.* 253 (1984). The authors argue that stockholders (especially older stockholders) use dividend distribution policies as an aid in keeping mental accounts. In this view, dividends can be spent, while "equity holdings" should be retained rather than partly sold off to finance consumption. A rate of dividends equal to zero would not place enough "expendable" money in the mentally constructed "accounts" devoted to spending or, worse, would tempt the equity holder to sell off some shares to meet urgent spending needs that he would actually like to keep segregated as part of his savings account. The idea that we keep distinct mental accounts for what economists would typically lump together as "money"—reflected in the notion that we may also, for instance, gamble money that we won gambling while we would not gamble that same sum of money even though we were not liquidity constrained—derives quite readily from the more modular views of cognition that F&F theorists favor.

It is clear, though, that H&B theorists have either been *influenced* by the modularists' ideas of domain specificity or independently arrived at the idea that cognition operates within spheres or that decisions are made within significantly separated mental accounts. It shows up even in the afore-cited work on the equity premium puzzle (see note 8 supra); the authors argue that to a considerable degree people assess the performance of *each* of their stocks rather than their portfolio as a whole in determining whether or not they have sustained especially dysphoric losses. Thus, the returns on single high-variance stocks may have to be even higher to account for loss aversion.

Similarly, H&B theorists believe that workers may not allocate time rationally over extended periods but make utility calculations based on targets for smaller periods, like days. Thus, cab drivers may not drive "enough" (from the vantage point of rational choice theorists who assume that people are able to make more global work/leisure trade-offs) on rainy days, when pay/hour is atypically high because they pick up more customers per hour. This seems to be the case because they meet daily income targets driving less. For a discussion, see Colin Camerer, Linda Babcock, George Loewenstein and Richard Thaler, "Labor Supply of New York City Cabdrivers: One Day at a Time," 112 Q. J. Econ. 407 (1996). It is not at all clear, though, either that the H&B authors believe that the separate mental accounts they describe are independent cognitive modules, or that one could develop a sensible modular theory of mind that separated, say, judgments about today's wages from tomorrow's, though one could imagine accepting the view that work intensity decisions are remitted to a module that is grounded in short-period calculations rather than that such decisions are made by a generalist mind that computed expected utility over time and context and simply applied the expected utility calculation to this particular problem.

Many of the other context-dependent elicitation effects that H&B theorists have emphasized in noting that evaluation is frame sensitive also seemingly occur only because subjects keep separate mental accounts. For instance, think about a typical instance of the so-called diversification bias; "trick or treaters" will select their favorite candy at two successive houses when asked to take one piece of candy at each but pick two different candies when asked to take two pieces at a single house. Diversification bias arises from the children's inability to determine a single ideal "candy portfolio" as rational choice theorists would predict. See Daniel Read and George Loewenstein, "Diversification Bias: Explaining the Discrepancy in Variety Seeking Between Combined and Separated Choices," 1 J. Exp. Psych: Applied 34 (1995). Instead, they have an ideal portfolio for a smaller framed category—an ideal portfolio for the house I am at now. (It is worth noting, just to remind readers how often such work on biases is used in conventional policy analysis, that some H&B-influenced scholars have argued that the portfolio allocation decisions that people make—e.g., between equity and bond-loaded finds—is not rationally related to risk preferences but follows from the use of a diversification heuristic. A plan that offer one equity fund and one bond fund will typically induce investors to put half ($1/n$) in each fund (where n = the number of funds), while a fund with four equity-loaded options and one bond-loaded one will typically induce participants to put 80 percent of total funds in equity because they follow the same $1/n$ diversification strategy. See Shlomo Benartzi and Richard H. Thaler, "Naïve Diversification Strategies in Defined Contribution Savings Plans," 91 Amer. Econ. Rev. 79 (2001).The case, say, for full-blown privatization of pension savings weakens rather markedly if choices are so elicitation-method sensitive.)

The Sunstein et al. work (see "Predictably Incoherent," supra note 2) on problems in contingent valuation and irrational awards of punitive damages depends as well on the fact that people compare events *within* particular mental frames rather than across categories. For instance, subjects can assess whether a defendant has engaged in an egregious act of securities fraud but find it difficult to determine whether the act is more egregious than a "typical" act of toxic dumping. I return to this point in the text in the consumer information context.

10. I think one of the clearest expressions of this view is in Linda Hamilton Krieger, "The Content of Our Categories: A Cognitive Bias Approach to Discrimination and Equal

Employment Opportunity," 47 *Stan. L. Rev.* 1161 (1995). The approach is further refined to take account of evidence of implicit bias in Linda Hamilton Krieger and Susan T. Fiske, "Behavioral Realism in Employment Discrimination Law: Implicit Bias and Disparate Treatment," 94 *Cal. L. Rev.* 997 (2006).

11. Such an F&F-based picture is not enormously far from the one presented in Reid Hastie and Bernd Wittenbrink, "Heuristics for Applying Law to Facts," in *Heuristics and the Law* 259, 272–74 (G. Gigerenzer and C. Engel eds., Cambridge, MA: MIT Press, 2006). Hastie and Wittenbrink themselves draw in some significant part on S. Christian Wheeler and Richard E. Petty, "The Effect of Stereotype Activation on Behavior: A Review of Possible Mechanisms," 127 *Psych. Bull.* 787 (2001), and Anthony G. Greenwald et al., "A Unified Theory of Implicit Attitudes, Stereotypes, Self-Esteem, and Self-Concept," 109 *Psychol. Rev.* 3 (2002).

12. This completely conventional defense for hiring by word-of-mouth, couched in F&F terms, is explicitly offered by Gigerenzer. See Gerd Gigerenzer, "Heuristics" in *Heuristics and the Law*, supra note 11 at 17, 30–31.

13. For examples of those who think that antidiscrimination commitments trump more general predispositions to extol heuristic use and users, see, e.g., Jonathan Haidt et al., "Group Report: What Is the Role of Heuristics in Making Law?" in *Heuristics and the Law*, supra note 11 at 239, 250–51; Donald C. Langevoort, "Heuristics Inside the Firm" on *Heuristics and the Law*, supra note 11 at 87, 96–97.

14. It would not be difficult to construct such an explanation for prejudice. A standard criticism of this sort of evolutionary psychology-influenced theory is that such "just-so" stories—of both adaptive traits and of maladaptive uses—are *never* very hard to construct. It is easy to make the case that "prejudice" worked well on the savannah when rapid judgments of who was friend or foe were useful, but that it is of considerably less use in making, say, potential productivity judgments in a post-industrial economy.

15. A terrific, and highly favorable, review of the scientific research on implicit bias can be found in Anthony G. Greenwald and Linda Hamilton Krieger, "Implicit Bias: Scientific Foundations," 94 *Cal. L. Rev.* 915 (2006). For a small sample of the extraordinarily large number of articles by academic lawyers arguing that the existence of such bias should lead us to reformulate antidiscrimination law in significant ways, see, e.g., Christine Jolls and Cass R. Sunstein, "The Law of Implicit Bias," 94 *Cal. L. Rev.* 969 (2006); Justin D. Levinson, "Forgotten Racial Equality: Implicit Bias, Decisionmaking, and Misremembering," 57 *Duke L.J.* 345 (2007); Ivan E. Bodensteiner, "The Implications of Psychological Research Related to Unconscious Discrimination and Implicit Bias," 73 *Mo. L. Rev.* 83 (2008); Jerry Kang, "Trojan Horses of Race," 118 *Harv. L. Rev.* 1489 (2005).

16. Krieger's work, supra note 10, expresses many of these preferences for reforming decision making processes rather than individual decision makers, but one sees it quite clearly as well in, for instance, Barbara Reskin, "The Proximate Causes of Employment Discrimination," 29 *Contemp. Soc.* 319 (1999), and in Susan Sturm, "Second Generation Employment Discrimination: A Structural Approach," 101 *Colum. L. Rev.* 458 (2001). There is work more influenced by F&F theory that shares this conviction that overcoming discrimination requires a shift in decision-making processes or in the cues that decision makers process, rather than relying either on exhortations or on conventional incentives (fines, damage judgments, or criminal penalties) to make less prejudiced judgments. See, e.g., Douglas A. Kysar et al., "Group Report: Are Heuristics a Problem or a Solution?" in *Heuristics and the Law*, supra note 11 at 104, 122–23.

17. Sturm's work is especially influenced by the enthusiasm for "new governance" that has especially characterized much of the work coming out of Columbia Law School in the past decade, with its emphasis on local experimentation and the generation of best practices that can be mimicked across organizations, while recognizing the intractable "local" and ever-mutable nature of many bad practices, that thus require organizations to have the capacity to constantly readjust, usually by establishing mechanisms that facilitate recognizing problems and using problem recognition as an occasion to improve. Sturm's suspicion of top-down, legal regulatory regimes designed to control subtle discrimination is significantly grounded in her supposition that people will be reluctant to discover biases within the organization if it subjects them to liability to have such biases uncovered, and discovery of problems is the key to revising behavior. Obviously the new governance work does not echo Gigerenzer's work in its assumption that individuals are inevitably first-rate problem solvers—quite to the contrary—but it shares a good deal of the same Panglossian optimism about human perfectability, if not native perfection.

18. A particularly nice account of work in this tradition can be found in Samuel Gaertner and John Dovidio, "The Aversive Form of Racism" in *Prejudice, Discrimination and Racism* 61–65, 67–73, 80–85 (S. Gaertner and J. Dovidio eds., Orlando: Academic Press, 1998).

19. See Ralph Richard Banks and Richard Thompson Ford, "(How) Does Unconscious Bias Matter? Law, Politics, and Racial Inequality," 58 *Emory L.J.* 1053 (2009). One of the strongest pieces of evidence for the proposition that those who are purportedly merely "unconsciously" biased are actually consciously biased, but typically won't *express* their conscious bias because of social desirability concerns, is that subjects who first take an "implicit bias" test like the Implicit Association Test (IAT) and are told that it reveals their true racial feelings and then answer questions about their racial attitudes reveal a good deal more conscious bias than those who are not alerted to the possibility that the researchers have already read their racist minds or are told the IAT is inaccurate. See Jason A. Nier, "How Dissociated Are Implicit and Explicit Racial Attitudes? A Bogus Pipeline Approach," 8 *Group Processes & Intergroup Relations* 39 (2005).

A much older, quite similar study, reporting similar findings (though not in relationship to the not-yet-invented IAT, but other measures of "unconscious" bias) is Harold Sigall and Richard Page, "Current stereotypes: A little fading, a little faking," 18 *J. Personality & Soc. Psychol.* 247 (1971).

20. The key works, I think, heavily grounded in the H&B tradition, are Cass R. Sunstein and Richard H. Thaler, "Libertarian Paternalism is Not an Oxymoron," 70 *U. Chi. L. Rev.* 1159 (2003), and Colin Camerer, Samuel Issacharoff, George Loewenstein, Ted O'Donoghue and Matthew Rabin, "Regulation for Conservatives: Behavioral Economics and the Case of 'Asymmetric Paternalism,'" 115 *U. Pa. L. Rev.* 1211 (2003).

21. For instance, one might recommend soft paternalist *nudges* to make retirement savings more attractive, or impose high taxes on goods that people consume impulsively, or without *effective* awareness of the risks that they pose, such as tobacco or foods chock filled with transfats, or make sure that people see the healthy vegetables in the lunch line before they see the greasy French fries.

22. See Amos Tversky, "Elimination by Aspects: A Theory of Choice," 79 *Psychol. Rev.* 289 (1972).

23. This argument pretty closely tracks the H&B-influenced argument in Russell Korobkin, "Bounded Rationality, Standard Form Contracts, and Unconscionability," 70 *U. Chi. L. Rev.* 1203, 1216–44 (2003).

24. This argument closely parallels arguments made in Jon D. Hanson and Douglas A. Kysar, "Taking Behavioralism Seriously: The Problem of Market Manipulation," 74 *N.Y.U. L. Rev.* 630, 724–33 (1999).

It might be worth tracing some of the arguments Hanson and Kysar make in just a bit more detail. (1) Consumers whose judgments of probability are unduly influenced by "representativeness" are likely to underestimate product risks if they have experienced a product as safe and reliable, if risks (even if, on reflection, unacceptably high) are unusual, or if they treat the problem-free use of the product they have seen in ads as "typical." (2) As I have frequently noted, availability may bias people to overestimate salient risks while underestimating less salient ones. Risk perception may be tied to how recently the consumer has been exposed to news of a salient risk if memory is a critical part of risk judgment (e.g., because the consumer implicitly samples from memory bad and good outcomes of product use). (3) If consumers seek to reduce cognitive dissonance, they will tend to process information in a fashion that confirms their initial preference reactions. Post-decisional bias may be especially strong— consumers will minimize the significance of product hazards discovered after purchase to reduce dissonance. They will do so even more if they overestimate their own abilities (i.e., if they are prone to optimism bias) and therefore underestimate the chance that they will be injured because "ordinary" users of the product are the ones who bear the high risk of injury. (4) If advertisers *anchor* consumers' risk estimates—presumably picking a risk estimate that is on the low end of one that could be accepted as rational—consumers will not readily adjust, given anchoring heuristics. Moreover, they are prone to be overconfident in their initial risk estimates, so that updating or education will do too little to shake their initial impressions. (5) People may perceive both very low and very high risks irrationally, underestimating quite high risks (e.g., the risks of smoking) while overestimating very low risks (e.g., the risks of living near a nuclear plant.) At the same time, they may compute *expected values* for very low risks too optimistically, ignoring low-probability risks that threaten catastrophic loss. (6) Because of hyperbolic time discounting, people may overvalue the benefits of immediate use relative to the losses or pains they will sustain later, leading to impulsive borrowing/credit card purchases, taking long-term health risks with drugs or tobacco, and so forth. Sometimes, of course, hyperbolic discounting problems will be aggravated by anchoring: Consumers who take on adjustable rate mortgages will not only unduly discount the pain of later payment simply because the payments will be made in the future but will wrongly assume the future pains will be no worse than the current pains, anchoring estimates to the readily available and representative pains of first round payments. (This may drive sellers not only to offer adjustable rate loans but to explain why so many sellers give introductory offers at low rates—e.g., cable or dish providers, cell phone companies.)

25. See Paul Slovic Baruch Fischhoff and Sarah Lichtenstein, "Response Mode, Framing, and Information Processing Effects in Risk Assessment," in *New Directions for Methodology of Social and Behavioral Science: The Framing of Questions and the Consistency of Responses* 21 (R.M. Hogarth ed., San Francisco: Jossey-Bass, 1982). Those reluctant to find irrationality would likely argue that subjects are wise to value the vaccine that utterly eliminates one strain of a disease entirely more highly than one that reduces vulnerability to both strains; subjects might well believe that there is more chance that a second vaccine will come along to wipe out the second strain if one has been developed that eliminates one strain than that a second vaccine can be developed that simply further reduces risk from undifferentiated strains.

26. See Howard Latin, "'Good' Warnings, Bad Products, and Cognitive Limitations," 41 *UCLA L. Rev.* 1193, 1239 (1994).
27. Cass Sunstein, "Selective Fatalism," 26 *J. Legal. Stud.* 799 (1998).
28. See Dan M. Kahan and Donald Braman, "The Self-Defensive Cognition of Self-Defense," 45 *Amer. Crim. L. Rev.* 1 (2008). For a more general overview of Kahan's efforts to contrast the idea that risk assessments are a product of cultural commitment with the more conventional H&B-influenced idea that they are a product of unreliable heuristic reasoning, see, e.g., Dan M. Kahan, Paul Slovic, John Gastil and Donald Berman, "Fear of Democracy: A Critical Evaluation of Sunstein on Risk," 119 *Harv. L. Rev.* 1071 (2006.).

   The studies by scholars like Kahan interested in "cultural cognition" are quite interesting, but they often seem somewhat harder to interpret to me than their authors imply. We cannot really get experimental subjects to report "pure" factual probabilistic estimates, utterly divorced from judgments of appropriate conduct grounded only in part in factual judgments. So the "egalitarian" feminist may *say* that she thinks the battered wife faced a high probability of harm, but we cannot tell whether she says that because that factual judgment is harder to assail than a more patently normative judgment that she is *entitled* to use deadly force to kill a known abuser (as long as there is some nontrivial risk that she is in danger of death). In this sense, of course, the experimental subjects intuitively "flip" traditional ideas that people can come to consensus on facts but not on values. They act as if all the real disagreement comes over the facts. Second, I think it is difficult to tell when the experimental subjects' judgment of probability is subconsciously influenced by deep cultural commitments and when the subjects are simply using a conscious heuristic or rule of thumb. If I have trouble figuring out how to vote on a ballot proposition in California that relates to alternative energy, I may simply decide to follow the rSierra Club. Similarly, people may make judgments about the unknown risk of things like nuclear power plants or global warming or guns in the home by conscious reference to the views of similarly situated persons: What the authors think of as "culture" may thus simply be self-consciously identified similar persons. That leads to the third problem. The account of "culture" in the pieces is rather thin and rather circular. For instance, subjects who think guns in the home lower rather than raise risks to their occupants are defined as coming from a "hierarchical" (more authoritarian) culture, but the association of guns with hierarchy seems to be deeply contingent; there is little way of telling whether subjects reevaluate the dangers of guns to express their cultural commitment to something like hierarchy or that we come to understand that a low estimate of gun risk in the particular American setting is "hierarchical" because persons with other more clearly hierarchical views have this view of guns. I am skeptical that if we didn't know the public opinion poll associations between issues in the American context, we could use cultural commitments *directly* to predict risk assessments or attitudes on many hot-button issues.
29. For critiques of Hanson and Kysar, supra note 24, that track this description reasonably closely, see James A. Henderson and Jeffrey J. Rachlinski, "Product-Related Risk and Cognitive Biases: The Shortcomings of Enterprise Liability," 6 *Roger Williams U. L. Rev.* 213 (2000).
30. For an excellent summary, with numerous applications, see Richard H. Thaler and Cass R. Sunstein, *Nudge* (New York: Penguin Books, 2008).
31. The canonical source on optimal punishment is Gary S. Becker, "Crime and Punishment: An Economic Approach," 69 *J. Pol. Econ.* 169 (1968). Becker's assumption is that punishment should not be set "too high" because criminals *should* commit offenses sometimes, when the

value of the offense exceeds the social costs the activity imposes. There are certainly situations in which we use criminal sanctions believing the optimal level of sanctioned activity is indeed positive, but plenty of situations in which we believe it is zero, or that the generally sanctioned activity would not be actually criminal, because it is subject to a justification defense, when it is non-zero. This is particularly true to the extent we believe it appropriate to launder preferences and discount, say, the pleasure criminals take in inflicting pain on others.

Optimal sanctions are not infinite for a different reason than Becker emphasizes. Legislators recognize, or should recognize, that the costs of suppressing crime are positive—incarceration, apprehension, and prosecution are all costly. They should compare the benefits from expected crime reduction with the incremental costs of obtaining that reduction.

32. For a discussion of such problems, see, for instance, Mark Kelman, "Hedonic Psychology and the Ambiguities of 'Welfare,'" 33 *Phil. & Pub. Aff.* 391, 395–97 (2005).

33. Strong versions of the argument that state actors in particular are not simply subject to the same biases that purportedly adversely affect consumers but are likely to make decisions that are subject to the many mishaps of collective decision making, are made, for instance, in Edward L. Glaeser, "Paternalism and Psychology," 73 *U. Chi. L. Rev.* 133 (2006). Others argue that it is unlikely that the state will be able to constrain itself from adopting unwarranted hard paternalist programs once it permits itself to engage in warranted soft paternalist ones, in significant part because the boundaries between soft and hard paternalism are poorly defined. See, e.g., Glen Whitman and Mario J. Rizzo, "Paternalist Slopes," 2 *N.Y.U. J. Law & Liberty* 411 (2007).

34. For a summary and critique of traditional politically conservative accounts of why ostensibly market-failure correcting safety regulations actually serve the perverse, competition-reducing ends of regulation-demanding entities, while doing little or nothing to enhance consumer welfare, see Mark Kelman, "On Democracy-Bashing: A Skeptical Look at the Theoretical and 'Empirical' Practice of the Public Choice Movement," 74 *Va. L. Rev.* 199 (1988).

For similar, standard politically conservative accounts of why purportedly consumer-protective antitrust regulation is prone to be "captured" for anticompetitive, welfare-reducing purposes, see, e.g., William J. Baumol and Janusz A. Ordover, "Uses of Antitrust to Subvert Competition," 28 *J. L. & Econ.* 247 (1985), and Fred S. McChesney, "Antitrust and Regulation: Chicago's Contradictory Views," 10 *Cato J.* 775 (1991).

35. It remains an interesting issue that I have simply been unable to untangle in my own mind whether the F&F school is most significantly distinguished from the H&B school on this, and many other, issues by rhetorical posture and/or disposition to emphasize Panglossian examples rather than analytical structure, It is hard to gloss over the rhetorical significance of things like book titles, though. It is perfectly plain that Kahneman and Tversky would not have written a book called, *Simple Heuristics that Make Us Smart* (New York: Oxford University Press, 2000). (The book co-authored by Gerd Gigerenzer, Peter M. Todd and the ABC Research Group.)

36. The resemblance between the F&F argument against unduly detailed disclosure and the standard rational choice arguments that unduly extensive disclosure fails to communicate because consumers won't bear the cost of processing more and more information is sometimes quite pronounced. See, for instance, Daniel G. Goldstein et al., "Group Report: How Do Heuristics Mediate the Impact of Law on Behavior?" in *Heuristics and the Law*, supra note

11 at 439, 459–60. For an H&B-influenced argument that is also nearly indistinguishable from the conventional rational choice argument, see Chris Guthrie, "Law, Information, and Choice: Capitalizing on Heuristic Habits of Thought," in *Heuristics and the Law*, supra note 11 at 425, 435.

37. The rational choice version of the idea that we would seek only finite amounts of information, given that information is costly to process and of declining marginal value, goes back to George Stigler, "The Economics of Information," 69 *J. Pol. Econ.* 213 (1961). There is an enormous literature in economics attempting to assess how consumers do and should sequentially search options, evaluating both options and the information needed to differentiate the value of options. For some examples, see Martin L. Weitzman, "Optimal Search for the Best Alternative," 47 *Econometrica* 641 (1979); Meir G. Kohn and Steven Shavell, "The Theory of Search," 9 *J. Econ. Theory* 93 (1974).

38. See, e.g., Gerd Gigerenzer, "Heuristics," in *Heuristics and the Law*, supra note 11 at 17, 23. For similar F&F arguments that simple search techniques perform as well or better than those in which agents sort through a good deal of information, see, for instance, Peter M. Todd, "Fast and Frugal Heuristics for Environmentally Bounded Minds," in *Bounded Rationality: The Adaptive Toolbox* 51, 62 (G. Gigerenzer and R. Selten eds., Cambridge, MA: MIT Press, 2002).

39. There are many examples. See, for instance, Gerd Gigerenzer and Adrian Edwards, "Simple Tools for Understanding Risks: From Innumeracy to Insight," 327 *Brit. Med. J.* 741 (2003). Such frequentist presentations are endorsed by legal policymakers more influenced by the H&B school as well. See, for instance, Chris Guthrie, "Law, Information, and Choice: Capitalizing on Heuristic Habits of Thought," in *Heuristics and the Law*, supra note 11 at 424, 434.

40. See Paul Slovic, John Monahan and Donald M. MacGregor, "Violence Risk Assessment and Risk Communication: The Effects of Seeing Actual Cases, Providing Instructions, and Employing Probability vs. Frequency Formats," 24 *Law & Hum. Behav.* 271 (2000).

41. See Kimihiko Yamagishi, "When a 12.86% mortality is more dangerous than 24.14%: Implications for Risk Communication," 11 *Applied Cogn. Psychol.* 495 (1997).

42. Think, too, in this regard of the standard findings that people may bet on outcomes where the "good event" numerator, rather than the probability, is higher. So, if given a chance to win a prize if they draw a red jelly bean, most subjects will pick the urn in which there are seven reds in a bowl of 100 beans rather than one in ten because they can more vividly picture drawing one of many reds from the bigger bowl. In this case, the affectively charged frequency presentation—7 in 100 vs. 1 in 10—leads to poorer performance than a percentage presentation would (I surmise no one would pick a 7 percent chance over a 10 percent chance if the options were presented in that way). See S. Epstein, "Integration of the Cognitive and Psychodynamic Unconscious," 49 *Am. Psychol.* 709 (1994). Once more, too, one recalls Over's observation, discussed briefly in Chapter Four, that frequency presentations that do not cue set inclusion may be of no use to people. In Epstein's experiments, subjects are not asked to compare bowls containing seven and ten red jelly beans, respectively, out of the same set of 100, and thus may do a poor job processing frequency information.

43. See, e.g., Callia Piperides et al., "Group Report: What Is the Role of Heuristics in Litigation?" in *Heuristics and the Law*, supra note 11 at 343, 362–63.

44. See Gerd Gigerenzer, Wolfgang Gaissmaier, Elke Kurz-Mileke, Lisa M. Schwartz and Steven Woloshin, "Helping Doctors and Patients Make Sense of Health Statistics," 8 *Psychol. Sci. in the Pub. Interest* 53 (2008).

45. The authors recognize that subjects might *underestimate* the significance of seemingly small absolute gains. (See id. at 90, discussing the fact that it may well be more clinically impressive and significant than patients are likely to realize that statins reduce the five-year mortality rate from four to three in 100 in men with high cholesterol but no other heart problems.) In most of the article, though, they are concerned that people *overestimate* the significance of relative shifts in phenomena with low base rates, and that this leads both to undue anxiety and to needless treatment.

 I return to this generic point later in the text, but once one argues, as a policymaker, that people may underestimate the efficacy of certain treatments if given absolute numbers and "more properly" estimate it in others, one invariably has already made a cost-benefit analysis of the financial and health costs of overtreatment, of whether to aggregate certain risk-reducing steps patients might take together so that they present, overall, a significant change in absolute mortality or morbidity risks. What the experiments are showing us is that people react *differently* to data presented in terms of relative rather than absolute risks; what is telling us that one reaction is desirable, though, is not internal to what it means to make "informed or prudent" decisions, but an external observers' judgment of "real" costs and benefits of taking the steps one is likely to take if alarmed or sold on the incredible improvement in one's odds of surviving a particular malady on the one hand, or less alarmed or unimpressed with the impact of treatment on overall mortality on the other.

 Obviously, as the authors clearly recognize (id. at 71), at the point at which many treatment decisions have to be made (those the authors describe as "the severely ill," id.), shifts in aggregate population mortality risk are no longer of any moment. Thus, assume that a patient has a very rare form of cancer that will kill him for sure if untreated but that can be cured in 50 percent of cases. Looked at over the whole population, "treatment" may change his risk of dying from the disease from a trivial 1 in 500,000 to an also trivial 1 in a million. But at the moment he considers treatment, the change is far more dramatic (looked at in absolute terms as well as relative ones) within the now-relevant sub-group (those with the rare disease). Thus, as the authors note (id. at 58,) it is important to present data relevant to actual decision-making points.

46. Oddly, the authors do not present what would seem to be more relevant age-specific mortality rates for prostate cancer, though those would seem more relevant than overall rates. I am not asserting that these would indeed reveal distinct patterns; I am merely noting that talking about the lifetime risk of dying from a particular cause (as the authors do, id. at 57), rather than dying *prematurely*, seems rather besides the point for most people making health care decisions.

47. The attention to proper graphical presentation grows out of work highlighted in Elke Kurz-Milcke, Gerd Gigerenzer and Laura Martignon, "Transparency in Risk Communication: Graphical and Analog Tools," 1128 *Ann. N.Y. Acad. Sci.* 18 (2008).

48. See Daniel G. Goldstein et al., "Group Report: How Do Heuristics Mediate the Impact of Law?" in *Heuristics and the Law*, supra note 11 at 439, 459.

49. See Thaler and Sunstein, *Nudge*, supra note 30 at 244–46.

50. Id. at 246–48.

51. See Archon Fung, Mary Graham and David Weil, *Full Disclosure: The Perils and Promises of Transparency* (New York: Cambridge University Press, 2007).

52. See, for instance, Konstantios V. Katsikopoulos and Gerd Gigerenzer, "One-Reason Decision-Making: Modeling Violations of Expected Utility Theory," 37 *J. Risk & Uncertainty* 35, 37–38 (2008):

Compensatory strategies were typically used only when the number of alternatives and dimensions were small or after a number of alternatives have been eliminated from consideration... when people had a choice between 32 SmartPhones that varied on six cues, non-compensatory decision making models predicted their choices better than Bayesian or other models that assume trade-offs did. Similarly, when people chose between cameras varying on seven attributes with two to six levels each, non-compensatory strategies again provided the best prediction: 58% relied on one attribute only, 33% relied on two attributes, and only 2% used three attributes. The experimental evidence... strongly suggests that heuristics that rely on limited search and do not make trade-offs are in people's "adaptive toolbox"... and that these heuristics are selected in a sensitive way according to the structure of the problem.

Chapter 8

1. I set aside completely quite distinct problems of incommensurability that have preoccupied some philosophers of science. Thomas Kuhn can be read to claim that evidence used to verify or falsify claims within a paradigm may be of no use in verifying or falsifying claims made within a distinct scientific paradigm; claims across paradigms could be deemed incommensurable in this sense.
2. Imagine that a person must choose between observing a religious holiday that forbids work and taking advantage of a great business opportunity that day. Some would argue that he may *compare* the options and think that observing the holiday is preferable without believing that he gets more hedonic utility out of doing so, or that he would have to be paid *more* than the business opportunity affords him to give up observing the religious holiday.
3. A crisp statement of this variant of the normative thesis can be found in Frederick Schauer, "Instrumental Commensurability," 146 U. Pa. L. Rev. 1215, 1227 (1998).
4. I essentially set aside in this chapter an interesting possible connection between the H&B school and incommensurability. While modularists might be especially prone to believe that the existence of domain-specific thinking *creates* the experience of facing incommensurable options, it is possible as well that the way in which we *solve* forced-choice problems when we seem to need to make trade-offs between plural ends whose values are not readily compared is by using not entirely rational heuristics, of the sort that H&B theorists focus on.
Following Bruce Chapman's argument, imagine, for instance, that we are on a scholarship committee that is trying to select recipients based on some "combination" of financial need, academic prowess, and community service, and that it seems difficult to know how to trade off a certain level of need for greater scholarly ability. Assume, too, that we think in some way that no one who is not at least minimally financially needy should win the scholarship, but do not want to use need level lexically (i.e., we do not think that the neediest applicant should necessarily win). We could use a sequenced decision-making process (e.g., select a certain number of people who are needy enough, a certain number of those who are scholarly enough, and a certain number of those with the highest level of community service). We might even choose to do so until, given the size of each group we have selected, there is just one person "qualified" along all the dimensions. See Bruce Chapman, "Law, Incommensurability, and Conceptually Sequenced Argument," 146 U. Pa. L. Rev. 1487 (1998).

Unlike Chapman, I am quite certain that this procedure well be irrational on many occasions if we are applying standard canons of rationality (e.g., if the "winner" is the most marginal candidate along all three dimensions and she beats out someone who is considerably more needy *or* academically gifted *or* community-service minded). But I agree with Chapman that it is one that is likely to be *used* quite a bit given our heuristic reliance on "reason-based" choice. The procedure is, if not rational, easy to *rationalize*. It also, like most reason-based choice decision processes, works by eliminating a person as soon as one has a reason to eliminate that person (e.g., not in the group of the five neediest). In making choices between two realistic options, the presence of a third irrelevant alternative may be quite influential: as I noted in Chapter Two, we choose a Mark Cross pen over $6 much more frequently when we are also allowed to choose a really cruddy pen that no one picks, seemingly because we first solve the easy problem (is the Mark Cross pen better than the cruddy pen?) and then anchor to the choice of the Mark Cross pen. Similarly, we on the hypothetical scholarship committee may think we have worked through a difficult choice situation (e.g., using the sorts of reflective pragmatic techniques that Anderson or Taylor argue that we use in these situations) but actually we are responding to *random* sequencing and list making. Thus, we've anchored to the neediest person if judgments about need are easiest to make and we make those first largely for that reason or we've arbitrarily selected some cut-off number along all the dimensions we care about and then treat membership in the groups whose size is fundamentally arbitrary as if it reveals something about the aggregate merit of each candidate. For the classic discussion of reason-based heuristic thinking, see Eldar Shafir, Itamar Simonson and Amos Tversky, "Reason-Based Choice," 49 *Cognition* 11 (1993). Context-dependent choices that violate "rational choice" principles against accounting for the presence or absence of irrelevant alternatives in choosing between two options are discussed in Amos Tversky and Itamar Simonson, "Context-Dependent Preferences," 39 *Mgmt. Sci.* 1179 (1993).

Note, too, that Chapman's recommended procedure bears a substantial relationship to an "elimination by aspects" approach. For my discussion of Tversky's view that people make decisions among options when distinct aspects of the option are inexorably bundled together by eliminating options that do not meet threshold levels of the most important virtue, then moving on to eliminate those that do not meet the threshold virtues along some second dimension, and so on, see the discussion in Chapter Two.

5. See, e.g., Gerd Gigerenzer, "The Adaptive Toolbox," in *Bounded Rationality: The Adaptive Toolbox* 37, 40, 46 (G. Gigerenzer and R. Selten eds., Cambridge, MA: MIT Press, 2002); Gerd Gigerenzer, *Adaptive Thinking* 191 (Oxford, UK; New York: Oxford University Press, 2000).

6. See, e.g., Bernard Williams, *Problems of the Self* 173 (Cambridge, UK; Cambridge University Press, 1973); Cass R. Sunstein, "Incommensurability and Valuation in Law," 92 *Mich. L. Rev.* 779, 859–60 (1994). I think one gets somewhat the same "flavor" of argument—using different words—in Lukes's plea to be attentive to the distinction between mere "trade-offs" and "sacrifices" of the sort we make when we have to abandon some commitment to meet another. See Steven Lukes, "Comparing the Incomparable: Trade-offs and Sacrifices," in *Incommensurability, Incomparability, and Practical Reason* 184 (Ruth Chang ed., Cambridge, MA: Harvard University Press, 1997).

7. Choices *could* be commensurable in the strong sense—each might be evaluated in terms of a single metric such as utility—but if we were not sure that the single metric were the only one we wanted to employ, it would not resolve the issue of how to choose. We could

decide how much utility we generated doing X and doing Y, but would not know to choose X rather than Y merely because it generated more utility if Y met some other goal. If the value of ends were commensurable along one or multiple dimensions, but not reducible to an all-things-considered single evaluative metric, it would not eliminate the difficulty of choice.

Arguably, though, "choice" may depend on some degree of incommensurability. As Brian Bix felicitously put it, "If all options were reducible to units of some good an individual sought to maximize, there would be no need for 'choice,' understood as an act of judgment. Any automaton can choose $500, when the alternative is $100 . . ." Brian Bix, "Dealing with Incommensurability for Dessert and Desert: Comments on Chapman and Katz," 146 U. Pa. L. Rev. 1651, 1652–53 (1998). Bix's point is not wholly convincing, though. Assume that one tries solely to maximize "utility" and will mechanically select the option that generates the "highest" level of utility. Unless the utility derived from each choice is obvious or can be measured by the simplest act of introspection, assessing options may still be effortful and require self-awareness and self-examination.

8. For a similar argument, see, for instance, Larry Alexander, "Banishing the Bogey of Incommensurability," 146 U. Pa. L. Rev. 1641, 1643 (1998).
9. I am not sure that a utility-reductionist need believe that utility judgments are actually readily made. It may take lots of work to figure out how much pleasure and pain, over time, one derives from certain end-states. See supra note 7.
10. See infra notes 14, 15, 17, 27, and 28.
11. Larry Alexander notes that deontological side-constraint theories all imply, in this sense, that consequentialist gains are not commensurable with rights violations. See Alexander, "Banishing the Bogeyman of Incommensurability," supra note 8 at 1644. For a further discussion, focusing on the need to exclude certain reasons from consideration in making decisions, so that a gain in Y may be of no moment, see Richard Warner, "Excluding Reasons: Impossible Comparisons and the Law," 15 Oxford J. Legal Stud. 431 (1995).

Though it is by no means always clear what he means when he refers to incommensurability, there are times when Gigerenzer plainly defines incommensurable values as those values that trump other values, and therefore, paradoxically, seem plainly comparable. See, e.g., Gigerenzer, *Adaptive Thinking*, supra note 7 at 190–191 ("One-reason decision making is not compensatory. Compensation is, after all, the cornerstone of classical rationality, assuming that all commodities can be compared and everything has its price. Compensation assumes commensurability. However, human minds do not trade everything; some things are supposed to be without a price. . . . For instance, if a person must choose between two actions that might help him or get him out of deep financial trouble, and one involves killing someone, then no amount of money or other benefits might compensate for the prospect of bloody hands.").
12. Eric Posner believes that people strategically either pose as, or even act as, the sort of people who are unwilling to make such trade-offs in order to gain reputational advantages as trustworthy in situations in which revealing one's trustworthiness is otherwise difficult. See Eric A. Posner, "The Strategic Basis of Principled Behavior: A Critique of the Incommensurability Thesis," 146 U. Pa. L. Rev. 1185 (1998).

For a very sharp attack on this understanding of what those unwilling to make trade-offs are doing, see Brian Leiter, "Incommensurability: Truth or Consequences?" 146 U. Pa. L. Rev. 1723 (1998).

13. The notion that individual rights are not to be balanced against social welfare gains resonates in the commitment to the idea that persons are so separate that to speak of gains to one counterbalancing losses to another confuses the nature of the entities one deals with, reifying social groups, or treating them as contained single organisms when they are not. I do not believe in any way that a foundational commitment to the separateness of persons—even if it were compelling as a foundational commitment—dictates the priority of any discrete sets of individual rights over the interests of any other person in any way, since respect for individual rights requires the rights-respecter to sacrifice her own interests in order to benefit the rights bearer. But this conventional legal realist point is ultimately neither here nor there for these purposes.
14. See Elizabeth Anderson, "Values, Risks, and Market Norms," 17 *Phil. & Pub. Aff.* 54, 61 (1988) (". . . wage differentials do not represent cash values people place on their lives, but rather reflect the risks people feel obliged to accept in order to discharge their responsibilities.").
15. See Elizabeth Anderson, "Practical Reason and Incommensurable Goods," in *Incommensurability, Incomparability, and Practical Reason*, supra note 6 at 91, 102.

    The argument I make in the text that theorists who claim to find incommensurability may not acknowledge that they have rendered action-options comparable in the course of thinking of reasons to act in a certain purportedly expressive way by specifying their true traits in further detail is suggested by Elijah Anderson, "Incommensurability and Practical Reasoning," in *Incommensurability, Incomparability, and Practical Reason*, supra note 6 at 151, 160.
16. Anderson, "*Practical Reason*," supra note 14 at 105–06.
17. For the classic elaboration of this position, see Joseph Raz, *The Morality of Freedom* 321–66 (Oxford, UK: Clarendon Press; New York: Oxford University Press, 1986).
18. For a very similar argument, see Leo Katz, "Incommensurable Choices and the Problem of Moral Ignorance," 146 *U. Pa. L. Rev.* 1465, 1466–68 (1998).
19. This argument is suggested by an argument in Donald Regan, "Value, Comparability, and Choice," in *Incommensurability, Incomparability, and Practical Reason*, supra note 6 at 129, 135, 137.
20. Ruth Chang, "Introduction," in *Incommensurability, Incomparability, and Practical Reason*, supra note 6 at 1, 4–5
21. Joseph Raz, "Incommensurability and Agency," in *Incommensurability, Incomparability, and Practical Reason*, supra note 6 at 110, 126–28.
22. For a far fuller discussion of a far subtler set of points, see Margaret Jane Radin, *Contested Commodities* (Cambridge, MA: Harvard University Press, 1996).
23. This argument bears a strong resemblance to an argument made in Matthew Adler, "Incommensurability and Cost-Benefit Analysis," 146 *U. Pa. L. Rev.* 1371, 1415–16 (1998) (the fact that juries, for fifty years now, have ordered defendants to pay money damages to parents for wrongfully causing the death of the parents' children has not compromised parent's affection for children or changed their relationship with them in any obvious way).

    Naturally, it is dubious that we should view juries as trying to "put a price" on the loss of a child or suggest in any way that the money the defendant pays truly "compensates" for that loss or is equal to it. One could think the jury is performing a whole host of consequentialist or deontological tasks that do not involve the claim that the parent would have found the sum of money—before or after the fact—just as "valuable" as keeping his child alive. The jury might be trying to give greater incentives for care in situations in which defendants risk children's lives, could be punishing a wrongdoer, could be trying to express an appropriate social attitude toward the grief-stricken. Whether there are other contexts in which we might

think we are "putting a price on children" in a way that might compromise the capacity to maintain certain sorts of attitudes toward children (e.g., facilitating the development of an active market in babies for adoption) would then be a wholly different question.
24. See Michael Walzer, *Spheres of Justice* 3–31, 86–91, 95–108 (New York: Basic Books, 1983).
25. Robert Nozick, *Anarchy, State, and Utopia* 233–35 (Oxford, UK: Blackwell, 1974). Nozick is responding more directly to an argument made by Bernard Williams that significantly animates Walzer's view.
26. It is a tremendously interesting question, outside the scope of this book, whether concrete choices (e.g., to enter into or accept certain contracts) made for expressive reasons ought to be treated the same way as contracts entered into with the expectation of engaging in traditional maximizing behavior. For a fascinating article claiming that the key problem with enforcing various contracts that we think women enter into "improvidently" is that entering the contract, at the moment of formation, contract formation had a symbolic meaning and was not thought of as a choice about projected future consequences, see Gillian K. Hatfield, "An Expressive Theory of Contract: From Feminist Dilemmas to a Reconceptualization of Rational Choice in Contract Law," 146 *U. Pa. L. Rev.* 1235 (1998).
27. See especially Anderson, "*Practical Reason*," supra note 14 at 94–95. See also Raz, "Incommensurability and Agency," supra note 21 at 113–15, 122–28, and Charles Taylor, "Leading a Life," in *Incommensurability, Incomparability, and Practical Reason*, supra note 6 at 170, 179–83.
28. See Anderson, "*Practical Reason*," supra note 14 at 98,
29. While rat-choice and H&B theorists treat the fact that people are willing to devote far more resources to save identifiable lives than statistical lives as one of the main poster children for the persistence of confusion and error, I think the case is complicated, even if people are not expressing symbolic commitments to the "life-saving" principle only when they happen to discern that the commitment to the principle is being tested.

Broadly speaking, subjects seem to prefer to spend more to "rescue" or "cure" those already in relatively immediate jeopardy than to "prevent" the development of peril, and to expend more to either save persons who are more "identifiable" or to prevent those who are more identifiable from becoming imperiled. The preference to save or cure rather than to avert peril may well be the product of a number of familiar heuristic-based biases (such as availability), but it is transparently irrational only if subjects' sole goal is to maximize life expectancy, setting aside physiological morbidity. In "Saving Lives, Saving from Death, Saving from Dying: Reflections on Over-Valuing Identifiable Victims," 11 *Yale J. Health Policy, Law & Ethics* 51 (2011), I argue that if people care not only about averting *death* (of themselves or others) but about averting situations in which they themselves or others experience heightened dread of *dying*, the preference need not be irrational. Furthermore, the preference to save or prevent the imperilment of identifiable others may grow out of two distinct forms of agent-relative anti-consequentialism; I argue it is worth considering whether such anti-consequentialist decision-making dispositions are justified only because they ultimately result in good consequences (in this case, a higher level of altruism).
30. See, e.g., Keith E. Stanovich, *Who Is Rational? Studies of Individual Differences in Reasoning* 148–52 (Mahwah, N.J.: Lawrence Erlbaum Associates, 1999).
31. The clearest statement of this "solution" to the problem of conflicting domain-specific modules is in Gigerenzer, *Adaptive Thinking*, supra note 6 at 231–33. The "solution" is not enormously well-specified, however, especially at the neurobiological level.
32. Id. at 231
33. Id. at 232.

Chapter 9

1. The key texts interpreting distinct schools of modern American legal thought for me are Thomas Grey, "Langdell's Orthodoxy," 45 *U. Pitt. L. Rev.* 1 (1983), and Thomas Grey, "Holmes and Legal Pragmatism," 41 *Stan. L. Rev.* 787 (1989). For those interested in decidedly different views of the Langdellian synthesis, it might be helpful to look at, among other sources, Duncan Kennedy, "Toward an Historical Understanding of Legal Consciousness: The Case of Classical Legal Thought in America, 1850–1940," 3 *Research in Law & Soc.* 3 (1980); Robert Gordon, "Legal Thought and Legal Practice in the Age of American Enterprise, 1870–1920," in *Professions and Professional Ideologies in America, 1730–1940* (G.L. Geison & L. Stone eds., Chapel Hill: University of North Carolina Press, 1983); G. Edward White, "The Impact of Legal Science on Tort Law, 1880–1970," 78 *Colum. L. Rev.* 213, 214–32 (1978).

    For those interested in distinct understandings of Holmes, it might be especially interesting to look at Yosal Rogat, "The Judge as Spectator," 31 *U. Chi. L. Rev.* 213 (1964); Robert W. Gordon, "Holmes' *Common Law* as Social and Legal Science," 10 *Hofstra L. Rev.* 719 (1982); H.L. Pohlman, *Justice Oliver Wendell Homes and Utilitarian Jurisprudence* (Cambridge, Mass.: Harvard University Press, 1984); G. Edward White, "The Integrity of Holmes' Jurisprudence," 10 *Hofstra L. Rev.* 633 (1982)
2. See, above all, Ronald Dworkin, *Taking Rights Seriously* (Cambridge, MA: Harvard University Press, 1977); Ronald Dworkin, "Is There Really No Right Answer in Hard Cases?" in Ronald Dworkin, *A Matter of Principle* 119 (Cambridge, MA: Harvard University Press, 1985).
3. This notion that a legal system must be rule-bound because rules are all that decision makers can implement and that citizens can readily learn appears repeatedly, albeit with numerous qualifications, in Gigerenzer and Engel's book on the relevance of the F&F school to law. See, e.g., *Heuristics and the Law* 146–56, 241–43, 255–56, 360–64 (G. Gigerenzer & C. Engel eds., Cambridge, MA: MIT Press, 2006).
4. Most of the virtues of formalism, or presumptive formalism, touted by Schauer refer to this sort of base-level formalism. See Frederick Schauer, "Formalism," 97 *Yale L.J.* 509 (1988).
5. There are innumerable tributes to the virtues of rules. Justice Scalia's has become reasonably canonical. See Antonin Scalia, "The Rule of Law as a Law of Rules," 56 *U. Chi. L. Rev.* 1175 (1989).
6. For a summary of some of the critiques of rules, see Mark Kelman, *A Guide to Critical Legal Studies* 40–54 (Cambridge, MA: Harvard University Press, 1987).
7. The idea that a small number of principles can generate concrete results in innumerable distinct cases is quite overt in Richard A. Epstein, *Simple Rules for a Complex World* (Cambridge, MA: Harvard University Press, 1995). Epstein argues that that one can derive a complete set of base-level rules from seven high-order principles. In some later work, Epstein explicitly defends the use of a small number of high-order principles in part on the grounds that subjects will best learn and understand the law if legal commands can be grounded in a few F&F-style heuristics and treats his high-order principles as quasi-heuristics. See Richard Epstein, "The Optimal Complexity of Legal Rules," in *Heuristics and the Law*, supra note 3 at 141.
8. For a fuller discussion of the problem that rules become increasingly inapt over time as parties tailor the form of their behavior to gain the advantages of being protected by the rules, see Kelman, supra note 6 at 41–42.

9. George Priest, "The Common Law and the Selection of Efficient Rules," 6 *J. Legal Stud.* 65 (1977).
10. See especially Friedrich Hayek, "The Use of Knowledge in Society," 35 *Amer. Econ. Rev.* 519 (1945).
11. Grey notes that the case method of pedagogy—which presses students to think about the acceptability of particular outcomes with particular sets of compelling facts as well as to consider abstract doctrine—ultimately helped to undermine the effort to do higher level conceptual ordering.
12. For a fuller explication of the argument, see Jeffrey J. Rachlinski, "Bottom-Up Versus Top-Down Lawyering," in *Heuristics and the Law*, supra note 3 at 159, 168–71.
13. For a summary discussion, see Robert W. Gordon, "The Geologic Strata of the Law School Curriculum," 60 *Vanderbilt L. Rev.* 339 (2007).
14. The classic Legal Realist discussion of such cases is in Edwin W. Patterson, "The Delivery of a Life Insurance Policy," 33 *Harv. L. Rev.* 198 (1919).
15. For a superb account of the most eloquent Realist thought on this point, see Barbara Fried, *The Progressive Assault on Laissez Faire: Robert Hale and the First Law and Economics Movement* 29–71 (Cambridge, MA: Harvard University Press, 1998).
16. Legal theorists like John Mikhail who advance the idea, heavily influenced by both F&F and MM theory, that there are moral universals, that we are born with the capacity to learn only a limited number of moral principles, just as we are born with the competence to learn language, believe that an important aspect of our moral competence is that we intuitively recognize that "harm-causing" is wrong, *prima facie*. It is plain that we can quasi-tautologically describe any moral judgment in terms of a judgment about an agent's morally causal responsibility for any culturally relatively defined bad consequence. But for us post-Coaseans, the claim that the mind has a very limited range of algorithms to process, represent, and compute *factual* unidirectional causal relations remains what could generously be described as a puzzling one

This point requires a fairly substantial digression. For most academic lawyers, the digression will be needlessly long because the point has become reasonably commonplace, but it is, I think, enormously significant, in large part because both Hauser and Mikhail assert that a substantial aspect of the universal moral grammar (UMG) is that it involves the purported capacity to identify when one party has caused another harm. See especially John Mikhail, "Universal Moral Grammar: Theory, Evidence and the Future," 11 *Trends in Cogn. Sci.* 143 (2007), and Marc D. Hauser, *Moral Minds* (New York: Ecco, 2006). The demise of the idea within the legal academy that people can make such stable unidirectional causal inferences can fairly be traced back to the analysis of legal relations provided by the Legal Realist, Wesley Hohfeld, in the early part of the twentieth century.

Briefly, the argument is this. All disputes between two or more parties basically involve conflicting desires about how to deploy scarce resources. The principle that we may do as we wish, provided we do not cause harm to others, is useless in deciding which set of desires should prevail, because, however we decide the dispute, one actor will be "harmed" as a matter of fact, either in the sense that the defendant will be free to make the plaintiff worse off or that the plaintiff will be told that he or she cannot do as he or she wishes with impunity. Thus, we cannot resolve the dispute as a matter of "fact" as to who has harmed whom; we can only decide it based on some implicit or explicit normative commitments that lead us to favor one side's interests over the other side's interests.

For lawyers, that way of looking at the problem of harm-to-others traces back (at least) to Hohfeld's early twentieth century reconceptualization of legal rights. Looked at functionally, Hohfeld argued, rights are constituted by the reciprocal duties that others bear to the rights holder. Thus, any expansion of one owner's protected sphere of unfettered action (the would-be user's use privileges) *must* come at the cost of contracting the rights of those adversely affected by that owner's growingly protected uses to be immune from the negative effects of such uses. To the extent that we privilege the owner of parcel #1 to barbeque freely, the owner of parcel #2 loses immunity from the losses that come from dealing with smoke. To the extent that we allow the owner of parcel #1 to build a tall building, the owner of parcel #2 stands to lose her view. Thus, however we resolve the dispute between the two owners, we must either interfere with the would-be user's "autonomy"—in the sense that we will limit her free action—or the "autonomy" of the party seeking to be protected from loss—in the sense that we will compromise our ordinary commitment to protecting people from non-consensual shifts in their baseline position. See Wesley Hohfeld, "Some Fundamental Legal Conceptions as Applied to Judicial Reasoning," 23 *Yale L.J.* 15 (1913).

Fifty years after Hohfeld, the economist Ronald Coase made essentially the same point, phrased in economic rather than legal terms, in his famous article, "The Problem of Social Cost," arguing that as a descriptive matter all social costs represent the joint costs of conflicting desires in a world of scarcity. The actions of each of the two interacting parties, he noted, are each but-for causes of the harm. A railroad emitting sparks does not cause a fire unless the farmer chooses to place his crops next to the train line: causation in this sense appears mutual, not unidirectional. See Ronald Coase, "The Problem of Social Cost," 3 *J. Law & Econ.* 1 (1960). For a further discussion of the material on Hohfeld and Coase, see Mark Kelman, "The Necessary Myth of Objective Causation Judgments in Liberal Political Theory," 63 *Chi.-Kent L. Rev.* 579, 581–86 (1987).

There is a more sophisticated reformulation of Coase's basic point, which better reveals the inadequacy of the unidirectional harm principle, uninformed by covert perfectionism or welfarism, to resolve disputes over which of two of conflicting uses to protect. The *cost* we are concerned with in the typical case of interactive harm, need not, either as a matter of actual social practice or normative theory, take the form of the physical damage that would occur if each party acted without either legal restraint or knowledge of the other's activity. Look again at Coase's famous example of interactive harm. A railroad wishes to run its trains on tracks that lie alongside a farm; if it does so, though, the sparks emitted by the train will set fire to the farmer's crops. It is true that if the railroad proceeds unimpeded, the consequence will be physical damage to the crops in the form of a fire, and we might intuit (in Mikhail or Hauser's sense?) that the railroad "caused" the fire.

But "damage" to the parties' interests need not take that form. The relevant damage—the true subject of moral judgment—that concerns Coase is what he labels the *social cost*, by which he means the difference in the sum of the values of the two parcels or activities in a world in which they did not interact and their value in the world in which they do interact. The social cost *might* take the form of a crop fire, but it might also take the form of added spark suppression costs for railroads, if they are forced to take preventive measures to prevent the fire in the first place, or lost profits for the farmer, if the farmer is forced to take preventive measures, for example, by ceasing to plant on land adjacent to the tracks. If farms were nowhere near trains (the non-interaction situation), the parties would not have to bear the cost of their interaction, in any form, whether fires, reduced crops, or spark suppression costs. But it is equally the case that if the owners were near one another but had different *desires*—if the farmer had no desire to use his land for crops or the train company's proprietors for spark-emitting transportation—there would also be no social cost. The social cost is thus the product of clashing desires, given interaction.

Naturally, not all uses of one's self or one's property compromise the interests of others, whether we measure the adverse effect by diminished property values or by decreased subjective utility. But the only time courts are asked to adjudicate or we are asked to make moral judgments whether or not the would-be user is privileged to act is when *someone* is adversely affected by the proposed use. To put it another way, the problem of law, like the subject matter of economics, morality, or distributive ethics, depends on the existence of conflict or scarcity. Unless we decide, as perfectionists, that one desire is more legitimate, more expressive of preferred human values, or decide as welfarists that one desire is *stronger*, we appear stuck.

In legal circles, a few people have tried to salvage a determinative role for an unmoralized notion of unidirectional harm-in-fact by limiting legal or moral liability to a subset of acts that cause harm-in-fact, with the subset defined by the objective unmoralized, natural) properties of those acts. In essence, both Hauser and Mikhail believe the UMG dictates that we compute harm-causation in this way. Two notable efforts in this vein have been Richard Epstein's argument that only physically invasive causes are culpable, and Hart and Honore's argument that only unusual causes are culpable. See Richard Epstein, "A Theory of Strict Liability," 2 *J. Legal Stud.* 151 (1973); Richard Epstein, "Defenses and Subsequent Pleas in a System of Strict Liability," 3 *J. Legal Stud.* 165 (1974); and H.L.A. Hart and Tony Honore, *Causation and the Law* 26–94, 109–29 (Oxford, UK: Clarendon Press; New York: Oxford University Press, 2d ed. 1985).

Epstein starts with a universalistic strict liability view of culpability for harm-in-fact: That you, as a matter of fact, harmed me is, *prima facie*, a sufficient reason to hold you liable for that harm. But he immediately limits the reach of this broad principle by invoking a limiting and quirky definition of cause. Only those supplying, threatening, or forcing others to employ invasive force are deemed to cause an event. Epstein's position is neither plausibly complete descriptively nor morally compelling. Its incompleteness is clear. If the defendant leaves his unlit car on a busy highway, it is the plaintiff's car that forcefully invades when it smashes into defendant's car. It is unlikely that Epstein really wants to suggest—or that Mikhail believes the UMG is "bound" to compute—that the plaintiff caused the crash, though. Similarly, Epstein acknowledges that a hypersensitive plaintiff is causally responsible for the atypical damages he suffers from defendant's routine invasive activities, even though the plaintiff plainly does not forcefully invade himself.

The more troublesome problem with Epstein's scheme, however, is the normative one: Why should we *care* about the physical properties of a causal factor at all, in determining culpability? It is easy to concoct examples that make that fixation seem absurd. One defendant erects a mirror which deflects sunrays that thereby "invade" a neighbor's property, causing it to be too bright, while the other builds a high fence, blocking light and thereby causing it to be too dark. Epstein would have us conclude that because only the first defendant's actions are invasive, only the first defendant is liable, although clearly the plaintiff is equally harmed, in similar ways, by either action. But even in the run-of-the-mill case (my car hits yours, stopped at a stoplight), where intuitively one feels that liability should attach to the cause that is physically invasive, that intuition cannot really ultimately rest on physical causation itself. It must come from some external value(s) that turn out to be served on some occasions by distinguishing among causes based on whether they are physically invasive or not. It is hard to imagine any theory of rights—other than the purely tautological claim that we have a right to be free of physical invasion—that would do the trick.

In another attempt to isolate some subset of causes-in-fact as morally culpable, Hart and Honore argue that liability attaches to those causes that cannot be taken for granted—that are unusual in the normal course of events. If Epstein's account forces us to draw distinctions that seem singularly unappealing, this account is unhelpfully circular. The question of which actor is simply "going about his business" and which one is interfering with the ordinary flow of events cannot *determine* the legal cause of the injury (or, in Mikhail and Hauser's sense be computed as a basic cognitive primitive) as it will be significantly determined by decisions about legal and moral cause. If the railroad is entitled to emit sparks, the farmer's decision to snuggle his crops right up to the tracks will disrupt the ordinary course of events and appear to be the fire's cause, just as the decision to park on the highway is doubtless routinely viewed as disruptive by American jurors. If the farmer is entitled to use all of his property for crops, and others must take steps to insure those crops remain undamaged, the spark-emitting train will look disruptive and therefore "cause" the conflagration.

Without recourse to perfectionist dialogue—about morally preferred uses—or welfarist dialogue—about subjective gains inherent in each use—we appear stuck. Moreover, just as with Epstein's physically invasive causes, the normative appeal of this distinction is unclear. Why do "ordinary" acts have a higher moral standing than more unusual ones? And as with Epstein's physical invasion test, whether an act is usual or unusual may be a tolerably good proxy for something else we might care about, on welfarist or other grounds (e.g., whether those harmed by the act should have anticipated it and thus protected themselves or the likelihood the act is socially useful). But it is hard to see why we would care about it in itself.

17. See Grey, "Holmes and Legal Pragmatism," supra note 1.
18. For an excellent summary, from an H&B vantage point, of the problems that people will have choosing those things that in fact turn out to make them happy, see George Loewenstein and David Schkade, "Wouldn't It Be Nice? Predicting Future Feelings," in *Well-Being: The Foundations of Hedonic Psychology* 85 (D. Kahneman, E. Diener, and N. Schwarz eds., New York: Russell Sage Foundation, 1999).
19. See Daniel Kahneman, Peter B. Wakker, and Rakesh Sarin, "Back to Bentham? Explorations of Experienced Utility," 112 *Q.J. Econ.* 112 (1997), and Daniel Kahneman, "Objective Happiness," in *Well-Being* supra note 18 at 3. For a discussion of some of the problems with both Benthamite hedonic utilitarianism and preference utilitarianism, see Mark Kelman, "Hedonic Psychology and the Ambiguities of 'Welfare,'" 33 *Phil. & Pub. Aff.* 391 (2005).
20. Holmes's intuition in this regard runs against the intuition of moral realists like Mikhail, who seem to believe, for reasons more complex than I will summarize here, that reactions that are easily cognized have some moral weight on that account alone.
21. Here is the fuller quote to which I refer in the text. After stating the aphorism that "the life of the law is not logic but experience," Holmes goes on to say: "The felt necessities of the time, the prevalent moral and political theories, intuitions of public policy, avowed or unconscious, even the prejudices which judges share with their fellow-men, have had a good deal more to do than the syllogism in determining how men should be governed." Oliver Wendell Holmes, *The Common Law* 5 (Boston: Little, Brown, 1881).

22. It is worth noting, but not central to my argument because, in my view, it is not terribly illuminated by reflecting on the heuristics literature, that the third famous aspect of Holmesian jurisprudence—the view that law is no more than a prediction of how courts will respond to the putative defendant's behavior—is also best understood not as a general theory of law but as an answer to a particular instrumental question. Viewed as a general jurisprudential theory, it is subject to a host of familiar difficulties: Most powerfully, why and how do we distinguish the commands of *legitimate* law from the predictions of what any powerful local bully will do? Instead, the prediction theory focuses on the view of law we should take acting in a certain role with certain purposes (just as we might view it appropriate to attempt to reduce law to conceptual systems as *teachers* of law but not as judges seeking a way to fill gaps in novel situations).

In this view, the prediction view is the apt one for an attorney counseling a client to take. It is the client-relevant form of Austinian positivism that is apt once one recognizes, contra Austin, that the law rarely acts through sovereign *commands* (injunctions and criminal penalties are at best the only even arguable exceptions) but generally merely establishes prices to engage in certain behavior. If all that law can be is prices, what the client needs to know or predict is what those expected prices are, just as he must know or predict when he will be subject to more absolutely constraining commands.

23. *The Holmes-Cohen Correspondence* in *Portrait of a Philosopher: Morris R. Cohen in Life and Letters* 313, 329–30 (L. Rosenfeld ed., New York: Harcourt, Brace & World, 1962).

24. In a similar fashion, the distinction between production and consumption gets blurred in his work. We do not produce merely for the sake of some separate activity (consumption), but should gain intrinsic pleasure in the act of producing.

25. *The Holmes-Cohen Correspondence*, supra note 22.

26. This theme is developed with particular force, if not necessarily particular persuasiveness, in the work of Keith Stanovich, who argues that the main side effect of developing the capacity to meet novel survival challenges is that people develop idiosyncratic, personal goals with no direct survival advantages. In a sense, System One maximizes the survival of genes, while System Two integrates a "whole person" with something more like utility-maximizing interests. See especially Keith Stanovich, *Who Is Rational? Studies of Individual Differences in Reasoning* 148–52 (Mahwah, NJ: Lawrence Erlbaum Associates, 1999).The argument is quite close in spirit to the argument I attribute in the text to Holmes.

27. Most legal scholars would argue, contra Arnold, that there *are* generalized issues of preparation versus attempt: that is, issues about when the behavior of the defendant is either proximate enough to consummation to cause legitimate social alarm, or alternatively, and in my view more persuasively, when the defendant's behavior reveals without reliance on extrinsic evidence about his intention his firm commitment to consummate an offense in situations in which he fails to do so only because of external impediments outside the defendant's control, rather than internal hesitations about completing the offense. The line can never be drawn in a fashion that is truly comfortable: When there is still *more* to do to consummate the offense (the preparation vs. attempt issue), we can never be truly sure beyond the proverbial reasonable doubt that the defendant really would have consummated the offense but-for external interruption. (To put it another way, we cannot be certain that he is indistinguishable, in terms of blameworthiness or dangerousness from the consummated criminal, just fortuitously unable to complete the offense). If we do not punish, though, simply because it always seems *possible* that the defendant would have changed his mind about proceeding, we

will allow many who are actually as culpable as those who have consummated offenses to escape liability simply because they happened to fail or be caught earlier. If Arnold is to be persuasive, he must convince us that this basic dilemma plays out quite differently when it arises in different "narrow fact patterns." It is this that I think he wholly fails to do.

It is equally true that it is hard to adjudicate the class of "impossible attempt" cases in which the defendant has completed her course of conduct and still not consummated the offense: Can we ever be certain that she intended to do something *different* than she actually did? Arnold, not atypically, treats these cases as about mental state—about the difficulty of specifying the precise object of the defendant's intention—but I think that is an analytical error. What seems more clearly an analytical error is that we can best decipher how these cases are decided by looking to distinguish various narrow fact patterns in which the general issue arises.

28. This is the very basic argument in Thurman W. Arnold, "Criminal Attempts—The Rise and Fall of an Abstraction," 40 *Yale L.J.* 53 (1930). Arnold's article, like most of the work that might be said to push the idea that the traditional legal categories are far too broad (like the conventional indicia of criminal attempt in this case, like consideration in attacks by Realists like Patterson on Langdell's work on contracts) is extraordinarily difficult to interpret. On the one hand, the piece can be read to imply that there are "real"—but still reasonably broad, overarching—concerns that actually govern practice and that these overarching concerns work out distinctly in distinct cases covered by the traditional category. Thus, in this view, "the traditional categories that animate attempt law"—on the act side, preparation versus attempt, on the mental state side, "specific intent"—are not too *broad* as much as they are the *wrong* categories. In thinking about the punishment of action without concrete harms it would be better to substitute some other category (e.g., the importance of implementing the scheme that is manifest in prohibiting the consummated offense). See particularly in this regard id. at 74 ("When we talk about the law of criminal attempts in general suppose we refer to it as a power of discretion that has been given to the courts either by the legislature or by common law precedent to extend the limits of prohibitions against certain kinds of conduct to conduct which does not quite fall within the terms of those prohibitions.").

On the other hand, the piece can readily be read to say that courts simply react to narrow categories—attempts to commit thefts of a certain sort, attempts to smuggle otherwise dutiable goods—and that these reactions then set precedents. See id. at 75–76 ("Certainly confidence games statutes, pandering statutes, prohibition laws, speed laws, laws against robbing the United States mail, sedition laws, etc. were all passed to meet entirely different problems. The court is given the power to extend the policy of these statutes to conduct not included within their specific language. Some of them will be extended to cover attempts, others will not. Very often, an emotional reaction toward the kind of conduct prohibited in the statute is about all that will guide us. Thus we probably will not punish an attempt to drive while intoxicated, but we will punish an attempt at statutory rape . . . (Questions as to whether the defendant's conduct was sufficiently blameworthy to deserve to be punished under the particular rule invoked (here we have the problem of "intent") or whether his conduct was sufficiently dangerous (here we have the problem of whether the means were adapted to the end, reasonable mistake in the means chosen etc.) or whether it was sufficiently far advanced towards its objective (here we have the question as to when "mere preparation" becomes an attempt) have no meaning or content when considered apart from the particular prohibition.").

29. Karl Llewellyn, "Some Realism about Realism—Responding to Dean Pound," 44 *Harv. L. Rev.* 1222, 1237 (1930). For a further explication of the point, see id. at 1240 ("A further line of attack on the apparent conflict and uncertainty among the decisions in appellate courts has been to seek more understandable statements of them by grouping the facts in new—and typically but not always narrower—categories. The search is for correlations of fact-situations and outcomes which (aided by common sense) may reveal *when* courts seize on one rather than another of the available competing premises. One may even stumble on the trail of *why* they do. Perhaps, e.g., third party beneficiary difficulties simply fail to get applied to promises to make provisions for dependents; perhaps the pre-existing duty rule goes by the board when the agreement is one for a marriage-settlement. Perhaps, indeed, contracts in what we may broadly call family relations do not work out in general as they do in business.").

30. See Leon Green, *The Judicial Process in Tort Cases* (St. Paul, MN: West Publishing Co., 1931).

31. See Jorge Luis Borges, "The Analytical Language of John Wilkins," in *Borges: A Reader: A Selection from the Writings of Jorge Luis Borges* (New York: Dutton, 1981) purporting to report the categories of animals contained in an ancient Chinese encyclopedia: (1) those that belong to the Emperor; (2) embalmed ones; (3) those that are trained;(4) suckling pigs; (5) mermaids; (6) fabulous ones; (7) stray dogs; (8) those that are included in this classification; (9) those that ramble as if they were mad; (10) innumerable ones; (11) those drawn with a very fine camel's hair brush; (12) others; (13) those that have just broken a flower vase; (14) those that resemble flies from a distance. He goes on to say, "Obviously there is no classification of the universe that is not arbitrary and conjectural."

32. Thus, in his primary analytical work on tort law, Green notes that the basic issues of tort law can be stated in quite general, policy-driven rather than fact-type driven, terms: "Persons have *interests* which are subjected to *harms*, against which the *judicial process* gives *protection*." Leon Green, *Judge and Jury* 9 (Kansas City, MO: Vernon Law Book, 1939). His division of "interests" is hardly enormously narrow—there are interests of the person, interests in use and enjoyment of property, and interests in the protection of various sorts of relations. Harms are divided into physical harms, appropriation, and defamation. The judicial process is analyzed in terms of divisions of authority between judge, jury and appellate review, with notes on the degree to which the process is highly rule-governed. Protection is divided into compensation, prevention, punishment and insurance. Id. at 9–10. His more concrete discussions of doctrine also track conventional categories rather than fact-driven ones—there are chapters on duty, negligence, causation, and the general distinction between law and fact judgments.

INDEX

acceptability
   criterion for judging judicial decisions, 204, 209, 210–14, 304n11
   product, 173
   threshold level, 39, 40
accidents
   information and risks, 168
   paying expected damages, 145
adaptive toolbox
   cognition, 62, 63, 203, 208, 233, 240
   fast & frugal (F&F), 84, 210, 224, 261n26
   hijacking basic adaptive capacities, 84, 203, 270n20
   recognition heuristic, 97, 109, 275n19
advertisers, capacity to manipulate, 4, 14, 40, 126, 164, 243n2
affect heuristic, decision making, 253n33, 254n41
agents
   implementing plans, 42–43
   principals, distinguishing from, 27, 42–45, 47, 257n62
ancestors
   environment of evolutionary adaptation, 59, 79, 156
   foraging, 80
   intuition, 247n13
anchoring
   "bundled valuations," 21, 24, 38–42
   company performance, 153–54
   consumers' risk estimates, 293n24
   convicted criminals, 149–50
   existence, 23
   expected value calculus, 23–24
   heuristic, 44, 250n18
   relationship to touch or concern requirement, 24
apt threshold level, 102
artificial intelligence, 9

asymmetrically paternalist, interventions, 175
attempt law, 220, 309n28
attention, internal mental process, 12
attribute substitution, 6, 58, 218
autonomy, consumer protection, 154
availability
   bias, 113, 249n6, 271n30, 284n21, 293n24, 302n29
   category, 85
   concept of, 7, 23, 84, 85
   H&B work, 102, 113, 262n28
   increasing the, of information, 160
   meta-, 85
   probability, 130, 138, 160, 169, 267n12
   recognition heuristic, 84, 262n28
   representativeness, comparison with, 21
   risk, 171
   voters, 45
availability heuristic
   accident, 58
   anchor-consistent information, 250n18
   error, 7
   F&F research, 249n9
   frequency, 22
   mortality rates, 113
   relationship to recognition heuristic, 84, 102

bad choices, regretting, 30–31
base-level rules
   cognition, 224, 240
   derivation, 303n7
   legal formalism, 206–8, 210, 212–13
base rate neglect
   capacity, 273n8
   HIV-positive test, 73–74, 150, 244n3, 266n6
   misjudgments of dangerousness, incapacitationists, 121, 147–50

behavior
  irrational, 32–38
  nudges, 162–63, 175
behavioral economics, 67, 154
behavioral finance
Benthamite, 215, 216, 307n19
biases
  durability, 287n45
  errors, 5, 35
  hedonic adaptation or desensitization, 135–36
  hindsight, 145
  implicit, 158, 291n10, 291n15, 292n19
  miscalculating punishment, 129–31
  perception of risk, 149
  probabilistic reasoning, 27
  reported happiness, 138
boundary conditions, heuristics, 96
bounded rationality, 51, 87, 258n4
brain
  hierarchical model, 198
  modular conceptions, 59, 63–65, 181–82, 197–98, 222
  System One/System Two, 33–36
building contracts, 222–23
"bundled" decisions, H&B school, 38–42
"bundled together," valuations, 24

capital murder 46
cardinal judgments
  end-state, 139
  value, 178–79
career criminals, 135–36
cheater detection
  abstract rule, 77, 78
  capacity, 270n20
  mate selection, 61–62, 222
  modularized view, 76, 79, 263n37
  precaution rules, 78
  selection task, 76–77
Cheater Detection Module (CDM), 76, 263n37
city population assessments, 55–56, 62, 93–96, 104, 106–7, 111, 112–13
city recognition, 101–5, 106–9
Classical Orthodoxy, 207–10, 212, 221, 240
Classical synthesis

critics of, 240
Langdell, 204–14, 224
cognition
  basic description, 230–31
  frequency mistake, 26–27
  incommensurability debate, 178–81
  massive modularity, 10–11, 57–60, 60–65, 180–81, 187, 206, 209, 222, 233
  modular theory, 289–90n9
  non-problem-specific mechanism, 12
  rational choice and F&F scholars, 237–38
  self-defense, 294n28
  System One/System Two, 33–36
  traditional vs. domain-specific theories, 10–12, 246–47n11
cognitive psychology, 119, 244n5
collective mechanisms
  decision making, 157–58, 265n3, 295n33
  jurors and juries, 72–73, 265n4
  overcoming individual discrimination, 157–58
colonoscopy, duration neglect and peak/end reporting, 143–44
commitment
  cultural, as alternative to cognitive fact assessment, 162, 294n28
  not comparison, 194–97
  resolving choices, 188–89
compensation
  commensurability, 300n11
  judgments, 44
  protection, 310n32
  strategies, 298n52
compliance with law, 68, 120
  fast & frugal (F&F), 122, 124–27, 128
  legal decisions, 9, 16, 62, 283n4
  regulatory, 163
comprehensiveness, legal system, 204–5
compromise
  outcome, 30
  rational-choice theory, 46–47
computation, limits, 87–88
conceptualization, legal rules, 218
conjunction fallacy
  F&F skeptical of H&B, 81, 250–51n20
  frequentist vs. probabilistic terms, 255n47

insurance market regulation, 20, 25, 123, 161, 213
judgment, 25, 247n1, 249n11, 250n19, 268n14
test, 35, 74–75, 82
consumers
  disclosure, 295–96n36
  errors, 176–77
  information, 164–65
  information form, 165–68
  manipulative advertisers, 4, 14, 40, 126, 164, 243n2
  market regulation, 155
  risk information, 171
  risk perceptions, 293n24
  tastes and circumstances, 168–74
  vulnerability, 174, 247n13
  welfare and autonomy, 154
contingent valuations, 31, 44, 152–53, 288n2, 290n9
contract
  categories, 220–23
  disputes, 153, 159
  family, 310n27
  formation, 212–14, 302n26
  Langdell's work, 212–14, 309n28
  mailbox rule, 212–14
  mutual consideration, 208
  rules, 264n47
contrast effects
  decision making, 29, 252n29
  intermediate punishments, 133–34
coronary care triage decisions, 87–88
cost-benefit analysis
  comparison of theories, 236t
  fast & frugal theorists, 68
  incommensurability, 16, 39, 178–82, 185–89, 301–2n23
  information to determine, 174
  migratory birds program, 31
  rational choice, 15
  valuations, 152–53
costs, gathering and processing cues, 51
criminal law
  deterrence, 45, 119–21, 130–31, 134–37, 143–45, 146, 282–83n1
  fast & frugal compliance, 124–27

  literature, 16
  optimal sanctions, 163, 294–95n31
  perceived vs. actual expected value of committing offenses, 127–28
  preparation vs. attempt, 308–9n27
  specific intent, 309n28
  timing of rewards and punishments, 131–33
criminal punishment
  behavior and expected, 124
  contrast effects and intermediate, 133–34
  "crime-prone," 285–86n30
  dangerousness and sentencing, 148
  designing optimal system, 119–21
  Due Process, 283n9
  duration neglect and peak/end reporting, 143–44
  errors in processing deterrence signals, 144–46
  fast & frugal approach, 121–27
  formal state mechanisms, 126–27
  frame-sensitive end-state evaluation, 131
  hedonic adaptation and desensitization, 134–43
  incapacitation, 147–50
  juveniles, 284n19
  miscalculation, 129–31
  professional criminals, 135–36
  retribution, 120–21
  retributive judgments, 146–47
  theory comparisons, 238–39
  timing of rewards and punishments, 131–33
  underestimating likelihood, 129–31, 135, 141, 149, 151, 284–85n21
cultural defenses 125–26
custody decisions, elicitation sensitivity, 30
cut-off threshold, 101, 102, 299n4

damages
  emotional and non-emotional, 222–23
  moral judgment, 305–6n16
  paying expected, for accidents, 145
dangerousness
  criminal, 148–49, 151, 308n27
  person on street, 156

death rate, 27
  mortality rate, 29, 113, 167, 174, 297n45, 297n46
  mortality risk, 38, 145–46, 160, 171, 188, 266n9, 296n41
debate
  heuristics & biases vs. fast & frugal school, 5–8, 20, 229–33
  jurisprudence and policymaking, 8–9
  probability matching, 79–81
  structure and implications, 9–16
decision-making
  affect heuristic, 253n33, 254n41
  bundled decisions, 38–42
  Classical legal orthodoxy, 240
  collective, 72–73, 295n33
  collective mechanisms, 157–58
  compensatory, 40–41, 47, 56, 93, 106, 121–23
  competing approaches, 9–10, 235
  contrast effects, 29, 252n29
  elimination by aspects, 38–42, 160, 169, 172, 181, 234
  expected value maximization, 5, 20, 39, 255n49, 260n15
  fast and frugal (F&F) school, 5, 7–8, 156–57
  good not bad, 240
  heuristics and biases (H&B) school, 4, 5–8
  judgments, contrasts with, 11–12
  lexical, 8, 15–16, 40–41, 56, 66, 108, 116, 121–22, 173, 176, 185–89
  non-compensatory, 8, 15, 66, 173, 272n1
  nudges vs. coercion, 162–63
  one-cue, 94
  organizations, 265n3
  principals, 42–43
  priority heuristic, 20, 247–48n3, 274n9
  prospect theory, 20, 29, 154, 248n3
  rational-choice theory, 187, 231, 233, 234, 237–38
  reason-based, 47, 215, 253n32, 299n4
  resolving choices, 188–89
decision utility, preferences, 31
decision weights, prospect theory, 20
dedicated informational encapsulated module, 94
default terms, negotiations, 153

desensitization
  adaptation to intensity, 137
  hedonic adaptation and, 134–43
  hedonic treadmill, 140
deterrence
  errors in providing, signals, 144–46
  F&F skepticism of, 121–22
  function of criminal law, 120
  H&B approach, 127–46
  hedonic adaptation and desensitization, 134–43
  punishment and, 127–28
  sentence length and, 119–20
  theory, 120, 282–83n1
devaluation, trading causing, 191–92
disclosure, consumers, 9, 44, 67, 119, 165–66, 176, 238, 295–96n36
discrimination
  antidiscrimination law, 291n15
  collective approaches to overcoming, 157, 291n16
  comparison of theories, 236t
  employment, 155, 187, 290–91n10, 291n16
  literature on regulation of markets, 155–58
  regulation, 292n17
diseases
  assessing risks, 160–61, 293n25
  mortality rates, 297n45
  overestimating risk, 166
disutility levels, 134–37, 143–44, 146
diversification bias, 290n9
dividends, 154, 289n9
domain specificity, massive modularity, 60–63
driving speed
  decision making, 123–24, 234
  information strategy, 168
  principals and agents, 257n62
Due Process, punishment, 283n9
durability bias, 287n45
duration neglect, peak/end reporting, 143–44, 287n47
dysfunctional heuristics, 12
  F&F theories of adaptive lag, 7, 69
  H&B theories of inapt generalization, 6–7, 81, 193, 230

ecological rationality, 37, 50–55
elimination by aspects (EBA)
　decision making, 160, 169, 172, 201
　Take the Best, relationship to, 160, 187–88
　theory, 38, 39–42, 181, 257n58
embarrassment, 82, 260n15, 278n29
emergency room, triage decisions, 57–58
employment, discrimination, 155, 157, 187, 290–91n10, 291n16
encapsulated module, 94, 264n46
endowment effects
　default terms, 153, 264n48, 288n5
　H&B heuristics, 29
　valuing end-states, 42
end-states
　distributive justice, 146
　evaluation, 29–32
　frame sensitive, evaluation, 131
　mistakes in evaluating, 25
　preferences, 28
　rational-choice theory, 47–48
　subjective valuations, 23–24
　valuations, 153
　value of attributes and features, 169
　value or utility, 20, 182–85
environmental issues
　best feasible technology, 15
　clean-up, 68
　climate change, 288n3
　forestation, 187–88
　valuations, 153
environment of evolutionary adaptation (EEA)
　ancestors, 59, 79, 156
　cheaters, 62
　F&F school, 236t
　hunter-gatherer, 74, 262n31
　input cue and mental output, 64
　real life, 75
　settings, 7, 84
errors
　accounting for, 6
　availability heuristic, 7
　biases, 5, 35
　consumers, 176–77
　costs, 6–7

deterrence signals, 144–46
　identifying normative, 28–32
　processing, 44–45
　regretting choices, 30–31
　shame/pride payoffs, 278n29
　systematic, and judgments, 247n1
evolutionary psychology
　cognition and action, 261n22
　critics of, 91–92
　fast & frugal (F&F) school, 7, 84–86, 219
　four-card Wason selection task, 75–76
　game theoretic equilibria, 93
　mate selection, 262n35
　prejudice, 291n14
ex ante risks and probabilities, 145, 152, 245–46n10, 255–56n51, 289n7
excessive optimism, 15
expected utility theory, 19–21, 248n3, 258n2, 290n9, 297n52
expected value
　calculation, 122, 174, 180, 241
　miscalculating, 25–32
　miscomputing, 21–25
　offending, 120
　perceived vs. actual, of offending, 127–28, 151
extremeness aversion, 46

failure
　literature focus, 43
　market, 5, 43, 67, 164, 175, 238, 295n34
　regulatory, 67, 164–65
false consensus effect, 36, 37, 256n54
familiarity
　city size, 8
　judgments, 102, 103, 105, 115, 277n25, 278–79n33, 280–81n35
　learning system, 280n34
　memory, 233, 246n10, 274n16, 276n21, 278n30, 278–79n33
　one-cue decision making, 94
　recognition heuristic, 92, 97–99, 246n10
　relationship to recall, 97–99, 103–4, 115, 278n30, 278–80n33
　repetition priming, 278n30

fast and frugal (F&F) school
  additional information, 172–73
  comparison to others, 236t
  conservatives, 13
  cost benefit analysis skepticism, 121, 180–81, 272n1
  criticism of heuristics & biases (H&B) mechanisms, 83–86
  debate vs. H&B school, 5–8, 20, 229–33
  decision making, 5, 7–8, 186–87, 200–201, 203
  decision making and treatment of outsiders, 156–57
  diminishing crime level, 121–27
  ecological rationality, 50–55
  established law and policy implications, 67–68
  evolutionary psychology, 7, 84–86, 219
  gap between real-world problems and lab, 231–32
  incommensurability, 187–88
  incommensurable values, 180
  information, 164–68
  irrationality of H&B school, 71–83
  Langdell and legal decision making, 202–3, 208
  legal compliance mechanisms, 124–27
  massive modularity hypothesis, 59–67
  observation of traits, 91–92
  performance variability, 92–93
  policymakers, 176
  product information, 170
  questions, 11–12
  rational choice theory vs., 238
  recognition heuristic, 90, 164
  structural features, 11
  structure of reasoning, 55–59
  tradition of thought, 10–11
foraging, ancestors, 80
forced-choice
  problems, 298n4
  recognition, 99–102, 114, 191, 276n20, 276n23, 276–77n24, 278n29, 281n35
  situations, 98, 194, 196
forest policy, 187–88
formalism. *See also* legal formalism
  Langdellian, 68, 202, 204–10

  presumptive, 303n4
four-card task
  abstract rule, 77, 78
  selection, 75–76, 269n18
fragility, non-commodity form, 192–93
frame-sensitivity
  contingent valuations, 288n2
  decision making, 132
  end-state evaluation, 131, 151, 290n9
  identifying, 28–32, 49
  judgments, 133, 185
frequency
  conjunction fallacy, 255n47
  judgment, 27
  presentation, 296n42
  probability, 27
  single events, 267–68n12
friendship, demands of, 194

gains, choices as, and losses, 182–85
gambler's fallacy, 86, 129–30, 271n31, 285n25
  impact on judgment of product quality, 154, 160
  relationship to hot-hand fallacy, 54, 86, 271n31, 285n25
gambling, bets, 251–52n27
gaze heuristic, one-input, 3, 245n8
g-loaded tests
  capacity, 93
  deliberative, 111
  intelligence, 34–35
  probability matching, 81
global warming, 153, 247n13, 294n28
"Grand Style" Ante-Bellum jurisprudence, 207, 217
granularity problem, 61, 187, 214, 218, 222, 223–24

habits of mind, evolution, 216
happiness and hedonics, 31, 286n33
  judgments of, 32, 139
  lottery winners and accident victims, 286n34
  measures of objective, 216, 253n38, 286n42, 307n19
  reported, and biases, 138

satisfaction, 140, 164
theories about sources, 141–42
harm principle, 304–7n16
Heart Disease Predictive Instrument, 87
hedonic adaptation
  adjusting to news that bad outcomes are certain, 31, 32, 119
  desensitization to punishment, 134–43
  peak/end reporting, 147
  phenomenon, 138
  satisfaction treadmill, 140
hedonics. *See* happiness
help the unlucky algorithm, 14–15
heuristics
  applicability, 261n23
  definitions, 3–9, 229–30
  diversification, 290n9
  existence of, 22–23
  imitation, 122, 283n4
  meta-, 64–65
  priority, 20, 247–48n3, 274n9
  selection problem, 67
  sociological critique of literature, 157–58
  System One/System Two, 39, 58–59, 253–54n39
  term, 243n1
heuristics and biases (H&B) school
  "bundled" decisions, 38–42
  commitment to principles, 302n29
  comparison to others, 236t
  conceptual overview, 42–48
  criticism, 50–51
  criticisms of fast & frugal (F&F), 93–115
  debate vs. fast & frugal school, 5–8, 20, 229–33
  decision making, 4, 5–8, 170
  deterring crime, 127–46
  elimination by aspects, 38–42
  expected utility theory and, 19–21
  factual vs. normative "mistakes", 25–28
  gap between real-world problems and lab, 231–32
  Holmes' proto-realism, 203, 215–20
  identifying normative errors, 28–32
  influence on legal theory, policy and practice, 42–48

  irrational behavior, 32–38
  labile judgments of value, 25–32
  legal academy, 152–55
  legal realism, 203
  liberals, 13, 14
  miscalculating expected value, 21–32
  miscalculating punishment, 129–31
  policymakers, 175
  probability misestimates, 21–25
  questions, 11–12
  rational choice theory vs., 238
  soft paternalism, 152–55, 159–64
  structural features, 11
  tradition of thought, 10–11
  "two system" models, 35–36
heuristics researchers, commonality and differences, 3–9, 229–31
higher order principles
  deriving base-level rules, 303n7
  legal formalism, 206–12, 217, 221
hindsight bias
  company performance, 289n7
  criminal punishment, 145, 288n1
  juries, 45, 72, 152
  literature on, 245–46n10
  overestimating culpability, 45, 46, 306n16
  varieties, 255–56n51
historicism law, 217
HIV-positive test
  base rate neglect, 73–74, 150, 244n3, 277n6
  chance and being informed, 142
  frequency, 268n12
Holmes' proto-realism, 16, 202–3, 215–20
homicide grading 46–47
hot-hand fallacy, 54, 86, 271n31, 285n25
  impact on judgment of product quality, 154, 160
  relationship to gambler's fallacy, 54, 86, 271n31, 285n25
housing vouchers, 14
human capacity, recognition heuristic, 96–97
hunter-gatherers
  environment, 13
  environment of evolutionary adaptation (EEA), 74, 262n31
  intuition, 13–14

identification tasks, modularity, 280–81n35
imitation heuristic
　forms of, 122, 188, 283n4
　meta-heuristic, 64–65
immune neglect, 141
immunity, punishment, 147
Implicit Association Test (IAT), 292n19
implicit bias, 158, 291n10, 291n15, 292n19
incapacitation, punishment, 147–50
incoherence
　end-state evaluation, 49
　identifying, 24, 28–32, 250n19
　judgments, 32, 45–46
　probabilities, 24
　thought, 194
incommensurability
　commensurability as reductionism to single metrics, 182–85
　commitment expression as mechanism of resolving incomparable choices, 194–97
　cost-benefit analysis, 301–2n23
　debate, 178–82, 239–40
　descriptive argument, 179–80
　H&B school, 298n4
　incomparability, 189–99
　inhibiting discordant impulses, resolving incomparable options, 206, 217, 238
　making choices, 39
　normative argument, 179
　problems of, 298n1
　rational choice theory, 199, 239
　trumping rules, 185–89
　values, 16, 178–81, 199–201, 300n11
incomparability
　arguments, 189–90
　commitment, 194–97
　criticizing comparability, 191–94
　devaluing or destroying traded good, 191–92
　fragility of non-commodity form, 192–93
　parallel processing, 197–99
　relationship to valuation, 190–91
　tradeoffs and sacrifices, 299n6
　tyranny and inapt reasons, 193–94
individual rights and separateness of persons, 301n13

inference, rational choice, 106–7
information
　additional, 172–73
　behavior and perception, 173
　consumers, 164–68
　economics, 296n37
　form, 165–68
　frequentist form, 166, 167, 244n3
　overload, 67, 165, 175–76
　product acceptability, 173–74
　rational choice theory and, 113
　retirement savings portfolio, 174
　single-event probabilistic presentation, 167
　stopping rule for cues, 55
　survival and mortality risks, 167, 171, 174, 184, 188
informational encapsulation
　cheater detection, 79
　F&F theory, 94, 114
　judgment and decision-making, 11–12
　massive modularity, 56, 60, 65–67, 181, 184–85, 261n22
　mate selection, 262n35
　reproductive sex, 254n40
　soft forms, 66
instrumentalism, law, 215–17, 218
intelligence
　conventional definition, 36–38
　differences, 36
　general, 34–35
　rationality, 256n56
　social, 260n15
　statements for negative event, 83
　Wason selection task, 75–76, 269n18
intervention
　heuristics and biases, 71, 152–53, 159–60, 175
　human behavior, 16
　medical, 266n6
　policy, 32, 44, 119
　paternalism, 159–60, 162, 175, 238
intuitions
　ancestral, 247n13
　choices, 169
　cognitive, 220
　desensitization, 140
　ease of retrieval, 85

elimination by aspects, 39
external values, 306–7n16
heuristic, 35
hunter-gatherer, 13–14
just resolution, 221–22
moral weight, 307n20
narrow category realism, 223–24
problem resolution, 196, 224, 240
public policy, 307n21
rational choice scholars, 5
System One, 34, 233
System Two overriding System One, 81, 112
training and, 211
unconscious, 33, 217
women and workplace, 157
investors
  dividends, 289n9
  loss aversion, 154, 289n8
irrationality
  F&F criticism of H&B, 71–83
  Heuristics and biases, 32–38
isolation effect, prospect theory, 20
item recognition, 92, 99, 115, 275n19, 277n25, 279–80n33, 280–81n35, 282n40

judgments
  accuracy, 258n6
  comparison of theories, 236t
  contrasted with decision making, 11–12
  expected utility theory, 21
  familiarity, 102, 103, 105, 115, 277n25, 279n33, 280n35
  few cues, 7
  frequency, 27
  heuristic approaches, 8
  incoherence, 32, 45–46
  incommensurable values, 179–80
  labile, of value, 25–32
  life satisfaction or happiness, 32, 139
  relative size, 245n7
  retributive, for punishment, 146–47
  self-defense, 294n28
  single events, 267–68n12
  systematic error, 247n1
judicial decisions

narrow categories, 218
principles of law, 240
jurisprudence
  debate implications, 8–9
  legitimate law, 308n22
  sociological, 202
jurors
  agents, 42–43
  collective decision making, 72–73, 265n4
  decision-making, 45
  experimental, 72, 133
  inter-jury unreliability and bias, 266n5
  neutrality, 243–44n2
juveniles, criminal punishment, 284n19

knowledge
  moral, 283–84n11
  sociology of, 10, 148

laboratory problems, F&F criticism of H&B, 71–83
Langdellian formalism, 68, 202, 204–10
Langdell's classical synthesis
  formal legal system, 204–10
  mailbox rule, 212–14
  normativity, 210–12
language acquisition, 63, 65, 259n11
legal compliance mechanisms, fast & frugal, 124–27
legal formalism, 16, 202
  base-level rules, 206–8, 210, 212–13
  higher order principles, 206–12, 217, 221
  Holmes' proto-realism, 203, 215–20
  Langdell, 202, 204–14
  mailbox rule, 212–14
legal literature, rational-choice theory, 44
legal realism, 68
  Classical Orthodoxy, 202–3
  fast & frugal (F&F) school, 203
  general statements, 220–21
  H&B school, 203, 215
  narrow categories ("case type"), 220–24

legal system
  antidiscrimination, 238, 291n13, 291n15
  comprehensiveness, 204–5
  heuristics and biases (H&B), 152–55, 160–62
  legal policy and theory, 245n9
  nature of formal, 204–10
  preparation vs. attempt, 308–9n27
  rules, 303n3
  soft paternalism and H&B, 159–64
  theory comparisons, 238
less is less, definition, 115
less is more, information, 115, 287n51
lexical decision making processes, 8, 12, 40–41, 66, 116, 173, 185–89
  elimination by aspects (EBA), 38–42, 160, 181
  household behavior, 126
  memory-based cues, 108
  non-compensatory, 15–16
  recognition cues, 104
  single-cue, 56, 121–22, 124, 165, 176
libertarian paternalist, interventions, 159, 175, 207, 214, 292n20
life satisfaction, judgments of overall, 32
loss aversion, 29, 154, 289n8
losses, choices as gains and, 182–85
loyalty, sense of, 184
loyalty-demanding module, cooperation, 184

mailbox rule, 212–14
mandatory
  arbitration term feature, 160
  disclosure, 44
  F&F heuristics, 274n12
  heuristics, 93
  incommensurability, 184
  massive modularity (MM), 10, 63–64, 180, 197, 206, 222, 261n22
  prison sentences, 128, 153
mandatory disclosure, processing errors, 44–45
manipulation, capacity of advertisers and lawyers, 4, 13, 45, 75, 230, 236, 243n2
market failure, 5, 43, 67, 164, 175, 238, 295n34
market regulation
  F&F theory, 155
  information, 164–68
  literature and discrimination, 155–58
  shifting behavior, 162–64
massive modularity (MM)
  basic conceptual problem, 61–62, 222
  cognition and judgment, 180–81
  cues, 261n22
  decision making, 187, 200
  hypothesis, 59–60
  modules, 60–65
  relationship to F&F school, 57–59, 62–65
  theory, 10–11, 59–67, 206, 209, 233
mate selection, evolutionary psychology, 261n22, 262n35
mathematical psychology, memory and perception, 4
medical care, 57–58, 193–94
memory
  binary familiarity, 246n10
  comparing items in and out of, 99–100
  mathematical psychology, 4
  misperception and distorted, 136
  recall v. familiarity, 97–99, 103–4, 115, 278n30, 278–80n33
  recognition, 57, 62, 99, 101, 156, 243n2, 275n19, 276n20, 277n27
  risk perceptions, 293n24
  searching, 261n21
  using information from, 97, 274n16
memory search, recognition cue, 55–56
meta-cognitive capacity, heuristics, 61–63, 95
Mills, John Stuart, *On Liberty*, 155
misestimates
  probability, 21–25
  probability of punishment, 129–31
mistakes
  factual vs. normative, 25–28
  fast & frugal (F&F) criticism, 73
mistaken evaluation concept, 171–72
mistake of law defenses, 125–26
modularity, identification tasks, 280–81n35
modules, massive modularity (MM), 60–65
money, sex and, 192–93
mood, aspects, 10
moral knowledge, 283–84n11
moral universals, 304n16

mortality rate, 27, 29, 113, 167, 174, 297n45, 297n46
mortality risk, 38, 145–46, 160, 171, 188, 266n9, 296n41
murder charges 46–47

natural disasters, probability, 24–25
natural frequencies, judgments, 74
negotiations, default terms, 153
neutrality principles, 170–71
non-commodity form, fragility, 192–93
non-compensatory decision making, 8, 15, 66, 173, 272n1
non-recognition, judgments, 101, 108
non-recognition information, 56, 105–6, 112–13
normative argument, incommensurability of values, 179
nudges, shifting behavior, 162–63, 175, 292n21

objective experience, incommensurability, 181–82
objectively preferable, end-state evaluation, 29
objective view, probability, 26–28
offending
   expected value, 120
   incarceration to prevent, 147–48
   perceived vs. actual expected value of, 127–28
opacity of judgments and decisions, massive modularity, 11, 60, 63–64, 206, 222, 261n22
optimal sanctions, criminal law, 163, 294–95n31
optimism bias
   bad events, 129, 171
   explain, 15
   forms, 43
   underestimating punishment, 284–85n21
optimization
   bounded rationality, 258n5
   fast and frugal (F&F), 51–52
   strategies, 3, 12
options
   commitment, 194–97
   neither equal nor unequal in value, 189–99
   on par, 190
outcome

   compromise vs. potential, 30
   probability and value, 19–20
overestimation, risks, 166, 171
overfitting
   compensatory decision makers, 165
   definition, 52–53
   experts, 236t, 237
   regressions, 68, 176, 211–12

pain/pleasure/indifference judgments, 139
parallel processing, incomparability, 197–99
pass the buck heuristic, 148, 149
paternalism
   asymmetric and libertarian forms, 68, 152, 159, 164, 235, 292n20, 295n33
   comparison of theories, 236t
   fast & frugal (F&F), 235, 236t
   H&B tradition, 159–64
   harder form, 164
   heuristics and biases as path to soft, 152–55
   nudges vs. coercion, 162–63
pathogens, restaurants, 172
peak/end reporting, duration neglect and, 143–44
pedagogy, 304n11
performance of groups, decision making, 265n3
performance variability, 34, 81, 83, 92–93, 197, 254n40, 255n43, 273n9
physical harms, category, 223
physiological mechanisms, 139–40
plausibility, testing theory, 119
policymaking
   debate implications, 8–9
   fast & frugal theorists, 67–68
   limits of psychological literature, 119–21
   literature, 154
   psychological theory, 285n22
political philosophy, heuristics schools, 13
political power, tyranny, 193
populations
   Asian cities, 95, 113
   comparing cities, 55–56, 62, 93–96, 104, 106–7, 111, 112–13
post-Darwinian view, nature of thought, 216
preference-elicitation procedure, 48

prejudice
  evolutionary psychology, 291n14
  F&F theory, 156
  literature, 155
  psychology-influenced theory, 291n14
  racism, 158, 292n18
  unconscious, 158, 217, 307n21
primary hindsight bias, 245n10, 256n51
principals
  contrasted with agents, 27, 42–45, 47, 257n62
  decision makers, 42–43, 257n62
  voters, 42, 43, 44–45, 49
principles, judges and law, 240
priority heuristic, 20, 247–48n3, 274n9
  contrasted with prospect theory, 20, 29, 154, 248n3
probability
  choices and conflicts, 247n3
  conjunction fallacy, 255n47
  ex ante, 245–46n10, 255–56n51, 289n7
  miscalculating punishment, 129–31
  misestimates, 21–25
  mistakes in assessing, 26, 251n23
  objective or subjective debate, 26–28
  outcome, 19–20
  representativeness, 24–25
  single events, 267–68n12
probability matching, 79–81, 255n49
probation, 29, 133
problem solving
  artificial intelligence, 9
  F&F criticizing H&B mechanisms, 83–86
product acceptability, taste, 173–74
products, safety and risks, 167–68
professional criminals, punishment, 135–36
prominence judgments, 105, 108–9, 112, 243n1, 282n40
  relationship to recognition heuristic, 103, 105, 108–9, 112
property crimes, decision and detection, 124
prospect theory, 20, 29, 154
proto-realism, Holmes, 215–20
pseudo-incommensurability, 200
psychological theory
  deriving policy from theory, 119–21, 285n22
  deterrence, 119–20

punishment. *See* criminal punishment

quasi-heuristics, rational, 64

rape, 91–92, 261n22, 272–73n7, 309n28
rational answer, definition, 37
rational-choice theory
  behavior of people, 32
  bounded rationality and information acquisition, 51, 87, 243n1
  comparison to others, 236t
  decision making, 187, 231, 233, 234, 237–38, 264n46
  deterrence, 121–23
  diversification bias, 290n9
  driver and driving speed, 123–24
  end-states, 47–48
  evaluating end-states, 30
  expected value, 120
  F&F vs. H&B researchers, 113–15
  homicide-grading, 46–47
  inference, 106–7
  misinterpretations by F&F researchers, 51–52, 54–59
  model, 256n55
  probability and value of outcome, 19–20
  reforming legal literature, 44
  rules of thumb, 15, 51, 57, 113, 123, 124, 205, 217, 233, 237, 241, 258n6
  suspicious of massive modularity, 66
rationality
  distinguishing from reason-based choice, 299n4
  ecological, 50–55
  intelligence, 256n56
  logical, 53–54
  rethinking, 258n5
  two-system strategy, 254n40
rational search, information and consumers, 165
realism. *See* legal realism
real-world problems, gap with laboratory and, 71–72
reason-based decision making, 47, 215, 253n32, 299n4
  custody decisions, 30, 47

reasoning
  intuition, 268–69n14
  two-system strategy, 253–54n39
recall, 97–99, 249n7
recidivism, criminals, 130, 134, 147–48
recognition
  availability, comparison to, 84, 85, 102, 113
  capacity, 92, 104
  familiarity vs. recall, 97–99
  forced-choice, 98–102, 114, 191, 194, 196
  memory, 57, 62, 99, 101, 156, 243n2, 275n19, 276n20, 277n27
  overvalue, 113
recognition heuristic, 11, 249n9, 259n7
  assessing applicability, 261n23
  assessment, 112–15
  availability, 84, 262n28
  capacities, 96–97
  city recognition, 88, 103–5, 106–9
  comparing items in and out of memory, 99–100
  critique of, 93–115
  fast and frugal (F&F), 90, 164
  judgment, 276n20, 278n29
  less is more, 52, 114, 115, 148, 259n7, 287n51
  preceding search for cues, 55–57, 260n20, 261n21
  rationality, 275n19
  size comparisons, 92, 93–98, 101–3, 111–15
  study of, 246n10
recollection
  memory, 97, 274n16, 277n25
  recognition heuristic, 97–99
reductionism, single metrics, 182–85
reformers, law, 45, 48
regret
  heuristic-based decisions, 253n33
  identifying, 28, 30–32
  initial response, 82
  misevaluating end-states, 45, 49
  renounced choices, problem of, 31
  vs. error, 171
regulation, discrimination, 292n17
regulatory failure, 67, 164–65
regulatory process, valuations, 152–53
rent control, 14

repetition priming, memory, 278n30
representativeness, 23, 24–25, 82, 86
representativeness heuristic, 35
  relationship to conjunction fallacy, 35
retirement savings, 174
retribution
  deterrence, 134–35
  policymaker seeking, 146
  proportionality of punishment, 120, 134
  punishment, 120–21, 143, 146–47
  utility losses v. capacity losses, 183
rights violation, 199
risk aversion, discounting, 132–33
risks
  assessing, of choices, 160–61, 293n25
  ex ante, 145, 152
  factual judgments v.cultural commitments in estimating, 162
  information about global, 171
  mortality, 266n9
  overestimation, 166, 171
  perceptions of, and bias, 149
  perceptions of consumers, 293n24
  products, 167–68
  smoking, 161–62, 171
  sub-risks and aggregate, 175
rule-of-thumb, 15, 51, 57, 113, 114, 123, 124, 205, 217, 233, 237, 241, 258, 294n28
rules
  base-level, in legal formalism, 206–8, 210, 212–13
  comparison of theories, 236t
  decision making, 6
  incommensurability, 185–89
  legal, for specific problems, 202–3
  legal system, 303n3
  mailbox, 212–14
  sequential, 248n3
  tributes, 303n5
  v. standards, 68, 203, 206, 221, 236t, 237–38

sacrifices, 299n6
SAT test
  intelligence, 34, 35, 36, 110
  probability matching, 81, 255n49
  recognition heuristic use, 110–12

search rule, recognition, 99
search/stop/decide schemas 56, 97, 122–23, 261n21
secondary hindsight bias, 245n10, 256n51
securities market, 154
self-defense, cognition, 294n28
sex
  consensual, 272n6
  mate selection and evolution, 261n22, 262n35
  money and, 192–93
  psychology of desire, 254n40
  violence, 272–73n6
single events, probability and frequency, 267–68n12
single metric
  commensurable choices, 299–300n7
  commensurable values, 178–79, 182–85
  comparisons, 186
  valuing ends, 200
size comparison, recognition, 92, 93–98, 101–5, 107–9, 111–15
smoking, risks of, 161–62, 171
social costs, moral judgment, 305–7n16
social intelligence, 260n15
social norms, positive law, 125
sociology
  heuristics literature, 157
  knowledge, 10, 148
  racism, 158
soft paternalism
  H&B tradition, 159–64
  heuristics and biases as path to, 152–55
speeding
  decision making, 123–24, 234
  information strategy, 168
  principals and agents, 257n62
Statutes of Limitations, 143
stereotyping
  group membership, 23
  literature, 155–56, 291n11, 292n19
  System One, 175
stock price, patterns, 153–154
stopping rule, informational cues, 55, 69
subjective experience, incommensurable values, 181
subjective view, probability, 26–28

suffering, punishment, 147
survival rates, 7, 34, 53, 89, 167, 197, 199, 288n52
System One
  adaptationist, 254n40
  automatic, 111
  heuristics, 39, 58–59, 162, 253–54n39
  initial reactions, 197
  intuitions, 233
  mechanisms, 219
  mixture of, and System Two, 217, 224
  stereotyping, 175
  survival challenges, 308n26
  System Two overriding, 34–36, 58–59, 81, 216, 233, 240, 256n51
  thinking, 33–36
System Two
  big-picture thinker, 197
  deliberative, 111
  heuristics, 39, 58–59, 253–54n39
  mixture of System One and, 217, 224
  overriding System One, 34–36, 58–59, 81, 216, 233, 240, 256n51
  survival challenges, 308n26
  thinking, 33–36
  utility-seeking ends, 254n40

Take the Best
  characterizing options, 187
  cognitive universe, 135
  elimination by aspects, 201, 257n58
  fast & frugal (F&F) strategy, 55, 64, 87, 88, 198–99, 244n2, 272n1
  F&F theory, 165, 167, 188
  rational choice, 282n43
  recognition heuristic, 260–61n20
  states of world, 160
talent, judging, 179
tastes
  heterogeneity and homogeneity of, 168–74
  neutrality, 170–71
  product acceptability, 173–74
tax law, 15, 44, 62, 162, 209, 292n21
tertiary hindsight bias, 245n10, 256n51
threshold level
  acceptability, 39, 40
  eliminating options, 299n4

probability, 129
recognition, 97, 101–2
torts
  distinction between, 208
  features, 218
  legal rules, 202, 310n32
  reform project, 223
traded good, devaluing or destroying, 191–92
tradeoffs, 299n6, 300n12
trait observations, fast and frugal, 91–92
triggering
  avoidant behavior, 128
  basic module, 197
  decision-, cue, 198
  mechanism, 139, 247n11
  third action-, cue, 182
trumping rules, incommensurability, 185–89
tyranny, criticizing comparability, 192–93

unconscious racism, literature, 158
universal moral grammar (UMG), 304n16, 306n16
utility
  expected utility theory, 19–21, 248n3, 258n2, 290n9, 297n52
  making judgments, 234
  maximization of, 10, 215, 308n26
  reductionist, 300n9
  single metric, 299–300n7
  utility-seeking goals, 254n40
  value of end-states, 20, 182–85

vaccination, accessing risk of disease, 161, 293n25
validity, value judgments, 28–29

valuation
  contingent, 288n2
  emotion, 198
  incomparable reactions, 190–91
value
  commensurability as reductionism to single metrics, 182–85
  commitment, not comparison, 194–97
  criticizing comparability, 191–92
  end-states, 169
  incommensurability, 16, 199–201, 300n11
  incommensurability debate, 178–81
  labile judgments of, 25–32
  options neither equal nor unequal, 189–99
  outcome, 19–20
value judgments
  incommensurability, 195
  labile end-state, 83
violence, 166, 272n6, 272–73n7
voters
  availability entrepreneurs, 45
  principals, 42, 43, 44–45, 49
vulnerability
  consumers, 174, 247n13
  disease, 293n25
  false consensus effect, 256n54
  framing effects, 83
  optimism bias, 43

Wason selection task
  abstract rule, 77, 78
  four-card, 75–76, 269n18
welfare, consumer protection, 154
workplace, market regulation, 155

zero point, reactions to life events, 139